D0903377

*A Short History of the Papacy
in the Middle Ages*

BY THE SAME AUTHOR

The Medieval Idea of Law

The Origins of the Great Schism

Medieval Papalism

The Growth of Papal Government in the Middle Ages

Principles of Government and Politics in the Middle Ages

A History of Political Ideas in the Middle Ages

Individual and Society in the Middle Ages

The Carolingian Renaissance and the Idea of Kingship

Liber Regie Capelle
(edited for the Henry Bradshaw Society)

Papst und König

A Short History of the Papacy in the Middle Ages

WALTER ULLMANN

*Professor of Medieval Ecclesiastical
History in the University of Cambridge*

METHUEN & CO LTD

LIBRARY
EISENHOWER COLLEGE

First published in 1972
by Methuen & Co Ltd
11 New Fetter Lane, London EC4
© *1972 Walter Ullmann*
Printed in Great Britain by
Butler & Tanner Ltd, Frome and London

SBN 416 08650 0

BX
955.2
U53
1972

Distributed in the U.S.A.
by Barnes & Noble Inc.

Contents

Preface

THE PRINCIPAL OBJECT of this book is to show in outline how the papacy as an institution developed in the Middle Ages. In time the book spans the history of the medieval papacy from its small and insignificant beginnings in the late Roman Empire to its eventual decline in the age of the Renaissance. The chief concern is the papacy, and not the individual popes. That personalities of necessity do figure prominently is understandable because an institution can be worked only by men, but they were organs who were charged with the application and execution of the idea which the institution itself embodied. Great and outstanding personalities there indubitably were, but in their official capacities they were shaped and guided by the institution itself. A history of the medieval papacy is not therefore a summary of individual papal biographies.

The history of the medieval papacy is the history of an idea, and this idea complex as it is in its genesis and structure, was a time and space conditioned conception of Christianity. The papacy was the embodiment and concrete manifestation of this idea. It was an organism or an institution that derived its sustenance exclusively from this transpersonal idea. There is reason to say that in the early and high Middle Ages it was on the whole the papacy which guided the popes – the papal office absorbed the papal personality. This is precisely the feature which makes the medieval papacy an institution *sui generis* and renders any comparison with other forms of government – for instance, of kingdoms, empires, towns, corporations, principalities, ruling dynasties, etc. – a fruitless task. For the papacy rested on a fairly closely defined programme, on a blueprint which was held to have been not of the papacy's own making but to have been given to it by a specific act of divinity. Whether this was, doctrinally, a tenable proposition is not for the historian to say. What is for him to say is that the papacy is the only institution within the European or

1

Western orbit of civilization which links the post-apostolic with the atomic age: as an institution it has witnessed the birth, growth, prosperity, decay and disappearance of powerful empires, nations and even of whole civilizations; it has witnessed radical transformations in the cosmological field evidenced by bloody revolutions, intercontinental wars and popular upheavals of such magnitudes and dimensions that wholly novel political and social structures appeared in their train.

Because the focal point of this book is the papacy, and not the popes, the emphasis lies on the organic development of the institution. Individual popes figure only in so far as they make their appearance as the transmitters and instruments of the papal idea itself. That consequently certain topics receive less attention than others and that, vice-versa, some topics such as how the papal idea unfolded itself in time and space, are given greater prominence, would in view of the subject of the book seem comprehensible. The attempt to present the historical development of the papacy as an institution had to be made: of histories of the popes there is no shortage. I also thought that the general reader and the student of history to whom the book is primarily addressed would be more helped by concentration on the essential features than by a sheer accumulation of mere facts which, as often as not, are, if at all, only rather tenuously held together by the fortuitous circumstance of a surviving source or still more frequently by their equally fortuitous occurrence within a specified stretch of time. Throughout the book I have stressed one feature which is particularly necessary in a work on the papacy (as distinct from the popes), and that is the role which Constantinople played in the evolution of the institution. The imperial régime in Constantinople played a crucial role in the orientation, structure and physiognomy of the medieval papacy: this is a point which is hardly ever given any prominence, but it is a feature which must be stressed if the history of the institution is to be made accessible to understanding. In more than one direction the history of the medieval papacy is co-terminous with the existence of the Byzantine empire. In brief, it was very largely the challenge by Constantinople and the response and reaction by the papacy which in vital and basic respects determined the path of this institution. Lastly, this book is also a modest attempt to integrate facts with ideas because the concentration on the one to the exclusion of the other would appear to be no longer adequate; in any case the two are too closely linked to be artificially divorced.

Over the course of the years it has frequently been suggested to me that I should write a book of this nature. I need hardly say that it was only after much hesitation that I resolved to undertake the task, for who would not be daunted by the prospect of treating, within a manageable compass, so long a period and especially so central a subject as the medieval papacy? What in the final analysis made me heed the many suggestions was that in one way or another for about a quarter of a century I had been lecturing on this subject; it formed the core of my teaching, has also been part of my own research work for many years and has resulted in publications which are germane to the topic of the book.

Only I know how much this work owes to others; how much stimulated and encouraged I have been by the kindness of colleagues and friends who have supplied me with copies and offprints of their own studies which to my great detriment may easily have escaped my notice; how much, above all, I am indebted to my many pupils, undergraduates and research students, who over the years bore with me in my classes and seminars and supervisions, but whose fresh and wholly unsophisticated manner always provided me with a wholesome stimulus. Here is the place to thank all of them warmly: they may not have been aware of how much I appreciated the points they in youthful enthusiasm put forward. Lastly, as on previous occasions, but this time all the more so, I am deeply grateful to my wife for not only the encouragement and indispensable assistance she has given me, but above all for the selfless forbearance and understanding patience she has shown throughout the period of gestation of this book, composed as it was in times of great stress and tension.

For those readers who would like to pursue certain points further I have appended a few 'Bibliographical Notes': these Notes contain references to primary and secondary source material. They are meant only as very rough guides and are no substitute for a full-scale bibliography.

Cambridge,
18 February 1971   W.U.

1 *The Papacy in the late Roman Empire*

THE MEASURE BY which the Emperor Constantine the Great not only granted the Christian Church freedom of religious worship in 313, but also decreed the return of ecclesiastical goods confiscated during the persecutions, had necessarily far-reaching consequences for the local church of Rome. Throughout the preceding century and a half this church had assumed some position of leadership in doctrinal religious questions. The Constantinean settlement acknowledged this state of affairs. Moreover, the Roman church had been credited with some pre-eminence by a number of earlier writers and theologians who applied certain biblical texts, notably in the New Testament, to this church. It is nevertheless worthy of remark that this biblically based pre-eminence of the Roman church was asserted by writers and ecclesiastics outside Rome. This is important to bear in mind if the historical situation is to be properly assessed: there was neither before nor for some considerable time after the Constantinean peace any reference by the church of Rome itself to any biblical basis of its pre-eminent role among Christian communities.

The consultative machinery which the Roman church had devised in the ages before Constantine was entirely in line with the principle that the law should be the vehicle of government. For the synods (or councils) held frequently in Rome under the chairmanship of the bishop of Rome, were assemblies in which differing points were debated and eventually formulated in the shape of canons, that is, decrees. This Roman device very greatly assisted the nascent local church, because the synods carried great weight not because they were chaired by the local Roman bishop but because no appeal could be made to any other tribunal. By the time of the settlement of 313 the Roman church had a somewhat superior but purely moral authority in comparison with other churches, just as Rome itself carried greater weight than, say, Milan or Marseille. There was, as yet, no suggestion that the Roman church possessed any legal or constitutional pre-eminence. However, the higher moral authority enjoyed by the Roman church was very important for the subsequent evolution of the theme of papal primacy.

The most immediate effect of the Constantinean settlement on the Roman church was that it – like any other church in the Roman empire – became a legal corporate personality within the terms of the Roman law. This recognition of the Roman church as a corporate body obviously had more important results than a similar recognition had for other churches. Thereby the Roman church became integrated into the Roman public law. The Roman church had become a body public – just as the whole Christian body, the universal Church, had become a body public – with all attendant legal consequences.

Moreover, by the early fourth century the Roman church had an internal organization at once superior to, and larger than, any other church in the empire. For instance, a generation earlier Pope Cornelius in a communication to Antioch (253) mentioned in passing that the Roman church had, apart from its bishop, 46 priests, 7 deacons, 7 subdeacons, 52 exorcists, lectors and door-keepers to whom must be added ancillary personnel and of course the Roman members without any official status. That this community needed organization, is self-evident. The Romans had always been noted for their organizational talent, and the available evidence shows in fact a respectably high organizational arrangement. When therefore Constantine conferred legal status on the Roman church, it had the inestimable advantage of already having a fairly advanced organization.

The fourth-century imperial government served as a classic example of monarchy. It was in the fourth century that the Roman church slowly began to pay heed to some of the so-called petrinological themes advanced by writers such as Tertullian and Cyprian. Their themes made the position and function of St Peter as the chief apostle their focal point, and these themes could not but help to crystallize the monarchic tendencies of the bishops of Rome. There was, in any case, a very articulate current of opinion in fourth-century Rome which showed keen aversion from polytheism and a corresponding preference for monotheism – the one deity replacing the many. This philosophic-religious orientation was of great advantage to the monarchic leanings of the papacy (as the Roman church came gradually to be known). As a matter of fact, in the edict of Milan (313) Constantine himself spoke of 'the deity on the celestial throne' and thereby underscored the theme of the one supreme God, the very essence of the Christian religion.

In his efforts to restore and maintain political as well as religious unity within the Roman empire, Constantine after removing his residence to Byzantium (the city on the Bosporus soon to bear his name, Constantinople) adopted the instrument which the Roman church had customarily used: the synod. The very year after Milan he convoked a council at Arles (314) which still ranks as the first Christian council summoned by a Ruler who was not a Christian. Its purpose was to find a common denominator for certain diverging dogmatic points of view relative to Christianity. As a result of the transfer of the imperial seat from Rome to Byzantium, the Eastern provinces of the empire gained at once in importance and weight, while on the other hand the role of the Roman church as the church situate in the capital began to be gravely affected by this move.

The great Council of Nicaea (325) convoked by the Emperor Constantine for the purpose of finding a common basis for the different Christian factions, was attended by nearly 200 bishops, though the church of Rome was merely represented by two priests. The balance was so much tilted towards the East that not more than four occidental bishops were present altogether, while the leader of this small group, the fifth western bishop, Hosius of Cordova, was an imperial appointee. The significance of this is not difficult to grasp: in the decisions of the first general council the church of Rome did not even play a minor part, although in a later age it was credited with the leadership of this council.

The convocation of this council, its composition and the predominance of Eastern participants were portents. It is of some considerable significance in this context to note that in his opening address Constantine referred to Byzantium as 'New Rome' – the opening bar of a major symphonic theme. If Constantinople was 'New Rome', the implication was clear for Rome itself and consequently for the standing of its church. Constantinople had become the empire's governmental and political centre of gravity. This factor was to a very large extent to determine the path of the Roman church.

Above all, because the Roman church – like any other church – was now part of the Roman public law which included the *ius in sacris*, the constitutional right of the emperor to convoke a council and to intervene directly in the affairs of the Christian Church, including the Roman church, could, from the constitutional standpoint, never be doubted. It was precisely part of the Constantinean settlement that the emperor attained this direct power in ecclesiastical matters. His designation as *pontifex maximus* (supreme priest) which according to the old Roman constitution he in any case was, was therefore no empty title. The traditional Roman monarchic imperial government thus received an enormous boost, partly owing to the influence of Christian monotheism on the one hand and partly to the 'incorporation' of the whole Christian Church into the sacred-public law on the other. The emperor had therefore a veritable legislative monopoly in ecclesiastical matters. It is advisable to draw special attention to these features because to some considerable extent they explain the growing tensions between Constantinople and the papacy, tensions which eventually led to a division of East and West. The drama that was to unfold itself in the subsequent millennium was very largely due to this constitutional legal framework of the Constantinean settlement. However little recognized, this constitutional aspect was of prime importance to the government at Constantinople.

The imperial government's aim to achieve and preserve unity throughout the empire explains why the Roman church as the principal and focal church in the Roman empire was particularly privileged by Constantine. He raised its material standards by special benefactions – which ten centuries later were the target of biting comments by Dante – and began a notable building programme which in its munificence was unsurpassed by any later Ruler. The bishop of Rome was now given a residence fitting for the bishop of the first city of the empire – the Lateran palace – and next to it the emperor began the erection of the Roman episcopal church. Mention should be made here of the other important church in Rome – St Peter's basilica – to which after its completion the earthly remains of the apostle were said to have been transferred.

This improvement of its external-material position was accompanied by internal, organizational measures. The Roman church now began the process of imitating imperial patterns. This was a feature which was to remain highly significant in the early part of the development of the Roman church. On the imperial model a chancery was established, and papal registers of incoming and outgoing mail were kept in the Lateran archives. Furthermore, as a result of imperial legislation the clerics of the Roman church began to enjoy a great many special privileges which amounted to exemption from public burdens, especially taxation as well as from the jurisdiction of the imperial courts in all cases involving faith, ecclesiastical dogma and discipline (23 June 318). Even purely civil cases had to be transferred from an imperial court to episcopal arbitration, if one of the contending parties demanded this.

Yet there was the paradoxical situation that the freedom of deployment granted to the Christian churches by imperial edict, resulted in the propagation of a great many doctrines by individual churches, especially in the East. This brought about serious internal rifts. What was lacking was a central authority endowed with the power of finally settling a controversial dispute. The only such authority was that of the imperial government. It was virtually forced to adopt a policy that imposed union on all churches, if Christianity was not to be fragmented and torn into numerous factions and sections and splinter groups, which would have nullified the basic aim which Constantine pursued in liberating the Christian Church. A council at Sardica (Sofia) was convoked by imperial order for 343 but it achieved little except an endorsement of the pre-eminent function of the Roman bishop because 'he upheld the memory of St Peter'. The vagueness of this statement, however interesting it is doctrinally, probably accounted for the small practical response to this decree, in which the primatial position of the Roman church was not unambiguously stated. The imperial policy of forcing through a union produced a situation in which the bishop of Rome was to all intents and purposes manhandled: the Emperor Constantius exiled Liberius, bishop of Rome, in 355 until he, so to speak, signed on the dotted line. This event showed clearly what great concern the imperial government then displayed in obtaining the agreement of the Roman church to the plan for unity of the

Christian faith, which was intended by Constantine to be the leaven of the Roman empire. Because it was situated in the capital of the Roman empire, the local *Roman* church had a special pre-eminence and superior authority, and its agreement to any ecclesiastical or religious measure proposed, was for this very reason held to be essential in the interests of the *Roman* empire. This position accorded to the Roman church by the imperial government to no small extent fertilized the ground for the later juristic pre-eminence and primacy of the Roman church.

In the history of the papacy – and of Christianity – the decree of the Emperor Theodosius I (27 February 380) was of fundamental importance. It made Christianity in the shape given to it by the church of Rome and the church of Alexandria the religion of the Roman empire. In substance this decree wholly accepted the point of view upon which the Roman and Alexandrian churches had insisted, that is, strict adherence to the decrees of Nicaea and condemnation of Arianism. The gist of the imperial decree was that all subjects of the empire must henceforward accept that religion 'which the apostle of God (i.e. Christ), St Peter, has delivered to the Romans and which is now professed by the pontiff Damasus and the bishop of apostolic sanctity Peter of Alexandria'. This was followed by the Nicaean declaration concerning the Trinity and the further declaration that any revolt against this religion was heresy and therefore an offence against the empire itself.

The equality stipulated in this Theodosian decree between the Alexandrian and Roman churches, did not survive more than a year. In 381 the place of the Alexandrian church was taken by the church of Constantinople on the occasion of the Second General Council. And most significantly this was called the church of New Rome and accorded a rank immediately after the Roman church. The church of Constantinople was raised to the position which Alexandria had hitherto occupied because Constantinople was the capital of the empire, and the pre-eminence which was still granted to the Roman church rested upon similar considerations: Rome was the old capital. Yet it is noteworthy in view of later developments that in his edict sanctioning the decrees of this synod (issued on 30 July 381) Theodosius did not even mention Rome or the church of Rome at all. Entirely in agreement with the Constantinean standpoint he emphasized that the imperial government alone was to be the authority which watched over the orthodoxy of the bishops (and hence of all Christians). Thereby the government made crystal clear that Rome and its church were to be relegated to an inferior place. Rome was to sink to the rank of a historical site. The inferior position now accorded to the Roman church found expression in the decree of the Council of Constantinople which stated that no bishop was allowed to intervene in the affairs of any other diocese. Translated into reality this excluded Rome from intervening in Constantinopolitan matters. The ecclesiastical centre of gravity was manifestly in Constantinople.

It is against this background that the subsequent development of the papacy as an institution of government can be understood. The period between the late fourth and the mid-fifth centuries was the age of gestation as far as the fundamental principles of papal government and the making of the institution itself were concerned. And it cannot be strongly enough stressed that this development was very largely the result of the challenge to its status issued by the imperial government of Constantinople.

A significant step in the institutional direction was taken by Damasus, the first pope to refer consistently to the Roman church as 'the apostolic see' ('sedes apostolica'). This designation was to become standard throughout the following millennium and claimed a monopolistic position for the Roman church according it superior rank and primary position among all other churches. As a counter-weight against the views expressed at the Council of Constantinople, the council held in Rome in 382 declared that the Roman church was not set up by any synodal decrees (a bold hit at the Council of Constantinople), but was founded by two apostles, St Peter and St Paul. Not only was the Roman church now credited with a double apostolic foundation – and no other church could raise a claim to so distinguished an ancestry – but this distinction conspicuously differentiated it from the church of Constantinople which, because of its recent establishment, was what it was solely by virtue of being situated in the administrative centre of the empire. The reference to a divinely willed foundation of the Roman church was a further assertion challenging the decree of the Second General Council of Constantinople. The great ideological advance which this Roman synod of 382 made was that the historic justification of the pre-eminence of the

Roman church was replaced by the assertion of a divine ordinance which had made St Peter (and St Paul, according to the synodal decree) its founder. Furthermore, this Roman synod of 382 also operated with the pregnant and potent terminology of the 'primacy of the Roman church'. In the history of the papacy no other term or concept or idea was to play such a crucial role as this. And a great deal of the subsequent papal history concerned the contents and the meaning of the 'primacy of the Roman church'.

By repeatedly emphasizing the function and position of St Peter, Damasus' pontificate officially introduced the basic petrinological theme. This was a theme that had been aired by theologians and writers and littérateurs before this time, but had not been made part of official papal doctrine or ideology. Only two such writers need be mentioned here, Cyprian and Tertullian, because their petrinological themes became integral elements of the papal programme and thus came to direct the path of the papacy. The former coined the very term of 'see of St Peter' ('cathedra Petri') specifically and exclusively referring it to the Roman church while the latter, a lawyer in the old Roman tradition, showed how Christian themes could in fact be advantageously shaped if the Roman law were brought to bear on them. Roman jurisprudence was harnessed to the service of Christian dogma and philosophy – the enduring bequest of Tertullian. The debt which the papacy owed to Tertullian is still not fully appreciated. For it was precisely the employment of jurisprudential principles which enabled the papacy to become an institution of government charged with the direction of Christians by means of the law. From its infancy the papacy had spent its life on Roman soil and in Roman environs. However much the legal complexion of the papacy has been misunderstood, the great legacy which the institution handed to later medieval (and modern) Europe is undeniable, for in the public field it was the papacy as primarily an organ of the law which formed the bridge-head between the raw, illiterate and barbarous Germanic West and the ancient, mature and fully developed Roman civilization. There was no other link between these two but the papacy in Rome. In transmitting the idea of the law as the vehicle of government the Roman papacy has made a fundamental and perhaps its most important contribution to the making of Europe.

It is therefore wholly understandable why the papacy as a legal and governmental institution readily borrowed a number of administrative features from the highly sophisticated imperial practice. Particularly conspicuous among these was the medium of communicating with the ecclesiastical authorities outside Rome. Pope Siricius, the immediate successor of Damasus, was the first to issue the kind of letter which was henceforward to be the papacy's vehicle of communication. The so-called decretal letter of the papacy was modelled on the 'decrees' or 'responses' ('responsa') of the emperor dispatched to provincial governors which decided controversial legal matters. In 385 the papacy sent a decretal letter to the Spanish bishops which is the oldest extant decretal and quite a formidable juristic document. As the name implies, a decretal was a letter which decided a matter finally and authoritatively ('decernere – decretum est'). In itself the device was at once a sign of the papacy's centralizing aims and a symptom of its authoritative standing. The decretal was a juristic decision in a concrete case, but – and this is very important to bear in mind – by virtue of the universality of papal authority, it came to be credited with universal validity.

This oldest surviving decretal of Siricius struck up themes which in the following ages were to become staple ingredients of the tens of thousands of papal decretals. Here the pope spoke of himself as the heir of St Peter and it was in this capacity that he carried the burdens of all, as he claimed, accepting thereby (on the Pauline model) responsibility for the whole Christian body public. In the spirit of the Roman synod of 382 this decretal associated the Petrinity of the pope with the idea expressed by St Paul that upon him the care of all the churches rested (II Cor. 11.28). Petrine and Pauline elements were conjoined and indissolubly linked with juristic precision and polish. From the purely juristic standpoint this Sirician decretal was a masterpiece of legal subtlety and shows the powerful influence which Roman jurisprudence had upon the nascent papacy. It is understandable that, once more in agreement with imperial practice, from the eighties of the fourth century onwards particular care was devoted to the papal archives. The archives were, so to speak, the readily available storehouse of the papacy's declarations.

Of no lesser significance in the history of the papacy was the suggestion made by Pope Damasus to St Jerome that he should translate the Bible into a Latin which was easily comprehensible and also up to date. The suggestion bore fruit in the translation which later became known as the Vulgate. The original Hebrew as well as the Greek texts of the Bible now became available in a Latin which was the language of the late fourth-century educated Roman classes. But since a good deal of the Old Testament especially was legalistic, the employment of Roman law terminology to convey the meaning of Old Testament expressions suggested itself. Roman legal terminology was thus unobtrusively disseminated thoughout the Bible text of the Vulgate. The readers of the Bible in the Middle Ages absorbed at the same time basic Roman jurisprudence. It is commonly overlooked that the Latinized Bible was one of the most influential transmitters of Roman law ideas to the European Middle Ages. That for the papacy the availability of a competent and elegant Latin text of the Bible was of vital concern, was self-evident. What needs stressing however is that the legal and institutional character of the papacy came to be strongly buttressed by the Vulgate: the service rendered by this translation to the nascent as well as the matured papacy is hardly recognized, but deserves to be properly appreciated.

Although by the late fourth century the pre-eminent position of St Peter was generally acknowledged in the local Roman milieu and although his death (and that of St Paul) as a martyr in Rome was commonly accepted, there had as yet been no attempt, certainly by the papacy, to argue the pope's function in exclusively juristic terms. It was all very well to speak of 'the apostolic see', of 'the heir of St Peter', and so on, but even if these were implicitly hinted at in the Bible, there was no explicit biblical declaration on the question of a successor to St Peter. Yet in view of the stand taken up by the papacy from Damasus onwards, the demand for a clear historical basis of these views and expressions became ever stronger. The deficiency of a provable original declaration was no doubt keenly felt at this very time. It is assuredly no coincidence that at the turn of the fourth and fifth centuries a document originally written in Greek towards the end of the second century, was translated by Rufinus of Aquileja who is better known through his translation of the *Church History* by Eusebius. It was this document in Latin translation which provided the missing link between St Peter and the popes in Rome as his legal successors. And it was in this document that the

crucial biblical passage was cited in full, according to which
Christ had handed to St Peter the keys of the kingdom of heaven
so that what St Peter loosed on earth, would be loosed in heaven,
and what St Peter bound on earth would be bound in heaven.
This conferment of powers by Christ on St Peter was a trans-
mission in thoroughly juristic terms and accorded well with
Jewish tradition. And the juristic tenor of this Matthean passage
(Matt. 16.18f.) was perhaps still more clearly discernible in the
Latin translation which employed the characteristic Roman law
terms and notions of *solvere* (to loose) and *ligare* (to bind) as the
operational terms of the passage.

The importance of this piece warrants a few more remarks.
Written by an unknown author, it purported to be a letter which
Pope Clement I – a historic personality – was said to have written
to St James, the brother of Christ, in Jerusalem informing him
of the last disposition which St Peter had made when he felt his
end near. In this spurious letter to St James, Pope Clement said
that St Peter had summoned the Roman Christian community
and addressed them in a quite unambiguous manner thus:

> I (that is, Peter) impart to him (that is, Clement) the authority of
> binding and loosing in order that whatever he (Clement) will decide
> upon earth, will be approved in heaven, for he will bind what must
> be bound and he will loose what should be loosed.

This was meant to be a last-will disposition announced in public
so that there could be no doubt about its intent. This was a
clear institution narrative according to which Clement was 'the
first pope' after Peter who appointed his successor in front of the
Roman assembly. This theme was so important to the anonymous
author of the (Greek) piece that he returned to it several times in
the same epistle. The specific institution of a successor established
the concrete and historical link between Peter and the Roman
popes. The Latin translation by Rufinus came at exactly the right
time. But as was his custom, he did not only translate, but also
embellished the original Greek text in his translation, touched it
up and enlarged some items presenting them in stronger terms
than the Greek text warranted.

What made this Epistle of Clement a vital document was that
in a skilful manner it focused attention on the juristic side of the
papacy. There had of course been other sees which had been

founded by St Peter, notably Antioch, but nowhere did St Peter institute a successor except in the Roman see. This document underlined the singularity and uniqueness of the one successor of St Peter, and it also took pains to refer to the successors of Clement – the whole chain of succession was presented in this Epistle. Further, although every bishop succeeded to the totality of the apostles, the bishop of Rome was the sole successor to the head of the apostles. The author of this document wished to pinpoint the juristic nature of Peter's one and only successor who stood thus in strong contradistinction to all the other bishops. As the only successor of St Peter the pope could therefore act in the same way in which St Peter himself would have acted by virtue of the powers given him by Christ. The idea of a legally conceived monarchy was certainly latent in this document. The subsequent juristic development of the papacy as an institution owed a very great deal to this Epistle which was cited over and over again right down to the sixteenth century. And it was from the early fifth century onwards that the crucial Matthean verses became the explicit and implicit staple ingredient of every official papal document, declaration or communication during the following millennium, if not beyond. In brief, the Latin translation of this Greek document crystallized attention on the ideological and juristic wealth of the Matthean passage. As a result it became one of the axiomatic tenets of the medieval papacy.

Moreover, the unique link of the Roman church with St Peter – its 'Petrinity' – was also expressed in allegorical language. Thus, for instance, the Pauline metaphor of all Christians forming one body was expanded by emphasizing the vital role which the head of the body, here St Peter himself, and his successors, played in the scheme. Further, in the already mentioned decretal of Siricius the pope declared that the members of the Church could always have recourse 'to the head of the body'. This allegory of head and members of the body was not to disappear again from the vocabulary and mental framework of the medieval papacy. Allegories were particularly suitable means by which some of the most fundamental themes could be driven home in an impressive way. The contribution which metaphorical expressions made to the entrenchment of the papal position should not be underestimated. They are reliable witnesses of a contemporary frame of mind, and also – as in this specific instance – factors which themselves propelled the historical evolution of the papacy itself. It was not, then, surprising that the papacy already in the early fifth century claimed to be the fountainhead ('exordium') of Christianity, both in a metaphorical and literal sense.

Some other factors in the early part of the fifth century helped the papacy towards the realization of the full monarchic position of the pope. The first decade witnessed the large-scale invasion of barbarian hordes under Alaric who sacked Rome in 410. The city was powerless, because the imperial government had more and more concentrated on the East at the expense of the West – a policy which left the Western half of the empire virtually defence-less and exposed to the attacks by the Germanic tribes. But because the centre of gravity was in Constantinople, the imperial government had less opportunity of exercising control over the papacy which, simply by force of circumstance, found itself assuming an actively leading role, at any rate in Rome. It is therefore understandable that the papacy made remarkable strides towards establishing itself as a governmental organ. The flow of decretals during Innocent I's pontificate reached a high-water mark both in quantity and quality. They were addressed to Italian, Spanish, Gallic, African metropolitans and bishops, and constituted the most ancient residue of decretals in all subsequent collections of the papal law. In style, structure and above all juristic penetration and refinement they were worthy equals of their imperial patterns (the rescripts). The tone of these early decretals was the language of authoritative government; they were suffused with juristic wisdom, detached and objective. Their underlying idea was frequently enough repeated: no bishop was at liberty to set aside with impunity a papal decretal and synodal decisions – a standpoint already expressed by Siricius in his decretal. Celestine I declared that 'the law (as embodied in the papal decretals) should be our master, and we as its recipients must not try to master, but to serve, the law'. Hardly anywhere had the idea of the rule of law found a more emphatic expression, at any rate at that time. And the importance of this viewpoint is only heightened if it is thrown against the contemporary brutality, horror and other by-products of the barbarian invasions. The message of the fifth-century papacy was that civilized government could be transacted only through the vehicle of the law. And the papal law embodied in the decretal letter decisively helped to form medieval society and gave it a complexion which is still not fully appreciated.

The core of the decretals was that according to the papal theme they made explicit and applicable to human, earthly conditions what divinity had laid down. Law was the emanation of divinity, but could be made known to mankind only through the appropriately qualified organs. This was a point which in the course of the fifth century was to acquire crucial significance when the Roman empire was, certainly not unjustifiably, equated with the *oikumene*, that is, with the world-wide union of all Christians. The law issued by the papacy in its decretals derived its binding character not from any humanly expressed consent or from historically binding considerations, but from the faith of the Christian in the divinely ordained government of the universe. Divinity was held to act through the instrumentality of its properly qualified officers. And since the monarchic idea of government had its strongest possible support in the petrinological argument, that is, the Petrinity of the Roman church, a centralized form of government evidently suggested itself, and this found unambiguous expression in one of Innocent I's decretals, according to which all major causes must be referred to the apostolic see.

The significance of this Innocentian constitutional principle was that it was to guarantee uniformity and unity of the Christian body public. From this standpoint what in actual fact was a 'major cause' could logically enough be defined only by the papacy. The device was to have a large share in strengthening the governmental functions of the papacy. What was furthermore noteworthy was that Innocent based the centralizing mechanism explicitly on a passage in the Old Testament (Ex. 18.22) according to which Moses was advised to set up judges over the people, but nevertheless to reserve any great matters for himself. The standpoint marked the beginning of the Bible as a *pièce justificative* of papal governmental pronouncements. In crucial matters papal principles were not to rest on tradition, history, synodal statutes, or other man-made organs. Among all historically evolved governments this was a unique phenomenon. Reality was to be subjected to the ideology enshrined in the law, and in its basic ingredients this ideology was the sum-total of the Christian faith. In a word, the government by the papacy of the corporate union of all Christians proceeded on lines which externally, that is, in form, were modelled on the Roman pattern of the imperial rescript, but which internally, that is, in substance, fundamentally differed from their prototypes. For the internal substance of the papal law was said to be biblically inspired and derived. This is the same as saying that the papacy interpreted and applied the divine law of the Bible to the exigencies of the government of the Christian body itself. Consequently, the antecedent historical process itself was, if not wholly disregarded, at any rate relegated to the background.

The complement to the constitutional principle according to which major causes had to be referred to the Roman church, was the explicit declaration by Boniface I that the papacy occupied 'the apostolic height' ('apostolicum culmen') from the verdict of which no appeal lay to any other authority or tribunal, a viewpoint already expressed by Pope Zosimus in 418. Thereby the appeal to a council or to the imperial court was excluded. The monarchic form of government was thus quite effectively shielded against obvious encroachments. This development within less than a generation and in the midst of most unfavourable external circumstances would go to show how prepared, alert and skilful the papacy was in establishing some of its crucial principles by the simple device of the decretal. In a seemingly routine decretal of 429 Celestine I laid down the principle of (papal) leadership in general terms. This thesis in one way or another reverberated throughout the Middle Ages and beyond: the people should be led, and should not lead itself (*Ducendus est populus, sed non sequendus*).

The authority of the Roman church was confined to the churches in the West. On the Eastern churches the papacy had very little influence. It is true that the Western half of the empire was always far less inclined towards theological and philosophical problems than the Eastern half. There a problem, such as whether Christ was divine as well as human, assumed major proportions. This christological question split the East into several contending factions. In order to find a compromise between the warring theological schools in the East, the emperor convoked a Council at Ephesus (431) which was to rank as the Third General Council of Christian antiquity. It was well attended by Eastern ecclesiastics, but did not attract many from the West. Nevertheless, a small papal legation of three spokesmen joined the assembly and also took some part in the discussions. They drove home the sonorous Petrine theme. Their leader declared in the session on 11 July 431 that everybody knew that St Peter as chief of the apostles was the foundation stone of the universal Church and that his successor and *locum tenens* was the pope in Rome, Celestine I.

This legatine declaration at the Council of Ephesus was of fundamental importance, evidenced by its re-appearance in countless official papal statements from Leo I right down to the Vatican decree of 1870 concerning the perpetuity of the primacy of St Peter. Yet despite these triumphant, though purely academic statements at the Council, in all other respects the role which the papacy and the papal legation played in the proceedings and in the making of the conciliar decrees, was negligible. Nevertheless, these abstract expressions were carefully stored in the archives of the papacy. The great advantage which the papal archives offered as veritable ideological storehouses – always readily available for reference whenever needed – began to show itself.

With Leo the Great the first phase of papal history comes to a conclusion. In his pontificate the primatial monarchic theme of the papacy received its final theoretical stamp. It was precisely by virtue of this finalization that the different aims, bases and structures of both the papacy and the imperial government in Constantinople came fully into the open. The gulf was too conspicuous to be disregarded any longer. Leo's imposing and yet very simple doctrinal edifice was to stand its test down to the modern period. He did not, however, invent the primatial theme but skilfully wove together a number of strains. By combining juristic, theological and biblical arguments he constructed a theme of papal monarchy which enabled the papacy to weather many a storm. A Roman by birth and upbringing he united in his person the practical diplomat and the man of abstract argumentation: one side complemented the other, and what characterized them both was true Roman simplicity.

In his function as pope he was a member of the Roman embassy which met the menacingly advancing king of the Huns in Northern Italy near Mantua in 452. This embassy (and not solely the pope, as later legend had it) dissuaded Attila from continuing his advance towards Rome, and Italy was spared a great deal of destruction. It was Leo who three years later persuaded Geiseric, the Ruler of the Vandals who had occupied the city, to abstain from murder, arson and tortures, though even so, Rome became for a whole fortnight the scene of plunder and of thousands of arrests by the invading troops. But the doctrinal attainments of Leo altogether overshadow the merits he had in mitigating the effects of foreign occupation.

Leo I used the Roman law in order to clarify the position of the pope as successor of St Peter, a theme that, as already indicated, had been struck up several times before. But Leo gave it juristic foundation in a manner which only a superb jurist could do. He operated with the Roman law of inheritance according to which the heir stepped legally into the place of the deceased person and thus in every legal respect succeeded him: the Roman heir continued in law the legal status of the deceased and took over his estate, his assets and liabilities, in short his rights and duties came to be possessed by the heir as his successor. The 'historic' link between St Peter and the pope was established by the letter which Clement I was said to have written to St James in Jerusalem (see above pp. 13f.). Upon this platform Leo imposed the juristic theme of inheritance so that the pope became St Peter's heir in regard to his powers, though not of course in regard to his personal status which was, understandably, not transferable or inheritable. In other words, the office, the objective legal status, the powers of St Peter were inherited by the pope, but not his subjective merits of having recognized Christ as the Son of God. Leo I expressed this juristic theme in the formula of the pope as 'the unworthy heir of St Peter' – a formula which has stood the test of time. In this succinct formula the objective element was that of succession or inheritance, the subjective element was that of the pope's personal unworthiness to inherit the office. And because the pope continued the status and office of St Peter, he was (not an 'apostolus' but) an 'apostolicus' – hence the ease with which the new adjectival form of 'apostolic' could be applied to the Roman see.

The great advance of this Leonine theme lay in the separation of the (objective) office of the pope (which was the same as St Peter's) from the (subjective) personality of the pope. And for governmental purposes it was the office of the pope, the papacy as such, which mattered, not the purely subjective personality, whether he was a 'good' or a 'bad' pope. Indeed, there can have been few governments in the history of mankind which had at their disposal so concise a programmatic theme as the papacy had from Leo I onwards. First, by the principles of Roman law the pope as an office holder was indistinguishable from St Peter himself. Second, the pope as office holder continued the *legal* personality of the first 'pope', with the consequence that, in his function as pope, no pope followed his immediate predecessor but St Peter directly: there was no intermediary between St Peter and the actual office holder. Third, the office thus inherited could be measured by purely objective criteria, or vice-versa, subjective standards and personal qualifications were irrelevant as far as the scope and extent of the office were concerned. In other words, within the terms of papal primatial doctrine the validity of a papal act or decree or judgment did not depend upon the morality or sanctity or other subjective-moral standards applicable to the person of the pope, but solely upon whether or not the judgment or decree was legally valid, and this requirement was measurable by objective standards.

This basic distinction between the (objective) office and the (subjective) office holder was of crucial importance to the medieval papacy, because what mattered was solely the objectively conceived law or judgment, and not the person of him who issued it. The office, in a word, absorbed the man. The cornerstone of the papacy was the office pure and simple: the pope as office holder was conceived to be an instrument to execute the office, that is, to translate the abstract programme of the papacy into reality. The Leonine bequest was the thorough de-personalization of the papal office. That this office (and the medieval papacy as an institution) suffered no damage from popes of extremely dubious or criminal character, was certainly due to the operation of this principle which disregarded the personality of the pope and concentrated solely on the papal office as a thing inherited from St Peter.

Seen from a different angle this Leonine theme culminated in the conception of the papacy as an organ of government. And government at all times concerned itself with authoritative guidance and direction of a community or group or association. Here, within the primatial thesis, the government as well as its form and purpose were, according to Leo I's interpretation of the

Matthean passage, laid down by Christ Himself. It was held to be the most exalted kind of monarchy because established by divinity itself. The purpose for which this government was set up, was the direction of the Christian community to its eventual goal, that is, salvation. The instrument of government was the legally conceived power of binding and loosing – a nomenclature of Old Testament origin and attractive to the legally trained Roman ear (see above pp. 11f.). The comprehensive powers inherited by the pope constituted according to Leo I a plenitude of power ('plenitudo potestatis' as he termed it). This papal plenitude of power was therefore a thoroughly juristic notion, and could be understood only from this angle and against the Roman law background. It was this side of the papal office which in later terminology was called jurisdictional power ('potestas iurisdictionis'). Hence in order to become, be and act as pope it was never (and still is not) necessary to be 'in holy orders', that is, to be ordained a priest or consecrated a bishop. The papal office did not presuppose any clerical status, hence any layman could (and can) become pope. At the time of their election or appointment very few medieval popes were priests or bishops.

This Leonine theme brought into clear relief the double foundation which the crucial Matthean passage contained. Christ founded a new society – the Church as the congregation of all the Christians – and in this same act also laid down the kind of government, that is, monarchy, to be exercised over the society. The society thus founded and its government thus established, were therefore tied together from the very beginning – that was the core of the Leonine and subsequent papal theme. Consequently, the Church was built upon the rock, that is, St Peter, and in order to build the society in agreement with the divine founder's designs Christ had given 'plenary powers' to St Peter. These were identical with those Christ Himself had. In the papal theme the pope therefore inherited the totality of Peter's powers. This Leonine kind of monarchy greatly resembled the kind of monarchy observable in regard to the contemporary Roman emperor. And Pope Leo I – as indeed Boniface I (in 422) before him – had no qualms in applying the Roman imperial term of *principatus* to the papal concept of primacy. The papacy was continually to refer to itself as possessing the *principatus* which indeed had been the constitutional term describing Roman imperial monarchy since the first century. It designated the supreme jurisdictional status which the papacy claimed to exercise within the Christian community, within the Church. The pope functioned on behalf of and in direct succession to St Peter, and St Peter himself was spoken of in papal quarters as the *princeps*, once more a terminology current in imperial usage since the time of Augustus in the first century.

Despite its terminological borrowings from the Roman government, this Leonine fixation of the primatial position of the pope drew a sharp distinction between the *principatus* of the papacy and the *principatus* of the empire. For the understanding of the evolution of the papacy it is essential to keep in mind that its *principatus* was held to have nothing to do with history, because it was the direct effluence of a unique divine act. The establishment of the Petrine papal monarchy was conceived as the exercise of the sovereign divine will. The *principatus* of the empire on the other hand was primarily a matter of history and of human organization and administration; this imperial principate was the outcome of an historical growth manipulated by purely human acts, and since all power stemmed from God, the imperial principate was only in a secondary way considered to be divinely willed. And a major historical point was that from immemorial times part of the Roman public law consisted of the 'ius in sacris'. Nothing had changed in this and nothing was to change in it throughout Byzantine history, namely that the public law contained as an essential ingredient the law relating to 'sacred matters' and among these in Christian times ecclesiastical matters figured prominently. The controlling organ of the public law was the emperor.

The point was that for the papacy historical contingencies were mere appendices to the supra-historical, divine volition, whereas for the imperial government history was of primary and the divine sanction of secondary importance. Differently expressed: for the papacy the historical development was no more than a confirmation of what was in the Bible and especially in the New Testament which established the institution of the papacy. For the empire the relationship was in all vital respects the reverse: the divinely willed order of things served as a powerful confirmation of the antecedent historical development. It was highly significant therefore that at the very time of Leo's pontificate the first imperial coronation by the patriarch of Constantinople took place (in 451): the imperial coronation was to show symbolically that divinity had approved of the emperor – the coronation was therefore always merely confirmatory and declaratory (quite in contrast to the later Western imperial coronation) (see below pp. 185ff.). Indeed, throughout the following millennium the strength of the Roman empire lay in its purely historical (as opposed to ideological) claims. Comparatively few historical facts spoke in favour of the papacy. All the stronger was abstract ideology, that is, the conception of the pope as direct successor of St Peter who was charged with the task of building the Church.

The relative importance allocated to history and doctrine by the empire and the papacy explains one more feature which emerged in the mid-fifth century and which was to exercise considerable influence on the relations between the two. One and the same body public could be viewed from two entirely different standpoints. The body under the control of the emperor was the Roman empire, of which the pope was a member. The body claimed to be under the control of the pope was the Church, of which the emperor was a member. Roughly speaking, the empire was co-terminous with the Church. The one – the empire – was a historically grown unit, in which the human element necessarily predominated, though the existence and sanction of the empire was divinely willed. The other – the Church – was a divine foundation, the government of which was simultaneously set up by a specific divine declaration, in which the human element played no role (see above p. 22). The consequence of looking at one and the same body from two different angles was that each standpoint necessarily impinged upon the respective government, for an empire could be governed only by an emperor, and a Church on the papal premisses only by a pope. It will presently be seen how much this twofold complexion shaped the history of both the empire and the papacy, leading eventually to the schism between East and West and finally to the rise of Western-Latin Europe.

In this context the meaning of the Roman-Byzantine imperial coronation deserves a further remark. Within the framework of this coronation as it was practised down to the fall of Constantinople in 1453 there is abundant evidence of the priority and primary role assigned to the historical roots and character of the empire and the purely confirmatory and secondary role allocated to divine and religious matters. In substance the imperial coronation added nothing whatsoever to the standing of the emperor or to his powers; and as regards his status as so-called 'God's representative' on earth, the coronation was wholly irrelevant. It solemnly declared a state of affairs that was already there, namely that the emperor was the representative of the Pantokrator (God) on earth. It was a mere ecclesiastical ritual, performed by the patriarch of Constantinople, himself an appointee of the emperor. In perhaps no other connexion does the essentially historical basis of the empire so clearly assume its predominance over religious considerations as within the imperial coronation: it was a solemn festivity and devoid of ideological meaning.

These differences between the relative role of history and religion (or faith) came to be epitomized in two of the most important decrees which the Fourth General Council, that of Chalcedon, issued in 451. This council was prompted amongst other things by the still unresolved christological disputes in the Eastern half of the empire. As the imperial convocation edict said, the council was summoned 'for the sake of fixing the true faith'. This council counted more than 600 participants, of whom however no more than five came from the occident: two African and three papal legates whose demand that they should preside, was flatly rejected by the imperial commission that dealt with organizational matters. The question which had inflamed Eastern theologians and ecclesiastics generally was the precise relationship between the human and the divine natures of Christ. Leo I's so-called 'Dogmatic Letter' which the papal legates read out in the session on 10 October 451, was the greatest triumph – it was also the last – which the papacy had achieved in the East. In this letter Roman prudence, statesmanship and delicacy in handling highly explosive material manifested themselves abundantly: the papal declaration, apparently reflecting the theological standpoint of the West, contained an ingenious formula which appeared to have satisfied all shades of opinion. The council rose in unison acclaiming the declaration by the famous words 'St Peter has spoken through Leo'. This was a triumph which no other pope had earned and received – the argumentation in this work of Leo's raised him some 1300 years later to the rank of a 'Doctor of the Church'.

But it was a short-lived triumph of the papacy. From these triumphant chords to the bitter and discordant notes at the end of this same Council of Chalcedon was only a short step. In its 17th chapter the council decreed that the civic status of a city also determined its ecclesiastical status which was a point of view already clearly hinted at in the Council of Constantinople in 381 (see above p. 9) and that had been decisively rejected by the papacy. The 28th chapter of Chalcedon (also elaborating the same Council of Constantinople) laid down that New Rome (Constantinople) had a status similar to that of Old Rome. Here indeed the whole Constantinean ecclesiastical scheme had won a resounding victory. What counted was the historical and political set-up. Because Constantinople was the residence of the emperor it was also the capital of the empire and this status of the city was reflected in the heightened status of its patriarch – that clearly was the meaning of the 17th chapter. What Rome and Constantinople had in common was the same honorary rank – that clearly was the meaning of the 28th chapter. That Rome was still accorded the same rank of honour as New Rome rested on the consideration that Rome gave the empire its name; and Constantinople possessed an equal rank of honour because it was now the administrative and political capital of this Roman empire. Taken together, these two chapters of the Council of Chalcedon effectively set in motion the fateful development which was to lead to the split between East and West.

This same council of Chalcedon was silent in the one respect that alone mattered from the papal standpoint, that is, the primacy of the Roman church. By implication, however, this claim was clearly rejected by both the chapters already mentioned. Rome was in any case hardly a city in which orderly conditions prevailed when the council was in session. It is not to be wondered at, however, that the Roman legates at the council at once fiercely remonstrated against the decrees, refused to sign them and left in protest. In perhaps no other instance could the gulf between the imperial Constantinean and the papal Petrine viewpoints be more convincingly demonstrated than in these two decrees. The acclamation by the council of the Emperor Marcian in the session on 25 October 451 as 'New Constantine' and as 'King and Priest' was indubitably intended as a rebuff to what the conciliarists and the government considered to be Roman papal pretensions, for the Roman church had raised its primatial claims with increasing insistency and frequency in precisely these years. It was also understandable why the imperial government steadfastly and consistently refused to refer to 'the principate of the Roman church'.

Inspired by the papacy the West-Roman Emperor Valentinian III (425–455) issued on 17 July 445 an edict which potently assisted the establishment of papal authority and primacy in the West. This imperial edict (which was not valid in the Eastern and by then much more important half of the empire) fully acknowledged the jurisdictional supremacy of the papacy, for 'nothing should be done against or without the authority of the Roman church'. According to this imperial rescript the Roman church had a threefold basis: 'the merits of St Peter'; the rank and dignity of the city of Rome; and a synodal decision (by which Valentinian referred to chapter 6 of the Council of Nicaea as later interpolated by Rome and which ran: 'The Roman church had always had primacy'). No doubt is permissible that one of the reasons for issuing this edict was to maintain an orderly ecclesiastical organization and to prevent, if possible, a recurrence in the West of what was observable in the East. For the papacy the edict was of major importance: it was the secular and imperial confirmation of the claim to primacy. In its significance this edict must stand next to the law of 380 by which Christianity was made the official religion of the empire. The papal claim to jurisdictional primacy was not, it must be emphasized, granted by this edict, but powerfully supplemented. The edict turned the papal claim into a constitutional law. It is of some interest to note that this edict laid down that whatever the authority of the Roman church should have decided or should in future decide, was to be binding and therefore was to be the law (*lex*). Moreover, the violation of this imperial edict and consequently the disregard of papal primacy constituted the crime of *lèse majesté*: after all, this was a constitutional law. Indeed, there is every justification for saying that by the middle years of the fifth century the subsequent development could quite clearly be discerned on the not too distant horizon.

B

2 *The Papal Conflict with the Imperial Government*

DURING THE PERIOD between the Council of Chalcedon and the pontificate of Gregory I the contours of the subsequent development began to show themselves distinctly. It was during this period that, as a result of the full implementation of the Constantinean plan (see above p. 7) by the imperial government, the papacy was forced to declare itself on a number of essential points: these were made in the face of what the papacy considered a serious challenge to its own vocation, *raison d'être* and purpose. Moreover, the principles which the late fifth-century papacy enunciated constituted the groundwork and framework of the papacy in the subsequent ages. It is therefore of prime importance to realize that the physiognomy and complexion of the medieval papacy were formed at this time and in specific relation to the imperial government at Constantinople. The papacy never lost these features – its path was determined by the imperial government which compelled it to clarify its own position within a Christian society. It was the fateful intimate link of the papacy with the city of Rome, the one-time capital of the empire, its absorption of Roman governmental themes and their integration into its own system which historically explains its clash with the imperial government. And to a very large extent the medieval papacy was the product of the fifth-century papal conflict with Constantinople. It was a struggle fought within the precincts of the empire itself and therefore on Roman terms. Shaped and structured in this severe confrontation with the empire, the papal programme and plan were given their contours, and the papacy that emerged from the conflict entered the medieval period.

Moreover, the Western parts of the empire experienced politically, economically, if not also socially and culturally, a very real

alienation from the East. The wholly ineffectual imperial governments in the West – and they appeared still more ineffectual in
comparison with the firm hands that were at the helm in
Constantinople – brought about a void in both Rome and Italy,
a contingency which not inconsiderably favoured the ascendancy
of the papacy as a governmental force. The weaker the West
became, however, the more stridently the East reaffirmed the
truly Roman character of the empire. The disappearance of the
Western half of the empire by the late fifth century, evoked all the
greater resonance in the East which considered itself the sole,
rightful heir and continuator of the grand, ancient empire that
bore the Roman name and originated in Rome. It is advisable to
point out how Byzantium became more and more aware of its
'Roman mission', not in spite, but because, of the sinking of
Rome to the level of a museum site: what was once applicable to
(Old) Rome, was now simply transferred to New Rome. Because
of the deteriorating situation in sixth-century Italy the Rulers at
Constantinople insisted upon their role as true 'Roman' emperors
with all the greater force. This role necessarily emphasized the
emperor's secular and ecclesiastical functions on the old-Roman
Constantinean model which was gilded with the Christian garb of
rulership. Although externally the ancient Roman *princeps* had
undergone a metamorphosis, in substance he remained what he
was: he was still 'King and Priest', at least as far as ecclesiastical
organizational matters were concerned; he was still 'divine'; his
laws were still 'sacred'; and he still bore the title of 'pontifex
inclytus' ('the most noble pontiff'). All this was evidently the
christianized bequest of the ancient Roman constitutional
arrangement whereby the *ius in sacris* as part of the public law
was controlled by the emperor (see also above pp. 5, 7, 23).

The ecclesiastical situation in the East was, in fact, particularly
apt to provoke imperial intervention. For there was, among the
higher ecclesiastics, considerable doctrinal unrest that involved
the imperial court. It again concerned christological controversies
which now had assumed alarming proportions, and they seriously
threatened the unity of the empire itself. The monophysites –
those who held that Christ possessed one nature only – and the
followers of the Chalcedonian settlement – which had pursued a
compromise solution – clashed and through the Patriarch Acacius,
the domestic-imperial prelate, the court came to be directly

implicated. In order to restore unity and to placate both camps, the Emperor Zeno in 482 issued an edict known by its formula of faith as the *Henotikon*. It was an imperially decreed edict which fixed the faith for the whole Roman empire, but – and in this lies its deep significance – it was issued entirely on the emperor's own authority, without above all any synodal consultation, let alone sanction, and profoundly affected both dogma and faith in a way that was to all intents and purposes opposed to the carefully worded Chalcedonian compromise. The *Henotikon* was indeed the first visible and concrete manifestation of the rapid advance towards an imperial régime that was a revised Christian edition of the old Roman monarchy. On the pattern of the ancient Roman emperorship, the emperor considered himself as the divinely appointed mouthpiece of Christ on earth: besides proclaiming what, in the interests of unity, he held to be the correct faith, he also realized that abstract pronouncements concerning the faith must be accompanied or followed by organizational and concrete measures against those who resisted the imperial formula of the new faith. Briefly, a number of hesitant or recalcitrant bishops were deposed by imperial verdicts, others and more compliant ones appointed in their place, and, in a number of instances, because of their opposition, high and leading ecclesiastics were charged with the crime of *lèse majesté*.

It was advisable briefly to depict the situation as it developed in the Eastern half of the empire during the latter part of the fifth century. For these (and numerous other) measures affected the papacy in Rome profoundly. Here for the first time the papal office had come into the hands of a member of the Roman senatorial nobility – Felix III was the first pope not to come from the lower sections of the Roman populace and hence to be conversant with the thought-processes of the ruling classes. The son of a priest, he was a widower when elected pope, had a number of children, had ample experience of civil life, and above all, was energetically assisted in his office by one of the ablest heads of the papal chancery, who was to be his successor, Pope Gelasius I. The pontificates of Felix III and Gelasius I constituted one unit and appropriately marked the concluding stages of the all-important Leonine papacy. They refined and defined in specific terms what was needed to be refined and defined. The situation as it had evolved called indeed for some clarification by the papacy, because the *raison d'être* of the institution of the papacy itself was indubitably challenged by the dogmatic and ecclesiastical measures enacted ruthlessly by New Rome.

Indeed, the policy pursued by the imperial government in Constantinople denied the very bases of the papacy and its governmental aim. The papacy held itself to be charged by divinity with the government, guidance and authoritative leadership of all Christians. And the recent imperial measures constituted a veritable challenge to the papacy which saw itself thwarted in the execution of its divinely imposed task. This imperial challenge forced the papacy to define and give precision to a number of governmental principles which were partly consequential to the Leonine primatial theme and partly grafted upon it. Moreover, it was also during the last decades of the fifth century that non-papal, private literary sources of Roman provenance began greatly to assist the papal theme; these were among the first unofficial Roman-Latin aids for the papacy. The result was the first serious schism between Rome and Constantinople, that is, outwardly between the papacy and the patriarchate of Constantinople, but in reality between the papacy and the imperial government which sheltered the Patriarch Acacius.

The problem presenting itself to the papacy in the eighties of the fifth century concerned the qualification for governing the Church as the congregation of all Christians. It was in this context that the twofold manner of looking at the Roman empire displayed its practical significance. It will be recalled (see above p. 24) that to the imperial government this Roman empire was the same as the ancient Roman empire, although Christianity had assumed a vital and cementing role within it. To the papacy on the other hand this same body public could be viewed as the Church which happened to be co-terminous with the Roman empire. Hence the fundamental clash concerning the right to govern, that is, to direct this unit. The papacy maintained that since this body was the Church universal, it had to be ruled in regard to the essential matters of the Christian faith – on all sides admitted to be the very buttress and cementing bond of the empire – by the only qualified organ, that is, the apostolic see as the divinely appointed governing instrument; the emperor, although playing an indispensable role within this scheme, had logically enough to follow the pronouncements of the papacy by translating them into practice, and this was to be done by turning the abstract pronouncement into the enforceable measures of the law. The imperial government on the other hand maintained that because within the Roman empire the Christian religion played a decisive role, it was the right and duty of the emperors to control all issues of faith, religion and the ecclesiastical organism, precisely the matters denied to the emperors by the papacy. The imperial stand was the residue of the old Roman principle that sacral matters were controlled by the emperor (see also above p. 29).

Government was understood by both the emperors and the popes as the authoritative direction of the corporate union of Christians in regard to the basic essentials of Christian life – it was at this point in fact that the ideology of the papacy showed considerably more strength and resilience than that of the imperial government: not surprisingly, because the papacy always gave precedence to ideas over facts, whereas the empire always stressed the priority of historical facts over ideas. What the papacy was insistent upon in this period was the exclusive right to enunciate the abstract ideas relative to the basic issues of Christianity. Once more the ancient Roman constitution served the papacy well: it chose the term of *auctoritas* which designated the final and supreme and unchallengeable ruling in any controversial matter. *Auctoritas* as claimed by the papacy from now onwards meant the faculty of laying down in a binding manner the fundamental guide lines that were to direct Christian society. That was the idea behind the (Roman) concept of the *principatus* of the Roman church which itself was the constitutional term for Roman monarchy.

It was these fundamental views which were set forth in a number of official papal communications in the last decades of the fifth century. Both as the draftsman of Felix III and as pope, Gelasius I formulated the idea of the papal monarchy with special reference to the actuality of the situation. In so doing he very greatly enlarged the storehouse of basic papal ideas which were to become the backbone of the medieval papacy. He maintained that both pope and emperor were necessary for the government of the 'world' (which to him was still the Roman empire), though each was called upon to function in a different way. The pope had the *auctoritas* which was moreover hallowed or sacred (*sacrata*) and which 'authoritatively' and finally determined those matters which were of direct concern to the Christian body public, such as the fixation of articles of faith, ecclesiastical organization, ecclesiastical jurisdiction – in other words, those very things which made any Christian society a living body. In this scheme of things the emperor had a mere 'royal power'. Gelasius thus considered that divinity had distinguished the emperor by conferring upon him the gift of the highest available power. It was this power which compelled him as the recipient of the divine gift and therefore as a Christian Ruler to enforce by his imperial law 'what the hallowed authority of the pontiffs' had laid down. And in order to make himself crystal clear and in terms readily understandable by his contemporary emperor, Gelasius emphasized the role which the popes had to play on the day of judgment, for it was they (and not the emperors) who had to render an account of how the emperors had discharged the trust which divinity had granted to them in the shape of 'royal power'.

The essential features of this Gelasian point of view – it has rightly been called the Great Charter of the medieval papacy – were first that within Christian society Rulership was a gift made by divinity, hence was a divine trust to be used in the interests of the divine foundation, the Church itself; and secondly the principle of the division of labour which should prevail in a Christian society: supreme guiding authority belonged to the papacy, as far as basic matters were concerned, but the emperor whose power indubitably stemmed from God (for there was no power but of God) was to function as the executive organ of the papacy, so that the purpose for which the emperor as a Christian Ruler existed, was to be realized. In Gelasius' thought pattern the emperor as a secular power pursued a definite and divinely fixed end, that is, to guard the Church universal and to protect the corporate union of all Christians. Hence the claim that the emperors should arrange their governmental actions and measures in such a manner that they fitted into the pattern fixed by the papacy.

The historic significance of this Gelasian doctrine was the clarification of the position of any secular power which was to function as an essential part of the Christian body public. The emperor, and later the king, was a member of the Church ruled by the papal monarch. The secular Ruler's role was to learn, not to teach, what is (and what is not) Christian. It was in order to perform the task of Rulership over the Church universal that according to Gelasius the pope had inherited from St Peter the right to bind and to loose. The petrinological argument thereby received precision. For according to the same Gelasius, the Petrine powers were all-embracing and comprehensive, since nothing was exempted from this power (which Leo I had already designated by the term of 'plenitude of power'). To cap his petrinological theme Gelasius also laid claim to the exemption of ecclesiastics from the jurisdiction of the secular courts: it may well be true that some of the bishops deposed by the imperial government had been guilty of high treason, but as ordained members of the Church they were not subjected to imperial jurisdiction. The principle of 'benefit of clergy' which was to play a major role in later medieval ecclesiastical history, was plainly pre-portrayed there. And hand in hand with this claim went its corollary that the papacy could not be judged by anyone – a governmental principle that had already made its first tentative appearance two generations earlier (see above p. 18). The papacy's fundamental petrinological and monarchic theme was classically expressed in the words of Gelasius himself:

> Nobody at any time and for whatever human pretext may haughtily set himself above the office of him who by Christ's order was set above all and everyone and whom the universal Church had always recognized as its head.

Statements such as these reveal the considerable degree of self-confidence that inspired the papacy at the end of the fifth century. They breathed, if not a spirit of defiance to the rulings of the 'divine majesty' of the emperor, at any rate a spirit of independence and also audacity. They show how both external factors, such as the collapse of the government in Rome, and internal factors, such as the recourse to unchallengeable biblical and divine reasonings, had contributed to the papacy's awareness of its own role and function as well as of its responsibility within a Christian society. These and many other contemporary papal expressions reflected the realization of the papacy's belief in the strength of its own foundation. However tender a plant the papacy still was, the emperor was told by Gelasius that because of the part he played in the schism dividing Old and New Rome, he should consider himself 'condemned' which was the same as saying that he was excommunicated – a bold challenge to the imperial authority by a pope who, after all, was constitutionally a subject of the emperor.

What the late fifth-century papacy indicated was that in a Christian society there was not only no room for an autonomous (secular) power, but also that the measures – doctrinal, organizational, disciplinary – recently initiated by the emperor, deserved outright condemnation. For the 'correct' scheme of things in a Christian world was the very reverse of what the imperial government had tried to enact. From its own point of view the papacy could not accept the recent imperial legislation or actions without firmly protesting: but this meant schism between the Roman and the Byzantine churches – the first serious split. With its strong biblical and religious backing the papacy indeed felt wholly justified in its remonstrations, even at the cost of causing a division. Although the statements relative to the governmental powers of the papacy must be classed as mere claims, by virtue of being incorporated in a number of collections of canon law they nevertheless were vehicles which decisively shaped the mind of later papal and non-papal generations. These statements did not always distinguish between the actual exercise of power and the mere claim to it, but this was a feature which characterized a great deal of the medieval papacy.

These magisterial pronouncements of the papacy were supplemented by two non-papal literary products. The one consisted of two closely related works allegedly written in the second half of the first century A.D. by a pupil of St Paul, but actually composed by an unknown author *ca.* 480 who is called Pseudo-Denys (to distinguish him from the genuine Denys, St Paul's pupil). What was of particular interest was that this author not only introduced the idea of hierarchical ordering, but coined the very term *hierarchy*. The essence of hierarchical ordering was that, according to this author, there was a divinely established order of ranks in the ecclesiastical and heavenly societies, and that these ranks designated different faculties and functions. It was the neatness of this scheme and the skilful combination of two hitherto unconnected terms (i.e. *hiereus* and *archos*) which indirectly assisted the papal programme. For the stern monarchic rule envisaged by the papacy could in practice exist and work only through a clean and tidily conceived system of higher and lower ranks and hence through delegation of powers from the supreme monarch. Indeed, one may go as far as to say that the petrinological system of the papacy received a powerful supplementation through the writings of Pseudo-Denys. From now on one could speak of a descending theme of government, because powers were held to descend from the supreme Being, that is, from God, to lower placed ranks and offices, each of which functioned according to its station and calling. It is unlikely that the identity of this author will ever emerge; and it is still more unlikely that he was in any way associated with the Roman Church.

The other literary product of the time moved on a more practical and mundane level. This was the so-called *Legend of St Silvester* composed between 480 and 490 by an unknown author. The piece later gave rise to one of the most influential forgeries in history (see below p. 77). Because of its vivid imagery and evident skill of narrative, the work was very widely read and well known throughout the medieval period. It depicted the conversion of Constantine the Great (who by this time had already assumed legendary proportions) with a wealth of concrete detail. But behind this innocuously apparent façade a very clear design was detectable. The author wished to indicate in a subtle manner how Constantinople had become the capital of the empire. It will be recalled that this function of Constantinople had played a vital role in the general councils, and this role of Constantinople as a capital supplied the imperial government with a justification of its policy in ecclesiastical and religious matters (see above pp. 26, 28). What quite obviously intrigued this author was the question of how Constantinople came to assume this function, and in trying to answer it he managed to harness the papacy under Pope Silvester to the task. In his novelistic product the author skilfully conveyed the impression that it was the papacy which in the last resort had been instrumental in raising Constantinople to its pre-eminent position. For since Constantine's move to Constantinople changed nothing in his status as emperor, the author depicted in lurid terms how the emperor showed his contrition before Pope Silvester. The author went even as far as to portray Constantine lying prostrate before Silvester without any imperial garments and emblems. Out of his charity Silvester forgave Constantine his sins and re-invested him with his imperial symbols and garments, so that he now moved to Constantinople with papal connivance: this, however, was not made explicit, but subtly hinted at. The more alert contemporaries and later readers nevertheless received the message.

It should be emphasized that there was of course not a shred of truth in the whole story and that Silvester played no role whatsoever in Constantine's decision to move to Constantinople. Yet it should also be stressed that the author's account may be read on two levels – on the sentimental novelistic and on the interpretative level. It was the latter which captured the imagination of the forger in the eighth century (see below p. 77). In brief, this product purported to show the hitherto non-existent link between the emergence of Constantinople as the capital of the empire and the papacy: the former owed its rise to the acquiescence of the papacy to Constantine's move. By implication therefore the claims raised by the 17th and 28th chapters of the Council of Chalcedon (see above p. 26) should be thrown against this background of how Constantinople actually had become the capital.

An event of major historical importance for the future of the papacy was the conversion of the king of the Franks, Clovis, to Catholicism. From the historical standpoint it is certainly noteworthy that this conversion (probably in 496) occurred during the period in which many basic papal themes were germinating. The role which Constantine played within the Roman empire and its ecclesiastical organization, was to be played in the West by Clovis, called the new Constantine. While however the real Constantine's ecclesiastical policy was grafted on the ancient Roman structure, the Franks were in course of time to become vital instruments in the hands of the papacy. The Roman parentage of the Frankish religious and ecclesiastical outlook prevented the outburst of anything approaching the deep christological and other theological controversies which had rent the Eastern half of the empire. Although the new Constantine drove out the military and secular remnants of Roman power from his realms, he nevertheless wholly accepted the ecclesiastical régime and organization of Roman provenance. Historically speaking, the conversion of Clovis provided the papacy with a platform from which it was able to deploy its own governmental schemes safely.

Yet at exactly the same time the first internal ideological

fissures began to shake the papacy in Rome. These were to lead to serious faction fights and tensions within the bosom of the Roman church. The significance of this internal papal situation was that two parties had constituted themselves, and these two parties were motivated by distinctly different outlooks, the one realizing the futility of carrying on within the confines and terms of the Roman empire, the other aiming at an appeasement of the imperial government in Constantinople. A majority of the electors preferred the deacon Symmachus as successor to the recently deceased Pope Anastasius II, while a not inconsiderable minority chose the Roman archpriest Laurentius. Both parties proceeded independently of each other to an election on the same day and at almost the same hour (22 November 498). The significance of this papal schism lay in that the Symmachan party stood for the strict observance of the Leonine-Gelasian papal principles, and therefore pursued a purely Roman policy, while the Laurentian party stood for accommodation with the empire and was not wholly averse to the acceptance of a modified *Henotikon* in order to restore unity within the Church.

Unable or unwilling to resolve the split, both parties appealed to the forces occupying Italy, that is, the Gothic king Theodoric the Great who however was not a Catholic, but an Arian. He declared Symmachus the lawful pope on the ground that he had entered the clerical status earlier than Laurentius and was elected by a majority. The intervention by a Ruler (who was not even a Catholic) in the affairs of the Roman church was viewed with considerable apprehension by some contemporary chroniclers. But the Laurentians backed as they were by influential members of the conservative Roman nobility, raised serious charges against Symmachus. The result was that Theoderic summoned a council – one of the earliest instances of a council summoned by a mere king – to investigate the charges. Most significantly, the synod ended with a strong endorsement of the sovereign position of the papacy, asserting that the apostolic see could not be judged by anyone. Only a firm order by Theoderic to deliver all churches in Rome to the charge of Symmachus ended the schism which pre-portrayed many a similar later contingency.

This internal papal schism was the occasion which stimulated forgeries on a hitherto unknown scale. One of the so-called Symmachan forgeries (the name did not imply that the pope himself was involved) invented a synod held at Sinuessa during the reign of Diocletian in which speeches and statements were made that were to serve as a justification of the synod held in Rome in 501. Another forgery concocted one more council summoned and chaired by Pope Silvester (who rapidly gained legendary fame) in which the recently baptized Constantine also took part. According to this forgery a great number of decrees were issued, of which the last in particular attracted attention: 'Nobody can sit in judgment on the first (apostolic) see which distributes rightful justice to all. Neither the emperor nor the whole clergy nor kings nor people can judge the supreme judge.'

These Symmachan forgeries exercised a very powerful influence, because they dealt with topics of direct concern to the papacy. They were included in a number of collections of canon law and formed, so to speak, the backbone of the constitutional position of the pope. The sentence 'The first (apostolic) see cannot be judged by anyone' showed persuasively how clearly the forger had grasped the notion of the pope's personal sovereignty: he had not received power from those who had elected him, and hence they could not take it away. The pope, in other words, formed an estate of his own. One cannot be surprised that this statement still forms a vital element in the present-day canon law (can. 1556). Yet it should also be noted that, if the forger had acquainted himself a little better with earlier papal material, he would have had no need to have recourse to forged or invented statements. For less than two generations earlier two popes, Zosimus and Boniface I, had expressed a view which in substance was identical with the one contained in the forgery (see above p. 18). Where the forger scored was in his better and more concise and impressive diction.

The early sixth century was also a period that became important for papal historiography. One of the most precious sources for the period from the early sixth to the mid-ninth century was the so-called Papal Book (*Liber Pontificalis*) which was begun at this time and was kept up by contemporary compilers who in all likelihood were clerks in the papal household. The entries for each pontificate were a mixture of pure narrative and interpretation of events and movements; they also contained indications of the motives of the acting popes. This was, perhaps, the first 'official historiography', inspired no doubt, but not for this reason untrustworthy. On the contrary, the compilers did not tell obvious untruths or falsify a picture or a situation, although they touched up and emphasized certain trends or events at the expense of others. The modern reader of these entries has constantly to be on his guard, because behind often innocuous statements some important clue to the true motives of the acting persons sometimes lies hidden. The aim clearly was to provide, probably only for domestic use, a record of papal policy in regard to the principal activities of the time. The style of the entries is matter-of-fact, does not aspire to any literary beauty or perfection and is at times quite crude, though the immediacy and freshness of the recorded activities at once strike the modern reader. Because they were strictly contemporary accounts, however much seen through the eyes of the papacy, they constitute the most valuable source material for some long stretches of papal history.

None of these observations, however, applies to the entries preceding the pontificate of Anastasius II (496–498). In striking contrast to the subsequent accounts they have little resemblance to reality. From the first century onwards these entries were characterized by a combination of historical imagination, wishful thinking, fiction and the promptitude to supply ready-made facts when this was felt necessary. They can overwhelmingly be disregarded as proper sources of papal history. But from the early sixth century onwards the emergence of a group of compilers who may well be called official historians of the papacy was one more testimony to the growing self-awareness of the institution itself.

There was nevertheless a considerable gulf between the highly developed governmental doctrine of the papacy and actual reality: concrete papal actions in the early sixth century can hardly be detected. On the contrary, the paradox emerged that despite its elaborate programme in the first three decades of the century the papacy was very much under the heavy influence of the Goths. It was they who put up those popes whom they considered pliable. Meanwhile the Acacian schism came to be settled during the pontificate of Hormisdas, which coincided with the reign of the Emperor Justin I (518–527), himself already decisively guided by his nephew, Justinian. Indubitably due to Justinian's persuasive efforts Justin made overtures to Pope Hormisdas in 519 to which the latter eagerly responded. The imperial government now recognized the function of the Roman church as the supreme tribunal concerning all questions of Christian faith and ecclesiastical dogma. After lengthy negotiations this and other points were fixed in the so-called Formula of Union (519) which marked, on the surface at least, the end of the Acacian schism that had lasted about thirty years. What gave the Formula its specific historical note was that it referred to the Roman church as the one apostolic church in which, according to the promise of Christ (in Matt. 16.18f.), the true and pure catholic faith had always been kept. This formulation of the primacy of teaching (*primatus magisterii*) of the Roman church was some 1350 years later invoked for the infallibility decree in the First Vatican Council.

But in its immediate effects this Formula was no more than an *ad hoc* arrangement which lacked the force of conviction on the part of the imperial government which spoke of 'two empires' and the 'two churches' of Old and New Rome. Externally it may have seemed a victory for the papacy, but even this may be open to doubt, because the accommodation was no more than a well calculated measure on the part of Justinian. His was the real moving spirit that wished to prepare the ground for his policy of re-conquest: if he was to reconquer Italy and drive out the alien Goths, and if the Roman empire in all its ancient glory was to be re-established, assuredly the church situated in Rome and for centuries considered the principal church of Christendom, had somehow to be pacified and given an appropriate status. In the scheme of Justinian the Roman church was an integral part of the Roman empire, but one whose role was to be confined to the tasks defined by the emperor himself.

In this renaissance of the Roman Empire the church of the historic city which had in fact given the empire its revered name, was to be accorded an appropriate rank. Just as the city of Rome was graded higher than other cities by contemporaries, in the same way its bishop, the pope, was to have a rank higher than that of the other patriarchs. The settlement of 519 was never intended to accord to the papacy anything even faintly approaching a jurisdictional primacy – and the history of Justinian's reign was to prove this abundantly. Considering its ancient Roman background with its bequest of the *ius sacrum* forming part of the imperial public law, and in view of more recent history, how could the imperial government have agreed to an acknowledgment of a papal *principatus*? The accommodation reached between Justin and Hormisdas did indeed end the Acacian schism, but as the similar accommodations between Rome and Constantinople in later ages down to the fifteenth century were to show, these unions were at best temporizing measures and at worst achieved nothing, however much they were applauded publicly.

One of the reasons why the 'peace' of 519 was greeted with enthusiasm by the papacy was that it appeared to give some relief from the oppressive government by the Gothic king. With the Goths the papacy had in any case far less in common than with the imperial government in Constantinople with which it shared the common bonds of the ancient Roman heritage despite the basic differences in matters of ecclesiastical government. Nevertheless, the Goths continued to use the papacy as their instrument, as was clearly evidenced by the peremptory order of Theodoric the Great to Pope John I that he should plead personally for the followers of Arianism with the imperial government. Recent imperial legislation had affected the Arians adversely, and the papacy was to supplicate for imperial favours for them. The journey of John I to Constantinople was the first undertaken by a pope, and from now until 710 in the pontificate of Constantine, when the last papal visit to Constantinople took place, there were frequent papal journeyings to the imperial court: few of these fulfilled their expectations. Not unexpectedly, John I secured no imperial favours, and on his return Theodoric threw him into his dungeons where he died in the same year as that in which the king ended his own life (526). That a pope should be compelled to intervene on behalf of the adherents to erroneous and heretical doctrines, such as Arianism indubitably was, must constitute one of the most humiliating situations in which the papacy found itself and can be explained only by the threat of brute force.

Meanwhile the Emperor Justin's nephew, Justinian, had gained even greater influence upon the policy of the imperial government. When after the death of his uncle in 527 he became the sole Ruler, a new phase in the history of the Roman empire and in that of the papacy was to begin. Justinian I's reign constituted the high-water mark of the idea and function of the Roman emperor in a Christian garb. This makes understandable his epoch-making codification of the Roman law and it is also comprehensible from his Roman-imperial standpoint that the monarch as the divinely established Ruler of the whole universe could not tolerate any other Ruler who claimed to have final authority in precisely those matters which the emperor himself considered to be necessary for the well-being of the empire and therefore within his governmental competence. With some justification had his government been somewhat inelegantly designated a caesaropapist Rulership. In actual fact it was no more than a refurbished Constantinean government with a Christian complexion. Justinian had fully inherited the ancient Roman axiom that the public law contained the sacral law and that therefore from the public standpoint it was his right and duty to deal with 'sacral matters' (see also above pp. 5, 7, 23). The Christian emperor had absorbed the ancient Roman emperor.

It is therefore understandable why Justinian who reigned for nearly 40 years, had profound effects upon the fate of the papacy and herewith on medieval – and eventually also modern – Europe. His aim was the re-establishment of the ancient Roman empire with a heightened glory and splendour. To this end he undertook the reconquest of Italy; to this end also the ancient city of Rome was to be given a status commensurate with its being the birthplace of the empire. Thrown against this background the acknowledgment by Justinian of the exalted rank of the papacy as the Roman church *par excellence* was comprehensible. But this did not amount to a recognition of its jurisdictional primacy. No Ruler was more insistent on the law as the vehicle of government than Justinian. But this clearly excluded the ascription of jurisdictional primacy (of the papal *principatus*) to the papacy. In its long history the papacy has hardly found a more determined challenge than in the governmental programme of Justinian which, it should be borne in mind, was fully supported by the whole ecclesiastical hierarchy in the Eastern half of the empire. In fact, at the conclusion of one session of the council at Constantinople in 535 the participants exclaimed that nothing could happen in the Church without the consent and approval of the emperor himself. Indeed, from the angle of the imperial government no other viewpoint was acceptable.

Precisely because the law manifested the emperor's will relative to all matters of public concern and because Justinian considered himself as much a theologian of exceptional calibre as a Ruler, he made numerous pronouncements on purely theological matters: these imperial views he turned into the law whenever appropriate or advisable. Furthermore, in these legislative acts, ecclesiastical organization itself became a favoured topic. This could not help but arouse the antagonism of the papacy. Imbued as he was with the idea that he alone was the vice-gerent of Christ on earth, that he alone was the divinely appointed Ruler of the universe, that it was his divinely inspired will which governed the world – hence his designation as the kosmokrator – his legislation affected virtually every department of the Christian Church, and in a quite special way the papacy which had no means of realizing its claim to jurisdictional primacy. As he himself laid down in one of his legal enactments it was his duty to see that in his laws his subjects were given 'the true faith'. The emperor as legislator was indeed 'divinity walking on earth'. Yet Justinian's legislation concerning heresy, the extermination of the remnants of paganism and the practice of Judaism, strongly influenced later Western developments: all these legislative measures were transmitted in his own codification supplemented by his additional laws. That his numerous interventions in the highly involved theological disputes in the Eastern half of the empire in the end brought about serious intellectual unrest, is not difficult to understand. After all, every pronouncement had considerable 'political' repercussions, because of the lack of a distinction between 'religion' and 'politics' at Constantinople.

The Justinianean standpoint is best summed up in one of his own legal enactments. In it he declared that both the priesthood and the imperial government proceeded from the one divine source. For divinity had established these two organs so that the one looked after 'the divine things' and the other after 'the human matters'. As he said in this same law, the imperial government exercised therefore particular care in the selection of ecclesiastical officers precisely because they concerned themselves with 'the divine things' which were the foundation of the empire itself. Thereby he had not only laid down his imperial principle of division of labour – remarkably like that propounded some 30 years earlier by Pope Gelasius I (see above pp. 32f.) and yet its very opposite – but also established the right of the imperial government to take the necessary ecclesiastical, disciplinary and organizational steps, notably in the matter of appointments, promotions and dismissals precisely because these were matters of the public law of which the sacral law was merely a part (see above pp. 5, 7). The papacy was simply another patriarchate within the Roman empire. This was the classic application of Constantinean principles to Christian conditions. To this law the Byzantine empire was to adhere until its extinction in 1453; it was also a law that served royal and imperial governments in the West of Europe as a theoretical model to be implemented as occasion warranted it.

What immeasurably enhanced the authority of the emperor at Constantinople was the very elaborate ceremonial and ritual with which from the early sixth century onwards he was surrounded. This ceremonial was itself a highly associative combination of oriental, Jewish, Hellenistic and early Christian ritualistic features. They presented the emperor almost as a divine personality. After all, Justinian himself declared that the laws poured forth from his own divine mouth. He alone as God's representative on earth could guarantee the unity, peace and concord of the empire as well as of the Church. The celestial monarch – the Pantokrator – had found in the emperor his earthly vice-gerent in the shape of the kosmokrator: in slightly modifying the statement of St Paul ('One lord, one faith, one baptism', Eph. 4.5) Byzantium expressed the same monarchic and unitarian theme in 'One empire, one law, one church'. The palace buildings were sacred; the meetings which the emperor held with his closest advisers were called 'sacred consistories'; on certain days he received the adoration of his chief officers; on other feast days he feasted the patriarch of Constantinople (whom he had appointed himself) and other dignitaries in a way reminiscent of the Lord's supper; imperial decrees and orders and writs were symbolically ornamented and provided with miniatures pointing to the semi-divine nature of his personality; hence on receiving an imperial decree the subject bowed and kissed the roll reverently. This rich symbolism was only another way of expressing the basic imperial ideology: the abstract law and the concrete symbolism supplemented each other very well. Moreover, protests and remonstrations against the imperial rulings could result in a charge of high treason committed against the divine majesty of the emperor. And it was this which was of particular and most direct concern to the papacy.

That the papacy was profoundly affected by Justinian's régime was understandable. Not only in the imperial laws, but also in synodal decrees the papacy's claim to jurisdictional primacy was, for ostensible imperial reasons, rejected. And even mere magisterial primacy – concerned as it was with mere doctrine, and not with jurisdiction – also came under attack during the pontificate of Vigilius, who had become pope in 537 exclusively with the help of the military conqueror of Rome, Belisarius. His rival, Pope Silverius (536–537), who was a son of Pope Hormisdas, was exiled by the imperial government. Vigilius managed to withstand the overtures of the Empress Theodora who worked hard in the interests of monophysitism and tried to transplant the monophysite views to the Occident, in which endeavour she sought the help of Pope Vigilius. Not surprisingly, her efforts were in vain. Vigilius withstood the temptation, though another attempt two years later showed the calculation and cunning of the imperial régime.

In order to pacify the monophysites and to harness them to the imperial cause in the interests of imperial unity, Justinian condemned the writings of three theologians (all of the Antiochean school) who were hostile to monophysitism. These were the literary works of Theodore Mopsvestia, Theodore of Cyrus and Ibas of Edessa. The edict of condemnation referred to 'the three chapters' (that is, three headings) and this was the name by which the matter has become known. But the papacy held firmly to the christological fixation made by the Council of Chalcedon (see above p. 25). When approached by Justinian, Vigilius refused to give his consent to the condemnation. Now the government put the pope under severe pressure. He was brought before the imperial presence in the palace of Constantinople. Here Vigilius collapsed, and in agreement with the emperor's edict he now also condemned the 'three chapters', though protesting that the orthodox view was that of the Council of Chalcedon (Easter 548).

Not without justification the Occident considered that this papal connivance was extorted, and some African bishops went as far as to excommunicate the pope. This was the signal for the opening of some very embittered African polemics against the basic assumptions of Justinian's ecclesiastical policy. The spokesman of this African opposition to the imperial régime was Facundus of Hermiane whose literary products bitterly attack the very bases of the Byzantine governmental scheme. Frightened by this rebellion which his agreement had stirred up, Vigilius withdrew his condemnation of 'the three chapters', declared the latter orthodox and prohibited opposition to them. Justinian however at once made sure of further 'support' by the papacy. Imprisoned, deprived of all his counsellors, sick, Vigilius collapsed for a second time in December 553 and once more declared opposition to and condemnation of 'the three chapters' legitimate: he wholly endorsed the decrees of the Fifth General Council (June 553). Only now was he allowed to return to Rome although he never saw it again, as he died on the journey.

The Vigilian affair was a *cause célèbre* and also a portent. Byzantine governmental policy went to any lengths to secure the agreement of the Roman church in the interests of 'Roman' policy. Whether or not under the same duress as Vigilius, the papacy under Pelagius I and John III continued the imperially decreed opposition to 'the three chapters', with the consequence that the provinces of Milan and Aquileja were separated from the Roman church for some decades. It is understandable that the authority and prestige of the papacy suffered greatly, not only in Italy, but also in other provinces and regions, especially in Africa. If ever a government exercised terror under the cover of law issued by a 'divine' monarch, it was the Byzantine variety in the sixth century. Against this kind of external pressure no doctrine or programme, however well worked out, could prevail. It was the stark and bleak contrast between the maturing governmental doctrine of the papacy and the cruel reality facing the institution which strikes the distant observer. Yet the aim pursued by Justinian – the unity of the 'Roman' empire – was so much a chimera that it only too starkly contrasted with mid-sixth century reality.

In order to assess the situation correctly, the cultural separation of the West from the East must be appreciated. In reviewing the institutional development of the papacy it is pertinent to consider the general animosity of the population that was prevalent in Italy in the years of the Justinianean re-conquest. It is equally important to realize the bearing of popular sentiments upon the papacy which in that age of insecurity was seen as one of the few stable institutions. The removal of the residence of the imperial governor in Italy from Rome to Ravenna must also be adequately appraised in this context. Although the armies of Justinian had come as 'Romans' to re-conquer and to re-incorporate Italy into the body of the Roman empire, the native population saw in them nothing but occupying forces. Neither did they speak the language of the indigenous population nor did they themselves show much respect for the institutions and customs which they were supposed to defend. They were looked upon by the Italian population as 'Greeks' rather than as 'Romans'. Can one wonder, then, that both Rome and Italy looked at the Byzantine forces askance and not at all as liberators from a foreign yoke? The invasion of the Lombards in 568 virtually put a stop to any further fantasies aiming at a re-conquest of Italy. The Lombard advance was to play a decisive role in the fortunes of the papacy.

The appearance of the Lombards on Italian soil greatly accelerated the process by which the papacy became aware of its own Roman past and of the potentialities which this historic contingency harboured. Of imperial power and authority very little was left in Rome, once the exarch had finally taken up his residence in Ravenna. In this context it should be kept in mind that for purely administrative reasons Justinian conceded some considerable power to the Italian bishops and also to the papacy in Rome. This enabled the papacy to act as a kind of intermediary between the imperial government in Constantinople and the invading Lombard armies – and when the necessity arose the papacy treated with the conquerors as a more or less independent organ. Then not only the decimation of the actual military strength of the empire in Italy, but also the poverty and slowness of communication with Constantinople were factors advantageous to the growth of the papal institution as a *de facto* independent organ in Italy. In contrast to earlier Germanic invaders the Lombards did not come as friends of the Roman empire, but as its destroyers. Wherever Lombard power was established the imperial administration ceased to function. In the place of an urban administration, a purely agrarian one now arose. In rapid succession the Lombards founded duchies in the North, Trent and Friuli, as well as in the South, Benevento and Spoleto, so that Rome and its immediate environs were hedged in between Lombard strongholds: this was the so-called Duchy of Rome (the 'ducatus Romanus') which together with the southernmost part of Italy, Naples and Sicily still nominally remained imperial territory.

To the different kind of public administration – the one urban, the other agrarian – was added a deep religious difference. The Lombards came partly as pagans, and partly as Arians, but were gradually converted to Catholicism. Since the papacy had become a very wealthy owner of large estates, it had plenty of direct contact with the Lombards. These papal estates were called patrimonies which consisted of a number of large manors with appropriately extensive lands around them. Here in these patrimonies, located all over Italy and also in Dalmatia, Gaul and Africa, Sardinia and Corsica, the papacy built up a first-class administrative system entirely on the Roman pattern: Roman clerics, Roman law, Roman procedures, Roman fiscal administration, characterized these patrimonies. They were models of 'business' administration amidst half-barbarian Germanic settlements.

Indeed, by the end of the sixth century the papacy was the biggest single landowner in Western Europe. The patrimonies brought the papacy not only into close contact with the conquering Lombards in Italy, but also precisely by virtue of their first-class administration provided a hinterland for the city of Rome and its environs. The revenues of the patrimonies served to support the indigent native population as well as needy monasteries and churches and the papal household itself. The erstwhile sharp difference between urban and agrarian administration gradually diminished, and this development went hand in hand with the decrease of Arianism and the increase of the Catholic Lombard population. But the Lombards remained for a long time an alien element in the Italian peninsula.

From the point of view of institutional history the imperial legislation in the mid-sixth century left an important legacy concerning the creation of the pope. Hitherto the creation of popes proceeded almost wholly on the same lines which characterized the creation of any other bishop. After all, the pope was essentially nothing else but the bishop of Rome. That is to say, he was elected by clergy and laity assisted by the neighbouring bishops, especially those of Ostia, Albano and Porto. It was these latter who consecrated the elected candidate a bishop and they were to do so throughout the medieval period. There is ample evidence that the more prominent the papal office became in public affairs, the more it attracted the ever vigilant eye of the imperial government. Hence the emperor actively intervened when the election was alleged to have suffered from some irregularity or when a candidate was elected who was known for his opposition to some imperial religious or ecclesiastical scheme. Throughout the sixth century members of the ancient Roman nobility strongly preponderated among the papal candidates.

The legal forms of papal elections came to be fixed by imperial decree in 555. These forms have been transmitted in the so-called *Liber Diurnus*, the handbook of the papal chancery which contained the papal formulae for the most frequently occurring constitutional and legal measures with which the chancery had to concern itself. The procedure laid down in this formulary book required that on the occasion of a papal vacancy the exarch at Ravenna was to be notified. The election itself was to take place three days after the funeral of the dead pope. The higher Roman clergy and the lay nobility played a prominent part in the election, so that one could speak of a Roman oligarchy which manipulated papal elections. There was to be a notarial protocol of the election procedure, and this had to be sent to the imperial chancery in Constantinople for confirmation of the election by the emperor himself. No consecration of the elected candidate could take place until the imperial *fiat* had arrived. It was not until 684 that because of the delays caused by adverse travelling conditions the exarch at Ravenna was empowered to confirm the election on behalf of the emperor. There were some isolated instances in which, on the imperial model, the living pope 'designated' his successor, but both the higher Roman clergy and aristocracy opposed this device which never assumed any practical importance. The procedure outlined in the *Liber Diurnus* was constitutional law and remained so until the break with the imperial government in the eighth century when for a time the place of the exarch was taken by the Frankish king.

3 The Papacy and the Conversion of England

IN THE HISTORY of the medieval papacy it would be difficult to find a pontificate of greater historical significance than that of Gregory I. With every justification it can be said that by the end of the sixth century a train of events had been set in motion which had repercussions far beyond the medieval period; and for the development of the papacy as a governmental institution the period at the turn of the sixth and seventh centuries became one of crucial importance. Gregory I still belonged to the ancient imperial Roman world, but he also realized the inherent potentialities of the Germanic nations. He became instrumental in bursting the narrow confines within which the papacy had hitherto led its existence. It is a mere truism to say that Gregory I was one of the few historic personalities who had learnt a lesson from history, who in accordance with this lesson initiated action, and thereby attained achievements of world-wide significance.

Born and bred in Rome – he was a descendant of an old Roman aristocratic family his ancestor being Pope Felix III (see above p. 30) – he embodied in his person all the characteristic features of what Rome and Romans ever stood for: intellectual tidiness, orderliness, loyalty to the law which he himself had perfectly mastered by virtue of his training, a sound practical commonsense and realistic assessment of a situation as it was (and not what it should have been). Yet he was no original thinker, and though his Latinity as expressed in his official letters to the imperial government in Constantinople was in no wise below the standard of his great predecessors in office, such as Leo I, he nevertheless was quite capable of descending to an uncouth Latin when it was necessary to reach the semi-literate lower clerical sections in distant regions. Despite his donning the monastic habit for a time he was thoroughly familiar with Roman public law and the way public business was transacted. Moreover, he possessed all the requirements which an ambassador at an exposed mission should have: skill, tact, flexibility coupled with firmness, discretion and discernment and above all a gift for detached observation. Pope Pelagius II had sent him to Constantinople as so-called papal apocrisiary, that is, papal ambassador, a mission which opened the future pope's eyes. Here in Constantinople he saw clearly how firmly entrenched imperial history, ideology and practice had been. Realist as he was, he drew the obvious conclusion: it would be both dangerous and futile to protest against this historically conditioned imperial scheme of government however regrettable was the interference of the government with ecclesiastical organization and doctrine.

Gregory I's clear realization was that the claim to primatial authority in matters of jurisdiction had no hope whatsoever of being acknowledged by Constantinople, particularly towards the end of the sixth century, when the ancient ties between Constantinople and Italy were being very rapidly loosened. And as a jurist he realized that to press the papal primatial claim would only expose the papacy to serious charges of subversion and the individual pope, as a subject of the emperor, to severe punitive measures because by raising a protest the pope impugned the 'divine' authority and status of the emperor. The reasons upon which the papacy advanced its jurisdictional primacy – the petrinological theme – had made not the slightest impression upon the government and the ruling circles in Constantinople. During his sojourn as ambassador he had ample opportunity of observing the lack of impact which Roman reasonings had on New Rome.

Elected pope on 3 September 590 Gregory showed all the qualities of a Ruler from the very beginning of his pontificate. What evidently was of great assistance to him was the quite respectable development of the institutional apparatus of the papacy, notably the chancery, registry, and the household offices concerned with the economic and financial administration of the patrimonies, large and dispersed as they were. The ability of the man was powerfully supplemented by an efficient administrative set-up. His over-all control of matters of direct concern to the city of Rome and its environs (the Duchy of Rome) and his determination and tenacity of purpose in the face of adverse circumstances gained him the affection of the Roman populace.

Attention to detail did not make him lose sight of the eventual aims of his 'grand strategy'. What is particularly noteworthy from the historical angle is that his was the first pontificate from which the official papal Registers have been preserved, albeit in the shape of a later, though authentic copy. These Registers are an invaluable source of knowledge, because they contain almost the whole official correspondence of Gregory I both to the East and the West. A man of exceptional energy he also wrote a number of books which might nowadays be said to be written for popular consumption, partly as edifying instruction and partly for pastoral purposes. However low in intellectual contents his books and above all his sermons and interpretations of the Bible were, they exercised a powerful influence on the thought processes in the medieval period. It is no exaggeration to say that the strong Augustinian complexion of medieval thought-patterns was largely due to the influence of Gregorian writings which 'popularized' a great many Augustinian ideas. It is however no longer tenable to credit Gregory I with the advances in liturgy and in church music which legend and pious exaggeration have foisted upon him.

Gregory's preoccupation with the papal patrimonies deserves special mention. It was through skilful management and organization that they yielded sufficient revenue, particularly food with which to feed the indigent population. The complete collapse of the imperial administration in Rome and its neighbourhood had seriously threatened the maintenance of public order and quite especially so when the vast proletarian masses were exposed to famine. The situation was saved by the generous distribution of necessities from the papal patrimonies to the starving population. Unwittingly, therefore, the papacy was drawn into the administration of public and social affairs. This feature became more and more pronounced during Gregory's pontificate when not only large sums of ransom had to be paid to the Lombards, but also when thousands of refugees reached the city of Rome. To these contingencies must be added natural disasters caused by the floods which made hundreds of families homeless. For a time even the imperial garrison stationed in Rome depended for its maintenance on papal supplies. In brief, administratively and socially Rome had become a responsibility of the papacy. It was therefore understandable that the papacy evolved new forms of organization, which, however improvised, nevertheless by virtue of their success served as the basis for further development, notably in the financial and social welfare sectors. That these developments greatly assisted the growth of the institution itself, is comprehensible.

Where however the pontificate of Gregory the Great assumed its profoundest historical significance was not within Rome but outside it. For the papacy now began the process of opening up the fallow Western Germanic soil to Roman ecclesiastical influences. It is difficult adequately to measure the impact of the unprecedented papal approach to the still half-barbarian Western nations. In some respects the missions to Gaul and Britain might well be likened to the discovery of the new world by the old on the threshold of the modern period. The reasons which prompted Gregory to undertake so hazardous an enterprise as the missions to the West, must be found in the experiences which he had while ambassador in Constantinople. As already indicated, these experiences showed him the futility and the danger of attempting to push Roman primatial claims against the imperial government. This was a historic realization on the part of an individual which has changed the map of the world.

The dilemma as it presented itself to Gregory was this. Either the papacy accepted the governmental scheme of Constantinople, which tried to relegate the papacy to the role of a patriarchate without any worth-while right to govern. Or the papacy insisted upon its vocation and freedom of governmental action (in the Leonine and Gelasian senses), in which case it had to protest against the numerous measures of the imperial government in the ecclesiastical and religious fields. But here the papacy was confronted with a very serious situation, for challenge and protests against the rulings of the 'divine' imperial majesty entailed serious charges. Not surprisingly, Gregory I chose the second alternative. He decided to insist upon the papacy's freedom of governmental action and the exercise of jurisdictional primacy. He decided further that if the papacy was to fulfil its true vocation without interference by the imperial government and without being constantly exposed to serious accusations, it could do so only if it extended its concrete influence to regions and districts which were of no concern to the imperial government. In practical terms this meant the beginning, or intensification, of papal operations in Spain, Gaul and Britain. The solution was as simple as it was effective.

The despatch of the advance party of the mission took place in September 595 and prepared the way for one of the most successful missionary enterprises undertaken in the Middle Ages. England became converted to Roman Christianity at the hands of Roman missionaries, headed by St Augustine (of Canterbury), and was to become one of the regions most devoted to the early medieval papacy. In Gaul the already existing ties with the papacy were considerably strengthened while in Spain the brilliant mind of Gregory's contemporary, Archbishop Isidore of Seville, powerfully combined Roman and Germanic elements: Isidore's influence in the medieval period can hardly be measured in quantitative terms. The Visigothic kings of Spain had by then been converted to Catholicism and became practical exponents of Roman Christianity and therefore strongly susceptible to Roman influences. In a word, in these three stable Western kingdoms no obstacle presented itself to the application of Roman primatial claims.

But with the disappearance of the Visigothic kingdom in Spain just a century afterwards (in 711), the religious and ecclesiastical leadership of the West began to be effectively assumed by Anglo-Saxon England. In fact, it was from the farthest corner of Western Europe and also the most recently converted region from which came the most powerful missionary impetus which eventually converted large parts of what was later to become Germany and also central Europe. Between the end of the sixth and the mid-eighth centuries firm foundations were laid for the impressive ideological edifice of what was later to become Latin Western Europe. This indeed was the conspicuous and concrete result of Gregory the Great's mission to England. Rarely can an undertaking have been crowned with such outstanding success. As Gibbon once remarked, while Caesar needed six legions for the invasion of Britain, Gregory achieved the same purpose with 40 monks.

With every justification Gregory can be called 'Father of Europe'. Its parentage and physiognomy were Roman, and its cementing bond was the faith as expounded by the Roman church. A merely physical or geographical entity was to become an ideological body which was sustained by its own inner forces, of which none was more resilient than the Christian faith in its Roman ecclesiastical shape. In prophetic vision Gregory himself saw this European union as the union of a Christian common-wealth ('societas reipublicae christianae'), the basic ingredients of which were of Roman and ecclesiastical provenance.

As already noted, a very great deal in the history of the papacy was due to the challenges issued by the East, challenges, that is to say, which forced the papacy to clarify its own point of view and thereby to develop its own programme. A further instance of this self-same process could be seen in the official papal title. The adoption of the title 'Servant of the servants of God' by the pope was the result of what Gregory I considered – perhaps erro-neously – a provocation on the part of the patriarch of Con-stantinople. Certainly from the early sixth century onwards the patriarchs had called themselves 'ecumenical patriarch'. They held that as the chief ecclesiastical officers their own status reflected the universality of the emperor himself – it was the old imperial point of view according to which the civic status of a locality also determined its ecclesiastical status (see above p. 26). Clearly the implication of this patriarchal title was that the patriarchs claimed that same kind of universal primacy which the papacy had always considered its own on biblical and historical grounds. By calling himself 'Servant of the servants of God' Gregory pointed up the contrast between his own view of Christian humility and that revealed in the pompous patriarchal designation. Yet in this very manner the pope exalted the papal office (possibly alluding to Matt. 23.11–12; Luke 9.48).

It is not without interest to note that by protesting against what he called the patriarch's arrogance in using the title (Gregory conveniently forgot that his contemporary patriarch had not coined the intitulation), Gregory's long friendship with the Patriarch John the Faster abruptly ended. The quarrel between the two men broke out – and this is highly significant – on the very eve of the departure of the advance party to Gaul and Britain. Although John the patriarch could not possibly know what had enraged his papal friend so suddenly, there were nevertheless some good reasons for the papal protests. The purpose of his mission was to make real the primatial claims of the papacy, but it would have been highly prejudicial to these claims, if the papacy had not protested against the 'arrogance' of the patriarch. For the papacy would by implication have admitted – had it not protested – that the patriarch's title correctly reflected his status and function. There can be no doubt that knowing the situation in Constantinople intimately Gregory never expected any result from his protests, but in order to ensure the success of his mission, he was forced to remonstrate and adopt the contrasting title. In assuming a title of humility the pope not only translated the Christian virtue into highly official terms, but also modelled himself on the great Justinian whose own intitulation as emperor occasionally manifested very similar sentiments of humility. The title coined by Gregory remained throughout the medieval period and beyond.

During the pontificate of Gregory I the papacy laid the foundations of its later potent influence in the European West. The greater this influence became in the West, the more it receded in the East. In fact, a clear difference in approaching Eastern and Western Rulers could already be noticed in Gregory's pontificate. Towards the Western Rulers Gregory spoke the language of the Roman governor who gave orders, commanded and expected the execution of his orders by those whom he called his 'sons'. In his official correspondence with the East he always appeared as the subject of the emperor who was never addressed as a 'son' and who never received any orders. While the idea of the papal *principatus* was in the foreground in Gregory's dealings with Western governments, not once did the term appear in all his official communications with the imperial government. All this must not be seen as a double-faced approach but as one which was prompted by a realistic assessment of the situation as it was. The supreme principle that guided Gregory was to avoid any trouble with the government in Constantinople at the time when he was building up his position in the West. A policy of bifurcation – one fork to the East, and one to the West – was this pope's unique contribution to the history of the papacy.

The actual military and domestic situation in Italy was evidently of great help to the papacy. Gregory conducted negotiations with the Lombards as if he had been the independent viceroy in Italy. This became particularly conspicuous during the Lombard siege of the city of Rome and the Lombard occupation of the neighbouring Roman districts. Upon payment of the astronomical sum of 500 pounds of gold, Gregory warded off further attacks by the Lombards – a humiliating and yet at the same time also a realistic move. Imperial policy was against all negotiations with the invaders, and the official communications of the government to Gregory left no room for doubt on this score. The eventual aim was clearly to recommence the reconquest of Italy and to establish a firmer imperial régime than that under Justinian. By tact, circumspection and adroit manœuvring Gregory arrived in 596 at his goal – peace with the Lombards whose king and queen, Agilulf and Theodolinda, were Catholics. This conduct of affairs by the papacy and the resultant *de facto* governorship of the pope in Italy contributed greatly to the authority, standing and reputation of the institution itself – and not only in Italy. In his function as virtual governor of Italy he welcomed the upstart and successor to the Emperor Maurice, the assassin and usurper Phokas – again, the overriding aim was not to provoke the new emperor to actions which might well prove deleterious to the overall papal strategic concept.

The inscription on Gregory's tomb called him 'Consul of God' ('Consul Dei'), a designation in which both the pagan and the Christian Rome found a persuasive expression. He was the diplomat, negotiator, man of practical wisdom and missionary rather than the thinker and scholar of the type of Leo I or Gelasius I. Taking their ideas as a basis however Gregory made the revolutionary breakthrough to the Germanic peoples. And it was to be the union of Latin Rome with the unsophisticated Germanic nations which was to yield that Europe of which the spiritual parent was Gregory the Great.

There is a very strong contrast between the objective historical significance of this Gregorian pontificate and the virtual absence of any recognition of its achievements by contemporaries. The source most directly and intimately concerned, the semi-official Papal Book, ranked Gregory in no wise differently from the popes who immediately preceded him. And indeed, in the succeeding decades the papacy displayed very little influence. This was the age, in which the papacy found itself in what might well be called 'Byzantine captivity'. Moreover, the popes immediately succeeding Gregory had neither the sagacity nor the vision nor the realistic wisdom to continue the paths which Gregory had delineated. But this to a considerable extent must be attributed to the very short pontificates. In the first twenty years after Gregory's death (on 12 March 604) there were not less than five popes; and between the individual pontificates there were long vacancies due to the delays caused by obtaining imperial confirmation of the elected candidate. In these circumstances a consistent and coherent pursuit of a Leonine or Gregorian policy was hardly to be expected. Further, the insecurity which pervaded the whole of Italy, was aggravated by the now emerging hostility of the Italian population to the remaining Byzantine officials who were wholly Greek and detached from the native people. A further aggravating factor was the enmity of the Italians to the Lombards. All these circumstances combined to make the peninsula hardly the platform for deploying governmental skill on the part of the papacy.

It was the wretched state in Italy and Rome which largely accounted for the weakness of the papacy in resisting Byzantine interventions in purely religious questions. Once more the imperial government used the papacy as a mere instrument in the pursuit of its own domestic policies. The emperor, Heraklius (610–641), was hard pressed in the beginning of his reign by the Persians' menacing advance towards the Bosporus. Towards the end of his reign the Muslim threat added further to the difficulties of the empire which in rapid succession had lost valuable provinces to the conquering Arabs. The parts of the empire which were particularly sensitive were Egypt and Syria, but in both the dogma of monophysitism was still very strongly represented. These dogmatic standpoints concealed deep political tensions, because they directly impinged upon the position and status of the emperor himself. Further, in order to ward off the very real Muslim advance, unity of the empire was a peremptory governmental demand. Now, in order to accommodate the monophysite followers the patriarch of Constantinople, Sergius, no doubt inspired by the emperor, attempted to solve the problem tangentially by presenting the christological question in a new light: the question was to be not whether Christ had one or two natures, but whether Christ had one or two energies (a human and a divine) and one or two wills (a human and divine will). The patriarch solved the problem by asserting that there was only one energy and one will in Christ. How far this was distinguishable from monophysitism, is of no concern in this context.

What is of concern is that in order to lend greater weight to

c

this ruling, the papacy was approached. The ruling pope, Honorius I, quite obviously unaware of the wider dogmatic and political implications of this new doctrine, appeared in a somewhat simplistic manner to endorse the view held by the patriarch. This view came to be known as monenergism and monotheletism (one energy; one will). Thereupon followed in 638 one more imperial decree fixing the faith – the so-called *Ekthesis* – which it was hoped would settle all christological disputes for good. In this same year Honorius I died. Opposition, however, arose in the West. The renewed fixation of the faith by imperial verdict was at once assailed in the West which considered that this violated the orthodox doctrine set forth by the Council of Chalcedon now approaching its two hundredth anniversary. And in order to quell any further debate which might weaken still more the internal fabric and resistance of the empire, the Emperor Constans II issued the so-called *Typos* in 648 by which any further debate of the problem was forbidden. In this decree the emperor said that 'inspired by divine light, we wish to extinguish the flame of discord. That is why we decree for all our subjects (and it should be noted that this included the popes) that from now on it is forbidden to debate whether Christ had one or two wills. Whosoever acts against this order, will have to face the terrible judgment of divinity and will furthermore incur our own penalties, that is, if he be a bishop deposition, if a nobleman confiscation of his estate, and if an ordinary subject exile and torture.'

The very year after this law was published, the papacy guided by Martin I summoned a synod to the Lateran for 5 October 649. This was clearly the action of a pope resolutely determined to oppose imperial rulings on a matter of faith. The synod not only endorsed the doctrine that Christ had two wills and two energies, but also – and considering the situation this was a very bold and courageous step – openly condemned the patriarch of Constantinople and a number of leading Eastern ecclesiastics by excommunicating them. Martin himself had already incurred the displeasure of the emperor, because he had begun to act as pope and allowed himself to be consecrated bishop without having first obtained imperial confirmation of his election.

Both from the imperial and the papal points of view the situation was extremely tense and serious. On the one hand, there was a pope who, despite the dire sanctions threatened, explicitly refused to accept the verdict of the imperial majesty, although strictly speaking it was not the papacy, but a Roman synod which had opposed the imperial decree. On the other hand, the *Typos* as published was constitutionally an imperial law. The synodal decision was a deliberate defiance of this law in which the emperor who held himself to be God's representative, had pronounced on a religious matter. Hence the imperial government ordered the exarch Olympios to arrest the rebellious pope and to take him to Constantinople. The emperor seemed to have been unaware of the unreliability of his own officer, the exarch who, as soon as he appeared in Rome to execute the warrant, revolted against the emperor with the help of the remnants of the imperial militia stationed in Rome. He proclaimed himself emperor of the West with a co-emperor called Valentinian. That Martin I did nothing to prevent this from happening, should surely not have been made the basis of a criminal charge against him. But it was precisely this which the imperial government did after Olympios had been killed while fighting the Arabs in Sicily in 652.

The most serious of all serious charges, that of high treason, was raised against the pope. It was the successor of Olympios who with a strong and reliable contingent of militia marched to Rome and executed the arrest of the pope on 17 June 653. The exarch's military escort behaved themselves as barbarians rather than as imperial soldiers smashing the chandeliers and furniture in the Lateran palace. According to the warrant of arrest the pope was deposed by the exarch and at once taken to Constantinople. After the pope had been kept in prison for 93 days, the trial began which was to be one of the great show trials of Byzantium. The witnesses for the prosecution were all officers from the militia contingent which had made the *putsch* and had been led by Olympios. They saved their own skin by this alibi, for if anyone was to be charged with high treason it should have been these officers. Martin I exposed this manœuvre for what is was, but without avail. When referring to dogmatic or religious questions he was cut short by the presiding judge: 'Nothing of dogma – you stand here on a charge of high treason.' The end was predictable. Martin was found guilty and sentenced to exile in the Crimea. There he died on 26 September 655. This pontificate shows to what lengths the imperial government was prepared to go in order to uphold it own governmental scheme; but the pontificate also shows what danger faced the papacy if even within very narrow religious terms it attempted to fulfil what it itself considered its vocation in a Christian society. Indeed, it was not only futile, but dangerous to protest against the rulings of the self-styled divine majesty represented in the emperors at Constantinople.

This was not an isolated episode. Not only did the West with admittedly inadequate means resolutely oppose the dogmatic rulings of the emperor, but opposition arose also in the East. One of the writers critical of the imperial government was Maximus, later called the Confessor, who in trenchant, biting, and well argued writings fiercely attacked the assumption of 'papal authority' by the emperors. He as well as his collaborators were arrested in Rome and brought before the imperial tribunal. In May 655 he was sentenced to exile, and despite several attempts to persuade him to give up his 'pro-papal' standpoint, he remained firm, declaring in the face of threats that the emperor had no right to fix the faith or to interfere in matters of religion which, he maintained, was the vocation and specific function of the papacy. When all persuasion had failed, he together with his collaborators experienced the full wrath of the imperial government: their tongues were cut out and their right hands cut off. Seven years after his trial Maximus died in exile on 13 August 662.

It is obvious and also understandable that these and other actions by the government intimidated the papacy. This intimidation accounted a great deal for the growing 'Byzantinization' of the papacy in the following decades. Thus the papal chancery came to adopt the characteristically Byzantine obsequious and subservient modes of address and tone in its official communications; outwardly at all events the papacy through its chancery began to refer to the imperial majesty as though it acquiesced in the government's scheme of things. It was indeed a macabre display of imperial power – elongated shades of the past – when the same emperor who sentenced Martin, paid a visit to Rome where, in a somewhat ghostly manner, he was received with due pomp and ceremony by Pope Vitalian. It was the last visit of the 'Roman' emperor to the city which gave his empire its name: a farewell visit which symbolically preceded, by five decades, the farewell visit of the pope to Constantinople. To a contemporary observer the sixties and seventies of the seventh century might well have appeared a period in which the papacy had finally succumbed to the terror exercised by the imperial government.

The serious losses suffered by Constantinople as a result of the Arab advances and the occupation of imperial territory by the Bulgars in the Balkans prompted the imperial government to have recourse once more to the same tactics which it had tried in similar earlier contingencies, though this time the religious move was in the reverse direction. That is to say, in order to harness the imperial West (as far as one could still speak of it as an administrative unit) to the government and its policy, the papacy had to be somehow appeased. Hence ways and means had to be found to make legal what had hitherto been proscribed religious doctrine. The emperor convoked the Sixth General Council for November 680. In the Easter synod of 680 held in Rome the papacy under Agatho made its views clear by defiantly striking up the claim to magisterial primacy. The Emperor Constantine IV was told in unambiguous terms that the Roman church was his mother and that it had never been proved that it had erred. After taking account of the views of the papacy on the dogmatic question of the two wills in Christ, this general council overturned all that had been decreed and acted upon before. The dogma now proclaimed was that Christ had two wills, and those who had held the opposite view were condemned as heretics – including the Patriarch Sergius and Pope Honorius I. Nevertheless, the establishment of a common religious platform in the East as well as in the West was an unrealizable aim. The council convoked by the emperor, Justinian II, for 692 was to be merely an appendix to the Sixth General Council: it was to issue purely supplementary regulations.

The papacy was not even invited, and yet the numerous decrees (which were to regulate the life of the Eastern church until this very day) re-enacted many earlier laws which had offended the West in general and the papacy in particular. That these decrees were to deepen the already sufficiently wide gulf between East and West is of lesser significance than the stern demand by the emperor that – though neither invited to, nor consulted by, nor represented at, the council – the pope should sign. Six large rolls embodying the record of the proceedings and the signatures of the participants were dispatched to Rome and the pope was peremptorily ordered to sign which he flatly refused to do, despite having been threatened with the fate of Martin I. Two high papal officers, Bishop Peter of Porto and the papal counsellor Boniface, were at once arrested and taken in chains to Constantinople. The imperial officer and his soldiery were however unable to execute the warrant to arrest the pope (Sergius I) because of the open hostility of the Roman crowds who were so enraged by this attempted arrest that the commanding officer fled and found a safe refuge under the bed of the pope. The bishop of Ravenna, Felix, was arrested, taken to Constantinople, tried with other 'rebels', sentenced, blinded and exiled.

The recourse to such measures by the imperial government showed the real weakness of Byzantium. And no bold assertions on the part of this same Justinian II that he had been specifically chosen by divinity as the guardian of the true Christian faith could hide the essential instability of this kind of régime. For the real target of such imperial protestations concerning the emperor's intimate link with divinity was the Roman church. The papacy, however, now seemed unaffected by intimidation and declared the decrees of the council of 692 unacceptable and therefore invalid. In order to discuss the matter Pope Constantine was therefore summoned to Constantinople, a summons which he accepted only under the condition that he was given safe conduct, a condition which the government fulfilled. It was to be the papacy's farewell visit to Constantinople (711). No pope ever set foot again in the city founded by the great Constantine.

The imperial summons of the pope to Constantinople clearly indicated at least in appearance a change of policy from terror to suave persuasion and negotiations. They had however one aim only, that is, to achieve the acquiescence of the papacy to the quite far-reaching decrees of 692. Indeed, the pope was ceremoniously, almost pompously, received at Constantinople by the highest officers of the government, and finally by the emperor himself who even performed the proskynesis (that is, his prostration before the pope), kissed the papal feet and confirmed the privileges of the Roman church, all this quite obviously to soften the resistance of the pope. There were some long drawn out negotiations between the emperor and the pope in the vicinity of Constantinople, but their result, if any, was meagre. At any rate, the pope remained adamant on the main point, and because of his refusal the decrees never had any force in the West.

The succession to Justinian II gave the papacy an unexpected chance to show its latent fibre, even in these unfavourable conditions. The successor was Phillipikos Bardanes who condemned out of his own plenitude of power the christological decision of the Sixth General Council and decreed a return to the earlier (heretical) view that there was only one will in Christ. The papacy was not slow in sharply protesting against this imperial standpoint – one more turn-about within the same generation. The papacy went even so far as to refuse to acknowledge Phillipikos as emperor. His name was not mentioned in papal documents, nor was his portrait shown on papal coins nor his picture carried through the streets of Rome, as was the ancient custom; nor were prayers said for him in the services at the Lateran. The result of this papal opposition was quite a serious unrest in Rome with consequent street fights in which more than 30 people were killed. For the papacy made common front with the Roman populace against the imperial garrison. Further bloodshed was prevented by the personal intervention of the pope who indeed acted against the advice of his own counsellors and the city officials who were all for a further 'show down' with the militia. What from the historical point of view is significant is that the papacy was strong enough to refuse recognition of an emperor in Constantinople: it was as if the roles between emperor and pope had been reversed. To understand this it may be profitable to cast a glance at the 'other end' of Europe.

While the papacy was the object and target of a tyrannical imperial government which never ceased to boast of its superior civilization, in the Western European regions it was accorded a totally different treatment. The West accepted St Peter's authority wholly and without discussion and therefore St Peter's link with the church of Rome and the pope. England and Gaul saw in the papacy an institution divinely willed and established: an institution that was specifically charged with carrying out the commission given by Christ to St Peter. The genuine veneration which the papacy received from Gaul, England and the recently converted Germanic tribes, provided a stark contrast to that treatment it had experienced at the hands of the lawful imperial government for more than two centuries. Yet it is worth pointing out that both Western veneration and imperial intimidation had the same root: the Petrinity of the papacy. Because of its close link with St Peter and the pope's succession to his powers the West looked with reverence and awe and profound respect upon the papacy. It was that same link and succession which made the East treat the papal institution despotically. The situation may be seen, once more, in terms of faith and history. For the West which in this context had no relevant history, the faith stood in the foreground; for the East it was (Roman) history and the historical continuation of the Roman empire which primarily mattered, and the faith was relegated to a role subordinate and subservient to the interests of the empire (see also above p. 23).

In concrete terms strong ties especially between Anglo-Saxon England and the papacy came to be forged at exactly the same time as that at which the imperial government had begun to terrorize the papacy. Numerous pilgrimages to the burial place of St Peter were undertaken by kings and princes; the Roman church was the recipient of many and large gifts; and when the Anglo-Saxon missionary efforts to the Frisians and other Teutonic tribes had been put well under way the papacy was credited with a directive role by the missionaries themselves. They allocated this role to the papacy, not because it demanded to play this role, but because the ecclesiastical organization to be set up in the mission fields naturally called for authoritative guidance and orientation by the papacy. This process began under Sergius I who conferred plenary powers on Willibrord, the great missionary of Frisia and North Germany. He was in fact consecrated archbishop of the Frisians by the pope himself in 695 and changed his Anglo-Saxon name into that of the allegedly first successor of St Peter, Clement. In itself this is hardly a significant event, and yet it highlights the powerful pull which the purely religious idea of rebirth exercised on man at the turn of the seventh and eighth centuries. The same could already be witnessed in a previous instance: on the occasion of his pilgrimage to Rome, the Anglo-Saxon king Caedwalla abdicated in 689 to be baptized 'Peter' by Pope Sergius.

Of profound historical impact was the conversion of the Germanic tribes East of the Rhine, a task of considerable complexity and danger demanding great tactical skill, by the head of the mission, Winfrid, who was consecrated missionary bishop of the Germans by Gregory II in 722. Again to demonstrate his rebirth he substituted the name of Boniface, the Roman martyr, for his native name. The creation of Boniface as bishop was parti-

cularly significant, because he took a special oath of obedience
to the papacy. Thereby still stronger ties were forged between the
newly established ecclesiastical organization in the converted
German lands and the papacy. The importance of this development in the early eighth century can hardly be exaggerated. The
undoubtedly sincere love which the missionaries entertained for
St Peter – hence the irresistible attraction of Petrine Rome – also
accounted for a number of new churches north of the Alps mostly
dedicated to St Peter (some also to St Paul). Numerous monastic
settlements followed, and they too manifested the same spirit of
dependence on Rome. The claim made by the papacy in the late
fourth century that the Roman church was the head and fountain
of Christianity (see above pp. 10, 16) was given practical and concrete shape by the Anglo-Saxon missionaries, notably by the
effects of their own ecclesiastical creations in the converted lands.
Of this abstract papal claim uttered by Damasus and Innocent I
the missionaries assuredly had no knowledge.

In 732 Boniface was made archbishop and German legate of
the apostolic see responsible for the whole ecclesiastical organization throughout the vast Frankish and Frisian regions. The result
of this rapid expansion of Christianity throughout the length and
breadth of central, Northern and North-Western Europe was that
from the very start of the missions the papacy had an opportunity
to exercise a very potent and enduring influence on these realms
and their ecclesiastical organism. It would seem superfluous to
emphasize this point. What needs stressing, however, is that
because they show Roman papal influence concretely, the councils
held in the Frankish realms and the decrees they issued exhibited
unadulterated Roman Latin Christianity. The German church, in
brief, was from the beginning the one territorial church which
came into being through the joint efforts of the papacy and the
organizing missionaries. The note of papal defiance to imperial
terror measures at the turn of the seventh and eighth centuries,
can be understood without effort. It was now the papacy which
began to issue a challenge to the imperial government. In view of
the very powerful and unquestioned security which the papacy
enjoyed at the hands of the youthful and virile Germanic nations,
the stand which the papacy took against Constantinople from the
second decade of the eighth century onwards, was wholly understandable.

The refusal on the part of the papacy to acknowledge the new emperor can be viewed as a preliminary to the later attempts at a fully-fledged extrication of the papacy from the imperial framework. This refusal by Pope Constantine was little else but the exercise of primatial rights by the papacy. On this basis it had condemned the decrees of an imperially convoked synod; and it refused to acknowledge an emperor who in papal eyes was a heretic. The actual constellation of circumstances which greatly helped the papacy were the ineffectual imperial régime in Italy and Rome and the strong moral support by the Germanic nations. Yet it is necessary to point out that no change whatsoever had occurred in the constitutional situation of the city of Rome and therefore of the papacy. Both were legally still part of the empire, however insecure the latter's hold was and however secure the papacy felt itself in the knowledge that the Franks and others were devoted to the Roman church and St Peter's successor. The situation was without a doubt fraught with dangers and demanded delicate handling as well as foresight and courage.

For by the twenties and thirties of the eighth century the conclusion had become inescapable that within the framework of the empire there was no future for the papacy as a governmental institution. The very hallmark of any government worth the name is the right to lay down what should and what should not be done. Within the terms of a thoroughgoing Christian society the norms were Christian, and the papacy believing as it did that it alone was qualified to lay down these norms, was denied by New Rome the exercise of this basic governmental right. What was at stake was the existence and future of the papacy as an institution that authoritatively guided the Christian body public, the Church. The dilemma which faced the papacy in the third and fourth decades of the eighth century was: should it continue to stay within the empire or should it leave the soil – literally or allegorically – which had nurtured it for so long?

On the one hand, the papacy's thought-patterns, its ethos, its very structure were thoroughly Roman. This feature linked it, on the purely intellectual level, with the imperial régime with which, after all, it had a great many premisses in common. On the other hand, there were across the Alps the Germanic nations with whom the papacy had virtually nothing in common, who were culturally and intellectually far below the level of the Roman or Italian populace, let alone below that of Byzantine society. But if one tries to focus attention on the one function which the papacy had always considered vital, that is, the authoritative guidance of the Church by means of the law, one will at once comprehend that the dilemma was capable of a solution. As long as the papacy remained part of the Roman empire, there was, as the dismal history in the seventh and eighth centuries had shown, no hope of ever exercising any primatial rights. And this exercise the papacy considered necessary for the good of Christian society. The acceptance of the Petrinity of the papacy by the Germanic nations in fact strongly suggested the solution to the dilemma. Consequently, the path which the papacy was to tread, ended with its releasing itself from the fetters and ties which the constitutional link with the empire imposed upon it. The aim was to gain freedom of governmental decisions and actions, freedom of deploying its primatial position which meant however in actuality the severance of the centuries-old ties with the Roman empire. To tread that path meant the extrication of the papacy from the constitutional framework of the Roman empire. On a realistic assessment the papacy had no other choice but to tread that path. Thereby an altogether new chapter opened, not only in the history of the papacy, but also in the history of Europe.

This grave situation confronting the papacy can also be seen in another way. As an institution the papacy had, so to speak, grown into the texture of the already existing Roman empire. After all, the papal church was the church of Rome when Rome was still the capital of the empire. But, and this is the vital consideration, as an institution charged with the leadership, guidance and government of the Christian people by the law which was based on faith, the papacy fundamentally differed from any other government. It had no army, no soldiery, no police forces and the many other paraphernalia of a public government. It could operate only when its primatial position was not obstructed by those who had physical power at their disposal. But what the imperial government had amply proved was that not only did it not co-operate with the papacy – as indeed more than two centuries before Gelasius I had postulated in a communication to the emperor (see above pp. 32f.) – but that it actually obstructed it and treated it with contempt, opposition and finally terror. No other solution presented itself in the thirties and forties of the eighth century than to harness the unquestionable Germanic veneration for St Peter and his successor to the purposes of the papal government. By following this path – which indeed was fraught with very grave dangers for the papacy – the institution not only fulfilled what it thought to be its mission and vocation, but also effected a profound change in the religious, ideological and finally also political map of medieval as well as modern Europe. Indeed, that path had already been indicated by Gregory the Great.

4 The Western Orientation of the Papacy

INTO THE HEAVY and sultry atmosphere which enveloped the relations between the papacy and the imperial government a fresh and cleansing breeze blew at the time when at the head of both institutions stood two new men – the second Gregory, a true Roman, and the third Leo (717–741), a Syrian, founder of a new dynasty and as an army leader the saviour of Constantinople in the face of deadly Arabic onslaughts which if not repelled might well have changed the course of history. In order to execute his plan of re-establishing Byzantine sovereignty in Italy Leo III issued stern taxation decrees for Italy and Sicily and thereby gravely affected the economic position of the papacy which was the biggest single land owner. Once again, the papacy refused to bow. The native population was wholly on its side. This open defiance was all the more courageous as the pope was to all intents and purposes the emperor's vice-roy in Italy. Understandably, the threat of serious charges to be brought against the pope produced only further stiffening on the part of the papacy. The imperial government – perhaps wisely in view of earlier experiences – offered to abstain from pressing any charges if the pope would promise to publish the imperial decree forbidding the veneration of images. The dogmatic scene had changed from christological pronouncements to liturgical and doxological questions. In the East there had always been some opposition to the use of images for religious worship, first by the orthodox Jews, then by Islam and also by some Christians who considered it pure idolatry to represent pictorially the Son of God. In his decree Leo III ordered first the removal, and in 726 the destruction of all images demanding at the same time from the bishops a declaration of support. Though there was even some opposition to this law in Constantinople, the West unanimously condemned it.

The leadership of the Western opposition belonged to the

papacy under Gregory II, who was in every respect worthy of his name. He point-blank refused to accept the bargain offered by Leo III, whereupon the government despatched ships and soldiers to Italy to arrest the pope. They never arrived, because they suffered shipwreck. More effectively, the emperor ordered the confiscation of all papal estates in Calabria and Sicily and separated the whole of Sicily and all the Balkan regions from the jurisdiction of the papacy and transferred these districts to the patriarchate of Constantinople, a measure which was never revoked. It was obvious that these two steps – the confiscation and the ecclesiastical reorganisation – vitally affected the papacy both ecclesiastically and economically.

The papacy now attacked the emperor himself in official communications which in rudeness, contempt and the disregard of all diplomatic niceties and polish must have reached a high-water mark. In them the whole governmental scheme was mercilessly torn to pieces. Most important, the papacy now openly spoke of a secession from the empire. That the pope ventured upon this highly perilous ground, showed how secure he felt – despite the threat uttered by imperial officers that Martin I's fate would befall him. Indeed, in the matter of images he had the whole Occident behind the papal opposition. Here again, the difference between East and West was very largely conditioned by the different cultural levels. The West was still primitive and pictorial presentations of biblical or religious themes were particularly appropriate to explain difficult religious points to an overwhelmingly illiterate population. The stand which the papacy took in this matter was, from the contemporary angle, wholly understandable. Moreover, these imperial decrees were one more flagrant violation of papal jurisdictional rights. In his attacks on the emperor Gregory II went as far as to declare that 'The whole Occident offers the prince of the apostles proof of faith, and if you should send men to destroy holy images, then I had better warn you: we shall be innocent of the blood that will then flow . . . you have no right to issue dogmatic constitutions; you have not the right mind for dogmas; your mind is too coarse and martial.' To which the emperor replied in the stereotyped phrase that rung hollow under the circumstances: 'I am king and priest.'

What raised these communications of the papacy to first-class historical documents was that they in fact renounced allegiance to the empire and revealed the innermost intentions and thoughts of the papacy. Indeed, from the papal point of view, there were two practical alternatives which would bring to an end this dreary relationship between pope and emperor. The papacy could physically leave the framework of the empire and take up residence somewhere in the Frankish realms. This clearly was the plan which motivated Gregory II. Or the papacy could leave the empire not by physically removing itself, but by excising from the body of the empire a portion of territory which in public law was no longer under imperial, but solely under papal jurisdiction. In the event, the papacy chose the second alternative, and for good reasons. For despite the security which the papacy would have enjoyed in Frankish realms, the adoption of the first alternative would have inflicted irreparable damage on the institution. The papacy without a direct and concrete link with St Peter and Rome would have suffered gravely – the very fate which befell the papacy six centuries later when it resided at Avignon and after its authority had reached the highest point. How much more deleterious to the papacy would a severance with Petrine Rome have been in the mid-eighth century when the papacy was a comparatively tender plant. The adoption of the second alternative was to lead to the establishment of the papal state in central Italy, partly co-terminous with the Italian papal estates, but fundamentally different from them in that they constituted a sovereign entity governed not by private, but by public law and, what is most important, whose existence was guaranteed by the kings of the Franks.

Amongst the Germanic nations the Franks had since the turn of the fifth and sixth centuries maintained continuously good relations with the papacy. In his communication to the emperor Gregory II had in mind the Franks whom the Byzantines liked to call 'barbarians' but whom the papacy had every cause to extol for their devotion to St Peter and his successor: this was the theme of the first Gregory and it was a very effectively deployed stratagem by the second Gregory. During the latter's pontificate the connexions between the papacy and the now firmly established Frankish ecclesiastical organisation became especially close. This was also the time when the ineffectualness of the imperial régime in Italy and Rome was particularly marked. By contemporary standards, the stability of the papal institution compared very favourably with the instability of the imperial administration.

That papal-Frankish relations developed satisfactorily was no doubt due to the firm bonds which tied the missionaries and newly appointed ecclesiastical officers to the Roman church. Precisely because imperial rule became feebler from year to year, the Lombards resumed in earnest their attacks on imperial territory and began apparently to threaten Rome itself.

The Lombards in fact became a source of considerable anxiety to the papacy, though papal fears may at times have been wildly exaggerated. The Lombard threats – real or imaginary – prompted the papacy under Gregory III to initiate its programme of extrication from imperial jurisdiction. Specifically addressed to Charles Martel, the recent victor over the Arabs at Poitiers, in 738–739 the first papal appeals to the Franks went out asking them to free the papacy from the Lombard menace. Obviously as a bait Charles was offered the position of Consul of the Duchy of Rome by the pope who also despatched large gifts to the Frank as well as the chains of St Peter himself. But despite the distinctions with which Charles Martel was singled out, he categorically refused to be drawn into Italian or Lombard affairs. After all, he was on perfectly friendly terms with the Lombards and he was not shown why he should intervene in Italy and make them his enemies. The papacy learnt a lesson from this. If the programme it pursued was to succeed, it had to be prepared very much more carefully and with far greater attention to detail.

The situation in Italy steadily deteriorated. In 751 the Lombards expelled the exarch from Ravenna and the imperial garrisons from North-Italian soil. They now made active preparations for an advance south, their spearheads being directed at Rome, and occupied large districts from which all remnants of the imperial militia were driven out or made prisoner. At exactly the same time unrest also grew in the Frankish kingdom. By the forties of the eighth century the old Merovingian dynasty had proved itself wholly effeminate and incapable of governing the kingdom. For several decades effective power had been in the hands of the mayors of the royal palace who not unjustifiably considered the situation anomalous. During the reign of King Childeric III the mayor of the palace, Pippin the Short (a son of Charles Martel) resolved to put an end to this situation. His plan was to remove the reigning dynasty and become king himself. Because this obviously was a step of major dimensions Pippin sought some approval for his design from what the West considered the highest moral authority, the papacy. In order, therefore, to have some sanction and legitimation for what was nothing else but a *coup d'état* Pippin approached the papacy. This step taken in no less a matter than the envisaged removal of a legitimate king, gave manifest proof to the papacy of the degree of esteem in which it was held across the Alps.

The pope, Zacharias, replied to the well-framed question of Pippin that the man should be king, and be called king, who wielded actual power and not he who was only nominally king without effective power at his disposal. In the same communication the pope ordered that Pippin should be made king. Backed by this sanction and explicit papal approval given in 750 Pippin had himself formally elected king of the Franks at Soissons, at the same time deposing Childeric. The year afterwards Pippin was anointed king by Archbishop Boniface. This was the first royal anointing of a Frankish ruler. In adequately assessing the action of the papacy, the somewhat refined moral standards of the twentieth century are out of place. The action must be judged by the standards of the mid-eighth century, according to which no reprehensible character was attributable to the kind of sanction readily supplied by the papacy.

Indeed, the Frankish monarchy appeared to the papacy as the most suitable instrument for its plan of gaining that freedom which it had sought. For even a purely nominal imperial rule constituted a latent danger to the papacy, because it had not full freedom to deploy its primatial functions. That the papal approval to the Frankish *putsch*, the expulsion of the exarch from Ravenna and the consequential Lombard threat to Rome occurred simultaneously, should be borne in mind. All these events took place within little more than a year: the papal communication was dispatched in the late spring of 750, Ravenna fell exactly a year later, and Pippin was anointed in the early autumn of 751. This was precisely the situation which offered plenty of opportunity to papal initiative, and the papacy was not slow in taking the lead. Accompanied by a special Frankish escort for which he had asked, Pope Stephen II left Rome for the Frankish kingdom in mid-October 753; he arrived at Ponthion (near Vitry-le-François) at Epiphany 754. It was just over 40 years since a pope had undertaken the last journey to Constantinople – this journey to the

Franks was the first of a pope westwards. These two journeys symbolized the end and the beginning of an epoch.

That this papal journey had been long and well prepared is sufficiently proved by the Frankish escort which Pippin had sent upon papal request. That the papacy attached greatest urgency to the journey is demonstrated by its beginning just before the onset of wintry conditions which were bound to be met while crossing the Alps. What did not lack a certain irony was that a fortnight before the papal-Frankish party was to have left Rome, an embassy from Byzantium somewhat unexpectedly arrived, ordering the pope to intercede on behalf of the emperor with the Lombard King Aistulf for the return of territory to the empire. As ordered Stephen II and his party (in which the imperial ambassador was now included) proceeded to Pavia, the headquarters of Aistulf, who not unexpectedly refused to enter into any discussions concerning a return of conquered territory. Pavia conveniently lay in any case on the route to France. The refusal by the Lombard king was of course what the papacy had anticipated. Nothing could have been further from the pope's intention than a return of territories to imperial rule. The pope travelled from Rome to Pavia in a twofold capacity – he was to plead on behalf of the emperor from whose rule he wished to extricate himself. The one mission was the very antithesis of the other.

The result of the negotiations between Stephen II and Pippin at Ponthion was that the king promised to restore to the papacy, or rather to St Peter, the territories robbed by the Lombards (such as the exarchate of Ravenna and many other districts). In return for this promise the pope prohibited under pain of excommunication the choice of a king who did not belong to the family of Pippin. A little later at St Denis in the spring of 754, the pope anointed the king and created him patrician of the Romans. The great ideological significance of this papal anointing – and it should be borne in mind that the pope himself was not anointed, since papal anointings were unknown at the time – was that the hitherto prevailing charisma of blood (represented in the Merovingian dynasty) was replaced by the charisma of divine grace that was conferred by the pope on the usurper, King Pippin. In the event, Pippin fulfilled his promise in two campaigns. He crushingly defeated the Lombards and donated the lands he had conquered from them to St Peter and hence to the papacy in a solemn document which was deposited at the tomb of St Peter in his basilica (early summer 756). This, in short, was the action which created the papal state incorporating as it did the exarchate of Ravenna and a number of regions in central Italy.

Both the right to create King Pippin a patrician of the Romans, that is, their military defender, and the claim to the districts which he 'restored' to the papacy, were based upon the forgery known as the Donation of Constantine. This rested on the novellistic product of the late fifth century (see above pp. 36f.) and asserted that before departing to Constantinople, the Emperor Constantine had handed over to his contemporary pope, Silvester, large, though unspecified provinces and regions in Italy and in the Western hemisphere as well as all islands, in addition to the Lateran palace which was to be the official papal residence. Constantine also gave the pope the right to wear all imperial insignia and garments and to create consuls and patricians. This forgery was the document upon which both Stephen II and Pippin proceeded, though it is safe to assume that Pippin was quite unaware of the character of the document which provided the archival title-deed for the papal restoration claims. The essential point was, however, that as far as Pippin was concerned, he acted as a defender of rights belonging to St Peter. It was in this capacity that he wrested the stolen territories from the Lombards and handed them over to St Peter through the medium of the papacy. At the eleventh hour through a special embassy to the victorious conqueror the rightful owner, that is, the emperor, announced his claims and asked for a return of these selfsame regions. This request was flatly refused by the Frank who maintained that though he had taken possession of the territories by his own conquest, he had done so on behalf of St Peter. Since the imperial ambassador did not of course know of the 'documentary' title-deed for the papal claim to these territorial restorations, he could not but have been thoroughly bewildered by Pippin's reply: what should St Peter have had to do with these lands?

In brief, Pippin acted as an organ that righted a wrong inflicted by the Lombards on St Peter and the papacy. The Lombards had wickedly stolen property from the owner, the papacy, to whom the Emperor Constantine had made over these territories as a gift in perpetuity. Pippin's campaigns and actions were entirely within the framework of that faith which the papacy conceived to be necessary for eventual salvation. He was the avenger of St Peter, because only in this way could he obtain eternal salvation. As the papacy made crystal clear in numerous communications to him, if he were to refuse help to the papacy, all the churches in his own kingdom and herewith the whole of the Christian faith and religious practice would disintegrate, if not disappear altogether; his own kingship would also come to grief. Pippin's military campaigns and the resultant establishment of the papal state were the concrete manifestation of Frankish veneration for St Peter and his successor. This papal state incorporated not only parts of the (privately owned) papal patrimonies, but also regions and districts which had never been the property of the papacy. The donation effected by Pippin was an overt confirmation of the fictitious grant by Constantine.

This papal state (or patrimony of St Peter, as it was called throughout the medieval period right down to 1870) was now protected by the Frankish king, and the papacy was to be its undisputed master. The frontiers were by no means firmly fixed, and precisely because of this fluidity the papacy continued to press the Franks for further grants, though without immediate avail. As is natural with all youthful things the young state wanted to grow. For some years after the creation of this entity in public law the papacy still depicted the emperor's portrait on its coins; and the papal chancery also continued to date official documents according to the regnal years of the emperor; there were also other signs which did not overtly reveal the magnitude of the change that had occurred.

In one respect, however, there was an almost immediate result of the papacy's becoming the sovereign in large parts of Italy. The old Roman aristocracy very much came to the fore and demanded a greater share in the making of the pope, now that since the demise of the exarch imperial approbation had at least in practice fallen into abeyance. Hence there were troubled elections which prompted the papacy to issue its first proper election decree. Chaired by the pope the Roman synod of 769 was seized of this matter and passed a decree according to which no layman was allowed to take part in the election of the pope. This decree was to form the basis for a later and much more effective papal election arrangement. What the original enactment lacked, however, was any kind of backing by a power that was willing and capable of providing support when this was needed to prop up the authority of an elected pope.

The Frankish king clearly suggested himself for this role of a protector. Though Pippin was never persuaded to assume the title of a patrician of the Romans, however much he acted in this capacity, his son from the moment of accession (768) designated himself as such and lived up to the expectations of the office. Here must be noted the impact which the papally expounded faith had made. The difference between Romans and Christians was totally obliterated in the West. A Roman was a Christian and a Christian was a Roman. This ideological feature with which contemporary sources are replete, was an important presupposition for the development of the West of Europe as a body with a pronounced Roman complexion in contrast to the Greek Byzantine configuration of the 'Roman' empire. At any rate, Charlemagne in his function as patrician of the Romans, that is, as a military defender of the Romans who were identified with the Christians in general, confirmed the donation of his father and also added a considerable portion of Italian districts to those regions already 'restored' to the papacy. The whole of Venetia and Istria, though nominally still Byzantine, as well as the Duchies of Spoleto and Benevento and the island of Corsica, were now part of the papal patrimony. In parenthesis it should be noted that Venetia and Istria had not been in the hands of the Lombards. The presupposition for this large scale transfer of property was that Charlemagne had effectively subdued all remnants of Lombard power in Italy and had himself assumed the title of 'King of the Lombards'. Whatever had remained of the Lombard kingdom ceased to exist from 774. Nevertheless, repeated demands urging Charlemagne to restore further territory to the papacy which – it claimed – had all the documents in its archives, met with little success. His request to be shown the documents in the papal archives was refused which put an end to further papal territorial claims.

The historically most conspicuous and significant result of Charlemagne's overlordship in Italy was that the papacy gradually came to sever its last ties with the empire. Adrian I no longer dated papal documents according to imperial years, but according to the regnal years of Charles; coins in the papal patrimony no longer presented the emperor's effigy, but the pope's; of some significance was the mosaic in the Lateran which showed how St Peter himself handed a standard to Charlemagne and the pallium to the pope. These and other signs increased as the century drew to a close. In some respects it is true that the Frankish king stepped into the place formerly occupied by the emperor at Constantinople, and it was due to this change that papal elections came to be notified to the royal Frankish court instead of to an imperial officer.

Yet the purely external substitution of one Ruler by another concealed a most profound difference, because Charlemagne, in sharp contrast to the emperor, did not impugn the Petrine basis of the papacy. On the contrary, it was his genuine and deep veneration for St Peter and his successor which militated against any kind of opposition on the model of Constantinople. In fact, where the emperor had taken repressive measures Charlemagne generally supported the papal institution as such. Yet, although he was convinced that in essential questions the papacy was the divinely chosen repository of the true Christian faith and that the papacy – and not necessarily an individual pope – was the proper organ to enunciate doctrine, he nevertheless was also sure that as far as the effective government of the Christian people was concerned, doctrine alone did not suffice. What Charlemagne in general conceded – and here lay the real contrast to Byzantium – was magisterial primacy, that is, primacy in matters of religion, faith and dogma. This attitude of Charlemagne made understandable the rapid infiltration of papal ideas, particularly those relating to details in liturgy and ecclesiastical discipline, through the length and breadth of the Frankish realms. The sacramentary ascribed to Gregory I as well as the ecclesiastical law book of Dionysius (early sixth century) suitably expanded by Adrian I, were specifically requested by Charlemagne who took great care to disseminate these and other sources of papal authority in his kingdom. Roman liturgy became firmly established in the Frankish realms, and in his own plentiful legislation he was anxious to stress the papal substance of the individual decrees.

But despite this strongly marked Romanism of Charlemagne in religious matters, the papacy was all too soon made aware of the direction which Charlemagne's government was taking. Upon closer inspection there were considerable affinities with some Byzantine features which the papacy had hoped to have escaped.

This similarity of both Eastern and Western governments was not indeed surprising, since both exhibited a stern monarchic rule. And because Charlemagne's abiding aim was to be in the West what the emperor was in the East, a similarity of his government to that exercised by the emperor necessarily emerged. Not only in the government proper, but also in some peripheral matters the resemblance was rather close. When the pope, Leo III, had considerable difficulties with the local Romans in 798–9, he undertook the arduous journey to Paderborn in Germany to implore the patrician of the Romans to render him help in Rome.

On the occasion of this visit he became acquainted with the building programme which engaged Charlemagne's attention at this time, that is, the building of the palace at Aachen to which contemporaries had somewhat ominously referred as 'The Second Rome'. Uncomfortable memories of 'New Rome' must have crossed the pope's mind, especially when he further learned that next to the minster envisaged there was to be 'a sacred palace' for the king himself and another building, called 'The Lateran', was expressly designated 'the house of the pontiff' – all this could not but evoke and provoke comparisons with Constantinople and the imperial régime. What this building programme signified was a transfer of Rome to Aachen, where the pope's role might well have to be reduced to the level of that generally allocated to the patriarch of Constantinople, the domestic imperial chaplain. Although Charlemagne did undertake the campaign to liberate Leo III from the hostile clutches of the Roman population, the pope himself took the initiative in a different direction. There is no warrant for saying that Charlemagne had Leo III formally tried. What in actual fact happened was that at a large meeting of high ecclesiastics, Frankish magnates and other high-placed laymen in St Peter's basilica, the accusations raised against the pope by the Romans were discussed at great length, but the pope upon a solemn oath denied all the crimes and charges. The reason why the pope took this oath, was the unanimous endorsement which the whole meeting gave to the ancient, but hitherto never applied principle that the pope could not be judged by anyone (see above p. 39).

It was the first time that this principle had been invoked. The significance of this invocation can hardly be exaggerated. In his function as pope and as successor of St Peter he stood above the law. The application of the principle was historically and, from the papal point of view, governmentally far more important than the events to which it led. It was also this meeting which on 23 December 800 decided that Charlemagne, the king of the Franks, should be called emperor. And Charlemagne agreed to this suggestion in all humility, as the contemporary record has it. For according to contemporary views the throne at Constantinople was vacant, because a woman, Irene, ruled there.

The understanding of the subsequent events presupposes the proper assessment of this point in conjunction with the deep Frankish veneration for St Peter and the somewhat unpalatable impressions that the pope had received on inspecting the building projects at Paderborn. In any case, Charlemagne was indisputably the acknowledged Ruler of Europe between the Pyrenees and the Elbe, and without exaggeration could be spoken of as the Ruler of the West as far as this had been opened up. That all these circumstances and facts were easily capable of being turned to the advantage of the papacy, was a conclusion which the extremely alert, realistic and perceptive Leo III quickly reached. It was he who seized the initiative. Thereby he continued the dynamic lead which had characterized the actions of the papacy during the last decades. And as subsequent history was to show, as long as the papacy kept the initiative in its own hands, and thus utilized the emerging constellation of circumstances in the service of its programme, its success was generally assured.

The instrument which enabled the papacy to take the decisive step in the realization of its programme of extrication, was ready at hand. The Donation of Constantine which, in its transmitted form, had been fabricated in the early fifties of the eighth century (see above p. 77) was harnessed to the papal plan. The Donation had already served the papacy well in its claims to territorial restitutions. Extracts of the forgery unobtrusively found their way into official papal communications. Further, it was this 'document' which on the basis of its source (above pp. 36f.) tried to show how 'in reality' Constantinople had become the capital of the Roman empire. It clothed the reasons for Constantine's transfer of his residence from Rome to Constantinople in symbolic events and gestures of which the essential and relevant feature was briefly this: Constantine gave the imperial crown to Pope Silvester who did not, however, wish to wear it. The meaning was obvious. The crown was the pope's own as a result of the emperor's gift to him, but he allowed its use to Constantine who then left for Constantinople. The crown went from Rome to Constantinople with papal acquiescence, and it was in Constantinople only for so long as the pope suffered it to be there. That was, according to the Donation, how Constantinople became and continued to be the capital of the Roman empire. It will be recalled what great ecclesiastical significance Constantinople assumed in the decrees of Chalcedon and later councils (above p. 26) as well as in the government of the emperors themselves.

Since in 800 the throne in Constantinople was considered 'vacant' and since everything else indicated that the situation was propitious for papal initiative, Leo III in accordance with a concerted plan acted during Christmas Mass. That Charlemagne had readily agreed to 'accept the name of emperor' only two days earlier, was no doubt a particularly weighty circumstance. Leo III celebrated Christmas Mass, not in the expected church (in Santa Maria Maggiore) but in St Peter's – the very place held in the highest esteem by the Franks. During this service the pope put a 'most precious crown' on the head of Charlemagne just as he was rising from his kneeling position, whereupon the assembled crowd shouted the acclamation in a prearranged manner, so that now (to quote the most reliable source) 'he was set up as Emperor of the Romans'. It was the meaning that was given to the 'coronation' by the crowd at St Peter's which took Charles somewhat aback, for the role he had accepted was that of an emperor, but not that of an 'Emperor of the Romans'. This embodied a very special function. The emperor of the Romans was in fact the one in Constantinople, the historic successor of the ancient Roman emperor, who as such inherited the claim to universality of his Rulership. But this was not the function which Charlemagne wished to play. To be an 'emperor' was no more than a streamlined king who ruled over several nations, and it was this role which he had agreed to accept before Christmas. Clearly there was a wide gulf between papal and Caroline views. For if Charles had accepted the function of a universal Ruler as represented in the fully-fledged Roman emperor, the consequence would have been – as was certainly intended by the papacy – that the empire in the East would have been considered to have ceased to exist as a legitimate Roman empire, and that Charles himself would have now been the 'true' emperor of the Romans. His intention, on the contrary, was to be in the West what the emperor was in the East. His aim was parity or co-existence with the empire in the East.

But the step was taken and herewith a new dimension was introduced into the contemporary as well as the subsequent political configuration of Europe. The deed could not be undone, although liturgically and dogmatically it had no meaning whatsoever. The Frankish king was not anointed and no special prayers were said over him: it was a merely symbolic gesture that was performed by the pope. It is worth noting, however, that no pope had ever crowned an emperor in Rome. Although no doubt the coronation of the emperor at Constantinople by the patriarch served as a model, especially for the acclamations, there was on the other hand very little that the pope could borrow from the Byzantine ritual, for this focused conspicuous attention on the emperor as kosmokrator and supreme Ruler in all questions, including those specially affecting the papacy. Hence, apart from the acclamations, there was virtually nothing that could suitably be adopted for the Roman 'coronation'. Thus the bareness and shapelessness of this 'coronation' at Christmas 800 and the absence of all prayers for the emperor, can easily be explained. The report by one Frankish source that Leo III 'adored' the newly crowned emperor, in all likelihood referred to a merely symbolic bowing of the pope before Charles.

This stroke of the papacy neutralized possible dangers from the imperial government in Constantinople. Above all, the action completed the process of extrication begun just 50 years earlier. The centre of the Christian world was to be Rome, not Aachen nor Constantinople. Charlemagne's views, expressed long before these events, had greatly assisted the papacy in its resolve to re-instate Rome as the centre of Christianity, for a Christian was identical with a Roman. His military conquests were undertaken to propagate the Christian faith as expounded by the papacy; he was called 'Rector of Europe' since he governed 'the kingdom of Europe'. But this Europe was no longer an ideologically unshaped and amorphous territorial mass. It was slowly being welded into a coherent ideological entity that was built on the foundations of the Christian faith. And this faith was of Roman papal provenance. The Roman empire which he now governed as emperor (as his official title showed) was only another name for 'Christian empire', and this again was the same as the kingdom of Europe. Moreover, the inscription on his imperial seal demonstrated that the ancient (pagan) Roman empire was now reborn as a Christian empire – in a word it was a unit which was held together not by ethnic or historic ties but by the cementing bond of the faith enunciated by the church of Petrine Rome.

Yet on a wider plane the Christmas action raised a very serious problem: who was the rightful and legitimate emperor of the Romans? This is a point of which due historical notice should be taken. Was this Roman emperor the one created by the papacy or the one ruling from Constantinople? It was at this juncture that the papal action produced what would nowadays be called global repercussions. For the emperor at Constantinople could never imagine an emperor who was not an emperor of the Romans, and as such embodied universality of rule and dominion. The papal action was first ridiculed in Constantinople and later viewed as arrogance without meaning. According to Eastern reasonings, the emperor at Constantinople was the one and only historical successor to the ancient Roman Caesars, and no religious consideration entered into this at all. On the other hand, the West viewed the same matter, not from the historical angle, but from the religious standpoint. Here once more the antithesis of East and West showed itself in the antithesis of history and faith (see above pp. 17, 23, 26). This antithesis now assumed practical dimensions on the largest possible scale. The East viewed the empire as a historic, the West as an ecclesiastical unit based on the Roman faith.

It stands to reason that when the empire was seen as a historic unit, the presuppositions for becoming its Ruler were different from those which qualified the Ruler of an empire that was a manifestation of faith. Within the former the army, senate and people were to be at work at the creation of the emperor; within the latter it was an ecclesiastically qualified organ which created him. And since the concept of a Roman emperor embodied the idea of universality, he could only be made by an ecclesiastical organ that similarly embodied the idea of universality, and this was the papacy. Furthermore, this fundamentally different view on the character of the empire accounted also for another crucial difference in regard to the coronation of the emperor. As already noted, the coronation by the patriarch of Constantinople was never constitutive. The constitutional position of the emperor was quite independent of a coronation which therefore was merely declaratory. This is to say it proclaimed to the world in a solemn and public ecclesiastical ritual the already functioning emperor. On the other hand, the coronation by the pope in Rome was to become constitutive, and the emperor had to be a king before he received the imperial crown: not until the coronation was he an emperor. The pope constituted a special officer on a universal scale. This officer was seen by the papacy as still essentially a patrician of the Romans, that is, a military organ to whom through the papacy divinity had entrusted the physical protection of the Roman Christians. It stood to reason why the emperor at Constantinople could never qualify for this office. He not only did not acknowledge the standing of the Roman church within a Christian world, but he also remonstrated and protested against its rulings and had terrorized the popes. The papacy consequently applied the principle of suitability, a principle that had no meaning at Constantinople at all.

Nothing illustrated the basic difference between the Byzantine and the Roman emperor better than the adoption of a specifically Western feature on the occasion of the making of a Roman emperor. Since he was charged with the protection of an essentially ecclesiastical unit (though named 'Roman empire'), he had to have a special ecclesiastical and religious stamp. And this stamp was found to be the anointing carried out by the pope from 816 onwards. It was this feature – the unction – which made perfectly clear that the unit over which he was set up as emperor was of divine provenance and therefore essentially religiously conceived. Through the unction the link between the emperor and divinity was established by the officiating pope. The emperor was said to be in receipt of a divine favour in the shape of divine grace transmitted or mediated in the act of unction by the pope. This anointing element distinguished the imperial coronation in the West most conspicuously from that practised in Constantinople. For at Constantinople there was no unction, and understandably so, because the empire was conceived on the historical level. The emperor at Constantinople was a successor of the ancient Roman emperors. The administration of unction on the Byzantine emperor would have been quite meaningless.

From the religious as well as ideological point of view the action on Christmas Day suffered from quite serious shortcomings. In addition, there were incontrovertible signs that Charlemagne came to imitate a great many Byzantine features, so as to demonstrate by external means the parity of his empire with that in the East. The newly crowned emperor never again went to Rome. Amongst the features imitated and adopted was also that of creating a co-emperor. In 813 without regard for any papal views on the matter Charles created his oldest son Louis I his co-emperor. The papacy had some reason to be concerned about the trends in Charlemagne's government which clearly revealed at least the possibility, if not the likelihood, of a repetition in the West of the Byzantine scheme. The deployment of the dynamic initiative which had distinguished the papacy when a situation looked dangerous, suggested itself.

The motive of Stephen IV's (V's) journey to Rheims in October 816 – barely two years after Charlemagne's death – was to crown Louis I emperor although his father had already three years earlier raised him to that dignity, and above all to anoint Louis, and thus to make known to the world in a visible and unambiguous manner the vital difference between him and the Byzantine emperor. Thereby the pope also remedied the shortcomings of Charlemagne's coronation 16 years earlier. Eye witnesses reported that Louis I was crowned with the crown of Constantine I which the pope had brought with him – one more proof of the efficacy of the Donation of Constantine. Special liturgical prayers were said over Louis – one more proof of careful preparation. Further, the Romans were excluded altogether, as the papal party was very small. How singularly well the proceedings were prearranged could be seen in the threefold prostration of Louis before the pope as soon as he arrived at Rheims. No less significant was the pope's greeting Louis as 'a second David'. But what made this coronation at Rheims especially noteworthy was that it combined Western and Eastern elements: the coronation (which was of Byzantine provenance) became attached to the unction. The anointing was, on the model of the Old Testament, understood to confer divine grace on the recipient in the shape of ruling power. It was in fact this idea which had been applied by the Visigoths in Spain to the unctions of their kings, whom very likely the Franks imitated in the eighth century when **beginning** with Pippin the Short their kings were anointed. In actual fact Charlemagne himself was anointed by the popes three times.

But what was important was that hitherto unction had been administered to a king only. Now from October 816 onwards it was administered by the papacy to emperors. It was the first time that such use had been made of the unction. It should furthermore be emphasized that this was also the very first occasion when unction and coronation formed the two essential pillars of the ecclesiastical making of an emperor. Henceforward these two parts were to form the skeleton of every imperial (and royal) rite. Yet it should also be realized that the central feature of every Western imperial (and royal) coronation was not the crowning but the anointing of the Ruler. The purpose of the imperial unction was specifically to create the military defender of the papacy as the 'fount' and 'mother' of the universal Church. The unction was counted among the sacraments which could be administered only by the appropriate ecclesiastical officer. Hence also the emperor crowned by the pope was said to be 'the special son of the Roman church', a feature which distinguished him clearly from the emperor at Constantinople who was never willing to accept this filial relationship. In this designation the overtones and undertones of orthodoxy and heterodoxy could plainly be heard, and it was only a few decades later in this ninth century that precisely because he had received unction from the pope, the Western emperor claimed to have the 'right', i.e. the orthodox faith, whilst the Eastern emperor had not. The methodically pursued line of the papacy in the late eighth and early ninth centuries demonstrated the utilization of purely religious issues and sacramental matters for concerns which a later age would have had no hesitation in calling 'high politics'. The papacy had carefully cultivated the ground. Ecclesiastical ways of thinking and acting had penetrated all spheres of public and private life in the European West.

The dynamic initiative taken by the papacy in the matter of the imperial unction can be all the more appreciated if it is realized that there was – at the time – no anointing for bishops and that the popes themselves had not received this sacrament. The popes were not anointed until well over a century later while North of the Alps the episcopal unction as an integral part of the episcopal consecration was largely modelled on that administered to kings.

As it was a sacrament the unction conferred some kind of sacrality on its royal or imperial recipient. His whole inner being was said to have changed as a result of the unction which made him 'the Lord's anointed' (*Christus Domini*). This was Old Testament doctrine and was also the view attributed to medieval unctions. The recipient had, so to speak, shed his primitive attributes as a warrior and in his function was raised onto the pedestal of an athlete of Christ (to use an often employed contemporary term) to defend and protect the Church as Christ's own organized community in general and the papacy as the Church's governmental organ in particular.

Yet in course of time some vital differences between royal and imperial unctions emerged. Whilst for royal anointings chrism was used, for imperial unctions a liturgically inferior oil came to be applied which did not necessarily constitute a sacrament; the king was to be primarily anointed on the head, the emperor on the right arm and between the shoulder blades to sanctify the seat of his physical power. As it was maintained by the papacy in the ninth century (John VIII), what Christ possessed by nature, the emperor now possessed by grace, and that grace was conferred on the occasion of the imperial coronation. The development of the imperial unction (as distinct from royal unction) tended to reduce the great advantage which the emperor had as a 'mere' king: it brought into clear relief his role as the protector specifically created by the papacy on a universal scale (see also below p. 187). It is therefore understandable that later the imperial coronation was symbolically considered to be on a lower level than the royal coronation.

It is difficult today to appreciate adequately the great advance which the papacy had made at the turn of the eighth and ninth centuries. The whole ideological and 'political' map of Europe had been changed by the methodical, purposeful and vigorous application of an abstract programme to concrete reality. And this reality was singularly favourable to the reception of the papacy's ideas, doctrines and programme. For the presuppositions were entirely religious. And the instruments the papacy employed came evidently from the same religious reservoir from which the presuppositions stemmed. In a word, there was a rare correspondence between presuppositions, means and end. Seen from a wider historical perspective, however, all this was the fruit of

Gregory I's epoch-making missionary enterprise. It was he who had taken the decisive initiative in opening up the fallow Western soil to Roman ecclesiastical influences which came to full fruition in the ninth century. It was the age which saw the beginning of the process by which Europe became a firmly knit ideological unit resting on the faith enunciated by the Roman church.

5 *The Papacy and Latin Europe*

SEEN FROM THE purely intellectual angle the advance made by the papacy in the early ninth century coincided with the completion of the process of amalgamating Roman, Christian and Germanic elements in the West. The inextricable fusion of these three disparate strains resulted in the elimination of the harsh and abrasive contrasts which divided them, and in the emergence of a more or less homogeneous synthesis. The consequence was the great civilizing effect which the close connexions between the North, West and South of Europe brought about. The papacy itself through its intimate contact especially with the peoples north of the Alps came in course of time to absorb a good many non-Roman, purely Germanic features into its own system. This was particularly noticeable in the realms of liturgy, symbolism and also in questions relating to property of land. On the other hand, this pronouncedly Western orientation of the papacy also affected its relations with Constantinople. For in addition to the constitutional and 'political' that is, legal independence from the empire at Constantinople which the papacy had indubitably achieved, the cultural and intellectual estrangement already noticeable for a long time, rapidly increased. One could speak of a severance of the bonds which had hitherto linked papal Rome and imperial Constantinople. It was this twofold detachment of the papacy from Constantinople which contributed a great deal to the acceleration of the process of creating Latin Europe as a viable unit. It is advisable to keep these mutual Western influences in perspective if one wishes to understand the strong and resilient ties which joined the papacy with the virile Northern nations.

That from the first decades of the ninth century the papacy and the Frankish monarchy became mutually dependent upon each other, is not difficult to grasp. The Franks were necessary

D

as the military protectors of the papacy against the unruly Romans, and especially against the Roman aristocracy which considered itself 'cheated' of success by the combined forces of the papacy and the Franks. The tension between the papacy and the local aristocracy had already made itself felt in the turbulent scenes at the election of Stephen III as well as during the pontificate of Leo III. On the occasion of the election of Eugenius II in 824 severe disorders broke out again. On behalf of his father, the co-emperor Lothar I issued a Constitution in 824 which was intended to protect the papacy from the machinations of the local Roman aristocracy. This document stipulated that the pope should notify the Western emperor that an election had taken place, so that his consecration as a bishop could proceed in the presence of imperial legates who would serve as guarantors of public order. It will readily be seen that the old stipulation according to which the elected pope had to notify the Byzantine emperor and later the exarch, was the model for this Constitution, with this qualification however that the purpose of notifying the Western emperor was to secure peaceful conditions in Rome on the occasion of the new pope's consecration. The Constitution was issued in the interests of the papacy. No Frankish control of the papacy as an institution nor approval of the elected pope by the Frankish court was envisaged.

On the other hand, the papacy exercised considerable influence upon the Franks, and this quite especially as Louis I was more distinguished by his piety than by his governing abilities. His weakness together with his outlook inculcated by a narrow clerical upbringing, produced disastrous results in his realms and understandably offered the papacy a large avenue for exercising influence in matters on which papal thought had not yet had an opportunity of concentrating. The intervention by the papacy in the quarrels of Louis I's sons with the emperor himself, cannot by any stretch of the imagination be counted among its successful measures. This was not only because the papacy intervened in a somewhat hamfisted manner in these unedifying quarrels – the intervention of Gregory IV in 833 in France was a deplorable and pitiable episode siding as he did with the rebellious sons – but also because the papacy trod (with long-term effects) on the susceptibilities of the Frankish episcopacy. The tension between papacy and episcopacy emerged for the first time in the thirties of the ninth century precisely because the bishops considered that papal interference constituted an infringement of their rights.

At that time the episcopacy began to emerge as an adversary of the papacy, and it was an opponent with whom in the subsequent centuries the papacy found it increasingly hard to cope. At the base of this tension and later conflict stood a problem of interpretation: was the power to bind and to loose given exclusively to St Peter (and therefore to his successors, the popes) or was this power given to all the apostles and hence to the bishops as the successors of all the apostles? The former viewpoint was unswervingly held by the papacy, the latter equally unswervingly by the episcopacy. And each standpoint appealed to the same gospel, that of St Matthew, though to two different passages: for the papacy it was Matt. 16.18f., and for the episcopacy it was 18.18. As can readily be seen, the question directly affected the very core of the papal function and position as a monarchic institution. As the history of papal–episcopal relations showed, reconciliation of the standpoints was not found possible, nor even seriously attempted by either party. The problem remained unresolved throughout the medieval period. The papal standpoint tended towards monarchic centralization, the episcopal aimed at a decentralization of closely defined territorial units in the shape of the dioceses.

Yet, as far as the ninth-century papacy was concerned, it had to make sure that its plan so auspiciously inaugurated in October 816 was brought to a successful conclusion. In the execution of this plan the papacy was greatly assisted by the designs of the Frankish kings which ran on lines almost parallel to those of the papacy. The kings had every reason to fortify their position against the rising Frankish nobility which, indeed, found its most powerful supporters in the Frankish bishops. Stage by stage and within exactly 75 years of Charlemagne's coronation the papacy achieved a decisive victory in that sphere which it considered the most vital. It concerned the creation of a Roman emperor, because only thereby could it convincingly demonstrate the Latin character of the empire itself or, conversely, could it point to the essentially Greek complexion of the Eastern realm unjustifiably styling itself 'Roman empire'. Moreover, in contemporary conditions this creation of the Roman emperor was also the most persuasive means of proving the sovereign independence of the papacy from the empire of Constantinople.

As far as it concerned the papacy the evolution begun in the fifth century was concluded in the ninth. Whereas then the challenge of the imperial government forced the papacy to clarify and fix some of its basic principles (see above p. 28), now in the ninth century the papacy took the step of translating these principles into reality, and it did this now on its own initiative challenging the imperial government at Constantinople so much so that the latter's existence as a Roman empire was if not explicitly, at any rate implicitly, denied. The concentration of the papacy on the imperial question at the expense of many other tasks in which the institution might well have shown a more positive interest – for instance, missions, conversions, creating stable internal local conditions, expansion and development of liturgy, encouragement of learning, promotion of social welfare measures, to mention only a few of these tasks – was, though incontrovertibly a legacy of its own past, also a portent for the future. Having spent, so to speak, its formative years within the Roman empire, the papacy was unable to escape this strongest of all environmental influences. Constantinople stood in the fore when the papacy entered the historic scene, for papal principles were first clearly formulated after Constantinople's measures were conceived as a challenge, but these principles were now in the ninth century turned into an operational policy which had 'world-wide' repercussions. It is not for the historian to judge and evaluate this development. All he can try to do is to explain why and how papal policy, throughout the medieval period, constantly and consistently revealed the ineradicable influence of the papacy's infancy and adolescence, overshadowed as they were by Constantinople. The traumatic experiences of its youth left an indelible imprint upon the medieval papacy. Directly as well as indirectly Constantinople exercised a decisive influence on the papacy in the Middle Ages and offered some explanation for papal pre-occupation with matters of 'the empire'.

Although Charlemagne had made Louis his co-emperor and had crowned him in 813, three years later Stephen IV travelled to Rheims and set the seal on the policy initiated by Leo III. Louis I made his son, Lothar I, co-emperor in 817, who nevertheless six years later received an invitation by the pope, Paschal I, to come to Rome to receive the imperial crown. The anointing and coronation were performed on Easter Sunday 823, and this was the first fully-fledged coronation that took place in St Peter's basilica, henceforward to be the rightful place for imperial coronations. On this occasion the pope for the first time conferred a sword on the emperor. The symbolism was unambiguous, for it showed for what purpose he had been created emperor. The sword was henceforward an essential imperial emblem at every imperial coronation. In 850 it was the father, Lothar I, who petitioned the pope to anoint and crown his son, Louis II, a petition graciously granted by the pope. On this occasion some further and significant symbolic development took place. As the Donation of Constantine had suggested, the emperor led the pope's horse for a short distance as a sign of his humility and submission. It was this symbolism which was for the first time introduced here. The significance of the coronation of 850 was that it was no longer necessary for the pope to issue an invitation because Lothar himself had humbly supplicated the pope. Nor had Lothar made his son a co-emperor. Since he was not even a king, Louis' coronation by the pope in 844 as 'King of the Lombards' (another name to designate rulership in Italy) was particularly important, because it was the royal status of Louis II which enabled the pope to create him also emperor. In contrast to Constantinople, the emperor in the West always absorbed an already functioning king.

Twenty-five years later, in 875, the papacy had so much advanced in its status and authority that it was now in a position to fill the vacant imperial office by 'electing, nominating and postulating' Charles the Bald, the West-Frankish king. It was, as Pope John VIII claimed, 'divine inspiration' which made him offer the imperial crown to Charles, king since 838. When he died two years later, the papacy took the opportunity to advance its claims still further by telling the Italians that they must on no account accept anyone as king without prior papal consent. In other words, the idea of the 'Italian king' was to replace the Lombard king. The importance of the king of Italy lay in that this office was a preliminary to emperorship. This rulership over the 'Italian kingdom' ('regnum italicum') was another source of the later papal claim to examine and confirm the imperial candidate who after all disposed of actual power over Italy and was therefore of vital interest to the papal state in central Italy. The imperial creations by the papacy at the turn of the ninth and tenth centuries added nothing of importance, because the men made emperors were barely shadow Rulers.

This rapid development in the ninth century manifestly showed the victory of the papal theme in the West. The Frankish kings thereby tacitly accepted the papal presuppositions and premises in relation to the creation of the Roman emperor. That is to say, in the West it was generally accepted that the 'true' Roman emperor was the one who was made by the papacy. And the 'true' Roman empire was that territory over which this papally created Ruler presided. This was to prove a powerful support for the concomitantly emerging idea of an independent Europe which in its physiognomy was Roman and Latin and which in its substance rested on the faith as expounded by the papacy. Vice-versa, the territories governed by Constantinople were not 'Roman', because they did not follow the Roman faith, and consequently did not belong to Europe. The division of Europe into two separate halves now became concrete reality. One half was Latin; the other was Greek. And at once the conclusion was drawn that the Greek half had, so to speak, opted out of Europe because it was not Roman. Europe was Roman and Latin. What was outside the Latin precincts was no longer Europe.

In this scheme of things the Western emperor played an important role. He was meant to be the military supra-national protector of the realms which were religiously nourished by the faith of Rome. On the other hand by this same token the Franks themselves were catapulted onto the global plane. They had accepted the papal premises and were therefore bound to enter into a state of rivalry with Constantinople and its government. And the more the papal theme relative to Roman emperorship crystallized and came to be practically accepted, the more this rivalry with Constantinople bordered on conflict, for there could not be two Roman emperors each claiming to be a Ruler on a universal scale.

From the ninth century onwards each of these two Roman emperors symbolized the external, governmental manifestation of an essentially religious idea. This was adherence to, or rejection of, the faith as proclaimed by the papacy. The important point to bear in mind was that through the dynamic policy and initiative of the papacy the ecclesiastical and dogmatic divergence between Rome and Constantinople was transferred onto the level of 'world politics'. It is hardly possible to exaggerate the significance of this development. Two blocs began to face each other, and each embodied pure ideology or, in contemporary ninth-century terms, religious and ecclesiastical views. Europe as a Western and Latin concern started its triumphant career in the ninth century.

The papacy's need of an effective military protector was perhaps at no other time felt so acutely and pressingly as in the ninth century when Italy, and especially the city of Rome and with it the papacy, were seriously threatened by the Saracens. After having occupied Sicily where the Byzantine administration was to all intents and purposes wiped out, they devastated Southern Italy and continued their advance on Rome. There they laid waste suburban districts in 846 sacking St Peter's and other ancient places. Even the papal archives suffered from the plundering Saracens. The creation of a universal protector in the shape of the Roman emperor was a measure which (apart from its ideological motivations) necessarily suggested itself to the papacy in view of the actual Muslim menace. But the papacy had also recourse to self-help. For defence purposes against the Saracens Leo IV built a strong wall and additional fortifications in the vicinity of the Vatican. The part of Rome that was walled in, is still today called the Leonine City. At the hands of Greek naval forces the Saracens suffered in 849 a decisive naval defeat near Ostia, though Sicily itself hardly profited from this. The Western Roman emperors were unable to render any effective help to the hard-pressed papacy, because the Frankish Rulers were themselves victims of aggression. Almost simultaneously the Normans had begun their depredations in Frankish realms where the outlying regions were particularly exposed to Norman attacks.

Yet it was also during the middle years of the ninth century that in the Frankish empire an ideological force arose which in course of time was to exercise a most potent and decisive influence on the papacy. Precisely because Charlemagne and his successors had laid firm stress on the Roman and Latin character of the Frankish kingdom and quite especially of the ecclesiastical organism, ecclesiastical law and literature received thereby a very strong stimulus. They came to be studied, collected and interpreted, and soon became directive agencies in the Frankish empire. And this law and literature were indubitably of Latin provenance and Roman ecclesiastical parentage. For the improvement of Frankish education produced a result which was not foreseen by Charlemagne and his educational advisors. Those who benefited from the broadened and deepened education developed a heightened critical spirit. In the first half of the ninth century an intellectual élite emerged in the Frankish realms. The outlook of this wholly clerical élite had been shaped by the revived or recovered ancient ecclesiastical law and patristic literature. The views which this Frankish intelligentsia came to hold in matters of public government were by no means identical with those held and enacted in laws by the kings themselves. As a first notable sign of the awakened critical spirit must be mentioned the numerous and very well attended Frankish councils of the early part of the ninth century. Although most were convoked by the emperor, these councils issued decrees and set forth doctrines which by no means explicitly or implicitly supported the royal or imperial scheme of government.

The synodal decrees propounded in these lively councils showed how fertile the soil had become for the reception of the 'new learning' nourished as it was by law and literature of distinguished ancestry. The message which these Frankish councils attempted to bring home was that a royal government in order to call itself Christian, must translate into reality Christian doctrine as interpreted by the educationally qualified ecclesiastics. But – and this was the critical point – what doctrine was to be translated into enforceable law, was evidently to be left to the ecclesiastics. They, literally speaking, claimed to assume a leading and decisive role not only in matters of ecclesiastical law and doctrine, but also in matters of public and social concern. The acute and penetrating minds of the Frankish élite did not fail to drive home the stark contrast that was detectable between idea and reality, that is, between the ecclesiastical, spiritual, religious set of norms and the actuality as seen in the mundane, secular, royal field.

It is well to keep this Frankish background in perspective, because it provided a very fertile ground for the already mentioned Frankish episcopalism. The general tenor of conciliar views and decrees was episcopalist. Of the papacy there was very little mention. On the contrary, a distant observer might not have realized that the papacy existed at all as an ecclesiastical organ. The main grievances of the bishops against the Frankish royal system was the appointment of clerics (of all ranks) to their offices by the kings (or lower placed lay lords). This was the so-called proprietary church system, according to which the owner of the land had a right to erect a church on his land which because it remained his property was provided by him with a cleric whom he simply appointed to it. The clerics thus appointed came under the jurisdiction of the lay lord. The situation led to another grievance by the Frankish bishops, namely that by virtue of the proprietary church system their freedom was restricted in that they had to submit to royal control. According to their contention, clerics were immune from secular jurisdiction and law. They were 'the lot of the Lord' and should only be judged by their own ecclesiastical tribunals. However forcefully these views were set forth – and Agobard of Lyons was one of the most outspoken critics of the prevailing system – they lacked proper support from the law. There was plenty of doctrine upon which they could call, but doctrine without a corresponding law was – and is – of little use.

It was precisely in this context that the new educational standards bore concrete – and far-reaching – results. Armed and equipped as these highly educated clerics were, they had at their disposal a vast arsenal of doctrine which by virtue of their superior educational attainments they were able to shape into what purported to be law. For, and this was clearly their view, if the law was missing, it could be invented. And it was created in the heart of the Frankish realms, in or near Rheims, in the middle years of the ninth century. The great forgery which is of particular interest in papal history, was the so-called Pseudo-Isidorian collection of ecclesiastical law: in the preface the compiler called himself Isidore Mercator. The collection was concocted by an extremely able and gifted team of ecclesiastics. Although at least a third of the papal decrees and other legal material was pure invention, and although the remaining parts consisted of garbled or falsified as well as genuine material, it would be quite un-historical to apply modern standards of moral evaluation to this product. The substance of this material was no invention. What was fabricated was the law. What was not fabricated was the doctrine or ideology that was embodied in the law. This ideology had been broadcast for a very long time indeed. And that was also the explanation why this very large forgery fell on fertile soil, because that soil had already been cultivated in precisely the direction in which the forged material pointed. Moreover by asserting that their collection of papal and synodal decrees was an amplification of a collection of the ecclesiastical law which the forgers wrongly ascribed to Isidore of Seville, they surrounded their own concoction with the aura of respectability.

To attack the lay or royal jurisdiction was the main object of the forgers. But they realized that an effective onslought on this wide-spread and universally accepted practice would be of little avail if they did not anchor the law, which was their sole instrument of attack, in the Roman church as the pivot and fountain of Christianity. Only by pretending that the laws they 'collected' (in reality forged) stemmed from the papacy, could they provide the law with the necessary authority and support. And that authority and support were all the stronger the older the decree or other papal law was – and it was also less accessible to control and check. The recourse therefore to the 'decretals' of the papacy from its earliest times onwards was to supply the stamp of pristine Christian authority. However repeatedly put forward in Pseudo-Isidore, the theme of papal primacy was only a means to an end. Considering the actuality of the situation and the weakness of the papacy in the years when the forgeries were made (845–853), in the views of the authors of these forgeries there was no danger that the primatial theme would ever be practically applied. The real winner, however, was eventually the papacy, and not the episcopacy.

The forgers clothed their ideology and aims in very ancient papal decrees or canons of the councils of Christian antiquity. In this collection the 'papal decrees' began with Clement I's letter to St James in Jerusalem (see above pp. 13ff.) which was doubled in size by the forgers. The ostensible aim of the work was the establishment of the independence of the episcopacy from lay control and the weakening of metropolitan power. The ancient decrees were to show the uncontaminated pristine Christian point of view manifested in papal decretals. The ever recurring emphasis on Roman primacy in Pseudo-Isidore played only an auxiliary role. The papal decrees served as a *pièce justificative*. The forgers took infinite care to demonstrate in virtually every single 'papal decree' that the Roman church was the mother of all churches, that Christianity was epitomized in the Roman church from which all jurisdictional and governing power flowed downwards. It was the papacy which distributed some of its own powers to lower placed churches, and especially to the bishops. The bishops therefore partook in papal power, whence they could claim the same kind of immunity which was accorded to the papacy. Stress was laid on the 'papal' law according to which accusations against bishops were for trial purposes to be referred to the papacy. No decrees of a council had any validity unless it was summoned by the papacy. Accusations by lay people of bishops were made virtually impossible. The decrees insisted on a strict hierarchical ordering both within the ecclesiastical body and of society at large. That the Donation of Constantine also made its appearance in this volume, went without saying.

As already noted, in substance these forged decrees contained virtually nothing that had not been said before, or had at least been implicit in earlier and perfectly genuine sources. But by clothing earlier and current points of view with the halo of the law in the shape of a papal decree, the forgers unwittingly made a most welcome gift to the papacy. This collection of 'canon law' had also the advantage of having every relevant papal decree or synodal enactment from the earliest times down to Gregory II contained in one handy reference book. The respectably extensive ideological material was moulded into these numerous 'decrees' – all within two stiff covers. As their subsequent history proved the pseudo-isidorian decretals exercised an unparalleled influence on the papacy. They provided what the papacy had lacked until the mid-ninth century, that is, the ancient law in the form of decrees issued by the first-century as well as second and third-century papacy.

Pseudo-Isidore must be classed as one of the most influential fabrications in the history of medieval (and possibly also modern) Europe. In the current and by no means final edition of Pseudo-Isidore the material fills over 750 closely printed pages. But Pseudo-Isidore was not the only forgery concocted at that time. The other product also fabricated in the forties of the ninth century, at Mainz, was of negligible interest to the papacy. This collection by a deacon of the cathedral of Mainz, Benedictus Levita, pursued the same end as Pseudo-Isidore, that is, the

LIBRARY
EISENHOWER COLLEGE

liberation of the bishops in particular from the control of secular lords and metropolitans, but Benedictus' *pièces justificatives* were royal and imperial decrees of 'ancient' standing. They too were a means to an end. Benedictus Levita was a notable companion volume of Pseudo-Isidore supplementing the latter by secular laws, all showing what was the 'ancient' state of things in royal and imperial laws. And they too dealt with the same topics as Pseudo-Isidore, such as papal primacy, synodal supervision by the papacy, immunities, and so on. But the work (consisting of 1721 chapters) never reached so wide a public or had so great an influence as Pseudo-Isidore.

To the papacy Pseudo-Isidore proved a heaven-sent gift, because the work contained in legal language exactly what the papacy had postulated for so long. The papacy understandably shared the primary aim of Pseudo-Isidore, though the forgers' secondary aim became of prime importance to the papacy. The roles, in other words, were exchanged. What to Pseudo-Isidore was a mere *pièce justificative*, was the main concern of the papacy. What mattered from the papal point of view was the law that was now seen to be of unique antiquity and ancestry. And as far as the making of Europe was concerned, these forgeries very powerfully contributed to the emergence of a uniform pattern of thought which was at once ancient, legal, Christian and papal. This unifying effect of the great forgeries should not be underestimated. Pseudo-Isidore became one of the most important source books for later collections of canon law down to Gratian in the mid-twelfth century. Pseudo-Isidore's 'decrees' were disseminated in copies made all over Europe down to the fourteenth century. The contemporary papacy fully realized this potential of Pseudo-Isidore. Although Leo IV had possibly had recourse to the forgery in 853-4, Nicholas I certainly was the first pope who borrowed explicitly from Pseudo-Isidore. It should be kept in mind, however, that he was unaware of the true nature of the work on which he drew. Nicholas also saw the potentialities of the work as a force that greatly assisted in the process of welding Europe into a homogeneous ecclesiastical unit under the Roman papal aegis.

In the history of the papacy the pontificate of Nicholas I was on the same level of importance as that of Gregory I before, or Gregory VII after, him. This short pontificate of barely nine years left its mark upon contemporary ecclesiastical and social life. Nicholas' temperament was that of a born governor and master, as his many decrees made abundantly clear. To him kings, emperors, patriarchs, metropolitans, and bishops were subjected as the recipients of his orders. His instructions had to be obeyed without questioning. He envisaged an autonomous, supra-regal body of Christians which received its authoritative guide-lines solely from the papacy. His pontificate marked the beginning of that papal ascendancy which eventually and after many vicissitudes was to reach its zenith under Innocent III. On the papacy in Rome rested the whole religious and social order of the world – that was how Nicholas I himself viewed the role of the papacy, and in that spirit he governed. His was not an original mind, but one who in a masterly fashion knew how to use ancient material and shape it into one consistent whole in order to apply it to contemporary circumstances. Numerous extracts from most of his decrees were embodied in later collections of canon law. His collaboration with the learned librarian Anastasius was a practical example of harmonious team-work, the one supplying authority and strategy, the other the intellectual and tactical equipment. To label Nicholas the 'creator' or 'builder' of the medieval papacy, would be misleading – the papal edifice was built of many stones by many architects, though among the latter Nicholas certainly stood in the front rank.

The practical application of the Petrine theme was the hallmark of Nicholas I's pontificate. Actuality afforded plenty of opportunity to translate the abstract theme into concrete measures. One of his early measures was to reduce Archbishop John of Ravenna to his proper size. This archbishop had tried to erect something akin to a papal state with the consequence that the province of Ravenna was becoming largely independent of the papacy. At the Roman provincial synod in 861 the archbishop was made to retract these steps which had offended the tenets of papal primatial rights. While Nicholas here showed himself acting in the interests of ecclesiastical discipline, the marriage affair of Lothar II, the king of Lorraine, gave the papacy its first concrete opportunity to intervene effectively in a matrimonial matter which was, however, linked with the assertion of papal over archiepiscopal authority. For the king was strongly backed by two of the most powerful archbishops and their suffragans.

The point at issue was that Lothar when he became king in 855 was married according to ancient Germanic law to Waldrada, an aristocratic woman, by whom he had three children. This kind of freely dissoluble marriage was in current opinion considered to be of lower standing than an indissoluble union. Soon after becoming king, Lothar entered into an indissoluble marriage with another noble woman, Theutberga, who bore him no children however. Hence he wished to return to Waldrada and have this marriage raised to the level of an indissoluble union. Here the archbishops of Cologne (Gunther) and Trier (Thietgaud) and their suffragans supported and justified the king's intention, but the papacy, powerfully supported by Hincmar, the great archbishop of Rheims, sternly came out in favour of the second marriage. Waldrada was declared a mere concubine, and Theutberga the one and only legitimate wife of Lothar.

The significance of this papal intervention was that it pronounced only one kind of marriage valid and thus drove out the ancient Germanic custom of entering into a matrimonial relationship that could without formality be dissolved. The Roman council of 826 had allowed the dissolution of a marriage in the case of the wife's fornication. Moreover, the two archbishops were deposed by the pope and summoned to appear before him in the Lateran (October 863) – a step that created a very strong precedent and also showed how greatly the authority of the papacy had increased. Further, these two vacancies were to be filled only with his consent. Two generations previously no pope would have dared to depose two of the most powerful archbishops in Western Europe. Part of the explanation for this was the changed temper of the time. However loudly the two archbishops protested, they evoked no support. What did evoke favourable reaction was the step of the papacy which in the contemporary opinion had shown itself as the protector and guardian of a defenceless and innocent woman. Lastly, this marriage affair was also significant in that the papacy for the first time sat in judgment over a king who found himself unexpectedly threatened with excommunication, a fate from which the death of the pope preserved him. But it was a portent.

Nicholas even considered himself strong enough to deal with so powerful and resourceful an ecclesiastical prince as the archbishop of Rheims, Hincmar, who had excommunicated one of his suffragans, Bishop Rothad of Soissons, for (amongst other reasons) refusing to accept a ruling of the archbishop in his own diocese. Rothad appealed to the papacy, and Nicholas re-instated him (864). Nicholas could not but welcome the course the incident had taken. Episcopal matters as so-called major causes had always been claimed by the papacy to belong to its sole jurisdiction, even if there was no appeal. That metropolitan rights thereby suffered, was from the papal standpoint not in the least regrettable, because thereby the papacy had more opportunity of direct intervention. It was in this *cause célèbre* that Nicholas ostensibly referred to Pseudo-Isidore where indeed he found strong support for the weakening of metropolitan power. Hincmar considered that he had lost this battle with the pope not on legal grounds, but solely on those of papal authority and prestige. Indubitably, the assistance by Pseudo-Isidore was of considerable weight. Hincmar's case was quite instructive, as he himself was an otherwise effective supporter of the papacy's claims. His position highlights the dilemma of many ecclesiastics at the time. Quite in contrast to the decision of the Roman synod in 826 which had endorsed the proprietary church system, in common with Frankish writers Nicholas fiercely attacked the system which he called criminal and sacrilegious. The lands assigned to a church, just as the church itself, were divine things and thus removed from the disposition by laymen.

To the authoritative assertion of papal primatial rights in the West corresponded Nicholas' emphatic insistence on the papacy's rights in the East. And circumstances in Constantinople were particularly favourable for the sonorous intonation of all the papal Petrine chords. The patriarch, Ignatius, had publicly refused to give communion to the emperor because (the patriarch alleged) he had committed incest. Moreover Ignatius belonged to the ultra-conservative faction in the court circles. Imperial wrath deposed the patriarch without much ado and replaced him with Photius, the imperial secretary, commander of the imperial guard and one of the best brains and finest scholars of the time, who after his appointment ascended in five consecutive days through the various clerical ranks and stages to the dignity of the capital's patriarchate. This elevation however resulted in further internal Byzantine conflicts. The adherents of Ignatius deposed and ex-communicated Photius, whereupon he and his followers retaliated in kind. This rift within the Byzantine church barely concealed the very serious political tensions which lay behind it. In this difficult situation the emperor, Michael III, invited the papacy to send legates to a council which he intended to hold in the matter of the still unresolved iconoclastic problem that in the last hundred years had produced entirely contradictory legislative and dogmatic enactments in the East. At the same time Photius in accordance with custom, informed the papacy of his elevation.

Nicholas I at once saw the potentialities which the situation offered. To him the deposition of Ignatius and appointment of Photius was a matter which was of direct concern to the papacy and was solely within its competence. This was an episcopal matter, therefore a 'major matter' which was always held to be the exclusive concern of the Roman church. He cited the Matthean passages relative to the primatial function of pope as successor of St Peter and drove home the decree of the Council of Sardica which, in his reading, established the papacy as the lawful tribunal for settling 'major causes' (see above pp. 8, 17). He also dispatched legates to Constantinople to investigate the matter. This reaction showed how strong the papacy considered itself, in fact so strong that it could initiate a course of action which the patriarch and, more importantly, the imperial government behind him could only view as a papal challenge.

Although Nicholas had reserved to himself any final judicial verdict, after a short investigation the legates in Constantinople confirmed the sentence of deposition on Ignatius that had shortly before been solemnly pronounced in a large council at Constantinople. After receiving a full report, Nicholas in a Roman provincial council dismissed the legates, declared their decision to be without any validity because *ultra vires*, and reinstated Ignatius as patriarch of Constantinople – a step in which the imperial government was bound to see a deliberate provocation. Photius was ordered not to continue in his 'patriarchal' functions, since he had been invalidly ordained and consecrated, and was threatened with excommunication in case of his disregarding the papal verdict. As in similar earlier conflicts the real target was evidently the emperor himself, and only in a secondary sense the patriarch. And the emperor upon notification of the papal sentence, at once and in harsh terms demanded its withdrawal.

With all his characteristic intellectual superiority Nicholas –

now that he was sure of his position in the West – set forth the arguments for the primatial position of the papacy. In Photius, however, Nicholas found a worthy equal. With all the well-worn Byzantine arguments he defended his position and attacked the papacy in so fierce and passionate manner that the papacy on its part was forced to reply in kind. In a frontal assault on the emperor himself, Nicholas pungently drove home the Roman primatial theme, not without impugning the very function of the emperor as emperor of the Romans. 'You call yourself an emperor of the Romans and you do not even know the language of the Romans, Latin, which is despised by you.' Nicholas went so far as to tell the emperor that the Roman church was his mother which had graciously granted him ruling powers. The divine will was transmitted only through the instrument of the papacy. From a wider historical perspective this acrimonious, if not ferocious, exchange between Constantinople and Rome signified that neither side entertained any hope of a reconciliation. And indeed there was none. Backed by the imperial government Photius assembled a large synod at Constantinople in 867 in which Nicholas was declared a heretic (without having been given a chance to defend himself against the charge), excommunicated and deposed as pope. What was hitherto detached alienation, gave way to a virtual schism between East and West.

The situation was aggravated by the Bulgarian mission. The king of the Bulgarians had become a Christian in 864. His god-father was actually the Emperor Michael III, but Photius refused the king's wish to erect a Bulgarian patriarchate. Thereupon the king turned to the papacy, and Nicholas welcomed the opportunity by agreeing to the dispatch of Roman missionaries. At the same time he sent a very long and most detailed epistle to the Bulgarians in which virtually no important point was left untouched. Hardly before or afterwards did the papacy in so minute a manner lay down vital religious and ecclesiastical points in what was technically a mere missionary instruction. Photius on his part stigmatized the Roman mission and papal efforts not only as an uncalled-for intervention, but as outright interference in regions which by law belonged to the jurisdiction of the patriarchate of Constantinople. To Photius all this papal initiative was nothing but arrogance. He declared some of the central Roman tenets to be damnable heresy and impetuously castigated the haughtiness of the papacy for not recognizing the validity of Byzantine ordinations.

What the Photian schism signified was that the gulf between East and West had gone too far to be capable of repair. All that could reasonably be expected was a patched-up truce. The deep significance of this schism was that the Latin West confronted the Greek East. Or to express this differently, the division between East and West was religiously and ecclesiastically conditioned. It was a division that was to shape the future of Europe throughout the medieval period and beyond. In the eyes of the West to be a Greek had become synonymous with being a heretic. The papacy realized the potentialities which this situation harboured, and exploited it fully. And, indeed, by the sixties of the ninth century the West had made great and effective progress towards constituting a homogeneous unit. To a large extent this was the result of the movement usually called the Carolingian Renaissance which in its basic presuppositions was exclusively Latin orientated.

Throughout the ninth century the intellectual level of Frankish society reached remarkable heights in all fields of activity – dogmatic, liturgical, devotional, biblical, historical, hagiographical. For the first time in European history the period saw books specially devoted to questions of public government. The intellectual upsurge resulted in liveliness and vigour of contemporary literary productions. They were the first flowering of a specifically European culture with its own physiognomy and complexion. It was structurally a combination of divers and often disparate strains, notably Germanic, Christian, Roman and papal. The essential point was that this culture was fundamentally a religious culture which effortlessly explained why it was also Roman directed and Latin orientated. That the papacy had begun to play its part in this making of Europe (in the Western Latin sense) has already been noted, but the Photian conflict provided a particular stimulus for the papacy. It was the acumen of Nicholas I which assessed the ideological preparedness of the West correctly and which utilized the situation in a conspicuous effort to harness the whole of the articulated West in the struggle against Eastern pretensions. And the presuppositions were quite exceptionally favourable, especially after Photius had attacked the whole Western Church in a vicious manner. Nothing was more effective than concerted action. In a circular letter to important sees the pope asked for comments on the Byzantine-Roman conflict. The significance of this papal step lay in its anticipation of the Western reaction which totally rejected the Eastern point of view and strongly rallied to the assistance of the Roman church. What should be borne in mind is that although the issues themselves were of ancient standing, they had now reached truly 'global' dimensions. What previously was a mere ecclesiastical issue between Rome and Constantinople, now engulfed what then was Western Europe and the whole Eastern empire.

What was remarkable was the readiness with which in the West both kings and ecclesiastics responded to the circular letter of Nicholas I and supported the papacy in its fight against Constantinople. Hence also the promptness with which the Western replies were formulated. The West now spoke a uniform language and had an identity of outlook. The work of both the papacy and the Frankish Rulers bore fruit in the unanimous condemnation of the East both as regards substance and the methods employed. There is nothing more conducive to achieving unification than a common opponent. What the Byzantine challenge and the resultant Acacian schism in the fifth century (see above pp. 29f., 40) effected in regard to the clarification of basic papal principles, the Photian challenge and schism effected in the ninth century. Subsequent patching-up operations could not conceal the depth of the rift dividing the West from the East. In brief, the idea of Europe was held to apply only to that part of the Continent which manifested the basic Latin substructure. Europe was an ideological concept, and no longer a merely physical term. It was welded together by the Roman Christian faith fixed by the papacy. But because the empire governed from Constantinople did not accept this faith enunciated by the successor of the prince of the apostles, it no longer belonged to Europe and therefore was heretical. Europe had come to mean the Latin West. The East was outside this Europe.

Despite the quite ostensible cleavage between Rome and Constantinople, attempts were made to reach some accommodation. Soon after the death of Nicholas I a change of imperial government in Constantinople – Michael III was murdered by his successor, Basilius I the Macedonian – made possible the re-instatement of Ignatius. In its usual temporizing manner the government and the patriarch suggested the convocation of another council at Constantinople. This moderately attended council took place in the winter months of 869–870. Convoked by the emperor the presidency was in the hands of three papal legates. Ecumenicity to this council was not accorded until the twelfth century, whence it ranked as the Eighth General Council. Its decrees were never published in the East where they never had any legal validity. It once more professed a formula of union which was as little effective as similar earlier attempts. It was also the last council to which the papacy dispatched legates. Hardly had the council closed when the Bulgarian situation once more cast a deep shadow over Rome and its relations with Constantinople. In the event, Bulgaria came to be irretrievably lost to the West.

This setback for the papacy was accompanied by renewed and quite determined Saracen attacks in the South of Italy. Louis II as the Western Roman emperor and thus as the military defender of the 'Romans' rendered signal service to the papacy as well as to Western Christianity by his military stand against the invaders, but his early death in 875 put an end to a gallantly fought resistance by the imperial forces. Pope John VIII himself commanded a fleet equipped by the papacy from its own resources and successfully led the naval forces against the Saracens in several raids. Yet the papacy increasingly attracted the attention of the Roman nobility, especially since the Frankish Rulers were very hard pressed by the continuous Norman attacks in the North and West, and by Hungarian raids in the East, while the Arabs in Spain began to resume their attacks northwards. Moreover, Charles the Bald (who had succeeded Louis II as emperor) died after only two years as emperor – and the immediately following emperors were mere shadow figures, in no conceivable manner capable of fulfilling the role for which they were created. The papacy was therefore in a peculiarly vulnerable position at the turn of the ninth and tenth centuries.

In fact, the whole Italian peninsula seemed little else but the target for any enterprising warrior who was able to marshal some invasion forces. The frequent appeals of the papacy to Rulers north of the Alps brought men into Italy who had little appreciation of the cultural inheritance which they were supposed to defend. Left to itself in these decades the papacy became more and more the playball of the Roman aristocratic factions. What the early tenth century showed was that the institution was still in need of the active and efficient help of some secular Ruler. In order to prevent the ever recurring Roman riots on the occasion of papal elections, a synod under the chairmanship of John IX re-issued in 898 the Constitution which Lothar I had first enacted in 824 (see above p. 92). The synod insisted that the properly elected pope should not be consecrated unless and until imperial legates were present: they were to guarantee the preservation of public order. In the circumstances this decree – confirmed by the synod of Ravenna shortly afterwards – was barely an empty gesture, because the 'legates' were as powerless as their 'emperors' who were now Spoletan dukes and as emperors veritable nonentities.

Throughout the first half of the tenth century certain features became apparent. The Roman aristocracy had now gained far more power than it had before. The significant point was that – in strong contrast to the nobility north of the Alps – this Roman nobility was not primarily linked to landed estates but was overwhelmingly an outcome of urban and local Roman conditions. It was therefore not military at all, but indulged in power politics, intrigues, machinations and subterfuges. Hence since for the last two centuries the pope had been the governor of the city of Rome, the Roman nobility through controlling the papacy itself intended to be in effective control of the city, its revenues and finances. At the same time it is worthy of remark that more attuned to urban intrigues than to virile military exercises, the contemporary Roman nobles did not shine forth in knightly prowess by resisting the Saracens or other robber bands. It is clear that these adverse circumstances greatly tended to diminish papal authority. The papacy's 'natural' protector, the Western Roman emperor, had gone and was not yet replaced by any stable successor willing to continue the role as a military defender of Christendom.

There were, moreover, additional factors which arrested the development of the papacy in this period. From the nineties of the ninth century down to the mid-tenth century there was a very swift succession of popes, some of whom ruled only a few days, others only a few months, and very few more than ten years. This factor alone, especially when taken in conjunction with the disorderly conditions within and without Rome, prevented the pursuit of anything approximating a consistent line. Furthermore, the papal civil service though perfectly capable of coping with contemporary exigencies, was not yet resilient enough to withstand the severe and repeated shocks which the frequent changes in the papal headship inflicted upon the smooth running of the institution.

A further aggravating circumstance which deleteriously affected the papacy in this period, must be sought in the personalities of the popes themselves. The unstable external conditions and the utter insecurity in Rome and Italy obviously contributed to the decline of the fibre, stamina, and general morality of the contemporary popes. It was as if the personalities of the popes reflected the universally observable disintegration, conditioned by the change of dynasties, notably the disappearance of the Carolingian line, no less than by the wild attacks on the still very feeble core of Europe, Italy and Germany. This period is not without justification called the papacy's 'dark century' (the *saeculum obscurum*). It visibly, almost symbolically, began with the macabre scenes after the pontificate of Pope Formosus. The rule hitherto observed was that because a bishop was (allegorically) married to his diocese, he could not become pope, because he would then have been a 'bigamus', i.e. married twice. This rule (originally enacted in the 15th chapter of Nicaea) was first set aside by Pope Marinus (882) who had been a bishop at the time of becoming pope; but this was obviously overlooked. When elected pope, Formosus had been bishop of Porto. After his death this circumstance was made a charge against him by his successor Stephen VI. He had the dead pope exhumed. His corpse in full pontifical vestments and seated on a throne, faced a tribunal which enacted the 'cadaver comedy' and tried the dead pope. He was found guilty, publicly undressed and thrown into the Tiber (897). But soon afterwards the Roman mob broke into the Lateran, threw Stephen into the local jail where a few days later he was strangled by hired assassins. In quick succession (as a matter of fact Stephen's immediate predecessor, Boniface VI, ruled only three weeks) followed Pope Romanus ruling less than four months and Theodore II, pontificating twenty days, though both of them seem to have died a natural death. In 903 Pope Leo V was imprisoned by the antipope Christophorus who found himself ousted a few months later (January 904) by the former Roman deacon Sergius III, strongly supported as he was by Theophylact, the papal financial adviser and commander of the Roman militia. Elected pope, Sergius made short shrift with both Leo V and Christophorus and had them murdered in jail.

With the ascendancy of Sergius III a typical representative of the house of Theophylact came to the fore. The house was to exercise a decisive and baneful influence on the papacy which for the next decades became the plaything of this aristocratic Roman faction. Theophylact's wife Theodora and their daughters Theodora the younger and Marozia added sexual lust to his own lust for power. There is no direct evidence that Sergius himself had a liaison with Marozia and that the later Pope John XI was their progeny, although this was rumoured. Like Sergius III most of his successors were direct appointees of the new aristocratic régime which managed Rome and the papacy according to its own designs and intentions. This government exhibited all the traits of that petty tyranny of which local aristocratic cliques were always capable. After the death of Theophylact, Marozia herself took the reins of government into her own hands with a single-mindedness and ruthlessness characteristic of female tyrants. When Pope John X, Sergius' successor, raised some weak protest against the régime, he and his brother were thrown into jail and in due course murdered.

After the two short pontificates of Leo VI and Stephen VII Marozia managed to have 'elected' her own illegitimate son, John XI, one of whose first governmental actions was the despatch of legates to Constantinople to consecrate the imperially appointed patriarch Theophylaktos, aged 16 years (who was the emperor's own son) whose expertise throughout his 23 years as the patriarch in the capital of the empire, shone forth in equestrian pursuits rather than those belonging to theology or liturgy. The kind of government exercised by the regiment of women in Rome appeared even to Marozia's legitimate son, Alberic, to go beyond permissible limits. He objected to his mother's third marriage with Hugh of Provence and went as far as to incite the Roman mob (which was never difficult) against Hugh who was driven out of Rome. Alberic now had his mother imprisoned. From 933 until his death in 954 the true lord and master of Rome and of the papacy was the young Alberic who styled himself 'Duke and Senator of the Romans'. All papal appointments were made by him, including the personnel of the papal service.

None of the popes thus appointed showed much awareness of what the papal office required, though none sank to the level of Sergius III. There was even some evidence that the new spirit radiating from Cluny created some stirrings in Rome and found adherents, including Alberic himself. He made the Roman senate take an oath that after his death they would elect his young son Octavian pope. The contingency occurred the following year in 955 when Pope Agapetus II died. It would seem as if the Roman senator had modelled himself on the East-Roman emperor's appointment of his son as patriarch of Constantinople. Octavian became pope in 955. His pontificate initiated the practice of changing the papal name. Indeed, it would hardly have been fitting for a pope to have been called Octavian: he became John XII and despite his profligate character and youth was unwittingly to play a major role in the development of the papacy, if indeed not in that of Europe. He combined the functions of civil and spiritual Ruler of Rome (*princeps* and *pontifex*).

In view of the turbulent conditions in which Italy and Rome found themselves in the first half of the tenth century, the question might well be asked why the Byzantine government made no effort to re-establish its authority in Italy or Rome and to exercise some control over the papacy. The answer lay in the extremely delicate situation of Constantinople internally and externally. Internally, in these decades the government was engaged in curbing the rise of a feudal aristocratic power within the empire, a task to which all its domestic resources were dedicated, while externally the empire was just then severely threatened by the Bulgarian king Symeon who aimed at erecting a new empire in the place of Byzantium. Although this plan came to nought, imperial resources were nevertheless gravely taxed. Sporadic Hungarian incursions and attacks could be repelled, but what constituted the most serious external danger was the Arab menace on the Eastern borders of the empire necessitating the concentration of all available forces in the Mediterranean islands as well as in Syria and Mesopotamia. No worthwhile forces were available for the West, though this did not in the least affect the eventual imperial designs. That the papacy was at the time secure from any intervention by the imperial government was in part also due to the readiness with which some popes complied with requests made by Constantinople. This compliance could be explained by the policy pursued by the ruling aristocratic clique in Rome. Its aim was to avoid all possible friction with Constantinople. The popes who were mere appointees of the city governors, faithfully reflected the aspirations of their masters.

That the papacy was in fact able to survive this period at all – one of the darkest in its history – was due to the unquestioned historicity of its Petrine claims, to the undiminished fervent veneration which the Northern peoples had of Petrine Rome, and to the highly effective distinction between the person of the pope and the papal office itself. Perhaps no other papal axiom was to render such signal service to the papacy as this. However low the calibre of most of the popes about this time, however oblivious most of them were of their vocation, none of this affected the papal office itself, that is, the powers and authority contained in it. And for governmental purposes it was the office that mattered, not the character of the popes who occupied it. Whether they were saints, scoundrels, or just mere ciphers, made no difference. The law issued or the decree given was not in the least dependent upon the character of the ruling pope. What counted was that the law etc. was promulgated by the papacy as such, not whether the pope was a 'good' or a 'bad' pope. The institution kept up its wide-flung correspondence and issued grants or confirmations of immunities or of other exemptions, instructions for episcopal elections (though in isolated instances also endorsing the royal right of appointing bishops), reproaches to princes, requests to kings, and so on, quite apart from its task of drafting synodal decrees. The chancery personnel (chancellors, notaries, scriptors, etc.) is known through the surviving documents. Yet in quantity there was certainly a great reduction of governmental measures. The institutionalized apparatus functioned, of however low a calibre the popes were. It would be true to say that the papacy as an institution was greatly in need to be defended against the popes. And that protector was once more the Western emperor who was to rescue the papacy from the popes.

6 *The German Monarchy and the Papacy*

THE LOW STATE of the papacy's fortunes in the mid-tenth century contrasted sharply with the vigour displayed by the new dynasty in the East-Frankish realms of the former Carolingian empire. They formed the nucleus of what was to become medieval Germany. The Saxon dynasty, established by Henry I in 919, during the reign of his son, Otto the Great (936–973), had rapidly · become the leading European power, territorially, militarily, economically, and also to some extent culturally. There was · resolute drive, youthful energy, forward-looking policy, coupled with the realistic appreciation of the limitations imposed by the available resources. As a result of the successful defeat of the Magyars in 951 the role of a defender of the Latin Christian West · was virtually thrust upon the kingdom of Otto I. The most important reason for the internal advance and the domestic stability of the kingdom lay in the firm control which the king · exercised in the appointment of high-ranking ecclesiastics, notably bishops and abbots, who in one way or another were wholly dependent on the king himself. The basis of this royal strength was the proprietary church system (see above p. 99) · which was raised to a major constitutional and social principle. In effect, every important see, church or abbey, had by the tenth century become dependent upon the monarchy. The ecclesiastics provided a very efficient framework for the execution of royal policy – without these highly educated and capable men it would have been well-nigh impossible to administer and govern so vast a kingdom with any degree of efficiency.

It was in fact as a result of the rise of Otto I that the twin bequest of the Carolingian dynasty and of the papacy came to bear fruit. The very extent of the territories governed by Otto · suggested a resuscitation of the idea of the empire as it was structurally, even if not territorially, at the time of Charlemagne whose influence upon the minds of men became greater with the passing of time. This resuscitation of the imperial idea necessarily gave a further impetus to the idea of Europe as a homogeneous unit with its focus on Petrine Rome. Indeed ancient Roman and Christian-Roman ideas coalesced into one integrated whole. But an essential ingredient of this Latinized Western Europe and of the idea of the Roman empire was, if not overt hostility to, at any rate serious apprehension of, Constantinople. The main burden of the Western opposition was now understandably to fall on the shoulders of the Western emperor, because as previously noted, there could not be two Rulers each claiming to have universality of dominion. In this context it is of some interest that Byzantine forces had begun military operations in South Italy in the fifties of the tenth century.

The situation in Italy and in Rome was ripe for an intervention from outside. On 22 November 950 at Pavia Count Berengar of Ivrea was elected and also crowned king of Italy. He saw in the widow of his weak predecessor, Adelheid, a danger to his shaky position and imprisoned her. She escaped and petitioned Otto the mighty king of the Saxons for help. In September 951 Otto initiated the long and distinguished line of Italian campaigns undertaken by the German kings during the next five centuries. Having proclaimed himself king of the Lombards he married the widow. What was, however, most significant was that he also submitted a petition to the pope, Agapetus II, for the imperial crown. The request was turned down on the instructions of the Roman Senator, Alberic.

The opportunity came less than ten years later. Berengar had resumed his attacks and began to threaten Rome. The pope, John XII, appealed for help to Otto, an appeal that had momentous effects on the fortunes of the papacy, Italy, Germany and Europe. The appeal was reminiscent of that issued by the papacy exactly two centuries earlier (see above pp. 74f.). Its ready acceptance by Otto was based on the influence which the papal and Carolingian bequests exercised on him. As the mightiest Ruler in Europe he considered that his position as a mere king no longer adequately expressed his true status which, by contemporary standards, had indeed begun to assume universal character. The view he took of his own position was that it could appropriately be expressed only in a fully-fledged emperorship: the development in the ninth century had by now become a tradition both of fact and idea. Of quite especial concern to him in this context – just as it was to the papacy and the papal state – was the imminent threat of the Byzantine forces in South Italy where the Easterners had not only advanced and consolidated their position, but had also reached some understanding with the dukes of Benevento and Capua. This situation on the very threshold of the papal state and the menacing designs of the hostile forces which stood on the Garigliano less than 60 miles from Rome, was one of which notice had to be taken by both the pope and the Saxon king whose aspirations were conspicuously affected by the contingencies emerging in the South of Italy.

The confluence of papal aims and royal German aspirations produced on 2 February 962 the revived Western Roman emperor in the person of Otto I. The same cluster of problems arose now and in a very much more accentuated form than they had arisen in the time of Otto's great model, Charlemagne. According to John XII's intentions Otto was to become the military protector of the interests of the Roman church. That was the reason why the papacy now also played its trump card: in recognition of his services Otto was to become emperor. The eventual aim of the papacy was to use the Western emperor as an instrument of its 'global' policy. After all, the Western emperor was in the first place created in opposition to the government at Constantinople. The papal writ was to run unimpededly also in the 'empire' governed from Constantinople, a contingency that did not, however, come about until 1204.

Although the ideological initiative certainly lay with the papacy, Otto's aspirations were not without influence on the formulation of papal policy. Nevertheless, even a pope of so low a calibre as John XII managed to convey to the mighty Saxon the indispensable role which the papacy played in creating the emperor. John had an ornamental copy of the Donation of Constantine made, and this ornamental copy was handed to the newly crowned emperor. Whether the recipient of this gift appreciated its significance, it is impossible to say. But about papal intentions no doubt was possible. This 'document' reduced the papal theme and ideology to unambiguous and cold constitutional language.

Eleven days after the coronation Otto confirmed the Carolin-

gian donations and papal possessions in a solemn compact with
John XII. On the following day, 14 February 962, he set out to
subjugate the hostile forces in his role as the official protector of
the Roman church. In so doing he did not, as the papacy had
expected, force the inhabitants of the conquered regions to take
an oath of allegiance to the pope, but to himself – indubitably a
somewhat unexpected manner of protecting the Roman church.
The pope was enraged. He now called upon his erstwhile enemies,
including Berengar, to come to his succour. He even established
contact with the Byzantines. He instigated a revolt in Rome
against imperial officers. This course of things determined Otto
to return to Rome in the autumn of 963 to call a synod at which
he himself presided. The pope was summoned to appear before it.
He refused, whereupon on 6 December 963 the synod disregarding the principle that the pope cannot be judged, deposed him and
appointed a successor in the person of Leo VIII, a layman, who
within one day was rushed through all clerical orders. In the
papal actions enlisting the help of his enemies, Otto saw nothing
but treachery. In order to prevent a recurrence of similar papal
intrigues, Otto had the compact he had drawn up with John XII
18 months earlier enlarged on his own authority and without the
knowledge of the pope by inserting a stipulation that every
newly elected pope was to take an oath to the imperial legates. ·
In this oath to be taken before his consecration the pope was to
promise the fulfilment of his obligations to the emperor. Precisely .
because it was so vague, it was a very stringent stipulation, and
this compact (the so-called *Ottonianum*) was to remain the constitutional basis of the numerous imperial interventions in papal
creations for almost exactly a century. In practice the modified
compact served as a handle for the Germans simply to appoint the
new pope, if the situation in Rome made it necessary.

For the sake of providing the Roman church with more ·
suitable pastors than was the case in the immediate past the
imperial intervention was a virtual necessity. Otto I himself had
to experience the need to intervene. Hardly had he left Rome
when (the deposed) John XII returned, expelled Leo VIII with
the help of the Romans, and presided over a synod in February
964. This assembly reached exactly the opposite verdict to that
of three months earlier. Leo VIII was deposed and exiled, and
John took fearful vengeance on his adversaries. Having soon

afterwards been slain on the occasion of one of his nightly esca-
pades into the matrimonial home of a Roman citizen, John was
succeeded by Benedict V who did not find favour with Otto.
Returning to Rome in June 964 he sent the pope into exile and
re-instated Leo VIII. Two years later the troubles which the
imperially appointed John XIII experienced, necessitated a further
intervention by the emperor who had his son Otto II crowned
co-emperor at Christmas 967.

Frequent absences of Otto II from Rome were occasions for
many serious troubles there which embroiled the popes. The
aristocratic faction of the Crescentii exercised an undue influence
in Rome and on the papacy for nearly 40 years. Because it was
obviously impracticable for the emperor or an adequate imperial
force to be permanently in Rome, the papacy as an organ of
government was bound to function in a somewhat lower gear.
Not only frequent and short pontificates but also murder (for
instance, Benedict VI, Boniface VII, John XIV) and deposition
of popes were facts which though they affected the institutional
side of the papacy remarkably little (see also below pp. 123ff.),
nevertheless did not promote the expansion of governmental
activities. The Crescentian tyranny emboldened John XV, the son
of a Roman priest, to enlist the future emperor's help. Otto III
had been declared of age and reached Rome in 996 in time to
nominate John's successor. His choice fell upon the first German
to become pope, Brun, a twenty-four-year-old cousin of Otto
and a member of the royal chapel who as Gregory V in fact
crowned Otto emperor. But once more, as soon as Otto left,
Crescentius mobilized the Romans who expelled Gregory V and
installed the archbishop of Piacenza (John XVI) as anti-pope.
Upon his return Otto restored Gregory V, had John blinded and
incarcerated, while Crescentius was decapitated. No doubt,
despite his youth (he was only 16 in 996) Otto had made an
excellent choice in Gregory and after his death made a no less
excellent choice in appointing his former tutor and instructor, the
archbishop of Ravenna who became Pope Silvester II. It was due
to his overwhelming influence on the young emperor that the
latter was fired with the idea of the Roman empire which remained
a focal point of his policy. Rome was to be the capital of the
world, not Constantinople, and he, the emperor, was to be the
sole and universal governing authority. The wholesale transfer of

Byzantine symbols, ceremonials, officers, titles, and so on, was to express the emperor's eventual designs.

Because Rome was to him the capital of the universe, the papacy assumed in his scheme of things the role of a mother of all churches and the pope the role of a chief metropolitan of the universe, but – and this was the vital point – whatever rank, dignity, authority the Roman church and the pope had, was the effluence of the emperor's good will. In so far he was indeed a replica of his Byzantine colleague. He also proved himself a generous benefactor to the papacy by restoring the papal state. In a solemn document – still preserved – he declared all previous grants and conferments null and void, and quite especially the title-deed upon which the papacy claimed the territories constituting the papal state, he stigmatized as a figment of imagination. It was the first time in the Middle Ages that the Donation of Constantine was labelled what it was – a forgery. Otto entrusted to the papacy the territories forming the papal state out of his own imperial plenitude of power. He considered the territories to be imperial property which he made over to St Peter through the medium of the papacy.

Several years of royal or imperial absences from Rome encouraged further faction fights in the city which brought the Tusculan nobility to the fore, with results not different from those observable during the régime of the Crescentii. In any case the very short pontificates were all too frequently punctured by antipopes who were of no higher calibre than the 'legitimately' appointed popes. Rivalry between two popes (Benedict VIII and Gregory) brought the deeply religious German king Henry II to Rome, and with him the first concrete signs of a much wanted reform of the papacy and of the city government appeared on the horizon. Henry II (canonized by Eugenius III in 1146) was a close follower of the by now firmly entrenched reform programme advocated by the Cluniac monks. They had made the regeneration of Christian society its main propagandistic plank. The ecclesiastical policy Henry II pursued in Germany was thoroughly inspired by the Cluniac ideals. His firm control of the higher ecclesiastics by direct appointments and the exercise of disciplinary powers assured the succession of able and far-sighted men. It was this policy which he also wished to apply to the Roman church. The German king in his future role as

Western emperor suggested himself as the instrument of active reform and papal regeneration.

One of the first concrete signs in this direction emerged subsequent to Henry II's coronation as emperor by Benedict VIII in 1014. Henry had prevailed upon the pope to insist that papal officers in Rome and in the papal state conducted themselves in a manner which did not bring discredit upon the papacy and the clergy in general. Above all, the wide-spread alienation of clerical property, the lascivity and immorality of the lower clergy, marriage or concubinage of priests, simony (that is, purchase of ecclesiastical offices) were some of the manifestations of conduct which ill-became ecclesiastics and officers of the papacy. For how should a regeneration of Christian society take place when its clerical functionaries showed such grave and objectionable defects in their own bearing? The large Council of Pavia in 1022 presided over jointly by pope and emperor, issued a number of decrees precisely aiming at this regeneration of society in general and of the clergy in particular.

Yet nothing illustrated the feebleness of the papacy in the first half of the eleventh century better than its utter helplessness during the reign of the first Salian king in Germany. Conrad II evinced extremely little interest in the fortunes of the papacy, with the consequence that the Tusculan party once again came to set the tone in Rome. The result was the creation of another youth of 18 as pope (Benedict IX) whose scandalous conduct provoked even the Romans to take matters into their own hands. In 1044 another Roman revolt set up the bishop of Sabina, Silvester III, as pope but he was unable to assert himself against Benedict. Having been assailed by the Romans, Benedict renounced the papacy against a consideration of 1000 pounds of silver in favour of his god-child John Gratian who became within a year the third living pope in Rome – Gregory VI. It was indeed a spectacle which showed to what depths the 'mother of all the churches' and the 'successor of Peter' had sunk. Yet it was noteworthy that even at this nadir of the popes the papacy itself did not appear to have suffered in prestige and authority, at least not in that quarter from which alone effective help could reasonably be expected – from the German monarch. Not only had the papacy as an institution not shown any signs of damage as a result of the conduct and personalities of the popes themselves, but above all the imperial idea itself had remained unshaken, that is, the idea that only the pope in Rome, of whatever low personal standing he might in actual fact be, could validly confer the imperial crown and create a Roman emperor.

Despite, even by contemporary standards, the exceptionally low · calibre of individual popes who were 'successors of St Peter' in these 150 years, the papacy as an institution was nevertheless helped by factors outside Rome. To begin with, the papacy's administrative apparatus, its civil service, so to speak, was functioning, however greatly reduced its output was. Nevertheless, papal letters still came forth from the papal chancery in comparatively speaking respectable quantities, and advice, exhortation and orders were still given by the popes in all sorts of matters and addressed to all sorts and conditions of men. Bishoprics and abbacies were founded by kings and laymen after receiving the approval and sanction of the papacy. To churches, monasteries, and other ecclesiastical establishments all over Europe, solemn privileges were granted, and existing ones, such as immunities and the like, confirmed in documents which had all the elegance, sonorousness and loftiness of language and contents for which papal documents had always been noted. In brief, the office continued to function as heretofore, however low the personal standard of the individual popes might be.

What mattered to the outside world was the institution as such, · not the personality of the pope who evoked extremely little interest from contemporaries. In this way the ancient papal principle (to which reference has already been made, see above pp. 20ff.) of a distinction between the papal office and the individual incumbent, was vindicated in a most striking manner in this century and a half. Moreover, as the available evidence makes clear, there was very little slackening of pilgrimages to Rome. The incentive of the pilgrims was to visit the graves of the apostles Peter and Paul. The veneration of the other relics which were to be found in Rome was only a further motive which attracted many pilgrims to the 'eternal city'.

One more and highly significant feature should be borne in · mind in this context. In little more than 60 years the popes crowned no fewer than five German kings as emperors of the Romans in St Peter's basilica. The first coronation was that of Otto I in 962 and the last that of Conrad II in 1027, at which the

E

presence and assistance of two kings, Cnut of England and
Rudolf of Burgundy, demonstrated the significance of the event
in European terms. It does not need much historical imagination
to visualize not only how impressive these imperial coronation
ceremonials were, but also how many people – and they constituted the responsible section of contemporary society – witnessed these occasions and took part in them. What, above all,
must be properly assessed was the ideology which the imperial
coronation ceremonial enshrined in an unambiguous language
and which was expressed in equally unambiguous symbolism.
Not even the most dull-witted contemporary could have misunderstood the meaning of an imperial coronation and the ideology
it embodied. Prayers, gestures, symbolic actions and emblems
showed one thing, and that was how essential and indispensable
the pope's coronation of a king as Roman emperor was. Without
the pope's active intervention there was no emperor in the West,
a vital and highly significant difference from the situation in the
East (see also above pp. 24f.). But, and this is the fundamental
point, it was not the pope as a person, it was not John, Silvester
or Benedict, who mattered, but the office which enabled him to
act. It was the institution of the papacy, not the individual pope,
which alone stood in the foreground and which, on precisely
these memorable and incisive occasions, engraved itself upon the
minds of contemporaries. The 'moral depravity' and 'the scandalous conduct' of some of the popes were, within this framework,
of negligible, if any, concern. It was the objectively conceived
office, the institution of the papacy, which alone mattered, and
not the subjectively conceived personality of the pope. That the
low moral bearing of the popes in these decades did not affect the
institution of the papacy, can be understood only in a medieval
environment in which the criteria of subjective evaluation had far
less meaning than today.

For the incontrovertible esteem in which the institution was
held there is also evidence in a different field. Missionary enterprises had effectively been undertaken since Charlemagne. What
was noteworthy was that with the exception of England in the
late sixth century the papacy did not initiate any missions in early
medieval Europe. The conversion of pagans was almost exclusively in the hands of kings, and here the Frankish and later
German Rulers could claim greatest credit. The essential point

about these missions was that when they had reached a stage of some finality, the converted regions or districts or countries had to be organized, and it was at this juncture that an approach was made to the papacy. A good many enterprises started in the ninth century. For instance, missions were sent to Moravia from Salzburg. Bohemia was brought into the Latin Christian fold, though the final conclusion of this mission was not reached until 973 when the bishopric of Prague was erected to come under the jurisdiction of Mainz, as Pope Benedict VI ordered in 973. The conversion of Denmark and Sweden was undertaken by Louis I in 831 with the newly established archbishopric of Hamburg as the headquarters for missionary activities further north, a plan specifically approved by Gregory IV (although the archbishopric was later transferred to Bremen which remained the metropolitan church for Scandinavia). Iceland as well as Greenland became objects of conversion, and were hence drawn into the papal orbit.

Of particular importance was the Slav mission which began in the tenth century and on which the Saxon emperors were especially keen. Otto I was instrumental in founding the arch- bishopric of Magdeburg as the headquarters of his mission, a plan finally sanctioned by the papacy (John XIII) on 20 April 967. Magdeburg was now a metropolitan see and also played a great role in the missions to Poland. Otto III founded the bishop- ric of Gnesen which was at once approved by Silvester II who also encouraged Brun of Querfurt to assume the leadership of the mission after he had been consecrated to the see of Magdeburg. Hungary became Christian in the course of the tenth century. Its leader Stephen had married Henry II's sister and was anointed and crowned as king of Hungary at Gran in 1001: whether he also entered into a relationship of vassalage with the papacy and whether Silvester II actually sent a crown (as was asserted in the eleventh century by the papacy), is doubtful. The archbishop of Gran became the metropolitan of Hungary under whom ten bishops functioned. The papacy always regarded both Hungary and Poland as advanced outposts of Latin Europe against the schismatic non-European Greek East. In brief, despite the low stature of the popes during this period, the authority, prestige and standing of the papacy had not suffered, as was demonstrated by its ecclesiastical and organizational measures in the North, West and North-East of Europe. All the countries converted came notionally under the jurisdiction of the papacy, however circumscribed its actual power was. But this was the backcloth of the later development which made the papacy an effective focal point of Europe.

It is also in this context that another factor came into play, that is, the exemption of monasteries from the control of the diocesan bishop (ordered by the Council of Nicaea, ch. 4). Although this law was never revoked, from the seventh century onwards upon request the papacy began to grant privileges to certain monasteries, according to which they were exempt, that is, freed, from the jurisdiction of the local bishop. One of the first to receive this papal grant was St Columban's monastery, Bobbio in Italy (628). This granting of monastic exemption was one concrete way of demonstrating in a practical manner the theme of papal primacy, and had, understandably, effect only in the West of Europe: at no time was the papacy requested by any monastic institution in the East to grant exemption – a practical difference between the Eastern and Western power of the papacy. In the West this grant of exemption of monasteries – exclusively the right of the papacy – became a major source of strength to the institution itself, especially after Cluny and its numerous dependencies had received this privilege. It does not need much historical imagination to visualize how close the ties were which the papacy had come to knit with monasteries all over Europe and how finely woven the net was which linked the monastic enclaves in the dioceses with the papacy. It thereby established direct contact with and control over wealthy and influential institutions and not inconsiderably weakened episcopal power, and this all the more so when in the twelfth century whole Orders became exempt from the control of the diocesan bishop. It was also in the eleventh century that a related development took place which was seen to supplement royal measures, that is, in addition to the royal protection which they received, the papacy granted its own special protection to certain monasteries which thus came – so it was expressed – 'into the property of St Peter' and enjoyed a heightened protection against baronial or ducal or other lay encroachments and exploitations: the monastery was said to enjoy the 'Libertas Romana'. These grants were also sources of additional income to the papacy, as the monasteries concerned had to pay an annual 'census'.

Few medieval Rulers possessed that depth and earnestness of religiosity or felt the burden of being a Christian king more acutely than the second Salian king, Henry III. To a man of his outlook, the spectacle of three living popes in the mid-forties was well-nigh intolerable. After all, the Roman church was of particular concern to him as a Christian king who had special obligations towards it, obligations, that is, which did not materially differ from those he had assumed towards the episcopal and metropolitan churches and abbacies in his own now greatly enlarged dominions. As a devout follower of the Cluniac programme he had taken the greatest care in his appointments to bishoprics and abbacies. Few medieval Rulers were as painstaking in applying the principle of suitability for the office as Henry III was. The result proved his principles of selection right. The German church disposed of men in the higher echelons of the clergy who, on purely subjective moral grounds, were far above some of the individuals acting as popes in Rome.

With a strong military escort the king advanced to Italy where he held court in a synod held at Sutri on 20 December 1046. The synod deposed Silvester III and sent Gregory VI into exile. The latter took up his abode at Cologne accompanied by the Roman deacon Hildebrand. Three days later, on 23 December, Henry III presided over another synod which deposed Benedict IX, so that the way was cleared for a new pope. In his function as patrician of the Romans, Henry III designated the bishop of Bamberg, Suidger, as the man to fill the vacancy. Another German ecclesiastic had thus become pope. On Christmas day 1046 Clement II crowned Henry III emperor of the Romans. Entirely in agreement with the *Ottonianum* and his renewed function as a patrician of the Romans the emperor was to appoint three more popes before his untimely death in 1056 plunged his empire and kingdom into one of its darkest periods. The popes appointed by him were all men of intellectual calibre and moral fibre commensurate with the institution they headed. That they were Germans only proved how correct Henry's own appointments in Germany had been. The prohibition against translating a bishop to the Roman church was no longer insisted upon and finally abolished in 1059 (see below p. 136).

Yet, paradoxically enough, it was these new men who were to usher in an age which vehemently impugned the very method by which they themselves had become popes. Indeed, the papacy as an institution had now been given appropriate incumbents. It was precisely they who became aware of the conspicuous cleavage between the institution of the papacy and the personalities of their predecessors. The new men knew all too well that the popes were created by lay rulers (or the Roman nobility). In fact, between 955 and 1057 there were 25 popes, of whom no fewer than 12 were straight imperial appointments and the others creations of the Roman aristocracy, while five popes were deposed or dismissed by the emperors. The calibre of most of these popes facilitated the disregard of the principle that the pope cannot be judged. One of the most pressing needs was to change the method by which the vacancy in the papal office was filled. This change could not, however, be mere adjustment or adaptation, but could only tear up a whole system by its roots. And that system of lay intervention and lay government of ecclesiastical matters, was based on the proprietary churches.

Two main presuppositions made it possible for this change to be put into practice within an astonishingly short time. The first presupposition was that because the institution of the papacy had been little affected despite the personalities of the popes, the official apparatus together with the various offices and departments had continued to function. What however was needed was greater efficiency and supervision and control of the already existing apparatus which was easily capable of expansion. Above all, the papal chancery as the nerve centre of the institution had not suffered any deleterious effect. The second presupposition concerned the easy availability of a body of doctrine upon which the change could be based. And that body was indeed readily available in a quite mature form: the programme of the papacy as a governing institution had been maturing since the mid-fifth century. In other words, the programme was there, and so was the apparatus which was to implement the programme. What the following decades showed was the determined attempt on the part of the papacy to apply this programme on a universal scale.

While the governmental apparatus functioned at the seat of the papacy, that is, the Lateran palace, the men who were to manipulate the programme and to make it a driving force of contemporary society, came from north of the Alps. On a

personal level these men came to mirror the idea of a homogeneous European society within the precincts of the Roman
church itself. This process of making the papacy an international
reflexion of European society, began with the pontificate of Leo ·
IX, 47 years old, a relation of Henry III who appointed him. It
was of the greatest significance that Leo – bishop of Toul –
made the acceptance of his appointment dependent on the fulfilment of certain canonical conditions, that is, that his appointment
should be ratified by his election by the clergy and people of
Rome. Henry III did not realize the significance of this condition.
Leo IX may well be viewed as a classical representative of the
Cluniac movement which, as already noted, aimed at a moral
reform of the whole of society and specifically of the clergy. The
evils most conspicuous to the adherents of Cluny at the time,
were simony, the buying of ecclesiastical offices, and concubinage,
that is, marriage of fully ordained clerics. But what Leo also
realized, as soon as he took up the papal office, was the need for
a far sterner and firmer central papal government than had
hitherto been envisaged. Leo's perspicacity and acuteness of
vision made him see the potentialities of the already existing
governmental apparatus of the papacy.

What in Leo's view was immediately needed, was the infusion ·
of some new blood into the main departments of the Roman
church. In order to achieve this, Leo called to Rome some of the
best brains from north of the Alps, and quite especially from
circles with which he as bishop of Toul had already had close
contact. From the monastery Remiremont in his former diocese
he called Hugh the White. From the Lotharingian monastery
Moyenmoutier he called Humbert. From the cathedral chapter of
Liège he called Frederick, the brother of Godfrey, the Duke of
Lorraine. And lastly, in the monastery of Cluny where he had
taken refuge, Hildebrand received a call from Leo, to accompany
him to Rome. They all as well as a number of lesser men eagerly
accepted the invitation and at once impressed their stamp upon
the institution in Rome. They began to apply their own ideas to
the problems of the day and achieved thereby a regeneration of
the governmental machinery within little more than a decade.
These outstanding men were charged with responsible posts and
had therefore ample opportunity to release their hitherto
untapped energies. A number of them were created cardinals.

Notably the chancery was transformed into one of the most efficient departments of the papacy.

Humbert distinguished himself also in his literary contributions all of which centred in the problem of how to achieve the right order within a Christian world. He was indeed outstanding in the way in which he dealt with this burning question. His works show a master mind that is thoroughly familiar with all the ramifications of this topic. He had a perfect mastery of the official papal programme as well as of ancient and early medieval litera-ture. No less versed was he in the law. That what he believed to be a virtually inexhaustible reservoir of papal law – that is, Pseudo-Isidore – was a forgery, he had no means of knowing. What, however, his writings, notably his long tract against the simonists, signified was the emergence of a new genre of literature, that is, the polemical or publicistic kind which was not only severely scholarly, but also a means by which to create and shape public opinion. Humbert's long book was one of the earliest which was strictly thematical as well as scholarly in its advocacy of the papal programme.

Humbert's clarion call was to do away with the proprietary church system, because it was diametrically opposed to the basic axioms which should prevail in a Christian society. In this society according to him no ecclesiastical office should be conferred by a layman, even if he were a king or an emperor. His forthright condemnation of simony and concubinage, no less than the arguments employed, presented a programme of social regenera-tion, and, above all, set the tone of subsequent legislation. But over and above all these issues, there was one that dominated the practical and literary work of Humbert and of all the newcomers, and that was the consistent, firm and repeated stress they laid upon the central tenet of the papacy – its primacy. The new men realized what potentialities this ancient and by then matured papal tenet harboured and how useful and beneficial it could be in the service of Christianity when applied to contemporary society. To them this papal tenet appeared the one and certain instrument with which the regeneration of society and of the clergy could successfully be undertaken. For they also realized what untapped and yet mature material had accumulated in the very bosom of the Roman church. These uncompromising and energetic men set to work with an enthusiasm, audacity and zeal which even in the long history of the papacy had few, if any, parallels.

From the pontificate of Leo IX onwards the papacy profited · from the élan and single-mindedness of this far-sighted group of men who were bent on making papal ideology a social reality. Hildebrand was at once recognized as a highly gifted and effective administrator who besides being rector of the Benedictine monastery of St Paul outside the walls, was in charge of papal finances. As a member of the inner council of the pope and by virtue of his forceful and incisive manner of putting across ideas, he began to exercise a decisive influence on the fortunes of the papacy from the moment he returned to Rome. He was also frequently employed as a papal legate. The new legatine system which now began its great career was a means of maintaining direct contact with distant ecclesiastical and secular authorities, especially in delicate matters. Papal decretals and papal legates became the chief instruments of papal policy. And the missions which Hildebrand and a number of other eminent men of the Roman church, such as Peter Damian, undertook, at once revealed the great advantage of these direct contacts in which points could be raised which easily lost their impact and precision in lengthy written communications, particularly when it is borne in mind how poor and also perilous communications were. The legate came to be the personal representative of the pope, that is, the personification of the primatial principle.

But Leo himself also put the primatial principle into practice · by his frequent journeys to France, Germany, let alone to places inside Italy. He thereby established personal contact by holding frequent meetings with the diocesan or provincial clergy and also summoned a number of synods on these occasions. In these meetings the main topic was the attack on simony and concubinage. In order to eradicate these the synods issued numerous decrees which the Emperor Henry III warmly supported. Such synods were held, for instance, in Pavia, Rheims, Mainz, Vercelli, Mantua, Salerno, and of course Rome. But more important than these frequent synods was the effect which the personal appearance of the pope as the living successor of St Peter had on the participating clergy and the observant laity. The primatial function of the papacy came to be witnessed in person, so to speak. Thus the Council of Rheims (1049) chaired by Leo, declared that the pope

· alone was the universal primate and the 'apostolicus', a highly significant statement when set against Byzantine views. Although the concrete and immediate result of synodal legislation should not be overestimated, the main effect was that the institution of the papacy was, as it were, physically transported to influential ecclesiastical centres of Europe. The papacy began not only to be heard and esteemed in the far distance, but also to be seen and respected in the flesh.

The clear realization of the duties inherent in the papal office also accounted for the initiative which the papacy during Leo IX's pontificate took against the continuing menace of the Normans who had begun to settle in South Italy since 1016 and plundered and devastated churches and monasteries. Leo's call for a war of liberation in the service of St Peter – very likely inspired by Hildebrand – was eagerly taken up. In 1052 the pope visited the emperor who handed over the duchy of Benevento to the papacy. Upon his return to Rome the pope recruited an army and himself joined the armed forces which suffered, however, a heavy defeat at the hands of the Normans. They took the pope prisoner in June 1053 and released him only nine months later. In actual fact, the South Italian situation in conjunction with the forcefully advocated tenet of Roman primacy involved the papacy once more in a conflict with Constantinople where the Patriarch Kerullarios (1043–1058) was in charge of ecclesiastical matters. For the papacy the loss of South Italy to the patriarchate of Constantinople in the eighth century (see above p. 72) had always been a very sore point and constituted a serious griev-ance. But the pursuit of an active papal policy in South Italy mobilized the suspicious patriarch of Constantinople whose ambitions apparently were insatiable.

Kerullarios closed the Latin churches in Constantinople in 1053 and confiscated the few Latin monasteries there. He and his party aggressively asserted that the Western custom of using unleavened bread was wholly uncanonical and unwarranted: the host, they said, was unconsecrated. In encyclicals and pamphlets and letters Kerullarios and his helpers fanned the last conflict with the papacy and the Latin West. The arguments which they used were all of old and seasoned stock but what was without precedent was the highly abusive language which they employed. As the draftsman of official papal communications, Humbert took up the challenge. In his fiery and passionate letters to the East he made the primatial function of the papacy the focal point and underpinned his arguments with lavish quotations from the Donation of Constantine and other questionable sources. The close argumentation and the hitherto unknown intimate familiarity with canonical sources and ecclesiastical history produced the predictable effect in Constantinople: their counter attacks lost even the last traces of 'diplomatic' language. What no doubt grated on Byzantine ears was the mastery with which the Roman chancery parried their attacks with a wealth of scholarly, historical, dogmatic and legal points. But in substance there was hardly any new material in either the Western or the Eastern communications.

In order to enter ostensibly into direct contact with Constantinople, a three-man papal legation consisting of Humbert as leader, Frederick of Lorraine (the later Stephen X) and Archbishop Peter of Amalfi, left for Constantinople in the spring of 1054, but neither the patriarch nor the legates could have had any illusion about the worth or even the feasibility of a truce. At Constantinople the patriarch incited the population against the Latins whom he forbade to celebrate mass. The meetings between the legation and the patriarch and the emperor, were cool and predictably achieved nothing. Thereupon, on 16 July 1054 in the full view of the congregation abruptly and dramatically Humbert put the already prepared papal decree of excommunication of Kerullarios and of his followers on the high altar of S. Sophia. Constantinople interpreted this step as sheer provocation. The patriarch on his part excommunicated wholesale the legates and all their supporters. The latent schism had become an open schism between the Eastern and Western churches. The dramatic staging of ecclesiastical censures in 1054 was no more than the final scene of a long drawn-out tragedy. Of all the dogmatic differences of varying grades and importance, the central feature of this conflict was the primatial position of the papacy. Now that this primatial question had become the pivot of papal policy, the open rupture with the East could not come as a wholly unforeseen event. Because of their dependence on Constantinople, the Slav kingdoms (Bulgaria, Serbia, as well as Russia) followed suit and declared their loyalty to Constantinople. Here too a latent state of affairs became now patent.

In view of the antecedent development which led to the open

schism, it is perhaps pointless to ask – as is frequently done – whether the excommunication of Kerullarios was formally valid. Whether Humbert was aware of the papal vacancy – Leo IX had died in April and no successor had been appointed by July 1054 – it is impossible to know, nor is it relevant, since, strictly speaking, he was a legate of the apostolic see, and not of the pope. Legatine powers could not therefore be affected by the pope's death. However, the question of the validity of the excommunication was not raised at the time.

In the history of the papacy the two short pontificates following Leo IX's constituted a very important period of transition. Victor II, imperial chancellor, was the last German bishop to become pope and, what was more important, the last pope to be appointed by imperial nomination; he was also a pope who retained his bishopric (of Eichstätt). He too had spotted the talents of Hildebrand whom he used as a papal legate on a number of missions. Hildebrand was especially prominent as papal legate in French councils which concerned themselves with reform measures. Nothing illustrated the change of temper in the Roman church better than the manner and speed of creating Victor's successor. With the death of Henry III in October 1056 the old imperial regime had vanished: it was a symbolic departure of the young emperor when on his deathbed he entrusted the care of his six-year-old son, the later Henry IV, to Victor II who followed the emperor into the grave on 28 July 1057. In order to forestall a move by any of the Roman aristocratic factions, the high Roman ecclesiastics speedily proceeded to the election of Victor's successor and four days after his death chose the abbot of Monte Cassino, Frederick of Lorraine. It was also highly significant that the Roman church now felt strong enough altogether to disregard the German court where the Empress Agnes had become the regent. Soon after his election the new pope, Stephen, dispatched Hildebrand as special papal envoy to the German court to notify it of the accession of the new pontiff. The plan clearly was to confront the court with a *fait accompli*. The German court which had in the preceding hundred years exercised such a decisive influence on the fortunes of the papacy, was now merely informed of what had taken place. The court made no attempt to invoke the constitutional basis of its by now virtually customary intervention. These two short pontificates witnessed unambiguous signs of the papacy's self-awareness. Stephen's pontificate especially tested in practice the strength and state of preparedness of both the Roman nobility and the German court. From their lack of reaction and apathy the men of the Roman church drew the necessary conclusion.

Although the Tusculans tried once more after Stephen's death to create their candidate (Benedict X), the group of men now guiding the papacy refused to have anything to do with them and, in accordance with the instructions of the dying pope, waited until the return of Hildebrand from his mission to the German court. The formal election of Stephen's successor took place in December 1058. The choice of the bishop of Florence who became Nicholas II, signified a cesura in the history of the papacy. From now on the institution began the steep ascent to the dominating position where it became a force that decisively shaped the destinies of Europe for the next two hundred years. The men surrounding the pope realized – and the most recent events leading to the appointment of Benedict X furnished additional proof – that if the papacy was to play the role which, in their view, it ought to play according to its own and mature programme, the most elementary prerequisite was that the pope himself should be elected freely, canonically and without any intervention by either the local aristocracy or, more importantly, the German kings or emperors. The time for the initiation of decisive measures was particularly propitious now that the regency in Germany was in the hands of the weak and conciliatory Agnes, Henry III's widow and mother of the future king.

The Lateran synod of April 1059 presided over by Nicholas II· went straight to the central issue of papal election. The decree it passed laid down that the pope should be freely elected: the cardinal-bishops should first confer about the candidate and should then summon the cardinal-clergy; the remaining Roman clergy and the people should assent to the choice. In a presumably deliberately vaguely drafted passage reference was made to the future king (Henry IV) and to his successors who were to be rendered the respect and honour that was due to them. This formula was to mean a great many things to a great many interpreters. With that decree the papacy had taken a long step forward in its quest for freedom. The decree persuasively showed how well prepared were the men now at the helm of the Roman church when they took the earliest opportunity to ensure the proper regulation of the election to the successorship of St Peter. The skeleton of the decree was the measure enacted in 769.

The significance of this synodal measure of 1059 can be summed up under several headings. First, it put on a firm basis the ancient papal point of view that only those qualified should function as electors of a particular office holder. Secondly, that election was to be free from any interference by organs outside the electing body itself. Thirdly, the decree abolished the prohibition against translating a bishop to the see of Rome; this prohibition had already been disregarded. Fourthly, if the freedom of the cardinal-bishops was restricted in Rome, they could proceed to an election outside Rome, and the pope thus elected and enthroned at once functioned as successor of St Peter. Fifthly, the decree marked the beginning of the College of Cardinals as a body specifically charged with the election of the pope. This body was also to attend upon the pope in an advisory capacity. On the model of the imperial court in Constantinople the official meetings of the pope with the cardinals were called consistories. As Peter Damian said the College of Cardinals became the senate of the pope similar in function to the ancient Roman senatorial body. This was one more instance which showed how much already existing offices were made use of, for nothing would be more erroneous than to think that this election decree established the cardinals as special dignitaries. The emergence of the College of Cardinals as a special body was an almost classic example of a steady evolution of an already functioning body within the Roman church.

The cardinals as specific dignitaries had certainly existed in Rome since the sixth century and had in course of time come to occupy distinct and prominent offices. There were now the seven cardinal-bishops, that is, the bishops of Ostia, Albano, Porto, Silva Candida, Palestrina, Sabina and Tusculum, the first named always having been (as today) the senior. In the antecedent period these had to perform certain weekly liturgical functions in the Lateran church whence they were also called 'Lateran bishops'. In addition there were 28 cardinal-priests who originally were the heads of 28 churches situated within the city walls and who also functioned at services in the Lateran according to a roster. Lastly, there were the cardinal-deacons. They were originally clerics who, since Adrian I, had been in charge of the so-called 18 diaconal churches in Rome and had been entrusted with public welfare matters, such as supply of food and corn to the poor in Rome, provisioning of needy pilgrims, and so on; they too took regular part in the Lateran service. As a fully corporate body these three orders (cardinal-bishops, cardinal-priests and cardinal-deacons) made up the College of Cardinals which functioned in its corporate capacity from the end of the century onwards and continued to function in this way well into the modern period. Had there not been the antecedent development, it would have been unthinkable that within less than half a century there could have evolved such a well-organized body. From the early twelfth century onwards individual cardinals began to be employed for delicate and important legations, and in the same century they also became the heads of some special departments in the Roman church, such as the chancery, chamber, etc. In a sense the cardinals in their corporate function resembled a cathedral chapter, and the election decree of 1059 in fact spoke of the cardinal-bishops as quasi-metropolitans (see also below p. 229).

Only after 1059 is it indeed possible to refer to a Roman curia. The term designated the corporate organization of the Roman church. The pope together with the cardinals formed the supreme governmental body of the whole of Christendom. Already under Leo IX a number of the outstanding men who had been called to Rome (see above p. 129), had been appointed cardinals by the pope, such as Humbert, Hugh, and shortly afterwards Peter Damian. It was these exceedingly capable men who from the moment they joined the papal entourage imprinted their own image upon the institution. The direction of the papacy lay to a very large extent in their hands and when in late 1059 Hildebrand became the archdeacon of the Roman church, the curia found in him not only a zealous if at times also impatient and impetuous reformer anxious to establish the papacy as the central government in accordance with ancient doctrine and law, but also a man who had become thoroughly familiar with conditions in different parts of Western Europe as a result of his numerous legations. These men had an iron will and energy, and also, by virtue of their superior intellect, had a perfect mastery of the programme they wished to see applied. The measure concerning the election of the pope was only a beginning. In the same Lateran synod of 1059 they also proclaimed what could only be called a lay strike, that is, they prohibited lay people from attending the services of priests living in concubinage. The priests themselves were threatened with excommunication if they did not dismiss their concubines. Above all, no cleric was henceforth allowed to accept his ecclesiastical office from the hands of a layman, no matter whether with or without payment: this was one of the earliest decrees solemnly proscribing investiture with an ecclesiastical office by a layman. That simony was also condemned, was understandable. As so often with medieval legislative measures, so here too: their effect was limited, and one of the reasons was that the machinery for their enforcement did not as yet exist. But they showed the state of ideological preparedness on the part of the Roman curia; they reflected the powerful influence of Cardinal Humbert.

The sagacity and statesmanlike vision of the men at the helm of the curia was best shown by the measures which the papacy took to secure its rear. There was no illusion in curial quarters about the real nature of the far-reaching decisions and decrees issued. Admittedly, there was no king in Germany but only a weak regency; admittedly, the Roman nobility happened to be in some disarray in early 1059, but these fortunate contingencies might well be of a merely temporary nature which made it advisable to seek military help where it might be obtainable. It was probably due to the initiative of Hildebrand and Abbot Desiderius of Monte Cassino (the later Victor III) that the Normans in Southern Italy were harnessed to the role of a military defender of the papacy: this was a veritable reversal of papal policy as pursued by Leo IX and Stephen. And for the Normans the curial approach immediately after the conclusion of the Lateran synod was by no means unwelcome, because in this unexpected way they greatly improved their own position which was strengthened by overt papal sanction and legitimation.

In July and August 1059 at Melfi (Apulia) the papacy not only concluded peace with the Normans, but on the same occasion also made the Normans vassals of the Roman church. This was the first effective infeudation carried out by the papacy. Count Richard received Capua, while Duke Guiscard was enfeoffed with Calabria and Apulia as well as Sicily (which was still in the hands of the Saracens). That as a result of this papal initiative the German court – however helpless and badly guided it was – showed apprehension was understandable, for the German kings Conrad II and Henry III had only a short while before handed over almost exactly the same territories to the Normans as imperial fiefs. The papal step was based on the Donation of Constantine. At any rate, both Norman princes promised annual payments of · feudal dues, but above all they undertook the military defence of the papacy when needed, and guaranteed freedom of papal elections. The historic significance of this papal-Norman concord was firstly that strong ties were now knitted between the papacy · and the Normans which were vitally to affect the papacy down to the fourteenth century and, secondly, that the papacy had begun to emerge as a feudal overlord. In strictest papal terminology it was St Peter who was the feudal lord, whose place the living pope took. The papal curia was to become the most powerful feudal court in Europe within the next 150 years.

The coronation of Nicholas II as pope served as a further and · very persuasive reminder of how greatly the self-awareness and self-assurance of the papacy had increased. This was, as far as the available evidence goes, the first papal coronation, and in this the papacy borrowed one more symbolic element from royal and imperial symbolism. But there was a great difference between these kinds of coronations. While the royal coronation or, strictly speaking, the unction created the king who until that moment was a mere prince, the papal coronation added nothing at all to the status, authority and function of the man elected pope who by accepting the choice of the electors at once became the successor of St Peter (hence the possibility, still existing today, of a layman becoming pope). Similar considerations applied to the imperial coronation performed by the pope, for the king to be created emperor, was not emperor until the anointment and coronation at St Peter's basilica. The papal coronation was meant to signify by visible, easily comprehensible and familiar means the monarchic status of the pope. Most literally, the coronation symbolized the monarchy of the pope.

On the other hand, there was a certain kinship between imperial coronations in Constantinople and papal coronations in Rome, because in neither instance did the ceremonial add anything to what the office-holder already had. In both cases the purpose of the coronation was to declare to the outside world the status of a Ruler. The coronation did not create the emperor at Constantinople nor the pope at Rome: it had a merely declaratory function, and was not constitutive as the royal and imperial coronations in the West were. The ceremonial of the papal coronation was later greatly expanded and also included the symbolism of the enthronement (for some other details see below pp. 230f.).

A comparison of the state of affairs prevailing in the Roman Church in the mid-forties of the eleventh century with those observable some twenty years later, will demonstrate that however propitious the circumstances for the papacy were – notably the absence of an emperor after Henry III's death – this astonishingly quick rise of the status of the papacy must be attributable to factors which can on no account be satisfactorily explained by a purely accidental contingency of favourable circumstances. The most readily available and convincing explanation is that the institution itself had not suffered in the dismal antecedent period. What was needed was to turn the already existing machinery into an efficient organism. In particular, there was available a fully matured programme of the papacy and an ideology with a very distinguished ancestry. There were also available the men who were to work the already existing apparatus in the exclusive service of this programme and ideology. The combination of both created a secure platform for the ascendancy of the papacy in subsequent decades.

What, in other words, was 'new' in the papacy from the sixties onwards, was not the programme, but the attempt to apply it to the contingencies of the time with a ruthless energy and logic. Evidently, this needed the men of the right calibre. The situation now allowed the emergence of the man who had already been a decisive influence on the papacy. Hildebrand-Gregory VII was the personification of the papal programme and ideology. He was to impress papal cosmology on the late eleventh century. The papacy had first been under the dominating influence of Hildebrand and was then directed by Gregory VII. What had hitherto been merely programmatic and an idea, was to be made concrete in the world at large. The papacy under his intrepid direction was propelled by its own inner strength and programme to become an institution of European dimensions. The papacy had made Hildebrand, and Gregory VII was to make it the focal establishment of Europe. The fifth-century view that the Roman church was the mother of all churches from now on began to approach reality, though at times she was a harsh mother and the pope as monarchic Ruler an exacting father.

7 The Gregorian Age

IN THE PERIOD immediately preceding the pontificate of Gregory VII the papacy guided by Alexander II kept up the initiative and impetus which had characterized its policy since 1046. In particular, the dynamic initiative of the papacy displayed itself in two ways and each, though in a different field, was to have long-term effects. The one was in part an extension of the measure which the papacy had already begun to apply, that is, the infeudation of weakly placed or insecure governments. The papacy now showed considerable interest in the military campaigns all too frequently undertaken at the time by princes and kings. And the latter welcomed this spontaneous papal interest, however much their motives and those of the papacy might have differed. By manifestly supporting the one or the other campaign, the papacy indubitably believed that it was gaining military allies – a belief not always borne out by subsequent facts – and that it was strengthening and extending its own authority and influence. The concrete means by which this papal approval of a campaign was shown was by the dispatch of the banner of St Peter. This papal banner symbolically denoted that the particular campaign was undertaken in the interests of Christian justice, of which the papacy claimed to be the sole and final interpreter. Alexander II on several occasions had an opportunity of sending the papal banner to warriors. The most famous case was that of William (the Conqueror) before he set out on his invasion of England (in 1066), while other contemporary instances were those of Roger of Sicily (in 1064), William of Aquitaine (1064–65) and of Erlembald of Milan; the cases could easily be multiplied. What they all signified was the blessing of St Peter through his successor, the pope, of the military action: it was a public 'sanctification' of war or warlike measures. There can be no doubt that this measure bore a revolutionary and dynamic complexion, and this was especially so when the military action was directed against a public authority which was, at least by contemporary standards, perfectly legitimately installed.

There was another manifestation of papal initiative in the Alexandrian pontificate. As already indicated the papacy had begun to realize that the most serious evil of the time was the proprietary church system, according to which the lay lord invested the cleric with his office: it was a system upon which the whole contemporary public order rested, and was of particular concern, not so much to the lower churches, as to episcopal, metropolitan and the great abbatial churches, for it was only through the bishops and abbots that any kind of stable royal government could be secured. The crucial point was that the established order could not but view with considerable misgivings the determined attempts by the papacy to do away with this system. As long as the papal programme remained merely doctrinal and abstract, it was held harmless. But as soon as the papacy began to apply the old papal doctrine in practice, the established order at once realized the threat inherent in this application. And the programme itself was of course silent about the means by which it was to be implemented and applied concretely. These means were devised by the men directing the fortunes of the papacy in the years under consideration, that is, from the sixties in the eleventh century onwards. That the landed aristocracy and the West-European kings, in combination with the beneficiaries of the system, that is, the bishops, abbots and so forth, formed the conservative backbone of contemporary society, is not difficult to understand. The proprietary church system was the most powerful governmental and economic instrument at the disposal of the wealthy land-owning sections of society. That the 'have-nots', including the lower clergy, formed the overwhelming part of the population, is only another way of saying that wealth was concentrated in the hands of the fortunate few.

Mention has already been made of the decree of the Lateran synod in 1059 which forbade lay people to attend the services of priests living in concubinage. Now this measure was clearly intended to be a serious challenge to the traditional recruitment of clerical officers who were to minister to the needs of this Christian society. And in challenging the method of recruitment the synodists struck or attempted to strike at the very roots of contemporary society. They were allying themselves with social groups who belonged neither to the class of the priests nor to that of the land-owning lay lords; by proclaiming a strike on the part of the laymen, the papacy attacked the wealthy who conferred the ecclesiastical offices and benefices.

Whilst this decree (and its subsequent re-enactment by various councils) was aimed at the landed section of the population, there was a simultaneous development in regard to the urban populations. This development was not initiated by any council, but solely by the papacy. The tenor of the papal and curial approach to the urban masses in Italy was once more an implicit attack on the conservative, traditionalist forces in the towns themselves, because here too it was these forces which secured the continuation of practices wholly condemned by the papacy: simony, concubinage, but above all the decisive part which these elements took in the appointments to ecclesiastical prebends, including episcopal and archiepiscopal and metropolitan appointments. A notable example of this alliance between the papacy and what may without fear of employing anachronistic terms be called the lower and lowest classes of contemporary society, was provided by Milan in the sixties of the eleventh century. For here the papacy powerfully supported the so-called Patarini (Italian *pattari* = scrap or old clothes dealers) who constituted the backbone of a movement at once economic, social and political, directed against the wealthy and influential forces in the city. This North Italian movement which had sprang up without any papal initiative or help, now found in the papacy a very potent ally, although the motives which joined the two together no doubt differed widely. But what mattered and what was common to them both was their opposition to the existing traditional social structure. The Patarini were the embryonic beginnings of a mass movement mainly of the lower lay and clerical masses against the mighty conservatives concentrated in the nobility.

By harnessing this mass movement to its own programme, the papacy took a step of a veritably revolutionary character. The city governors and high-ranking ecclesiastical officers, including the archbishops, in Milan – as elsewhere – came of course from precisely those sections of the populace which the papacy considered chiefly responsible for the diseases besetting society.

When Alexander II – before becoming bishop of Lucca he was one of the most powerful advocates of this movement – dispatched the papal banner to the leader of the Patarini, the knight Erlembald, a link was forged the strength of which could not in contemporary conditions be surpassed. The movement had received its Petrine blessing. The mundane and military camp marched alongside the papal and ecclesiastical forces. The initiative was Hildebrand's who during his mission to Milan came to realize the great potentialities of the movement and the great mutual benefits which a close alliance would bring. The papacy realized that an alliance with these forces was preferable to a frontal attack against the entrenched establishment.

The situation in Milan was to prove crucial and a pattern for the further development. Although the archbishop, Guido, had as a result of the legation of Cardinal Peter Damian, in 1060, accepted some of the papal programmatic points, his position became untenable in Milan and 10 years later he resigned sending ring and staff to King Henry IV, thereby acknowledging that he owed his position to the king's predecessor, the Emperor Henry III. This made a confrontation of the opposing forces inevitable, for in the meantime the papal alliance with the new revolutionary forces had struck deep roots. The German king was compelled to take an active interest in the situation, because Milan was economically and strategically an essential German linchpin for the domination of Lombardy. The ancient see of St Ambrose became the scene of fierce civil as well as ecclesiastical strife. Henry IV and the conservative elements disregarded all overtures on the part of the Patarini and appointed Godfrey, a descendant of an old Milanese aristocratic family, whom the Lombard bishops as staunch adherents of traditionalism and followers of Henry IV soon consecrated as bishop, after the king had invested him. The Patarini, upon papal suggestion and military as well as demagogic assistance by Erlembald in the presence of a papal legate (6 January 1072) elected Atto, another Milanese cleric, who was, however, a man of humble origins. Serious disturbances occurred in Milan and brought the papacy into open conflict with the conservative elements in the city. Alexander II formally recognized Atto and excommunicated five counsellors of Henry IV, because they (so it was pretended by the curia) and not the king had ordered Godfrey's consecration by the Lombard bishops.

Behind this step, however, was Henry's mother who wished to detach her young son from the influence of these counsellors, and hence no steps were contemplated against the king himself. This was the situation which Hildebrand as Pope Gregory VII inherited.

The dynamic activity of the curia, almost wholly dominated by Hildebrand during Alexander II's pontificate, showed itself also in strengthened papal relations with the Normans, after some difficulties had been ironed out, and these too were Hildebrand's achievement. Encouraged by the papacy, Robert Guiscard drove out the last remnants of the Byzantine occupation troops in Southern Sicily (1071) which now came also in organizational respects under papal influence. And by 1072 Sicily was cleared of the Saracens by the Normans, so that the pope's vassals dominated the whole of the South of the continent. It was on this occasion that Robert too received the papal banner. The subjection of Southern Italy and of Sicily to Norman-papal rule, was to be of crucial significance both to the papacy and the Western empire and to Europe at large. By the conquest of England the papacy hoped to exercise its influence on another Norman power, notably in the appointments to the numerous vacant English sees, though Alexander and his successors were to find the Anglo-Norman kings rather recalcitrant 'sons of the Roman Church'. Of no lesser significance was the connexion which the papacy began to establish with Aragon, then with Castille and Leon, the Christian kingdoms of Spain. King Sancho Ramirez of Aragon, in 1068, became a papal vassal and introduced Roman liturgy; from 1089 the kingdom paid annual feudal dues to the curia. Here again it was Hildebrand who was the driving spirit; he was also instrumental in providing papal support for the Norman and French military contingents engaged in the reconquest of Spain. It was on this occasion that the papacy granted the first indulgences to those who took part in this campaign which had all the external trappings, though not the name, of a crusade. It can readily be seen that through these territorial extensions by Christian princes and active papal participation the papacy from the early seventies onwards came rapidly to play the role of a focal point of Europe. Not only did the papacy stand in direct contact with virtually all European princes, but it had also established relations with forces which had hitherto been considered a *quantité négligeable*, that is, the socially and economically weaker powers, as instanced especially in the Lombard cities of Milan, Cremona, Piacenza, and so on. In brief, within less than 25 years the papacy had made its presence and influence felt throughout the length and breadth of Europe.

By the early seventies many of those who had been instrumental in raising papal authority and prestige, had died and their place had been taken by a new and no less virile generation. After the death of Godfrey of Lorraine (in 1069), his daughter-in-law, Mathilda of Tuscany, began to occupy a key position in Italy: she was an unwavering and staunch supporter of the papacy throughout the following stormy years. In 1072 Peter Damian, the cardinal-bishop of Ostia, died; in the same year the powerful German ecclesiastical prince, Anno, archbishop of Cologne, retired from active service, after having been the virtual regent of Germany; and several other prominent personalities closed their earthly careers. In 1073 Alexander II died, and apart from Cardinal Hugh the White and the cardinal in charge of the library and chancery, none of the other luminaries of the curia survived his pontificate. The man who had been the driving force of curial politics was Hildebrand whose curial career formed the bridge between the period which saw three popes as simultaneous successors of St Peter and the age in which the papacy had began to play a decisive role in European affairs. Upon popular pressure and in a wholly irregular manner, Archdeacon Hildebrand became pope as Gregory VII, on the very day after Alexander's death. He was one of the historical figures who left an indelible imprint on the papacy as well as on the course of European history.

However unimpressive he may have been as a man, as pope he · personified the papal programme as none had done before and as few were to do after him. He activated the programme of the institution as it had evolved and matured throughout the centuries, and he ruthlessly applied it to concrete reality. No doubt, there was something of a daemonic will-power in his personality, but in the world of harsh reality this would have counted for little if it had not been backed by a firm programme and institutional apparatus. These presuppositions existed in ample measure. Repeatedly and, as can be proved, correctly, he · claimed that he was simply the executor of ancient decrees, laws, views, the one who considered it his mission to translate pure, abstract ideology into papal actions in order to shape the reality of Christian life. What appeared new in his pontificate, was this impetuously pursued policy of application, but not the matter and programme that was applied. And the consistent application of an ideology hitherto expressed in merely abstract terms always tends to administer a shock to contemporaries who suddenly realize its effects.

The over-all aim of the Gregorian papacy – and of the succeeding pontificates – was to release the sacerdotal section of the Church from the fetters which the Germanic and wholly un-Roman structure of society had imposed upon it. In order to achieve this release, some drastic changes in the social structure were called for. And one of the means to carry through these changes was the reduction of royal-monarchic power to its proper dimensions which in its turn involved the crucial question of the standing and function of a Christian king within a Christian society. What was needed was the accommodation of this society to Christian laws and maxims. Their interpretation and final formulation was precisely the function of the papacy. Hence the consistent stress on the primatial function. The papal law or judgment was allegedly invested with the halo of divinity that had sanctioned it. The channel through which this device was to work was either direct instructions to subordinate officers or the mechanics of the legatine system. It is clear that this scheme presupposed a strict hierarchical ordering of society, at the apex of which stood the pope as monarchic Ruler. The stern application of papal monarchy was seen as the only means by which the chief defects from which contemporary society suffered could be eradicated. These were concubinage and simony, the investiture of ecclesiastical officers by lay lords, and the power of bishops, metropolitans and the provincial synods as legislative organs. Each of these obstructed the exercise of monarchic government by the papacy. The battle cry chosen – liberty of the Church – was to indicate the assumptions as well as the aims of the papacy.

Although not distinguished by great learning Gregory VII nevertheless mastered basic conceptions to a degree which few, if any, of his predecessors had attained. And it was precisely the basic axioms of the papacy which he had absorbed during the long, eventful and difficult years preceding his own pontificate. Among these axioms the one with which he constantly operated was that of the concept of the Church as an organic, corporate and public union of all Christians, clergy and laity alike, not confined within territorial bounds: it was a body which was universal and as much spiritual as it was mundane and earthy. This character of the Church necessitated government which could only be in the hands of those who were qualified by their ecclesiastical office to function as the directive organs of the Church. Hence the insistence on the freedom of these qualified officers. In this respect, too, the hierarchical ordering was necessary to achieve concord and avoid discord (as Gregory never tired of stressing) as was also the implementation of justice. The idea of justice from now on became operational in all governmental acts of the papacy. Justice in its Christian clothing was to inspire the law ordering society, and therefore only properly qualified officers could be entrusted with its interpretation and fixation. In the last resort this was the function of the papacy, and the appellation of the Roman Church as the seat of justice had some justification within the papal thought-pattern. Whatever emanated from the papacy, was said to bear the stamp of divine sanction, and unconditional obedience to the papacy was therefore demanded. Disobedience showed a conspicuous lack of a most vital Christian attitude – humility. Gregory held himself to be a re-incarnation of St Peter as well as St Paul. That 'apostolic' kinship also explains why he waited over two months for his consecration. Elected on 22 April 1073, ordained priest at the end of May, he was consecrated on 30 June, the Sunday following the feast of St Peter and Paul (29 June). Yet in the meantime he acted as pope, that is, as true governor, in no wise different from the manner in which he acted afterwards. This can serve as a particularly good instance of the constitutional position of the pope who, for purposes of government, became ruler from the moment of his election, although he may have been a layman or only a deacon, and therefore not even an ordained priest. If (which is not certain) Gregory announced his election to Henry IV, it was a mere notification and not a request for royal approval.

The early years of this pontificate showed all the energy and will power that had been stored up. There was an over-all bustling activity. Expansion of papal authority was the motto, and one of the means to achieve this was by infeudations which had recently been inaugurated so conspicuously. The despatch of papal legations to Spain and the appeal to French barons to assist in the reconquest of the country, fell into this category. Here the papacy also raised the claim, based on the Donation of Constantine, that Spain was its property, because given to Pope Silvester. The same claim was raised in regard to Sardinia and Corsica. If any new conquests were made, the conquered territory was to pay an annual census to the papacy. In France the papacy advanced similar claims to annual payments, especially in the shape of a tax imposed on houses. That these claims were not met favourably, was foreseeable, especially as Philip I was in any case no advocate of curial aims. The relations between the papacy and France at this time went from bad to worse. Papal charges of simony practised by Philip I, produced little tangible result, except the threat of depriving the king of his royal power. The attempt by the papacy to establish feudal relations with the new régime in England failed mainly because of a misunderstanding caused by the papal communication demanding payment of Peter's pence. The break with the East was not yet 20 years old when Gregory became pope, but his mind was already actively engaged in the planning of a military campaign against the East. This plan was the precursor of the fully-fledged crusading movement some twenty years later. As he avowed, his aim pursued the establishment of papal primatial authority in Constantinople in order to end the schism. The campaign which he himself was to lead as 'general and pope' and for which he appealed to the French barons and some Italian knights (who, he claimed, had already promised 50,000 soldiers) came to naught, because other and more pressing matters prevailed. But this plan also aimed at containing the restless Normans in the South whom, he hoped, the mere show of force would deter from further military attacks on papal territory.

Undeterred by miscalculations, the papacy also fixed its gaze on the outer-fringes of Europe. In order to establish links with Denmark, Gregory offered Croatia and Dalmatia as a fief to a son of the Danish king, Sven II; when the Danes were unresponsive, the papal vassal of these territories became King Zvonimir of Croatia. At the same time the son of the expelled Ruler of Russia, Isjaslaw, was promised the kingdom of Kiev as a papal fief or more correctly, as a fief to be held from St Peter.

Papal relations with Poland and Bohemia – the latter under the jurisdiction of the archbishop of Mainz – were overshadowed by German affairs. Hungary, on the other hand, aroused the anger of the papacy in the seventies. It had claimed a special relationship with Hungary because of the alleged gift of Stephen, the Hungarian king, to Silvester II (see above p. 125). The papacy considered this gift to constitute a papal fief. The reigning king, Salomon, had however married Henry IV's sister and became subsequently a vassal of Germany. In view of the importance which the papacy had come to attach to Hungary, Gregory VII was unwilling to tolerate this state of affairs and encouraged the Hungarian rebel, Geisa, to take up arms against Salomon, who, so the pope alleged, had alienated Petrine property 'against all law and religious discipline'; 'royal power was translated to the rebel by the verdict of St Peter himself' the pope now claimed when he transferred governing power from the legitimate king to his rebellious subject. Here was the first mention of the papal theme of a translation of a kingdom from one Ruler to another. The practical effects of this papally decreed transfer of power were not commensurate with the efforts spent upon the transaction.

The basic presupposition in all these instances was that the · pope as the direct successor of St Peter had inherited monarchic powers. They embraced every aspect of Christian life from the cradle to the grave: neither person nor matter was exempted from papal jurisdiction. This principle of totality also explained why Gregory VII was not satisfied with partial measures and results. The main instrument by which the papacy now began to imple-ment its theses was that of the law. Already as archdeacon Gregory had impetuously urged Peter Damian to produce a small volume which was to contain the law relative to 'all the preroga-tives of the Roman Church'. The first law-book that might have · satisfied Gregory, was not Damian's, but possibly the collection made by Cardinal Humbert, produced in the late fifties: it very largely consisted of excerpts from Pseudo-Isidore. During the seventies and eighties numerous other collections of what was considered to be the 'norm of right living' in a Christian society were made. Their theme was the primatial position of the papacy, · though all these works were private efforts. These numerous collections laid the foundations of the more professionally and more systematically treated law of the mid-twelfth century. By its definition this law was alleged to be the 'canon', that is, the norm of right living in a Christian society.

There is nevertheless extant the remnant of one official collection of canon law. This remnant is in fact part of the official Register of Gregory's pontificate and contains the chapter headings of a canon law collection since lost. In their pithy language and their terse, succinct expressions these chapter headings show some of the 'prerogatives' of the Roman Church as Gregory had wished them to be collected and as he applied them himself as pope. Enregistered in the second pontifical year immediately after the Lenten synod of 1075 they are known as 'Dictates of the Pope', though this is slightly misleading, since numerous other entries in the official Register of the papacy bear this designation. These 27 chapter headings dealt with the pope's and the bishops' power. Accordingly, the pope was the universal bishop, not (as the individual bishop was) confined to a particular diocese or territory, but capable of intervening throughout Christendom in all matters which were held by the papacy to be 'major matters'. The pope could judge all, but he could not be judged by anyone or by any council. He could depose, translate, restore bishops. He alone could issue laws valid for the whole Church, divide some dioceses and unite others; and erect new abbacies. He also claimed to be entitled to preside over synods through his legates, to summon general councils, and that no decrees of a synod were universally binding, until approved by the pope. He could receive appeals and finally give judgment on pending litigations.

Other headings focused attention on papal relations with Christian princes. The pope was entitled to depose emperors (kings were not mentioned; the only emperor who might have 'qualified' for a deposition was the one in Constantinople, because there was no emperor in the West at the time). The pope was further entitled to release the subjects of a Ruler from their oaths of allegiance and fidelity. Only the pope could demand that princes kissed his feet – an obvious reference to the already existing Western-imperial coronation ceremonial where, before the rite began on the steps of St Peter's basilica, the imperial candidate kissed the papal feet. As a true monarch the pope was alone entitled to wear imperial insignia – this was copied from the Donation of Constantine. Lastly, upon legitimately assuming office, the pope became a saint, by which of course no 'saintly' character in any personal or liturgical sense was meant: this character was simply to bring into relief the comprehensiveness of the Petrine powers which the pope had inherited – the binding and loosing powers displayed effects on earth as well as in heaven. To cap it all, the perhaps most important chapter headings were those which declared that the Roman Church alone was founded by Christ, and that it had never erred and was never to err. Infallibility was here ascribed to the institution, quite in agreement with the views expressed by Hormisdas and Agatho I (see above pp. 41, 63).

From the historical point of view these chapter headings contain nothing that had not been said before either in a papal decree or some literary product. The headings were a succinct legal summary of what the papacy considered to be its main and exclusive rights, and this indeed was the reason why they came to be written into the official papal Register. They constituted a guide to the understanding of most subsequent papal measures. Because their general complexion was thoroughly Roman-Latin, they stood in sharp contrast to the still efficacious Germanic practices. In challenging the latter lay the real and deeper significance of these 'Dictates'. They presupposed an ideological background which was in many and in vital respects opposed to the underlying Germanic basis of society, the hallmark of which was loyalty and fidelity, whereas in the Roman system it was a strict hierarchical ordering of society which was held to be of divine origin. Hence its law as promulgated by the papacy was also held to be of divine provenance.

Altogether the 'Dictates' contained a severe challenge to a great deal of the reality of social life. In concrete terms it was the proprietary church system that was attacked. Its visible and easily understandable manifestation – investiture of a cleric with an ecclesiastical office by a layman – signified the domination of the laity over the clergy. The system was one of the most resilient Germanic features which understandably deeply affected the social fabric. No orderly public government was considered possible without the king's (or other lay lord) conferring both the clerical office and benefice (the cleric's source of income) on the incumbent by investiture. The tenor of the 'Dictates' was a frontal attack on the exercise of this power. The already mentioned decrees against investiture (as well as against simony and concubinage) had very little practical effect in view of their ubiquitous practices. But the papacy was obviously unwilling to tolerate any longer these customs which it considered indefensible from the point of view of doctrine and harmful from the point of view of the well-being of society. Hence the re-issue of the decree prohibiting lay investitures at the Lenten synod of 1075 (in which the 'Dictates' had played a role), though this decree was not generally publicized nor apparently were the so-called lower churches affected.

The universal and unambiguous decree against lay investitures was promulgated in the Lenten synod of 1078. That the earlier decrees concerned all Rulers in Western Europe, was self-evident, but the Ruler who was most directly affected was the German king, Henry IV. Not only was his kingdom territorially the largest in Europe and also the best organized by contemporary standards – and for this reason liable to suffer from the effects which the recent decrees must have on public government – but he was also likely to be the next emperor to be crowned by the pope, if precedents were any guide, and had large interests in Italy and especially in Lombardy, interests which in turn were of no small concern to the papacy. The Milanese matter was far from being solved (see above p. 145). But to make the picture complete, in 1075 Gregory had forbidden Henry IV in no uncertain terms to continue with the investiture of high-ranking ecclesiastics, yet the king carried on as before, not only in Germany, which would have been, at this juncture, of lesser moment to the papacy, but above all in Italy. In this same year he appointed the bishops of Spoleto and of Fermo, and without further scruples nominated (whilst Godfrey as consecrated archbishop of Milan was unable to take possession of his see and even unable to maintain himself) a third man as archbishop of Milan, so that there now were three claimants (Godfrey, Atto and now Thedald), of whom two were the king's candidates. It was a situation on the very door-step, so to speak, of the papacy which no pope could have tolerated for any length of time.

The challenge which Gregory issued to Henry IV on 8 December 1075 was intended to be an ultimatum and it was understood as such. The king was peremptorily told to abstain from any further contact with his counsellors excommunicated by Alexander II (see above p. 145) (excommunication being held to be a contagious disease). He was reproached for setting aside divine and canon law by his episcopal and abbatial appointments and threatened with the fate of Saul should he disregard this warning. This constituted the opening of the perhaps most ferocious and bitterly fought battle between a medieval king and the papacy. And it was a battle that concerned basic principles on both sides – and one of them was the final control of the clergy. Was this, as hitherto practised, to remain in the hands of the king or other laymen, or in the hands of the papacy which based its claim on the refurbished canon law and the interpretation of divine law? In support of the former was history, tradition and custom – in support of the latter medieval Christian ideology and ecclesiastical doctrine. In some ways this was reminiscent of the fifth-century conflict between Constantinople and Rome which also concerned the challenge of history by faith.

Henry IV accepted the challenge, as every king was bound to do, because on the control of the clergy, especially the higher clergy, public government to a very large extent depended. Encouraged by the recent victory over the Saxons Henry summoned a synod of his bishops at Worms for the end of January 1076. Political sagacity and diplomatic skill seem to have deserted the royal government as well as the synod which were very much influenced by the scandalmongering of Cardinal Hugh the White (who for reasons quite unconnected with this issue had broken with Gregory). Because of Gregory's attacks on simony, concubinage and especially royal investiture the German (as well as Lombard) bishops were in any case hostile to the papal programme which they considered subversive. The assembly at Worms answered the ultimatum of the papacy with the charge that the pope was uncanonically elected – after having been undisputed pope for nearly three years – and as 'the false monk Hildebrand' he was ordered 'to descend from the apostolic chair'. The assembly viewed Gregory's ecclesiastical measures as wholly uncanonical. Instead of stigmatizing the pope the aggressor, this defiant, not to say desperate move turned him into one who, in the eyes of the world, was wantonly attacked by the Germans.

At the Lenten synod a few weeks later the papacy replied in kind, but infinitely more effectively: King Henry IV was excommunicated, (provisionally) deposed as king and his subjects released from the oath of allegiance and fidelity which they had

F

taken to him. In the twentieth century the dramatic nature of these steps can hardly be adequately appreciated. No king had ever formally been excommunicated nor the exercise of his royal power denied by the papacy – and all this barely 30 years after the young Henry's father, the third Henry, had deposed and installed a number of popes. Moreover, all the German bishops who had taken part at the Worms declaration, were to be suspended unless they made amends by 1 August 1076, while their leader, the archbishop of Mainz, as well as the Lombard bishops, were excommunicated. In the following weeks the king and his advisers showed a lack of wisdom and foresight which was really remarkable. At Utrecht where he celebrated Easter, Henry attended Easter services in full royal regalia in the company of a great number of bishops and declared Gregory VII, now a mere 'Monk Hildebrand', deposed as pope. At no time had a pope ever been deposed by a mere declaration made some thousand miles away. When popes were formerly deposed, the king was with his army in Rome.

All these defiant declarations on the part of Henry and his government could not disguise the weakness of his position, for despite a certain sympathy displayed by England, France, Southern Italy and an initial episcopal support, the subsequent months all too clearly proved that Henry had entered the theatre of war without adequate preparation. He had wholly misjudged the temper of the time which in any case (and not always influenced by the papacy) had largely accepted the premisses applied by Gregory VII. Large-scale defections took place in the summer months and, from the military standpoint, a very serious situation arose for the king when the recently defeated Saxons made common cause with some South German rebellious princes. Those who had not yet seceded by October 1076, were persuaded to do so by the papal legates who convinced many doubters of the correctness of the papal step and the indefensible measures taken by the king. In October 1076 forsaken by most of his followers, he promised to abstain from all governmental activity and to obtain absolution from the pope within a year and a day from the date of his excommunication, while the German princes invited the pope to preside over a diet at Augsburg in the following February 1077 to arbitrate between the king and themselves. Shortly afterwards the king, accompanied by his immediate household, set out on his journey to Italy in order to meet the pope who was already on the way to Germany. A very severe winter – even the Rhine was frozen – prevented Gregory from proceeding further than Lombardy where at the castle of Mathilda of Tuscany, Canossa (at the foot of the Appenines), he waited for the escort to be sent by the German princes.

It was here at Canossa that after a dangerous and excruciatingly difficult crossing of the Alps by way of the Mont Cenis, Henry asked to meet the pope. The meetings began on 25 January 1077 and ended after three days. The pope could hardly do anything else but admit Henry to union with the Church again, but, as Gregory explicitly stated three years later, he did not reinstate Henry in his kingship, because 'the whole matter was in suspense' until the projected diet at Augsburg. The king's release from excommunication was conditioned by his promise not to put any obstacles into the path of the pope on his way to Germany. That the pope still considered Henry a king, albeit denied the exercise of his government, is convincingly proved by his taking the oath ('I, King Henry') confirming his promises not personally, but through the medium of two bishops. Throughout the following three years Gregory referred to Henry as king. The problem of royal investitures was not discussed at Canossa.

The significance of Canossa and of the events leading to it, was that a king who had been excommunicated, not for any aberration from the faith, but for defiance of the papal law and disobedience to papal orders, and who had additionally been suspended from rulership, had sought (and obtained) absolution from the pope. It was the first time that the papacy was able to display this authority towards the most powerful king in Europe who was forced to appear in the guise of a penitent. This and the rapidity of events – it was not yet two years since the investiture decree had been passed at the synod of 1075 – convincingly proved how brittle royal power was and what strength and support the papacy had gained in the preceding two decades since Henry III's death. The situation also showed that the soil was in fact ready for the reception of and fertilization with papal governmental ideas. Otherwise it would be hard to explain how the papacy whose relations with the Normans, its only military ally, were not at that very time particularly cordial, could have advanced so swiftly and with such remarkable assuredness. The picture would not be complete, if no reference were made to the initially defiant support of Henry's cause by the Lombard bishops and nobility. But the German bishops who were soon followed by their Lombard colleagues, thought it prudent to leave the camp of their king one by one and join the winning side. Adherence to principles was rarely the hallmark of medieval bishops.

It is nevertheless understandable that the quick succession of these dramatic events and the spectacular conclusion at Canossa provided a somewhat severe shock to contemporaries. Some of them were apparently perturbed by the excommunication of a king who was king by the grace of God and by the release of his subjects from obligations contained in their oath of allegiance. Gregory took great trouble to allay these apprehensions explaining that the pope's power to bind and to loosen was all-embracing and that it exempted no one, not even a king, and that no matter was excluded from its jurisdiction. If, he said, the apostolic chair had the power to judge spiritual things, why not also worldly and secular things? Every cleric, including the lowest exorcist, had a superiority of rank in comparison with any lay Ruler, because he was 'a spiritual emperor' to whom lay persons were subjected. Behind these ideas expressed with great forcefulness and consistency lies a view of society and its structure which flatly contradicted the traditional and existing set-up. Here the conflict between tradition and history on the one hand and ecclesiastical ideology on the other hand, came to be sharply focalized on the two office holders themselves, the king and the pope. Seen from another angle, the conflict was a battle between Germanism and Romanism. In the long run it was ecclesiastical Romanism which was to conquer and this victory was overwhelmingly due to its innate intellectual superiority. Its Germanic-royal opponent had nothing in store with which effectively to counteract it.

One more significant feature of these epoch-making events must be mentioned, that is, that the situation in the seventies produced a special kind of publicistic literature in the shape of short tracts, pamphlets and topical treatises. Their aim was to create and to shape public opinion in support of one of the contesting sides. Some were frankly partisan, but the majority was severely scholarly. There was not, of course, any centralized direction of this what might in modern terms be called propagandistic effort. This upsurge shows that the men were available, that they had at their disposal the necessary intellectual equipment and that the conflict was – not unjustifiably – understood by contemporaries to be not merely concerned with the position of a king or a pope, but with all strata of society. The standing of the laity as such within Christian society came to be questioned, as also were its relations with the clergy. This indeed was the crux of the matter and readily explains why some contemporaries compared the effects to the tremors of an earthquake. It was a revolution from above. The pillars of established society seemed to crumble. The public addressed by these literary efforts was very small, although the circle of those who were influenced speedily increased. Whilst the authors on the side of the king were wholly on the defensive and largely taken unawares by the events, the writers on the papal side showed a state of intellectual preparedness in setting forth their aim which was to bring 'order' into society.

The immediate effect of Canossa was that, although not restored to kingship, Henry IV was no longer excommunicated and could therefore take part in public and governmental business, albeit with diminished authority. The pope's astringent action nevertheless antagonized a number of princes in Germany, because without having been consulted they were faced by a *fait accompli*. At Forchheim in Bavaria on 15 March 1077 they elected an anti-king in the person of Rudolf of Rheinfelden, a brother-in-law of Henry IV: the princes had not consulted the pope. The result was civil war in Germany. Although the weather had sufficiently improved by March for Gregory to continue the journey to Germany, conditions in Rome necessitated his immediate return. But he never gave up his plan of going to Germany to preside over a German diet. It was his stubborn adherence to this plan which not only prolonged the German civil war but also caused some recovery on the part of Henry's fortunes, because the waverers believed they could detect vacillation and irresolution in Gregory. Despite a bustling papal activity displayed on all sides, there was some danger of the papacy's losing the initiative in Germany, and it was this which prompted the pope to proceed to the second excommunication of Henry IV and his final deposition as king in the Lenten synod of 1080. The breach was complete and beyond repair.

Like its antecedent some four years earlier, this papal measure was preceded by a solemn prayer to St Peter and Paul. The pope invoked their help and proclaimed to the world the punitive measures against the German king, by declaring that the papacy had the right to take away empires, kingdoms, principalities and all possessions of man and to grant these to anyone who deserved them. The thesis behind this verdict was that whatever a Christian held – it might be a kingdom, an empire or simple possessions – he held through the working of divine grace (on the Pauline principle 'By the grace of God I am what I am') and, evidently, matters of divine grace came into the orbit of papal jurisdiction. It was precisely against this that Henry had protested earlier asserting his exemption from papal jurisdiction because he was an anointed king, the 'Lord's anointed', and as such could not be touched by anyone, including the pope. In support of this he invoked the psalmist's 'Do not touch mine anointed'. In his 'prayer' to the two apostles Gregory VII gave his reply and thereby formulated a principle of papal law that was to be valid for the rest of the Middle Ages.

The subsequent events completed what was begun in 1076 and 1077. Surrounded by some of his bishops – mostly those who had incurred papal censures – Henry presided over a synod at Mainz on 13 May 1080 which decided upon the final deposition of Gregory VII. At the synod at Brixen on 25 June 1080 attended also by some Lombard and Burgundian bishops, the archbishop of Ravenna, the former chancellor of the German king in Italy, and also one of those suspended and excommunicated by Gregory, Wibert of Ravenna, was elected as anti-pope in the place of Gregory. Culturally, educationally and also socially Clement III was far superior to his rival. He belonged to the conservative section of the North Italian bishops, and by accepting election the royal schism in Germany was now accompanied by a papal schism. It was not until four years later that Clement and Henry could set foot in the city of Rome. At Easter 1084 Henry was crowned emperor of the Romans by Clement III in the same basilica of St Peter in which he himself had been crowned shortly before (on 24 March 1084) as pope.

Meanwhile Gregory had taken refuge in the castle of S. Angelo, ever since the Romans and especially the Roman aristocracy had shown their animosity, if not hostility, to him because of the dangers to which the city had become exposed as a result of his pontificate. It was in fact the Romans who had invited Henry and his pope into the city. The general hostility prevailing in Rome against the pope can perhaps best be gauged by the wholesale defection of 13 of his cardinals together with some high-ranking curial officials. In this extreme hour of need Gregory appealed to the Normans, and Robert Guiscard responded to the call. Although they drove out the Germans, the subsequent devastation of Rome now made the Romans rise against the Normans, with the result that they had to flee, taking the pope with them. He was made responsible by the Romans for all the misery that visited the city. Gregory took refuge in Monte Cassino and later in Salerno, where on 25 May 1085 he died, deserted by virtually everyone. After one of the most eventful and dramatic pontificates the papacy seemed to have lost a decisive battle. What this pontificate left behind was, allegorically speaking, the havoc and ruin caused by a tornado.

There can be no legitimate doubt that Gregory's strategic (and not merely tactical) mistake lay in dealing with kingship. Henry IV was a mere king, and not an emperor, and the papacy had not by that time sufficient armoury at its disposal to tackle this most delicate of all delicate problems. Where the papacy was properly equipped and had all the necessary arguments available was in questions of Roman emperorship but this was never a problem during the Investiture Contest. It was the papacy under Innocent III which was to draw the lesson from Gregory's mistake: then indeed the papacy sonorously proclaimed that the question of German kingship as distinct from emperorship was not a papal concern. Yet it was Gregory's strategic error which must be held largely responsible for the serious doubt which beset a great many of his ideological followers some of whom deserted him, because they were not convinced of the rightness of his proceedings. It was not so much the prohibition of lay investiture and its attendant problems which caused a detachment from the papal standpoint amongst a number of his influential contemporaries, as his open attack on kingship and his claim to settle himself and finally the question who should be the German king which evoked so many misgivings amongst many of his followers. Moreover, the claim of the papacy to pronounce on the legitimacy of Rulership was one that was of direct concern to every Western Ruler.

Yet although the impression immediately prevailing at the end of this stormy pontificate was one of failure, if not outright disaster, the fearless and consistent application of ancient, mature papal-hierocratic ideas engendered its own momentum and potently contributed to the erosion and eventual reduction of royal power in ecclesiastical matters. For it was religious faith which provided the cementing bond of society and it was upon it that society was built: but the final verdict in this sphere was the papacy's. The over-all result was that the tradition enshrined in Germanic customs and deeply pervading the matrix of contemporary society had suffered so severe a blow by this frontal assault of Roman ecclesiastical ideology that despite its initial show of force and merely apparent success it could never recover from the wounds received. Indeed, the Germanic system was too hollow to withstand the attack of the sophisticated Romanism. And it was not long before practice and reality began to march in step with this ecclesiastical Romanism.

On the level of government the conflict had centred on the authority and proper function of king and pope within a Christian society. By introducing the ancient, albeit flexible, notion of order, the papal-hierocratic side had at its disposal a weapon against which the royal side had very little to set, except history and custom. It was in this context that Gregory VII was said to have made the highly significant statement: 'The Lord did not say "I am custom" but "I am the truth".' This epitomizes rather well what separated king and pope, the one reflecting history and tradition, the other mirroring a rationally conceived plan and aim. 'Truth' and 'custom' need not be identical. But the repercussions of this conflict went far deeper, for as already indicated, the king, in some not unimportant respects, stood so to speak as the symbol of the laity which not unjustifiably considered itself attacked by the ecclesiastics. Hence not only the already mentioned upsurge of the so-called publicistic literature, but also the search on the part of the lay public for a platform with the help of which it might be possible to answer some of the arguments employed by the hierocratic party.

In the present context it is only necessary to make a brief reference to two distinctive developments which the application of papal ideology conditioned. The one was the utilization of the Roman law in the shape of Justinian's Code. Since the hierocratic party so strongly insisted on the law the most promising counter-attack seemed to lie in harnessing the already available Roman law against the law created or applied by the papacy. For this Roman law was at least the law of lay Rulers. Yet in the end this source of assistance did not and could not render much help, for it was basically late-Roman imperial law that manifested exactly the same ideological premisses which the emerging papal canon law showed. To employ Roman law, especially the Code, in the service of royalty, was to use the wrong weapon for the right purpose, for nowhere did Roman law deal with royal rights: the whole concept of a king was unknown to the Roman emperors, the predecessors and successors of Justinian. In brief, the Roman law of which by 1084 the first use was made in the conflict, could not and did not supply the means with which the hierocratic ideology could be dislodged. To do this either a Germanic ideology – as distinct from custom – or an entirely different ideology was called for. The former had no articulated spokesman, even if there had been something approaching an ideology, and the latter was not as yet available in the shape of Aristotle. All education having been in the hands of ecclesiastics for centuries, it is not difficult to see why the royal side had so little with which it could fight back. The dice was heavily loaded in favour of Roman ecclesiastical ideology. What the royal side dimly grasped was the conceptual need of a body – the State – which was autonomous, self-sufficient and independent. But the royal foundations themselves (which were overwhelmingly theocratic and religious) militated against the construction of anything that approximated the concept of the State. The royal side lacked the tools with which to construct an effective counterweight against the ecclesiological assumptions. It was the revived Aristotle who was to furnish these tools in the thirteenth century.

The other development was directly linked with this resuscitation of Roman law. However little effective support it gave to the royal side, it nevertheless, precisely because it was a lay Ruler's law, contained some elements which, when skilfully used, could curtail the efficacy of the papal-hierocratic scheme. That is to say, the presupposition for a useful deployment of Roman law was scientific penetration into its structure, framework and maxims. This was scholarly technique which could be learned and mastered only by a long process – this, in other words, was one of the factors favourable to the growth of universities. Above all, the study of Roman law greatly stimulated medieval political ideas and became in course of time an indispensable requisite within the precincts of the science of government. In fact, initially the medieval universities were a specific response to the needs of the late eleventh and early twelfth centuries which also explains why the early teachers and pupils were all laymen. It was no coincidence that the first product using Roman law as a tool against the papal canon law came from Ravenna where indeed there had been a university which was however soon to be supplanted by neighbouring Bologna. This became the citadel of all legal studies in the Middle Ages and was a direct offshoot of the conflict between the papacy and the German emperor, Henry V, the son and successor of Henry IV.

In one more, and indirect, way did the contemporary papacy contribute to scholarship. It was Urban II, the next but one successor of Gregory VII, who in a seemingly routine administrative act gave birth to what shortly afterwards became a specific mode of enquiry. Precisely because the papacy laid such crucial stress on the law, and because there were many laws issued at different times and as often as not contradicting each other, the question naturally arose as to which of these laws should be applied. And the advice which Urban II gave, was that because the laws were emanations of the human mind and this in its turn a divine gift incapable of contradicting itself, it was the task of the interpreter and administrator of the law to solve the apparent contradictions. The means to do this was the mental operation of a distinction. A distinction should be drawn (he counselled) between laws which were immutable and laws which were not because prompted by the exigencies of time, place and persons. Thereby a firm footing was established and a principle laid down which was capable of infinitely varied expansion. In its fully developed state the method suggested by Urban was applicable to canon law and Roman law as well as to theology and philosophy, in short to all branches of learning, because they all suffered from the same weakness, that is contradictions. The much desired harmony of the intellectual and real world demanded a method by which the *contrarietates* (as the contradictions were known) could be solved, and Urban's advice when adopted became the dialectical method of enquiry. It was to fructify all scholarship.

What the post-Gregorian papacy needed was a period free from drama, sudden convulsions and embittered recriminations, a period in which the principles of Gregory VII could be applied without causing similarly drastic upheavals. While smoothness, flexibility, coolness and adjustability characterized Urban II's mode of the government, in its aim and substance it pursued the path laid down by his great predecessor. What differed was the external manner with which the papal-hierocratic ideas were put into practice: Gregorianism was tempered by the soft furnishings of aristocratic judiciousness and lofty detachment. The issues of the Investiture Contest had naturally been exactly the same in France and in England as they had been in Germany. Through the efforts of Ivo, bishop of Chartres, and the velvety diplomatic skill of Urban II, himself a Frenchman, an accommodation with France was reached by 1098: it rested on a distinction first made by an eminent Italian scholar, Guido of Ferrara, in the late eighties, according to whom the properly ecclesiastical functions of the bishop (or abbot) should be strictly separated from his mundane, territorial or secular functions. Consequently, only the competent ecclesiastical authority could confer the former, while for the conferment of the latter (the estates, judiciary, militia, etc. comprising the so-called regalian rights) the royal or other secular authority was competent. This was the formula adopted by Ivo of Chartres, and a few years later (1105) also for the English settlement (see below pp. 167f.). The pope himself was not directly a party to these arrangements, but approved them. It was in fact under Urban II that the papacy began to reach the position for which Gregory had striven. In a number of ways this pontificate accomplished and brought to a conclusion what his predecessor had begun, notably in France and in Spain where the restructuring of the ecclesiastical organism was set in train. The intellectual and moral leadership of Europe passed now into the hands of the papacy – the true bequest of Gregory's pontificate.

Nothing better illustrates the heightened prestige of the papacy than the highly successful resumption of the crusading idea – originally Gregory VII's – by Urban II. He assessed correctly the depth of the religious fervour and zeal amongst the French and Lorraine peasant masses and also took into account the fairly recently emerged knightly class – the *milites* – which recruited itself from the military administrators and higher servants of the powerful lords. He had the gift of appealing to, and influencing, the French masses and had also the skill to select the right preachers to propagate the idea of a crusade. The result was something approaching a mass-psychosis, to which the recently awakened religious fervour as well as the crusaders' privileges were contributory factors: indulgences were granted as was immunity from taxes and tolls as well as a moratorium for civil debts. The crusader entered the papal 'family' and enjoyed a greatly increased personal protection. The crusades were always a specific papal undertaking and under papal leadership, even if this was not directly exercised as Gregory had envisaged. They provided a release of pent-up energies in the service of a religious ideal and by means of a military aggression that was suitably buttressed by the convenient Augustinian theory of the just war. Yet it should never be forgotten that to the liberation of the Holy Land, universally held to be the prime objective, was joined another and at least as powerful motive, that is, the establishment of Roman primatial rights in Constantinople in order to end the schism. This, indeed, was what Gregory had proclaimed as the prime consideration.

That so many crusading enterprises ended in disaster, if not catastrophe, was due to faulty organization, defective preparations and inadequate leadership in the field. The papacy had successfully started the movement, but had not the means either to carry out the individual enterprise or to establish satisfactory conditions in the conquered districts. Leaving aside some temporary and isolated successes, it proved impossible to transplant the social conditions of Western Europe into regions totally different in their social and cultural structure – the liberators came to be looked upon more often than not as conquerors by the native population. To this difficulty must be added the related one of how to provide for suitable ecclesiastical personnel in the Church now organized on Western-Latin principles. And the distrust and suspicion with which Constantinople – not without justification – viewed the crusading armies, which as often as not plundered and marauded Byzantine territories, hardly helped the cause; and Constantinople had every reason to fear for the security of its empire in view of the aggressiveness of the Western imperially led armies. Most of these features were clearly discernible during the first crusade which, as far as Europe was concerned, established and confirmed the papacy in its undoubted leadership, one of the numerous Gregorian legacies.

What needs stressing, however, is that in the first crusade, so successfully launched by the papacy, there was virtually no German participation. The explanation was that the strife of the papacy with Germany was still far from approaching a settlement satisfactory to both parties. The reason why it was possible to effect agreements in France and England with comparatively little effort was that neither country had any economic or military strategic interests in Italy nor had their kings any aspirations towards an imperial dignity; their relations with the papacy itself never reached the closeness which characterized those of Germany. History bore hard upon the papacy in its relations with Germany.

That William the Conqueror made good episcopal appointments was certainly true, but this was not something that necessarily would have inclined the papacy favourably towards him, because it was primarily interested in upholding papal principles, and of these William took little notice. From the papal point of view the government of the Conqueror would have earned much severer censure than Henry IV's, and this not only on account of the numerous episcopal appointments made by him, but also in view of his legislation. Indeed, Urban II conceded to William II that only with royal permission could papal legates enter England. Anselm of Canterbury's relations with this king were characterized by the former's high-minded adherence to papal principles which found no response whatsoever in the latter. Anselm went into exile. After his accession Henry I recalled the archbishop who referring to the repeated papal and synodal legislation concerning investitures, refused to accept the archbishopric from the king; Anselm went into exile for a second time. This reaction of Anselm who after all had only recently taken part in synods which had reiterated the prohibition of lay investiture, met with opposition both from the king and the overwhelming part of the English episcopate, their point being that royal investiture had always been traditional. Realizing the strength of the English opposition Anselm suggested to the papacy that the general prohibition be relaxed in England. This proposal met with a defiantly negative response by Paschal II. In order to escape threatened ecclesiastical censures Henry I reached a settlement with Anselm (July 1105) renouncing investiture with ring and staff; Anselm conceded that the bishops could take the oath of fealty. This arrangement needed papal approval which was in due course obtained. Neither in France nor in England did any ancillary questions enter.

But the German king was, so to speak, the presumptive emperor of the Romans in whom as its own and specific creation the papacy always had taken – and was to take – a decisive interest. Having clashed with the German king, it would have been the height of unstatesmanlike conduct to exhibit an inflexible dogmatism also in regard to the other Western kings. This was a feature of papal policy which began in the late eleventh century and was to show itself ever more markedly throughout the twelfth and thirteenth centuries, with the result that the French and English kings were able to muster strength and pursue a policy almost unimpeded by the papacy whereas Germany with its Italian appendices and strong ties with the papacy was the main theatre of war, ideologically, ecclesiastically and militarily.

The main reason for a delayed settlement with Germany in the late eleventh and early twelfth centuries was not only this close and historically conditioned German involvement in Italian and papal affairs but also the wealth and power of the German bishops and abbots which was far greater than that of their French or English colleagues. Despite contrary appearances before his succession in 1106 the second oldest son of Henry IV, Henry V, had taken up a standpoint in the matter of investitures which in no way differed from that of his father. His desired promotion to the emperorship brought matters to a head. With a strong army he came to Rome to be crowned emperor by the pope, as only the pope could confer imperial dignity. Paschal II and the imperial aspirant, Henry V, reached agreement before the (abortive) coronation according to which the pope declared himself ready to order the bishops to renounce all their worldly positions embraced in the regalian rights and to live by the alms and oblations which they were to receive from the faithful. The bishops (and abbots) were to hand back to the king all their estates, goods, mints, hundred courts, and so on. In return the king was willing to give up the right of investiture – in itself an empty gesture because the bishops would in any case have lost all importance in the public field. But when on the occasion of the planned imperial coronation on 12 February 1111 Paschal read out the treaty, there was such an uproar in the basilica of St Peter's that it was impossible to proceed to the coronation. Both ecclesiastical and secular princes adamantly opposed the arrangement, the former because as powerful princes they would have been reduced to misery and poverty, the latter because they feared the sudden and respectable increase in power on the part of the king through the accumulation of economic wealth. The pope refused to officiate, whereupon Henry V made short shrift of the matter and had him and his cardinals imprisoned and taken to an 'honourable' detention outside Rome. After two months Paschal's power of resistance was broken, and he gave in by allowing Henry to continue with the investitures by ring and staff and by accepting the mere promise by the king that he was not to hinder canonical elections – hardly more than a gesture; he also received the papal promise of complete amnesty for the act of 12 February as well as the assurance that he would never be excommunicated by the papacy. The imperial coronation took place on 13 April 1111.

By any standards this what was technically called a papal *Privilegium* (because the papacy conceded rights) was invalid. It was the result of blackmail, since the pope as a prisoner was no free agent. But apart from this, as soon as the contents became known there arose a storm of protest throughout Western Christendom, except of course in Germany. The *Privilegium* was stigmatized a *Pravilegium* because it conceded what had been condemned for so long by the papacy, synods and the overwhelming ecclesiastical opinion. The detailed justificatory memoranda issued by Paschal II and independently of him by Henry V, in which both set forth the merits of the agreement, only fanned further protests. The opposition was particularly strong in France, where Archbishop Guido of Vienne and the abbot of Vendome (Godfrey) were bitter critics, not of the papacy, but of the pope. The primate of France, Archbishop Joscelin of Lyons, toyed with the idea of convoking a synod which was to condemn the *Pravilegium* as heretical. Ivo of Chartres managed to avert the danger of a schism.

In the Lateran synod held in March 1112 Paschal came to realize the strength of the opposition and virtually retracted his concession by declaring that whatever Gregory VII and Urban II had condemned and rejected, he too would condemn and reject. The French synod under Guido of Vienne in 1112 also rejected the document as being null and void, declared all investitures to be heretical, excommunicated Henry V as a second Judas and threatened Paschal with deposition, if he did not confirm these (French) synodal decrees. Although he did not at first openly do so – his reason being that he felt himself bound by his oath not to excommunicate Henry for imprisoning him – his legates, Cardinals Cuno (of Palestrina) and Dietrich, excommunicated the emperor. The Lateran synod of March 1116 chaired by Paschal adopted the view of the French synod four years earlier, also declared investiture by a layman heretical and confirmed the actions of the cardinals which therefore did not necessitate a repetition of Henry's excommunication by name. Even in Germany the climate of opinion had by now almost wholly swung round to the Gregorian point of view, and the anti-pope appointed by Henry V (Gregory VIII) led barely a shadowy existence. The long-drawn-out war of attrition was to show its fruits.

The resoluteness and consistency with which the papal standpoint had been pursued (although not always by the pope), made the soil receptive in Germany for a final arrangement with the papacy. In its essentials this was not different from the settlement reached with England and France a quarter of a century earlier. True, there were protracted negotiations which began in the spring of 1119, but in the end attrition and weariness on the German side inclined even the emperor and his counsellors to reach an accommodation. The settlement, a true compromise, preceded by months of intense and hard bargaining and negotiations conducted by patient and able legations, laid down that the king (or emperor) would renounce investiture with ring and staff and that the higher ecclesiastics at least were to be elected canonically, that is, freely and without influence by the secular Ruler, and inducted into their ecclesiastical office by the metropolitan. But the king was permitted to be present at the election; in case of differences of opinion, the so-called *pars sanior* (that is, the weightier and more important part of the electors according to their standing and authority – not the simple numerical majority) was to decide, and the king was to abide by the verdict rendered by the metropolitan and other bishops of the province.

Once elected, the candidate was then to be enfeoffed by the Ruler with the sceptre before consecration, in Germany proper, while in Italy and Burgundy consecration preceded the enfeoffment by the Ruler which had to take place within six months afterwards. It was an arrangement which was intended to be temporary, but as it often is with temporary arrangements, they have a habit of becoming permanent, and this was also true of the final settlement reached at Worms on 23 September 1122.

This so-called concordat of Worms bristled with difficulties. The rights conceded to the king were conceded to him personally, to Henry V, while the concessions he made were made to the papacy as such, that is, to the institution, and not to the pope, Calixtus II, the former archbishop of Vienne (see above p. 169). The principle of the *pars sanior* together with the possibility of the royal presence at elections was a virtual invitation to make the royal will a decisive factor, although the king himself was never an elector. Further, the electors themselves – usually the cathedral chapters – came overwhelmingly from the aristocratic families which thus obtained a legalized influence on elections. Some of these difficulties were not to be eradicated until the papacy was in a position to create its own legal machinery by which in certain respects control and supervision of elections to high ecclesiastical office could be secured. But this was not the case until nearly a century later. In one point the Worms settlement was clear and unambiguous. The proprietary church system – the most obnoxious Germanic feature from the papacy's point of view – was abolished. The ecclesiastical office and the ecclesiastical benefice were clearly distinguished. The former was to be exclusively a matter for the clerics, who were not to be defiled by lay hands, and ring and staff were to be returned to their original meaning as ecclesiastical symbols. The ecclesiastical benefice was to be exclusively a matter for the lay Ruler and was to be handed over by the usual contemporary means, that is in the form of the sceptre. But the over-all significance of this settlement was that in regard to the composition, structure and organization of the ecclesiastical electoral body the determinative influence of the Ruler was excluded. On the whole, precisely because it was a mere compromise, the settlement served its main purpose of bringing a dismal conflict to an end. What the compromise persuasively showed was that the German ecclesiastical and secular princes now fully acknowledged the jurisdictional and magisterial primacy of the papacy. Lay investiture was removed for good and as a result of this settlement the Italian episcopate became virtually independent of the emperor. That Worms signified the decline of royal as well as imperial power in Germany is evident. The First Lateran Council of 1123 ratified the settlement solemnly. Between Henry III and his grandson, Henry V, between 1046 and 1122, a radical change in the standing, authority and prestige of the papacy had taken place. What the institution now needed was both a constitution and a system of law that were commensurate to the tasks and functions of the papacy as a focal point of Europe.

8 *Tensions and Conflicts*

IN THE TWELFTH century the papacy had to face two fronts. Each was intimately connected with the development of the papacy itself. The domestic or curial tension leading to bitter animosity within the close circle of the Roman Church and finally to schism, was conditioned by the re-emergence of the rivalry of Roman aristocratic families. The consequent tension manifested itself within the College of Cardinals, since it was this body which elected the pope and was also his senate; it formed the platform where conflicting interests were bound to clash. Moreover, it was not a simple resuscitation of the old family feuds now merely transferred to the College of Cardinals. A new kind of aristocracy had emerged, the rich, moneyed cliques, whose assets were wide, and who had varied economic interests including the loan of money to clients on an international scale. The family which by the twenties of the twelfth century had come to the foreground was that of the Pierleoni, whose strength lay almost wholly in ready money which was loaned to the papacy, from Urban II's pontificate onwards.

The other source of tension was Germany, and frequently enough the domestic and the 'foreign' tensions combined and intertwined. For as a result of the Investiture Contest German rulership had been greatly weakened. The historically evolved bases of German kingship had been neutralized by the consistent application of Roman papal ideology. But – and this was the crucial point – now that kingship could no longer rely on its Germanic bases, the potentialities of Roman emperorship began to be grasped with all the greater clarity and alacrity. Not only was the whole body of Roman law readily at hand, but also the professional and highly skilled expositors of this legal system – they were trained at the universities, notably at Bologna. Yet this imperially conceived and legally supported Rulership raised claims which were wholly at variance with the essence of the same Rulership as perceived by its creator, the papacy. Hence the tension and acrimonious conflicts which cast such a deep shadow on both the papacy and the empire from the fifties of the twelfth century onwards.

The vacancy created by the death of Calixtus II in 1124 brought the two factions in the College of Cardinals to the fore. The party of the Pierleoni – the wealthy family which had only fairly recently been converted from Judaism to Christianity – managed to get their candidate, the cardinal-priest Theobald elected as Celestine II. Hardly had he accepted the unanimous election and hardly had the *Te Deum* finished when an armed group of the Frangipani party led by Cardinal Aimeric entered the Lateran and forcibly ejected the newly created pope. He resigned at once having suffered in the mêlée some injuries from which he soon afterwards died. The cardinals accepted the resignation, proceeded to another election and chose the candidate of the conservative Frangipani, the cardinal-bishop of Ostia, as Honorius II.

At exactly the same time the new king in Germany, Lothar III of Supplinburg, showed himself anxious from the outset to be accommodating to the papacy. The change of temper of the time was perhaps best illustrated by his supplication to the papacy to confirm his election which was certainly an extraordinary request, because thereby the papacy was offered a means to intervene in royal elections. This request in fact indicated how far the papal programme had been accepted. On the other hand, the Normans in Southern Italy and Sicily invaded Apulia, of which the papacy was the feudal lord. Moreover through the uniting of Apulia with Sicily a very powerful and well-organized Norman block had arisen – a situation which the papacy could not accept with equanimity. Immediately Roger II of Sicily found himself excommunicated by the papacy which began an ill-prepared military operation against him. Nevertheless, in the treaty of Benevento (22 August 1128) the papacy reached some accommodation with this powerful king: its terms were more in the nature of a truce than a final settlement: it was a compromise.

Precisely because the papacy's attention was concentrated on the Norman question, the pope himself spent a considerable time away from the Lateran where tensions within the College of Cardinals increased. Cardinal Aimeric had become the leading spirit in the curia and also exercised a great influence on the creation of new cardinals during Honorius' pontificate. It did not come as a surprise that on the death of Honorius II the tensions between the Frangipani and the Pierleoni factions in the College of Cardinals once more erupted. In a somewhat precipitate manner the 16 younger cardinals – created mostly under Aimeric's influence – belonging to the Frangipani party elected Cardinal Gregory Papareschi as Innocent II. The same night and only a few hours later (13–14 April 1130) the remaining 14 electors who had been confronted by this *fait accompli* and who had been left completely in the dark about the machinations of their colleagues, refused to acknowledge the validity of this 'election' and proceeded in the church of S. Marco in Rome to the election of Cardinal Peter Pierleoni as Anacletus II: the 14 electors were joined by 10 of the other party during the same night, so that it was possible to say the Anacletus had the majority of the College of Cardinals on his side. Anacletus II was a direct descendant of the rich banker who had been baptized only two generations earlier.

The difficulty which this double election highlighted lay in the deficiency of the electoral decree of 1059 which had made no provision for this sort of contingency. It should be added that the election of Innocent II was carried out immediately after the funeral of Honorius II who was buried without any ceremony, most hastily in the late hours of the 13 April. Certainly, chronological priority belonged to this election. He was also at once enthroned after the 16 cardinals had acclaimed him as pope, but on the other hand Anacletus was eventually elected by the majority of cardinals. As there was no inclination on the part of either 'pope' to withdraw, the schism which was already a distinct contingency at the election of Honorius, became a reality. Rome itself recognized only Anacletus II and this was wholly due to the great power and influence which the Pierleoni wielded in the city administration; their bankers spent considerable sums on supporting their candidate. Innocent II had to flee Rome.

As an institution the papacy suffered less from this schism than might have been expected. Principles were not conspicuously affected. What was conspicuous was the brutal management of the election procedure which in its turn showed how defective the election machinery really was. The significance of this situation was that wholly non-papal if not non-ecclesiastical interests had been allowed to influence the election decisively. The root of the uncanonical election lay no longer outside the curia but within its bosom in the College of Cardinals. Non-ecclesiastical pressure groups operated through the College and their interests became articulate in this closed body. The other point to be noted is that it depended entirely on the great European powers, and no longer on the city of Rome which of the two contestants was to be recognized. Paradoxically enough, this schism showed conclusively what standing the papacy had achieved in Europe. Because the schism hardly manifested any clash of great principles, the literary activity as well as the public addresses on behalf of each pope resorted with great facility to what might well be termed mud-slinging and unsavoury attacks, and in this the Innocentian side was particularly virulent, as in a somewhat un-christian spirit it made the Jewish descendancy of Anacletus II one of the main targets of its polemics.

Although Anacletus had undisputed control over Rome, there could be no doubt that Innocent II commanded overwhelming support abroad. The three powers which mattered most were France, England and Germany, and in all three powerful influences were at work on behalf of Innocent who had close links with the old and new religious Orders. In France especially it was Bernard of Clairvaux – soon to become the uncrowned emperor of Europe – who persuaded the French government and hierarchy to accept Innocent as the lawful pope: at the synod of Étampes in September 1130 Innocent was solemnly and formally recognized as the successor of St Peter. Only a few months later Henry I of England followed in the steps of Louis VI of France: Henry's recognition of Innocent in January 1131 was also the result of Bernard's persuasive powers. In Germany the founder of the Premonstratension Order, Norbert, was very active in the cause of Innocent, and Lothar as well as the German hierarchy and secular princes acknowledged Innocent as the head of Christendom; the synod of Würzburg in October 1130 formally decreed the adherence of the empire to Innocent, and so did large parts of Christian Spain as well as most of the Lombard bishops. On the other hand, although Anacletus found support only in Scotland and in Sicily (Roger II) – apart from Rome – the joint efforts of Bernard, Innocent himself and Lothar to oust him were quite unsuccessful. Lothar had meanwhile been crowned emperor by Innocent II at the Lateran basilica, because the Leonine city and the Vatican were firmly in the hands of Anacletus and his forces. But Innocent was too weak to maintain his shadowy existence in Rome, once his imperial protector had left: once more he had to take refuge abroad. Attempts at ending this schism by submitting the purely factual questions to a mixed tribunal consisting of 3 cardinals from each side, failed. It was the natural death of Anacletus on 25 January 1138 which to all intents and purposes brought to an end this macabre episode in which ideas and principles were conspicuously absent, for his successor, Cardinal Gregory Conti (Victor IV) submitted to Innocent after less than two months.

Yet despite the barrenness of the third decade in matters of ideological development there are nevertheless some features which deserve a few remarks. The first is the shelter which France provided for the papacy and which continued what was inconspicuously begun under Urban II, himself a Frenchman. Since Rome had proved itself an insecure place of residence for the papacy, individual incumbents had often enough to seek refuge abroad, and the country that most frequently acted as a host, was France. The relations between the papacy and France grew gradually but all the more firmly into intimate ties. For theocratic kingship the French soil was particularly fertile; this idea of 'the king by the grace of God' was potently engendered by the legend of the holy oil of Chlovis, according to which on the occasion of his baptism a phial of holy oil was brought from heaven with which all legitimate French kings were to be anointed. Although this legend of the holy oil was current in France certainly by the time of Hincmar in the ninth century, it was on the occasion of Innocent II's crowning the young King Louis VII at Rheims in October 1131 that the Chlovis oil was for the first time used for an actual anointing – and used it was by the pope. From then on this oil gave French kings the special distinction of being among all European kings 'the most christian king'; political and constitutional developments in France owed a great deal to the efficacy of this legend. There was much mutual fructification between the papacy and the French monarchy. Theological studies in France and the subsequent growth of French universities, notably Paris, accompanied by enormous intellectual and academic advances, were powerfully supported by the papacy which, especially in public affairs, had found the French kings particularly receptive to its own ideas. France was to become the citadel of medieval scholasticism as well as the kingdom in which the theocratic idea of rulership manifested itself most conspicuously. It was also from the French quarter that the papacy was later to receive shattering blows, precisely because the monarchy had struck such deep roots with the help of the papacy (see below pp. 273ff.).

It was assuredly no coincidence that in this third decade the papacy was called upon to play a not unimportant role in yet another intellectual sphere which had however repercussions beyond the immediate scholarly precincts. It was in France that one of the most subtle medieval minds, Abelard, was to leave its direct impact. He provoked the conservative forces to bitter reaction by his emphatic insistence on doubt as to the avenue for reaching truth: nothing should be believed unless it were first critically examined. A standpoint such as this could wreak havoc on the traditional outlook based as it was on pure faith. Abelard's teaching at once attracted adherents. It was bound to arouse fierce protests, since the foundations of society and the generally accepted cosmology were held to be seriously threatened. Through the passionate and harsh attacks by Bernard of Clairvaux at the Council of Sens in 1140 a number of Abelardian views were condemned as heretical. Abelard himself appealed to the papacy, and Innocent II upheld the verdict, decreeing permanent silence on Abelard. This instance showed, not only that the papacy had come to be regarded as the final arbiter in such difficult theological and philosophical questions as were treated by Abelard; it also showed the influence which Bernard had on the papacy and how well he and Innocent sensed the wider implications of the Abelardian standpoint for philosophy, theology, and above all government, notably in France.

At exactly the same time the first rumblings of a popular revolt against the higher clergy and directly involving the papacy became uncomfortably distinct in Italy. The leader of this movement, at first of purely local character, was the Augustinian monk Arnold of Brescia who appeared to translate Abelardian tenets into social-economic terms. First in Brescia, and soon through large parts of Italy, not excepting Rome, his demagogic attacks on the riches amassed by the higher clergy won him many adherents. His plan culminated in the proposal that the clergy should return to apostolic poverty and should live by the alms voluntarily given by the faithful. Here again the 'establishment' realized the dangerous nature of these views, and Innocent II condemned Arnold in the Second Lateran Council of 1139 as a schismatic and heretic – though on what exact grounds has never become clear – and decreed his exile from Italy. Having turned to France where he joined Abelard, Arnold continued his teaching in public and, not unexpectedly, attracted the attention of the higher clergy which had him condemned at Sens (together with Abelard) and, also not unexpectedly, the French king in his turn exiled him from France. The actions of the higher clergy, of the papacy and of the French king were predictable, because Arnold attacked the very foundations of all these institutions. Arnold's later career was to lead him to Rome where his prime target became the papacy and his principal aim the establishment of a Roman republic. Arnold and Abelard might well serve as harbingers of new developments which were to affect the papacy in a most direct way.

Lastly, it was also during the pontificate of Innocent II, though without apparent papal initiative, that another new force arose, one that was to be of decisive and immediate concern to the papacy – the emergence of the canonistic school of law at the university of Bologna. It was in 1140 that there the Camaldunensian monk Gratian composed what he intended to be (and what remained) a text book of canon law in which he employed the new dialectical method to solve the numerous contradictions expressed in the thousands of papal decrees and patristic statements and royal and imperial laws which he incorporated in his work. Rightly has Gratian been called the Father of canon law. Canonistic scholarship was henceforward to exercise potent influence on jurisprudence as well as on theology and the science of government. Besides Roman law, there now was also a canon law school in the university of Bologna. The development that had begun with the collection of canon law (possibly by Cardinal Humbert) in the fifties of the preceding century, was now brought to a highly successful conclusion.

The practical significance of this canon law school which began to flourish from the moment Gratian bequeathed his work to the world, was that the ecclesiastical organism and above all the papacy had at long last trained lawyers at their disposal, a profession that hitherto had not existed. This supply of jurists, versed in both Roman and canon law, was of crucial importance to the papacy. As a governmental institution it always operated with the law, but the technicians who had special legal training did not exist. What there was, was intelligent and industrious amateurishness within the curia, but assuredly this was no longer sufficient for the fulfilment of the ramified tasks which engaged the papacy. Hence the eagerness with which the papacy viewed the development of the canon law school at Bologna; hence also from this very same time the emergence of the great lawyer popes, beginning with Alexander III (himself a pupil of Gratian and a master at Bologna) down to the fourteenth century. This feature deserves special mention, because none of the European Rulers had that thorough legal training and that intimate practical expertise in legal matters which the popes had. As legislators and judges they had therefore an inestimable advantage over any of their contemporary secular Rulers – assuredly a feature which is unique in the history of governments.

Moreover, the curia could not only be staffed with properly trained personnel, but could also establish very much needed special departments to deal with the flood of appeals to the papacy as the supreme court in Christendom. And in deciding the myriads of cases, new canon law came to be made which was – in sharp contrast to Roman law – a living law directly arising out of the topical contingencies and actual situations. The papal law came to be stated in the decretal letter (see above pp. 12, 16) the tenor of which was the exercise and practical application of the papal primacy of jurisdiction. It was only now from the mid-twelfth century onwards that this primatial claim could find adequate and appropriate clothing, because the professional technique was available. And the thousands of papal decretals contained the law which was valid through the length and breadth of medieval Europe and applicable to all conditions of men and all matters of relevance to the well-being of Christian society. It was only from now onwards that the papal monarchy became in reality and in effect the central government of Christendom (as far as it acknowledged papal primacy) because it had the vehicle by which the monarchy could be translated into practice – the law and a court of law. This is not to say that Gratian's book contained any new legal material. Far from it, because in a diligent and conscientious manner he used in his work only legal material that had already been embodied in earlier collections, such as the hundreds of extracts from Pseudo-Isidore, but these other collections did not indicate how the many contradictions could be solved. Because of his superior knowledge of Roman law – not available to earlier collectors – and by virtue of his mastery of the dialectical method his work initiated a true scholarship of canon law which was the presupposition for the professional making and application of the papal law. What Rheims had given to Rome in the ninth century in the shape of a law book, Bologna was to give to Rome in the twelfth century in the shape of legal scholarship. Thereby the papacy was provided with an adjustable, practical instrument with which to govern Christian society. A new era in the working of the papal monarchy began.

The realistic appreciation of the papacy's jurisdictional function encouraged archbishops, bishops and other lower placed officers to submit as many controversial questions as possible to it for final decision. The result was an onrush, not to say a flooding of the curia with litigation from virtually every part of Christendom that was not subjected to Constantinople. No one gave a better or more vivid picture of this state of affairs prevailing in the Roman curia than Bernard of Clairvaux whose pupil, the Cistercian abbot Bernard of Pisa had become pope as Eugenius III. What had become quite obvious by the forties of the twelfth century was that notwithstanding local Roman difficulties, the papacy as an institution had been accepted as the organ of government throughout Western Europe. In his work *De consideratione* dedicated to the new pope, 'the uncrowned emperor of Europe' bitingly castigated the noise and the bustle which the visitor to the curia noticed: there was little evidence of meditation, of prayer, of life dedicated to the knowledge of God – in brief, the danger to which Bernard believed the papacy to be exposed was that of secularization. What particularly aggrieved the pope's former teacher was what he called the noise made by the laws of Justinian and the intermingling of the mundane with the divine. In Bernard's view it was not the function of the pope to descend to trivialities. The true vocation and function of the pope as monarch was to stand outside and above Christian society, so as not to be caught up in the myriads of squabbles affecting its members. Bernard's tract exercised a very great influence on succeeding papal generations, because in inimitable and concise language he laid down a number of basic points which are clearly traceable in the official output of subsequent pontificates.

Bernard tried to draw the consequences of the view that the pope was a mediator between Christ and man, for to him the pope was 'flesh from God's flesh, spirit from God's spirit' and hence 'the pope had no equal on earth in his function as pope'. Consequently, the pope's government embraced the whole world, as he was the sole vicar of Christ on earth. Both royal power and sacerdotal authority were uniquely combined in the pope, hence he was 'the supreme priest and king'. Bernard gave the theory of the two swords its final formulation and this became the commonly accepted medieval allegory expressing supreme governmental power. Accordingly, the pope possessed both swords (the passage in Luke's gospel served as the biblical basis, 22.38), that is, the so-called spiritual sword which he wielded directly, while the material (i.e. the real) sword he handed over to the secular prince for him to wield according to the will of the pope. Here the saint simply put forward in allegorical language the ancient Pauline view explaining why the prince possessed a sword at all, that is, to suppress and eradicate evil. As far as basic matters of Christian society were concerned, what was evil and in need of elimination could only be authoritatively fixed by the pope – that was the message of Bernard. Bernard's allegory had already been continuously and symbolically implemented since the imperial coronation of 823: during the coronation the pope handed over the sword to the emperor. The symbolism left no doubt as to its meaning, as the sword was taken from the altar of St Peter's (the corresponding symbolism was that of the pallium which too was taken from the altar of St Peter's). Precisely because he had an exalted view of the pope as universal monarch, Bernard detested the papal handling of all sorts of petty squabbles by the papal court: where papal authority should display its force was in those matters which vitally affected the structure, well-being and eventual aim of Christian society. Papal authority was to be directive – the execution of what was directed did not lie in papal (or for that matter, in priestly) hands, because this was precisely the reason why there was a secular prince who wielded the sword.

To Bernard the pope was to be the supreme monarchic overseer (the *speculator*) of all Christians. The underlying theme of Bernard's tract was that pope, king, or emperor, in brief everyone should fulfil the functions allocated to him. Christian society was an organic body which was viable only when every member worked towards the same end and within an allotted sphere of action – otherwise there would be disorder, anarchy and the eventual collapse of Christian society altogether.

The deep impact of this tract on the papacy has already been noted. It was therefore no coincidence that from now on the pope designated himself vicar of Christ, a notion which was substantially the same as that of the successor of St Peter, but which brought into the clearest possible relief that St Peter was given vicarious powers by Christ Himself and that as successor of St Peter the pope acted vicariously as Christ would have acted. This notion of the pope's vicariate of Christ merely clarified the position of papal powers in relation to Christ Himself. Eugenius III, the faithful pupil of St Bernard, succinctly stated that the whole world knew that St Peter had been entrusted by Christ with the laws of the earthly and celestial kingdom.

Nevertheless, the pontificate of Eugenius III did not provide abundant opportunity of deploying these claims, although it was during this pontificate that the papacy witnessed an expansion of its actual influence as far away as Ireland where the papal legate Cardinal John Paparo presided over a national-Irish synod in 1152 in which the Irish diocesan organization was fixed and Roman liturgy formally introduced. Direct papal influence was furthermore made concrete in the far North where in 1150 the papal legate Cardinal Nicholas Breakspear established the independence of the Norwegian Church by separating the bishopric of Drontheim from Lund and transforming it into an archbishopric with ten suffragans, including the Faroe and Orkney Islands, Iceland and Greenland. In the same year the Swedish Church began to pay Peter's pence, and in a large Swedish synod presided over by the papal cardinal legate, a number of Roman decrees were promulgated as the law for the Scandinavian Church. The papal writ from the mid-twelfth century ran from the sunny Mediterranean shores right up to islands enveloped in never-ending winter.

The second crusade (1147–8), which Eugenius III proclaimed,

though in the end an unrelieved fiasco, had nevertheless some noteworthy features: the appeal for it did not fail to underscore as its by-product the establishment of Roman primacy in Constantinople. Bernard's pleas were highly successful as not only the French – originally intended to be the sole executors of the crusading plan – but also the first Staufen king, Conrad III, and his nephew, the young Duke Frederick of Swabia (the later Barbarossa) and numerous other South German princes took part. A new crusade was proclaimed against the Wends in the North of Europe, against whom the papacy appointed as leader the eminent Anselm, bishop of Havelsberg.

In a negative sense too this pontificate was important for the papacy, because from the late forties the latent animosity of the Roman populace against the pope was channelled into real hostility as a result of the resumed activity of Arnold of Brescia. His movement won many adherents amongst the lower Roman clergy and the slowly emerging 'bourgeoisie' of Rome. With great oratorical skill he presided over 'people's assemblies', glorifying Rome's ancient past and bitterly attacking the riches and the wealth and avarice of the cardinals no less than that of the papacy: the pope was 'not an apostolic man, but a man of blood'. This sort of attack – assuredly too premature to leave any permanent mark – was nevertheless a clear indication of the sentiments of large sections of the Roman populace. Arnold's programme of establishing a Republic of Rome as the mistress of the world relieved of all papal and imperial connexions no doubt appealed to the Romans, but it was also this programme which brought into existence a firmly knit front of resistance consisting of the papacy and other traditionalists, a front which would also have included Conrad III, had he not been otherwise engaged. Despite its obvious strength the 'establishment front' was unable to secure a safe foothold for the pope in Rome.

Seen in retrospect this phase of papal history spanning the pontificates of Innocent II and Eugenius III appears as an age of transition in which the old was being slowly re-shaped by something new which itself was nevertheless also historically conditioned. For from the mid-fifties of the twelfth century the complexion of the papacy began to assume a much more sharply contoured profile than it hitherto had, and exactly the same can be said about the papally created protector in the West, the emperor of the Romans. The next decades were overshadowed by the bitter conflict between the papacy and the Western emperor. This conflict was not, however, concerned with the Roman or Germanic bases of government, but with Romanism in its twofold form, the ancient or secular Romanism and the papal or ecclesiastical Romanism. Seen from a wider viewpoint one might almost detect a transfer of the conflict which the papacy had had to fight in the fifth century with Constantinople. The internecine conflict between the papacy and the Staufen empire lasted over a century.

The Western Roman emperor now harnessed the Roman law to his own governmental scheme. The Roman law in its Justinianean shape, notably the Code, became a potent ideological buttress of this emperor. As so-called emperors of the Romans the German Rulers held themselves to be the direct successors of the ancient Roman Caesars – hence the readiness with which they embraced the ancient Roman law. Bolognese scholarship of Roman law became now of most direct concern to the Western emperors, who from the middle years of the twelfth century had at their disposal a professional class of lawyers in the very science which supplied the ideological pillars of their empire. There can hardly have been another instance in which a legal system had rendered such signal service to a government or that a government had derived so much ideological support from a legal system (which was essentially alien to this government) as did the Staufen Rulers, notably Frederick I, from Roman law.

For the proper understanding of the ensuing conflict it should nevertheless be borne in mind that that Western emperor was a papal creation. There never was a medieval emperor without the active participation by the papacy. Antecedent ideology, practice and coronation rites since the ninth century made abundantly clear this sole right and prerogative of the papacy. The Frankish and German kings unreservedly accepted this basic papal standpoint. They became emperors as a result of the papacy's granting their humble supplications. It was through the exercise of the papal 'good will' (technically called the *favor apostolicus*) that a purely German Rulership changed into a Roman universal emperorship. The very fact of submitting a supplication to the papacy revealed that the future emperor had no right or claim to be crowned emperor by the pope. This supplication in conjunction with the unambiguous preliminaries to the coronation as well as the rite itself excluded a claim or right to become emperor. Indeed he was created for special purposes only, that is, as a protector of the papacy and as a counterweight against Constantinople. That was the original plan which in the medieval period did not undergo a change.

In order to vindicate his claim as a Roman emperor and in order to assert his rights to universal dominion (for there could not be two Rulers each claiming universality of dominion) (see above p. 85), the Western emperor had to adopt an antagonistic, if not openly hostile, attitude towards Constantinople. And in so far papal and Western imperial interests were harmonious and identical. But from the mid-twelfth century a sharp and acrimonious dissonance between pope and emperor developed in the domestic sphere. This dissonance was overwhelmingly due to the confusion by the German Rulers between appearance and reality. In appearance this papally created emperor was indeed a universal Ruler and a successor of the ancient Roman Caesars. And precisely because the ancient emperor was autonomous and this role was amply elaborated in the easily available Roman law, the Western medieval emperor came to act governmentally in no wise different from the emperor at Constantinople (for whom of course the same Roman law was valid). This shift from German kingship to Roman emperorship was the most conspicuous feature in the Staufen age between the mid-twelfth and mid-thirteenth centuries.

In pursuit of this secular Romanism the active and beneficial interest which the Staufen Frederick Barbarossa showed in the study of Roman law at Bologna and in the well-being of that university, became understandable. This interest showed what vital importance the new dynasty attached to the ideological roots of their power. The ancient Roman law was so much their 'own' that Staufen laws and decrees came to be inserted into the body of this law with the consequence that they formed an integral part of the 'ancient' Roman law. Moreover, the crusading armies which the Staufen emperors put into the field, were called 'Roman armies', just as the imperial princes were sometimes called princes of the Romans ('principes Romanorum'). To the Staufen emperors the Roman law appeared superior to the Germanic customs: it was written, originated in the deeply Christian emperors of antiquity, embodied a model of legal culture, and was expounded in a scholarly fashion at the medieval universities. The governmental ideology enshrined in the ancient Roman law furnished the backbone and structural framework supporting the government, aims and aspirations of the emperor of the Romans in the West.

On the other hand, and on the plane of reality, the papacy had never intended to create an autonomous Ruler in the shape of the Roman emperor in the West. The intention of the papacy was to create no more than an officer in the person of a Ruler who was called emperor of the Romans. As a universal power the papacy claimed for itself the right to establish a protector on a universal scale, and that role could be filled by one Ruler only, the one called emperor of the Romans. According to papal intentions this papally created Roman emperor was one in name or appearance only, but not in substance or reality. The papacy never concealed that its own creation was not autonomous in the sense in which the ancient Roman emperor had been. The whole elaborate coronation ritual, its preliminaries and its symbolism including the kind of unction administered (see above p. 89) conveyed this basic papal ideology even to the most dull-witted contemporary. And the papally conferred sword (see above p. 182) signified physical power which the imperial candidate received from the pope, and the accompanying prayer texts made similarly clear why the emperor received it: they were the practical application of the ancient Pauline-Isidorian themes. Further, in order to leave no doubt about the role which this papally created emperor was destined to play, namely that of an officer, no provision was ever made for an enthronement of the Western emperor: of course not, because no officer ever sat on a throne. This deliberate omission of an enthronement ritual within the imperial coronation rite illustrated compellingly what the papacy intended to create in the person of the Ruler designated 'emperor of the Romans'. The enthronement was possibly the most solemn mundane act of a royal coronation. That it did not figure at all in an imperial coronation was therefore most revealing.

The imperial and papal standpoints reflected the secular Romanism (of antiquity) and ecclesiastical Romanism (of papal provenance) respectively. The adoption of secular Romanism by the Western emperor was highly artificial, because it arose

G

directly out of the confusion of reality with appearance. In reality nothing corresponded to this ancient secular Romanism. It was ecclesiastical Romanism which shaped reality and which alone mattered, including the making of the Roman emperor himself.

Put side by side, the German Ruler's conception of his status as a 'true' successor of the Roman Caesars and the papacy's conception of the emperor's function as a mere officer who had to draw his sword at the bidding of the papacy, it is not difficult to understand how explosive such a situation could be, if the issues were clearly brought to a head. And that contingency did indeed arise in the mid-fifties. Indeed, the year 1153–4 may well be taken as a crucial phase in the history of the papacy. Within 6 weeks pupil and teacher died: Eugenius III on 8 July 1153 and Bernard on 20 August; a few months later King Roger II of Sicily died (26 February 1154). In Germany Conrad III suddenly died on 15 February 1152 and was immediately succeeded (4 March 1152) by Frederick of Swabia, known as Frederick I Barbarossa, one of the most powerful and gifted medieval German Rulers who was to reign nearly 40 years, while in England the Angevin Henry II ascended the throne in December 1154 – two kings whose governmental aims were by no means dissimilar. Two weeks before Henry II crossed the Channel, his fellow countryman, Cardinal Nicholas Breakspear became pope: Adrian IV was diplomatically very well versed and experienced, dispassionate and purposeful in his government. Indeed, one can say that during his pontificate the papacy began the ascent to the dizzy heights it was to reach under Innocent III. And it was also during his pontificate that the first tremors of the conflict between the papacy and the Staufen dynasty became all too audible. In fact, Adrian inherited from his predecessor a mutual assistance pact concluded in early 1153 between the papacy and the German king – the treaty of Constance – according to which the imperial coronation was implicitly contingent upon the delivery of Rome from the threat of Arnold of Brescia and his followers; the king as 'the devoted and special assistant of the papacy' (its *advocatus*) was also to subject the city to papal rule, to defend the papal state and to help in the recovery of lost territories; and both parties promised mutual help in their efforts to ward off the Byzantine threat to Italy by the 'Greek King', Manuel Comnenos, who imitating Justinian was just then engaged in launching the last ever campaign to unite Italy with Constantinople.

In contrast to his immediate predecessors Frederick did not submit a formal request to the papacy for the imperial coronation, but in language clearly modelled on Justinian's bombastic phraseology, simply announced his election. The curia no doubt felt the sting and replied that the pope gladly approved the election 'with the benign favour of the apostolic see' – a gratuitous act which the royal court no doubt assessed correctly. During the preliminaries to the coronation in 1155 the first contretemps occurred when the king refused to perform certain ceremonial services from which, he held, wholly unacceptable conclusions might be drawn. Although in itself of little significance, this refusal was a portent. The curia was no doubt distrustful of the Staufen's intentions. However much the people's tribune, Arnold, tried to ingratiate himself with the king, even offering the imperial crown, Frederick was not having any truck with this revolutionary rabble. Arnold was captured, delivered into the hands of his adversary, the pope, and hanged. The Romans showed little enthusiasm for the new king. His self-confident, if not arrogant speech upon entering Rome received a chilly reception. Rome, he declared, its senate and its empire had been transferred to the Germans (he abstained from saying by whom and how this was done); it was he who was to give laws, not the people of Rome. Because of fear of Roman hostility and disturbances the imperial coronation on 18 June 1155 had to be performed secretly on a Saturday (instead of on a Sunday as usual) in order to mislead the Romans, all this being somewhat incongruous for 'the lord of the world and master of Rome' who was there with his armed forces. Naturally, to the Romans, Adrian appeared implicated and he left with the newly crowned emperor who had decided on a swift withdrawal.

Relations between the curia and the self-confident emperor began to go from bad to worse, when the papacy considered that Frederick had failed to implement the treaty of Constance against the Normans who were advancing in the South of Italy and threatening the papal state. In default of any assistance Adrian IV came to an arrangement (in 1156) with King William I of Sicily (Roger II's son), who acknowledged himself a vassal of the papacy. The earlier relationship between papacy and Normans was re-established. On his part Frederick now considered the treaty of Constance broken by the papacy. And amidst the charges and countercharges occurred a further incident which showed how deep the gulf was that separated the papacy from Staufen ideology. On his return journey from Rome to Sweden the archbishop of Lund, Eskil, was captured in the summer of 1157 in Germany, and despite repeated papal appeals Frederick delayed the release of the prelate. Brought by two legates to Besançon in October 1157 where the emperor happened to celebrate his wedding, special papal letters complained about his conduct: he should not show himself ungrateful for the benefits he had so recently received from the papacy. When these letters were read out by the imperial chancellor, Rainald of Dassel, the crucial term 'beneficium conferre' was translated into German (for the Roman emperor knew no Latin) by a feudal phrase which implied that the empire was a fief of the papacy and the emperor a vassal. It was a mistranslation. The papal chancery used these terms entirely in their ordinary and innocuous Latin sense. Considering the occasion, it was no doubt highly humiliating for the proud Staufen to be reminded that he had received the imperial crown as 'a good deed' (a 'beneficium = bonum factum' in the literal sense) from the papacy, hence not as a matter of right. This moved entirely within tradition and ideology, as also the subsequent correspondence made abundantly clear.

But the damage was done: there was great commotion – the legates' life was threatened, especially when one of them asked, perhaps not without justification, from whom but the pope had Frederick received the empire? In no uncertain terms the legates were told to leave the gathering at Besançon at once. The imperial chancery – one is tempted to say – welcomed the incident and issued manifestoes in which the Staufen standpoint was set forth: the emperor held his power directly from God and the imperial crown was a divine good deed ('divinum beneficium'); the imperial coronation by the pope was no more than a declaratory act of a certain liturgical solemnity and not, as the papacy asserted, an act that constituted the king an emperor of the Romans. In other words, the coronation was a pageant and devoid of all constitutive meaning. Thereby the Staufen theme approached the Byzantine thesis and practice where the coronation by the patriarch had that significance which the Germans pretended the coronation by the pope had. Frederick indicated this unmistakably when in isolated instances two and three years before his imperial coronation he styled himself 'Emperor of the Romans' in official documents. That one of these documents was even sent to the papacy was clearly intended as a counterstroke to the papal approval of his royal election (above p. 189). What the Germans maintained was that they had a right to the imperial crown for which assertion there was not a shred of support in antecedent ideology and practice which reached back to the ninth century. They stared at a phantom that did not exist – the ancient Roman emperor who had, however, only one successor, and that was the emperor at Constantinople who refused to acknowledge precisely that which the Germans fulsomely acknowledged at least before the coronation, papal primacy.

One of the legates, in fact the one who had asked the embarrassing question, was the papal chancellor, Cardinal Roland, who in less than two years was to succeed Adrian IV as pope. As already mentioned, he was one of Gratian's pupils and himself a master at Bologna. With him the dynasty of the great lawyer popes was to begin. However, the very year before his election the situation had grown very serious indeed for the papacy. Frederick during his Italian campaign in 1158 subjected the half-destroyed Milan and the whole of Lombardy to direct German rule. At the famous Diet of Roncaglia (September 1158) he proclaimed in juristic formulation the sovereignty of the empire over Northern Italy, thereby severely restricting, if not altogether abolishing, the well-developed municipal governments in the Lombard cities and, as far as the papacy was concerned, simply annexing parts of the papal state to imperial jurisdiction. It was here at the Diet of Roncaglia that the ideological alliance between the Staufen empire and the Roman lawyers of Bologna was cemented. The significance of this alliance has not yet been fully appreciated. In other words, the emperor powerfully supported by Roman law and its professional interpreters, governed in the manner of his Eastern colleague: bishops and archbishops were simply appointed, and the ecclesiastical organism in the empire, including Burgundy and Lombardy, played the role of an imperial civil service.

An iron hand of considerable ability had begun to shape the destiny of the empire – no longer on the basis of by now antiquated Germanic traditions and customs, but on the basis of secular Romanism, the Roman law and its ideology. From 1158 onwards the empire was the *sacrum imperium Romanum*, the holy Roman empire, a terminology which was to bring into relief its divinely ordained mission and to designate a territorial body that included also the *sancta Dei ecclesia*. The designation of the empire as 'sacrum' (and not as 'sanctum') was a further borrowing from Rome and its 'ius sacrum' (see above pp. 7, 23, 32). The soil was ready for the reception of not only the Roman law in Germany but also of the attendant nomenclatures and epithets for the emperor himself, now more and more donning the mantle of a Roman Caesar and adopting a number of ancient Roman attributes. The subsequent decades were overshadowed by the confrontation of the secular Romanism with its ecclesiastical counterpart.

In the Roman curia itself and notably within the College of Cardinals there was a small minority which did not look askance at this resuscitated brand of secular Romanism, however much it might have appeared contrived. This faction preferred, moreover, a Northern to the Southern-orientated Norman policy which Adrian IV had adopted. What is important to bear in mind is that it was now ideological standpoints, and no longer projections of Roman aristocratic feuds which brought dissension into the curia. This tension erupted on the occasion of electing a successor to Adrian. The election (some of its details are still not fully known) was a riotous and undignified spectacle. One thing is certain: overwhelmingly, the cardinal-bishops elected the papal chancellor, Roland, and they were joined by the great majority of the cardinal-priests and deacons. Hardly had Cardinal Roland been elected when the vociferous opposition faction angrily demanded that Cardinal Octavian should be pope; in this demand the faction was supported by a crowd of Romans consisting of clergy and laity. The upshot of these wholly unparalleled events was that Roland, that is, Alexander III, and the overwhelming majority of the cardinals were forced to take refuge in the Borgho in Rome. Only a handful of cardinals remained with Octavian (Victor IV).

Thrown against the secular Roman ideology so fervently pursued by Frederick, this situation might well not have been unwelcome to him. There is no direct evidence that either he or his chancellor, Rainald, had a hand in the election proceedings on

7 September 1159. Alexander's first papal action was the excommunication of Victor IV as antipope – just over 20 years had passed since the last schism had ended. But for Frederick this was the signal to act in the manner of the late Roman Caesars as arbitrators between contending factions. Specifically referring to his ancient models (as well as to Frankish kings) he convoked a synod at Pavia for February 1160 which was to be a meeting of the whole of Christendom to decide the issue between Alexander and Victor. In imitation of Constantine Frederick opened and addressed the synod, but did not take part in its deliberations. Despite all the flourish, the synod was no more than a small council in which a number of imperial bishops appeared: compared with Frederick's grand design it was a pitiable affair. Instead of appearing Alexander excommunicated the emperor and released his subjects from the oath of allegiance: the emperor had no right to sit in judgment over the pope, Alexander declared, for the pope was not to be judged by anyone nor had the emperor the right to summon a council. The English and French episcopate gave Frederick the cold shoulder: their absence indicated that the eventual designs of Frederick had dawned upon them. Predictably the synod decided that Victor was the lawful pope.

Apart from Germany and some Northern parts of Italy the synodal decision fell flat. Alexander was acknowledged virtually throughout Western Christendom. After receiving and studying reports concerning the troubles encountered at the election, Henry II of England and Louis VII of France recognized Alexander as legitimate pope in late July 1160 at Beauvais. In other words, the two great Western powers were not willing to be told to which pope they should owe allegiance. In the same year 1160 Spain also declared its adherence to Alexander. The patriarch of Jerusalem and his clergy, in a synod held at Nazareth, persuaded the king of Jerusalem to acknowledge Alexander as the lawful pope. Although Hungarian legates took part in the synod of Pavia and voted for Victor, the overwhelming European support for Alexander and quite especially the stand of the French and English episcopate and kings influenced the Hungarian king and the Hungarian bishops to take the side of Alexander. The Scandinavian countries too took up Alexander's side. Even Manuel Comnenos, the emperor at Constantinople, made overtures to the papacy and intimated that in order to solve the vexatious problem of the two emperors, he would be willing to be crowned emperor of the Romans by Alexander III. But the papacy was too much aware of the rift between itself and Constantinople – conditioned by the latter's refusal to acknowledge Roman primacy – to take this offer seriously, which in all likelihood was seen for what it was, that is, a mere manœuvre to outwit the dangerous Western Roman emperor of German complexion. Southern Italy, Sicily and Venice too acknowledged Alexander as pope, and even a number of Lombard towns did. Solely in Germany was support for Victor conspicuous where he could maintain himself 'by the grace of the emperor', though even this support soon weakened when a number of influential archbishops and bishops left the emperor's pope. Victor was no more than a cipher: only once did he leave Northern Italy for a brief sojourn in Germany; he was never able to reside in Rome.

It is not necessary to enter into the details of the serious conflict between the secular brand of Romanism represented by the Staufen emperor, and the ecclesiastical kind of Romanism represented by the papacy under Alexander III who in his 22 years of reign was often for long periods unable to take up residence in Rome or even in Italy, because they were at times very firmly controlled by imperial officers. Renewed attempts by Frederick to win over France failed, since Louis VII also began to realize that the emperor of the Romans pursued plans which in the end were bound to affect France adversely, for as emperor of the Romans he was 'the lord of the world' (*dominus mundi*) which carried some disagreeable undertones for France. France became not incomprehensibly rather nervous whenever Staufen ideology and its revived Romanism showed signs of being translated into reality. When, for instance, during the often protracted negotiations imperial legates apostrophized the French (and English) kings as *reguli* (i.e. as 'kinglets') imperial diplomacy revealed its scheme of things all too clearly. In England this imperial Romanism produced the same effect. Despite Henry II's strained relations with the papacy, he was not tempted by baits held out by Frederick.

The opportunity for ending the schism presented by Victor's natural death in 1164, was not taken by Frederick who simply adopted a successor in the person of Cardinal Wido as Paschal III. Frederick's stubbornness justified by no considerations other than the fanciful contrivance of the Roman empire ideology even made the German episcopate realize the emptiness of this Frederician policy. In order to suppress this incipient opposition, Frederick's adviser Rainald realizing that the French were the strongest support for Alexander, hit upon the idea of driving a wedge between Louis VII and Henry II. Rainald's legation to Henry at Rouen in April 1165 produced a treaty of friendship between the emperor and the king and some vague promise that Henry might in future recognize Paschal III. Thus fortified the emperor himself convoked a large diet at Würzburg in May 1165 at which also an English legation took part. The trump card held by Rainald at this diet was the successful outcome of the Rouen negotiations. And Frederick now took a most solemn oath – quite against all tradition and custom – that he would never recognize Alexander and would never seek absolution from him (in both cases the 'never' extended only over a short period); the secular and ecclesiastical princes had to take the same oath, though if credence can be given to contemporary sources, some of the bishops present did not do so without conscientious scruples. On behalf of Henry II the English legation agreed with these decisions, though the king did not consider himself bound by his legates' agreement; this was understandable in view of the English episcopate's (and his own) firm adherence to Alexander. The way in which the Würzburg decisions were put into practice revealed considerable ruthlessness on the part of the emperor. Intimidation and terror were not entirely absent. The 'canonization' of Charlemagne in December 1165 was no more than a gesture.

Frederick's attempt to bring Alexander to his knees followed the line he had pursued in Germany. As a result of a change of temper among the Romans Alexander was able to take up residence there late in 1165, at the very time when Frederick began to make active preparations for his fourth Italian campaign. Its purpose was the elimination, not of the papacy, but of Alexander as pope, so as to make real his claim that there was to be 'one God, one pope, one emperor'. The Lombards were made to take the same oaths as the German princes had taken at Würzburg and in some places Frederick replaced Alexandrian bishops by bishops of his persuasion. Strong German armed forces under the command of Archbishop Rainald of Cologne and Christian of Mainz appeared before the gates of Rome. Making a surprise move they occupied Tusculum on Whitmonday 1167. In a swift

and decisive attack the city fell to superior German forces in early
July. The attack was preceded by Rainald's demand that the
Romans should extradite the pope and all his cardinals, but they
refused. Frederick's demand that Alexander should abdicate,
whereupon he would drop the anti-pope, so that the way would
be clear for a new and unanimous election, predictably came to
naught: Alexander realized that this was nothing but a manœuvre
to re-introduce imperial control of the papacy. He fled. With
appropriate pomp and circumstance the anti-pope was now
crowned and enthroned at St Peter's basilica, and on 1 August
1167 he recrowned Frederick and his wife. An epidemic of malaria
decimated the imperial troops and forced Frederick to leave
Rome: among the victims of the epidemic were the faithful
Rainald and a dozen bishops as well as numerous princes. It is no
exaggeration to say that despite appearances Frederick was no
nearer to his goal: Alexander and his curia were free, and the
papacy was not under imperial control.

The German retreat was the signal for the formation of the
Lombard League of 22 cities to resist German domination in
Italy. The new anti-pope (Calixtus III) who was elected without
imperial participation but by a very small number of the anti-
Alexandrian party, received only tepid support from the imperial
government which nevertheless exercised, in Germany, an all
the stronger influence on the filling of episcopal vacancies which
went to anti-Alexandrian prelates: what counted was the imperial
good will, especially when elections were disputed. It was precisely this which caused the resumed negotiations between
Frederick and Alexander to break down (1169–70). Alexander
was not prepared to recognize the ecclesiastical appointments
which had been made in the meantime. The Lombard League and
the Alexandrian curia and adherents constituted by the early
seventies a formidable united front – a dangerous constellation
for the imperial government. In order to smash this combination
Frederick embarked upon his fifth Italian campaign: it was to end
in a further defeat of the emperor. The Lombard forces' overwhelming victory at Legnano made Frederick drop his anti-
pope altogether and seek in earnest a reconciliation with the
Alexandrian curia. After lengthy, difficult and protracted negotiations peace was at long last restored and the schism which had
lasted nearly 20 years, ended.

In the Peace of Venice (July 1177) Frederick was released from excommunication, after readily and fulsomely acknowledging Alexander III as the lawful pope and after promising to restore to the papacy all the estates and districts illegally detained by him. If ever imperial policy towards the papacy had suffered shipwreck, it was Frederick's, although by a curial concession the ordinations and consecrations in Germany during the schismatic time were generally acknowledged. The resuscitation of a secular Romanism was no more than an instrument with which to re-establish imperial control of the papacy. In Germany however the influence of the emperor on ecclesiastical matters did not immediately suffer greatly as a result of the Peace of Venice. The return of Alexander to Rome in March 1178 signified the restoration of the papal state. As it was done on previous occasions Alexander summoned the Third Lateran Council for the following year (for some details see below pp. 229, 239f.).

Although Alexander's pontificate was overshadowed by schism and conflict with 'the special son of the Roman Church' (the Western emperor), the authority of the papacy came to be effectively extended to the most western outpost of Christendom, to Ireland, which the English Henry II finally conquered in 1171, at the same time at which the relations between the king and the papacy were highly strained as a result of the Becket dispute. This dispute had arisen as a consequence of the measures which Henry II had taken at Clarendon (1164) to fix constitutionally the rights of the royal courts over the English clergy. Of particular concern was the prohibition of appeals to the papacy and journeys of prelates abroad without royal consent, the regulations of the procedure for the elections of bishops which had to take place in the king's chapel, and the severe restriction of clerical immunity from royal jurisdiction. It was especially this latter point which aroused great hostility, because the relevant constitution of Clarendon was interpreted by the archbishop, Thomas Becket, as a violation of an ancient right and privilege of the clergy, according to which a cleric was exempted from royal or lay jurisdiction. The king's standpoint was that the clerics were his subjects in no wise different from any lay person. Moreover, the procedure envisaged in the Constitutions was alleged to subject the guilty cleric to double punishment – one, the ecclesiastical, by the episcopal court, the other, the royal, pronounced by the secular court. Becket fled the country and declared the Constitutions of Clarendon null and void; he also excommunicated the royal advisers (such as John of Oxford, Richard of Ilchester, Hugh of St Claire, etc.) and threatened Henry himself with ecclesiastical censures. The pope, too, condemned a number of articles of the Constitutions.

The papacy's position was particularly difficult in these years, since they coincided with the grave measures taken by the emperor against Alexander in Germany, Burgundy and Italy; to this must be added differences among the English bishops as well as Henry II's firm resolve to maintain his power over the clergy (mainly to re-establish peace and order after the troubled times of his predecessor); the situation was further aggravated by Henry II's having his son (according to the French model but against English tradition) made a co-king and having him crowned by the archbishop of York (14 June 1170), since the archbishop of Canterbury was in exile. Nor did the temperaments of the chief contestants contribute to an early settlement: long, weary protracted negotiations led to some settlement and accommodation between king and exiled archbishop on 23 July 1170 at Fréteval. This settlement however evaded some of the main issues; nor did the king give any binding promise. Cardinal Albert de Morra (the later Gregory VIII) quoted Jeremiah 13.23 when examining the arrangements between Henry and Thomas. The latter's opponents, notably Roger of York and the bishop of London, had not however been silenced, when Becket returned in December of the same year 1170. On 29 December he was murdered by some knights who had taken in a literal sense an angry outburst of Henry II which he came to regret bitterly. This senseless murder nevertheless speeded the final settlement of the king with the papacy at Avranches on 21 May 1172: Henry revoked some of the obnoxious clauses of the Constitutions of Clarendon and made amends, as demanded, to Alexander III.

However frequently he was forced to leave Rome and to take refuge for lengthy periods in France, in the history of the papacy Alexander III must nevertheless be accorded the greatest importance. His pontificate marked the period of transition between Gregory VII and Innocent III. Precisely because he had none of the qualities distinguishing these two popes, and because he was not endowed with originality, vision or real statecraft, but was a conscientious administrator with the gifts of endurance and unemotional toughness, the papacy emerged at the end of his long pontificate stronger, more respected and resilient than when he had ascended the throne of St Peter. It was the very mediocrity, if not commonplace tenacity of the administrator which at the time strengthened the papacy in the face of the very serious onslaught launched upon it by the emperor. His aim of turning the papacy into a patriarchate of the empire was thwarted. Despite schism, despite the incontrovertible danger to the papacy, despite anti-popes and the general hostility of the Romans, and above all despite the long sojourns of the pope abroad, the papacy as an institution had not suffered in the least. On the contrary, it had shown that, as an institution it could weather the very severe storms afflicting it, and it could do so, because this mediocre and entirely unoriginal pope was also the first pope who was a fully trained jurist of considerable skill and reputation. It is rarely the vocation of a jurist to show vision. As a pope it was his prime duty to apply in practice the theory of canon law which he himself had ably propounded at Bologna.

The papacy as an institution depended on this kind of office-holder represented by Alexander III. It must be emphasized that in great matters Alexander did not shine forth and revealed no constructive or positive plan, but the significance of his pontificate lies in the consistent translation of theory into reality: his verdicts, decrees, in short his decretal legislation was precisely what the papacy needed most just at that time. Nearly four and a half thousand decretals of his pontificate are still preserved – and more are still coming to light – and his legislation was to be the largest contribution which an individual pope made to the later official canon law book. His decretals created living law, because they dealt with all the issues relevant to his contemporary Christian society. They were despatched to places as far apart as Durham and Salerno, Salamanca in Spain, Upsala and Linkoeping in Sweden, Braga in Portugal, Armagh in Ireland, Prague in Bohemia, Gran in Hungary and Cracow in Poland; while among frequent addressees were the kings of Denmark, England, France, Hungary, Portugal, Scotland, Sweden. Among the juristic topics with which his decretals dealt, were matrimonial matters, feudal, electoral, judicial, legatine, penal, disciplinary subjects, in addition to issues concerning collegiate ecclesiastical bodies, the rights of cathedral chapters, and the disposal of goods during a vacancy, oaths, clerical duties, appointments of officers, details of tithes, rents and dues, prebends, immunities, extensive and restrictive interpretation of the law, constitutional problems, appellate jurisdiction, to mention just a few of the more important legislative acts which remained the law until Whitsun 1918, if not beyond.

It was in this pontificate that a major development unobtrusively took place. This development concerned the proprietary church system which came to be abolished through the papal decretals: they turned the pure theory as set forth by Gratian, into the enforceable law. The lay lord was, so to speak, dispossessed of his church and became its patron (or *advocatus*, hence advowson) with specific duties attached. And this patronage of the individual church was said to be 'annexed' to a 'spiritual thing' (i.e. the church) with the consequence that all issues connected with the lay lord's patronage came under ecclesiastical jurisdiction. Through the Alexandrian legislation Gratian's theory became the universal law which put the final and legal stop to the Investiture Contest. Finally, the legislation of this pontificate also contributed to the consolidation of the papal administration. In a word, the mechanics, the actual machinery of government and its organization were to a very large extent developed during this reign.

While the papacy's able German antagonist created little that proved to be of more than temporary value, chased a phantom in the shape of an alien secular Romanism and had few constructive ideas, Alexander III by his steady, unostentatious and unobtrusive handling of government enabled the papacy by the turn of the century to become the focal institution of Europe.

9 The Zenith of the Medieval Papacy

THE HARVEST FOR the papacy from the formal peace settlement at Venice was not overwhelming, either in Germany where the papal demands for 'freedom of elections' remained largely on parchment – the German episcopate appeared to prefer imperial mastery to papal orders – or in Italy where imperial troops were stationed in large parts of the Mathildine territories claimed by the papacy as belonging to the papal state. Yet the effects of the long schism within the papacy and the quarrels between papacy and empire were not lost on contemporaries. These were facts which fanned criticism of the contemporary papacy that was easily to develop into opposition. For what the Western world witnessed in the seventies and eighties of the twelfth century was an upsurge of so-called heretical sects and movements and groups, the common denominator of which was aversion from the officially fixed and applied kind of Christianity. These manifestations grew quite spontaneously in different parts of Europe and were largely independent of each other. This phenomenon furnishes ample evidence of the deep social influence which ecclesiastical institutions had come to exercise, and in particular the papacy which by its thousands of decretals effectively and concretely intervened in the shaping of the social organism. Furthermore, these non-conformist sects flourished strongly where the theocratic or descending theme of government was firmly entrenched and applied in practice, such as in France, Flanders, Southern Germany and the Rhineland. Vice-versa, where this ideology was less developed, the reaction to it was correspondingly weak, which appears to explain the absence of heretical movements on any worthwhile scale in England.

By virtue of the theocratic thesis directly based as it was on religious principles, the non-conformist manifestations were bound to affect theocratic governments adversely. This explains why the papacy and the emperor, Frederick I, at once found common ground when these heretical manifestations had reached dimensions which were held to be dangerous to both of them. Then harmony was at once established, because both felt their foundations threatened. At the synod of Verona in October 1184 – convoked in order to settle the double election at the ancient see of Trier, a purpose which remained unfulfilled – pope and emperor issued a joint decree concerning heresy. The significance of this synodal decree was that it laid down certain guide-lines by which statements or views or expressions could be pronounced as heretical; they also decreed severe penalties for the adherents of these sects, especially for lay people who after sentence by the ecclesiastical court were to be handed over to the secular justice for special treatment (which was the stake). The other noteworthy point was that all secular authorities such as counts, barons, rectors, etc., were bidden upon request by the competent ecclesiastical authority to help clerics against the heretics. The sanction threatened against recalcitrant secular lords was excommunication, interdict and deprivation of their office, while refractory cities were to be cut off from trade with other cities. This decree was the first general law to combat heresy and remained the basis for future legislation against heretics. The criterion of heresy was non-conformity with what the papacy had fixed (this had already been stated by Gregory VII, see below p. 220) and the Staufen emperor accepted and endorsed this decree thereby implicitly acknowledging to what extent his own position was dependent on the papally fixed faith. And the legal duty of the secular power to extirpate heresy upon the bidding of the ecclesiastical officers was here unambiguously enacted.

Yet at the same time Frederick pursued his secular Romanism which was based on premisses wholly different from those which he himself had just endorsed at Verona. Throughout his reign Frederick tried to act as a master of the papacy rather than as the papacy's own specially created protector. Thereby the papacy was forced to take up a defensive position and to adopt corresponding measures. Nevertheless, as long as Frederick directed his Romanism outside, that is, against Constantinople, there was harmony between the papacy and him. Then indeed both papacy and Western empire followed identical aims, that is, the reduction, if not destruction, of the empire in the East, because thereby the goal of the emperor to be the one and only Roman emperor, and the goal of the papacy to have its primacy also acknowledged in the East, would have been reached. As already noted (see above p. 186), there was a sharp contrast to this harmony in the domestic sphere.

For in line with his secular Romanism, which viewed the papacy as an imperial patriarchate on the pattern of the Byzantine emperor, Frederick demanded from the papacy that his son Henry (VI) be crowned emperor. Both popes, Lucius III and Urban III, flatly refused to adopt this Byzantine device of a co-emperor, whereupon Frederick occupied virtually the whole of the papal state. That he himself conferred the title of 'Caesar' on his son, showed his programme clearly as did his arrangement of the marriage of his son with the Sicilian princess, Constance, Roger II's daughter. This was indeed a master stroke, because Constance was sure to become the heiress of the Sicilian kingdom and the Staufen Henry VI, her husband, would then rule that kingdom which the papacy had since the mid-eleventh century considered to be its safe refuge. One can say that the papacy was in danger of being encircled and isolated in a physical sense. Yet, in accordance with his secular Romanism Frederick's plan had also – and very likely primarily – strategic motives which would indeed make it understandable why the papacy under Urban III did not object to the marriage. On the contrary, papal legates were present at the wedding in the cathedral of Milan on 27 January 1186. For strategically Sicily was particularly valuable: it was the springboard to the East and the only useful maritime access which the empire had. In any event, this marriage was to be of crucial importance for the papacy (but no less also for the empire), because German power came to be established in Sicily and was profoundly to affect the fortunes of the papacy in the thirteenth century.

Although the third crusade was launched on the initiative of the papacy – Pope Gregory VIII successfully appealed in his encyclical for it, because Jerusalem had been lost to the Muslims since 1187 – the leadership, organization and management were entirely in the hands of Frederick I who commanded a large and well-equipped army of some 25,000 warriors. Powerful support had also come from the English and French kings who had raised the 'Saladin tithe'. This was the last crusade that bore a universal character. It was sheer military might which, so to speak, cata-pulted the emperor into his leading position. In actual fact the position of a supreme commander in the field gave him the opportunity to make real the claim inherent in his secular Romanism by boldly asserting that the 'kingdom of Greece' (Byzantium) should henceforth by subjected to himself. This indeed was what the emperor of Constantinople was told in 1189 by the crusader Frederick who, menacingly making active pre-parations for the assault on Constantinople, styled himself 'the one monarch' to whom all other rulers owed obedience; and among these other rulers was not only the Eastern emperor, but also the kings in the West who had already been designated by the derogatory epithet of 'reguli' (mere kinglets). For the last time the Byzantines were able to stave off the very real military threat to the existence of their empire by making concessions. Drowned on a crusade when crossing a river in the Middle East (10 June 1190) Frederick Barbarossa of all medieval rulers had come nearest to reducing the papacy to a patriarchate of the German empire.

The animosity which the curia harboured towards the Staufen dynasty on the domestic front was easily understandable and was to bear fruit in the reign of Innocent III. In any event, Frederick's death did not remove the threat to the papacy. On the contrary, Henry VI was resolved ruthlessly to continue the policy of his father in regard to the papacy, Sicily and Constantinople. The twenty-five-year-old king confronted one of the most experienced and skilled cardinals in the person of Pope Celestine III, who was exactly 60 years older than the Staufen whom he crowned emperor on Easter Monday, 15 April 1191. Despite papal remonstrations and warnings he began to take possession of Sicily which he claimed by right of the inheritance of his wife Constance. He was crowned king of Sicily by the archbishop of Messina on Christmas Day 1194, and on 26 December his only son, Frederick Roger, was born. The union of this southernmost kingdom with the empire was a deadly threat to the papacy.

Every Staufen was anxious to secure his succession. In the case of Henry VI this meant to safeguard Frederick's future royal (and imperial) position which at once involved the papacy directly. At the Diet of Würzburg in 1196 the German princes somewhat half-heartedly agreed to accept Henry's proposition to make the

'Roman kingdom' hereditary on the model of other contemporary kingdoms. Now, this term 'Roman kingdom' or 'King of the Romans' had been considered as the stage preliminary to the position of the fully-fledged emperor of the Romans who could be made by the papacy only. But according to German reasoning the 'King of the Romans' (the *rex Romanorum*) gave a title-deed, that is, a right to be crowned by the pope and, moreover, meant the exercise of actual physical, royal power in Italian districts, some of which were also those claimed or actually possessed by the papacy as part of the papal state. For the Germans this royal position in Italy was essential, for what sort of Roman emperor would this be who had no reality of power in Italy? He would be as much a chimerical Roman emperor as the one in Constantinople who, also, was without royal, physical control anywhere in Italy. Yet the existence of this 'King of the Romans' had never officially been acknowledged by the papacy, and – in view of the history of the twelfth century – this was not surprising, because it would at least have implied formal papal recognition of German rule in Italy over undefined regions, including in fact territories claimed or held by the papacy.

But now at the same Diet of Würzburg in which Henry VI had made preparations for a crusade, he was anxious to have the succession regulated and a formal papal acknowledgment of the successor was essential. Hence the negotiations between Henry VI and Celestine III in October of this same year 1196 which aimed at having the boy Frederick baptized and also anointed as King of the Romans by the pope. These negotiations took place in great secrecy and dragged on for nearly a fortnight, but had no result, because the papacy could never agree to a perpetuation of a state of affairs which would have been completely inimical to its own interests in Italy. After all, at that very time, most of the papal state was occupied by German troops. And to have made Frederick 'King of the Romans' would have given him precisely these rights which the papacy did not wish him to have, first, because of the legitimization of German rule in Italy where the territorial boundaries were in any case fluid, and secondly, because the imperial coronation of the King of the Romans would then indeed have amounted to no more than a mere formality or solemnity – and this would have confirmed the very standpoint which the Staufens had always taken up, and which diametrically conflicted with the papal view according to which the imperial coronation was the exercise of a papal judgment as to the suitability of its strong arm: the coronation would have been merely declaratory and no longer constitutive.

The breakdown of these negotiations was the signal for the rapid ascendancy of the papacy after the last decades had witnessed the harassment and defence of the institution. The middle-nineties of the twelfth century were crucial for the papacy as an institution. If ever there was a Ruler who conducted his government entirely on the basis of secular Romanism and to all intents and purposes was a true Roman Caesar, it was Henry VI. He ruled over Europe from the Tweed to the Bosporus (the English Richard I was his prisoner and vassal); he had successfully weakened and encircled the Byzantine empire; he had made the kings of Armenia and Cilicia his subjects. Yet it was the papacy to which the future belonged, not to the Staufen 'Roman' empire. It was the papacy which was the only real 'winner' in the centuries-long conflict between East and West when Constantinople was captured by the Westerners. Thereby the papacy achieved its aim of establishing Roman primacy in Constantinople. It was as if Constantinople and the Eastern empire had become a ripe fruit that dropped into the lap of the papacy. The Staufen designs and attacks had so corroded the Eastern empire that the erection of a papally orientated Latin empire in Constantinople did not call for superhuman efforts.

The constellation of circumstances after the unexpected early death of Henry VI on 28 September 1197 were wholly favourable for the papacy. The young emperor was soon followed into the grave by the 92-year-old Celestine III in early January 1198. The cardinals acting on the new election decree of the Third Lateran Council (see below p. 229) proceeded in a swift election to create Cardinal Lothar of Segni as successor of St Peter. Innocent III was presented with a situation as favourable as hardly any pope before or after him had been fortunate to meet. Frederick, the heir to the Sicilian and German throne, was a minor of just over 3 years old; the population in Italy was sick and tired of German rule, destruction and occupation. In Germany there was virulent party strife which in the course of 1198 produced a double election in the persons of Philip of Swabia, the candidate of the Staufen party and a brother of the dead Henry on the one hand,

and of Otto of Brunswick, the candidate of the prosperous Guelf party on the other. German power had virtually completely collapsed in Southern Italy and Sicily, and upon the death of the empress, Constance, in November 1198 the pope himself became the guardian of Frederick (II) and the feudal overlord of the kingdom as the widow had in fact stipulated. Constantinople was enfeebled by the heavy payments to the Germans as a ransom as well as by serious succession troubles. The schools of canon law had produced a mature governmental ideology and had greatly deepened the science of canonical jurisprudence – in fact, Innocent III himself had been a pupil of the eminent canonist Huguccio at Bologna as well as of Peter of Corbeil at Paris.

Innocent III moreover possessed exactly the right credentials and qualifications. An energetic, purposeful, tireless worker, a man of vision and yet always concentrating on what was feasible and practicable, a man whose methodical and tidy mind displayed an extraordinary lucidity in the spoken and written word as well as an unusual grasp of the essential elements of a matter. He was an ecclesiastical Ruler who appeared to be interested in the promotion of basic Christian tenets rather than in mere external formalism. Over and above these qualities he had a superiority of intellect which put him far above any of his contemporaries; it was this intellect which enabled him to analyse a complex situation in easily comprehensible terms. To these features should be added as highly characteristic of the man an excellent sense of humour and ready wit, especially when presiding as supreme judge in his judicial sittings held usually three times a week.

Yet, as is so often the case with men of outstanding intellectual qualities, he had quite a remarkable lack of knowledge of men and a corresponding inability to realize on what base motives men, even if they were archbishops, princes and kings, could be prompted to act. If there is one thread running through this pontificate, it is that mundane reality can be conquered by the force inherent in ideas. It was on this axiom that Innocent based his policy, and it was this axiom which made him suffer shipwreck in the very problems to which he applied himself with singular zeal and devotion. It is nevertheless remarkable that before his election – he was merely a deacon on being elected pope – hardly any of these literary, juristic and intellectual qualities were shown. Although he played a far greater part in the inner councils of the curia than he is usually credited with, his book written while a cardinal and entitled 'On the contempt of the world' is commonplace, lugubrious, emotional, platitudinous, and had it not had the later Innocent III as its author, would rightly have been consigned to oblivion. The election seems to have transformed Cardinal Lothar: he was, if ever there was one, a Ruler *par excellence* who superbly mastered papal ideology as well as its law.

The papacy had indeed a man who believed he knew how to utilize the favourable circumstances to the advantage of the institution itself. In brief Innocent III was the man who came nearest to accomplishing the task begun by Gregory VII – that is, the translation of abstract papal ideology into reality. During his pontificate the papacy became the focal point of Europe. He had the fortune to inherit the institutional framework of the papacy, the organizational, departmentalized and specialized apparatus of the curia. It had been preserved in its basic functions throughout the preceding decades of acrimonious conflicts. The actual machinery for governing Christian society was now entrusted to one of the ablest successors of St Peter who wielded his inherited powers as vicar of Christ.

As governor Innocent III realized that the personnel of the curia and certain malpractices which had begun to infest curial departments, needed his urgent attention. Even before he was consecrated and crowned (on 22 February 1198, that is, six weeks after his election), he started a re-organization of the whole curial apparatus, making short shrift of the parasites and hangers-on in the various departments and purging and streamlining the executive departments of the papacy. At the same time the civil administration of the city of Rome and its immediate environs was taken in hand and within literally speaking a few weeks the heads of the civil administration, such as the prefect and the justiciars, were replaced by men of his own choosing. Innocent laid the foundations for the exemplary curial civil service organization which was indeed necessary if the multifarious tasks of the curia were to be discharged properly.

But all this was part of the far larger plan to make the papacy an effective instrument of government which needed a secure base in Italy. Hence also in the very first weeks of his pontificate he began the so-called policy of recuperations, that is, the recovery of the territories claimed to belong to the papacy by right and wrongly taken away from it. As the territorial extent of the regions re-claimed was never precisely fixed, and as moreover numerous districts were claimed on the basis of documents which as often as not were spurious (such as the Donation of Constantine), plenty of elbow-room for manœuvring was left to a pope with diplo-matic skill. Although some of Innocent's claims in pursuit of the recuperation policy may seem fantastic, he nevertheless succeeded in central Italy in reconstituting the papal state which, from the curial standpoint, was in a sorry condition. German officers, rectors, administrators, and so on, were replaced by papal officers. The success of this policy was not a little due to Inno-cent's making skilful use of the very pronounced anti-German sentiments in Italy and by sometimes striking up tones which a later age might have termed nationalist, such as 'our dolce Italia' or 'the interests of Italy demand recuperation and papal rule', and the like, though a nationalistic sentiment was totally alien to a pope of Innocent's calibre. What these adulations aimed at was a diminution of German power in Italy, or in correct contemporary terms, the eventual abolition of the very idea of a 'King of the Romans'. It is not generally recognized that neither this idea, nor the term, nor the office of a 'King of the Romans' existed in Innocent's structure of papal programme or vocabulary. Not once did he himself use this term. To him there was a German, French, English king, but no Roman king who exercised legitimate power in Italian regions and who, above all, claimed to have a *right* to become Roman emperor. This policy of recuperations was indissolubly linked with this Innocentian rejection of a 'King of the Romans'. Not without justification has Innocent been called the second founder of the papal state.

The rapid initial success of the policy of recuperations was certainly due to the vacancy in Germany after the death of Henry VI in September 1197. Moreover, there was also a vacuum in Constantinople which was an added incentive for the papacy to act quickly. The election of Philip of Swabia in April 1198 by the Staufen party was followed by the election of Otto of Brunswick by the Guelf party which was determined, partly for ideological, partly for commercial-economic reasons, not to have another Staufen on the throne (the Guelfs had their main support in the Rhineland and were led by Adolf, the archbishop of Cologne, whence trade relations with England were important). Although this double election was of vital interest to the papacy, Innocent made no move to exercise influence in Germany for well over 2 years, however closely and keenly he watched the situation as it evolved. That his sympathies lay with the Guelf candidate was obvious, but as pope, that is, as the one who had to confer the imperial crown on one of the two contestants, he outwardly kept the unbiased attitude of an umpire until he considered that papal interests warranted his active intervention which was in the early part of 1201. How much importance he attached to the matter can be seen from his establishing a special Register which contained all the official communications received and dispatched by him on the imperial question. This correspondence shows the superb skill of this pope and his unsurpassed dexterity in handling explosive material.

The conflict between Philip and Otto gave Innocent an opportunity of stating in unequivocal terms the basic papal principles relative to the government of Christian society. Above all, he declared himself on the role and function of the emperor in this society. The Staufen thesis that the elected German king had a right to the imperial crown because he was 'King of the Romans' Innocent flatly rejected and made it plain that the conferment of the imperial position was an 'apostolic', that is, a papal favour which could be exercised only on the fulfilment of certain conditions. And history down to his time amply proved, he declared, that the papacy had always been opposed by the Staufen dynasty. Thus he rejected all claims made by Philip who had announced that he was to come to Rome 'in the near future' to obtain the crown from the pope. He also rejected the claim advanced on behalf of the young Frederick II, not only because he was a Staufen, but also because he was unsuitable on other grounds. Innocent therefore decided in favour of the Guelf candidate, Otto, and his main reason for so doing was that Otto was prepared to make a number of concessions which were attuned to the Italian programme of the papacy: Otto's promises virtually renounced German rights in Italy. Above all, fears of the dreaded Staufen union of the empire with Sicily were dispelled by Otto's promises which fully acknowledged the papal recuperations. Innocent's decision on the 'imperial' question in reality depended on which of the two contestants would be least troublesome in Italy.

But Innocent could not pose this problem in its brutal simplicity – indeed its immediate beginnings went back to the abortive negotiations between Henry VI and Celestine III in 1196 (see above p. 205) – without offending both aspirants to the imperial crown: hence Innocent's stress on his role as emperor-maker and the exposition of the papal theory of the emperor. The papal theme was set forth in its final form: the pope as the vicar of Christ alone had the right to create the universal protector of Christendom who therefore was no more than an assistant (or advocate) of the papacy in the pursuit of its aims on a universal scale. Innocent emphasized the right of the Germans to elect their king, but his promotion to emperorship was the exercise of papal judgment, because it was the apostolic see which had transferred the empire from Constantinople to the West in the person of Charlemagne (the so-called theory of translation of the empire). To the papacy the emperor was an officer specifically created by the pope as his strong physical arm on a universal scale: the Roman emperor reflected the universality of the Roman Church, his creator, hence also the repeated emphasis on the sun-moon allegory in this context, the moon receiving its light from the sun. He was charged with specific duties and was given by the papacy a plenitude of power in order to discharge these duties. How far the latter went was in the final resort to be decided by the papacy. That is why the creation of the emperor belonged to the papacy 'principally and finally' (*principaliter et finaliter*). Regally the emperor was a German king (hence Innocent's refusal to interfere in German elections), and not a 'King of the Romans' with regal powers in Italy, while functionally the emperor was a papal officer (hence the absence of an enthronement, see above p. 187) whose power notionally was as universal as the pope's who had made him. This imperial power should be exercised only when ordered by the papacy – the bequest of Bernard's teachings that the emperor should act at the bidding of the pope. That, in brief, was Innocent's theory of empire as set forth in the conflict between Philip and Otto. And this theory also furnished the appropriate background to the Fourth Crusade, the active preparation for which fell precisely into the early years of Innocent's pontificate.

Despite an initial success of Otto between 1201 and 1203 which was entirely due to Innocent's insistent diplomatic support, the

Guelf cause began to lose favour among the German princes, ecclesiastical as well as secular. Although he was still excommunicated – though the fact was not generally known in Germany – Philip made progress and, by 1205, Otto was virtually left alone. In the changing fortunes of the two contestants Innocent's personal deficiency – his inability to judge personalities correctly – played a major role. Otto was a worthless, inefficient, bungling, totally unreliable braggart, while Archbishop Adolf of Cologne, the main driving force of the Guelfs, dropped Otto after having pawned the treasures of his cathedral and fleeced the Guelf side: in 1205 he offered to crown Philip king of Germany or king of the Romans, after having crowned and enthroned Otto seven years earlier at Aachen: on 6 January 1205 Adolf as the legitimate coronator anointed, crowned and enthroned his formerly bitterly attacked, if not persecuted, opponent at the right place – at Charlemagne's seat of government, Aachen. Only now did the realization dawn on Innocent that it was impossible to govern by ideas alone and to master concrete actuality by subjecting it to the logically compelling force of the abstract idea.

Innocent was forced to recognize this state of affairs, especially when Philip and his party were now ready to make a number of concessions which they were unwilling to make in the earlier phases of the conflict. Just before a mixed commission of papal and Staufen legates was to assemble to finalize the agreement, Philip was murdered (June 1208). The assassination was entirely unconnected with the dispute with Otto who now left no stone unturned to revert to his earlier position. Since this German civil war had already lasted some ten years, a general weariness made itself felt. The papacy too was keen to put an end to this matter, and on 4 October 1209 Innocent III crowned Otto emperor of the Romans, only now to realize what kind of man he had distinguished by his support. Otto conveniently forgot all his earlier promises and changed from a Guelf into an emperor with Staufen aims. His attempt in 1210 to occupy Southern Italy and his dispatch of troops to Sicily as well as his efforts to restore a number of papally 'recuperated' territories to German jurisdiction by enfeoffing German officers with these territories (for instance, Spoleto, Ancona, Romagna, etc.) met with energetic sanctions by Innocent, that is to say, excommunication of the emperor less than a year after his coronation.

Despite a brilliant strategy and a perfect mastery of papal ideology and history Innocent's policy had suffered total shipwreck, as he himself acknowledged in his letters to the German bishops: he had forged the sword by which he was now smitten. He applied to himself the words of I Kings 15.11: 'It repents me that I have set up Saul to be king.' In numerous dispatches he could not mention the name of Otto without appropriate curses. The young Staufen, Frederick II, the pope's own ward, was now formally elected king by the German princes in 1211. He promised never again to unite Sicily with Germany. Crowned 'King of Romans' (that is, king of Germany) at Mainz in 1212 the Staufen renewed in the Golden Bull of Eger in 1213 the promise which the Guelf Otto had made more than ten years earlier in regard to the papal recuperations and the freedom of ecclesiastical elections. Otto's fate was sealed, not by papal policy or stratagems, but by the defeat which was inflicted upon him and his English ally by the combined forces of Philip II of France and of Frederick II at Bouvines in 1214.

The papacy under Innocent III came to be considered in this very same decade as the embodiment of law and order by those who would otherwise have become victims of anarchy and arbitrariness. But appeals to the papacy involved it also in interventions in the public sector of a number of kingdoms. Thus with France for which in common with many other pontiffs, he harboured a nostalgic predilection, Innocent's relations worsened as a result of the matrimonial affair of Philip II (Augustus). He had preferred Agnes of Meran to his legitimate wife Ingeborg of Denmark whom he dismissed. This affair had serious repercussions in the public sphere, because one of the few supporters of Otto was the Danish king Waldemar II whose sister Ingeborg was. Agnes was the daughter of the Duke of Meran, a staunch supporter of Philip of Swabia. Hence in order not to offend Waldemar and not to give unwittingly support to the Staufen cause, Innocent took severe measures and forced Philip to take his wife Ingeborg back. Yet Innocent readily legitimized the illegitimate children whom Agnes had borne – no doubt the significance of this gesture was not lost on France and Philip Augustus.

England too became the scene of papal intervention, especially as King John had close relations with Otto of Brunswick. Hence Innocent showed some forbearance towards the king in spite of some of his high-handed ecclesiastical measures. But a number of disputes compelled Innocent's intervention, after they had been brought to his attention and before his court. Among these was the Canterbury matter. The vacancy of the archbishopric in 1205 and King John's policy forced Innocent's hand. The election was indeed highly irregular. The monks at Canterbury had first elected their sub-prior Reginald, but soon afterwards and upon royal pressure dropped their candidate and together with suffragans elected the bishop of Norwich, a royal favourite. When the matter came before the papal court, Innocent quashed both 'elections' and the monks present in Rome elected Cardinal Stephen Langton, a contemporary of the pope at the university of Paris, whom he personally consecrated at Viterbo in June 1207. But the king refused to admit Langton whereupon he was excommunicated after the country was put under an interdict (March 1208), with the result that there was no divine service. Many bishops fled and prevailed upon the pope to release John's subjects from their oath of allegiance which Innocent eventually did. Philip of France was empowered by the papacy to invade England and to take possession of the country. Active French preparations made John compliant, and on 13 May 1213 he gave in, especially as his own barons had also begun to rebel against him. He resolved to become a papal vassal which meant that he was now under special protection of the papacy. Langton was admitted as archbishop of Canterbury. The papal interdict lasting for more than five years, caused great distress in the country, especially as papal taxation demands had in any case exacerbated the sentiments of the English towards the papal curia.

Papal vassalage of England was preceded by the enfeoffments of other countries. Bulgaria under its King Joannitza had become a papal fief. The Spanish peninsula became of particular importance for Europe. Aragon under its King Peter II renewed the arrangements which had started in 1089, but had lapsed in the course of the twelfth century, according to which the country was to be a papal fief. In 1204 he was crowned a papal vassal by Innocent himself who also obtained the king's promise of free and canonical elections. Portugal as well as Castile renewed feudal contracts with the papacy, and it was in fact the joint military effort of Navarre, Castile, Aragon and Portugal which sealed the fate of the Arabs in the peninsula. They were decisively defeated on 16 July 1212, and the papacy was able to start with the ecclesiastical organization of the districts liberated. This was a task which was greatly facilitated by these kingdoms having been fiefs of the papacy. In fact, the papacy in the early thirteenth century counted a greater number of vassals than any other European power.

Papal activity in the North and North-East of Europe took the form of supporting missionary activities, especially in Livland. In order to assist the resident bishop, Albert, Innocent appealed to the Christians in Saxony and Westphalia to take up arms against the pagans in Livland instead of a pilgrimage to Rome. This example of the North-East mission was later also followed by other popes and by the Germans. Both in Norway and Sweden the Innocentian papacy had cause to intervene in royal succession disputes. The Bohemian Duke Ottocar was allowed by the pope and in agreement with Otto IV to assume the royal title, functions and privileges. Thereby Bohemia became a kingdom which it was to remain well into the modern age. In Hungary, too, the papacy intervened in the conflict between King Emmeric and his brother Andrew. In short, papal activity and influence was displayed throughout the length and breadth of Europe. The papal curia became the busiest governmental centre in the 'world' as it then was.

The significance of the Fourth Crusade emerges only fully in this context. From the very beginning of his pontificate Innocent considered a crusade as one of the urgent tasks. He ordered a special crusading tax to be paid by the clergy (one-fortieth of their income). Led by Duke Boniface of Montferrat the crusading army (over 30,000 men) transported in Venetian ships left in November 1202, but instead of sailing for Egypt as originally intended the crusade first captured Zara (now Zadar) on the Dalmatian coast (despite explicit papal prohibition) and then took course for Constantinople – the very contingency which the Byzantines had always feared. The crusaders besieged the city and finally in April 1204 fiercely attacked and shamelessly devastated this ancient place of culture. Constantinople was occupied by the Westerners who erected a Latin empire with a Latin ecclesiastical organization there. Although this event was not planned by Innocent he nevertheless warmly welcomed the union of the Roman and Greek churches which was the immediate result of the fall of Constantinople and of its occupation. This brought to fruition the aim harboured by the papacy since the fifth century – the establishment of primatial authority in Constantinople. Indeed, from his point of view the pope had reason to exclaim that the church of Constantinople had now returned to her mother, the Roman Church; or as he also declared, the church of Constantinople was now reborn into a new infancy through its being subjected to Roman primacy. The papal writ now began to run into Asia Minor. What had eluded the Germans, fell into the lap of the papacy. Innocent even thought that if the empire had passed from the Greeks to the Latins earlier, the holy places would never have been lost.

The Latin empire lasted until 1261 and served the papacy as a firm base from which to undertake missions to Russia, in order to complete the union of the churches. The Latin patriarchate in Constantinople – inflated by an enormous (Latin) hierarchy and staff – experienced nothing but hostility at the hands of the populace, but at least on parchment the schism had come to an end. As far as the papacy was concerned, the organization of the Latin Church in the East put a very great strain on its resources, though initially the papacy was able to cope with the strain well enough. Innocent appealed for a new crusade against Islam in 1213: it was to have started in 1217.

In view of this far-flung activity of the curia and the kind of Christianity it reflected, the growth of an opposition to it cannot cause much surprise, although at first this opposition was not directed against the papacy as an institution. Better education of larger parts of the population promoted a certain critical attitude to a legally fixed and judicially enacted brand of Christianity. The chief grievances of the – admittedly – small opposition groups were that the higher clergy neglected their preaching duties and that they had amassed too much wealth. There was some affinity with earlier rebellious manifestations, instanced by Arnold of Brescia. This time however the main platform of the opposition was the substance of an officially decreed Christianity, and therefore much more serious than any earlier opposition. Hence the two battle cries were: itinerant preaching and apostolic poverty. There were signs of this spirit of opposition throughout Western Christendom. They were in evidence by the time Innocent became pope. In dealing with the adversaries this pope's intelligence, understanding of the needs of the time and his general humanity distinctly mark him off from all his predecessors and successors. The rigid, inflexible, dogmatic approach to the problem of non-conformity, perhaps best illustrated by Alexander III's unimaginative and hamfisted handling of the Waldensians, gave way to an individual approach on the part of Innocent. His general principle was to treat non-conformists and deviants in the manner in which a medical expert would treat a disease, that is, to seek out the symptoms in order to detect the causes. Treatment should concentrate on the removal of errors which might affect the substance of Christianity. Unessential differences should be left untouched. The aim was to bring back to the ranks as many of the deviationists as possible by making concessions where they could be made without infringing upon the substance of dogma or doctrine. But if these efforts should fail and the deviationists should still persist in their practices and teachings, the full rigour of the law relative to heresy was to be brought into play.

This basic policy showed considerable success, though by no means to that extent which its originator had hoped, partly because the disease had gone too far to be treated in the way he suggested, partly because the non-conformists had no firm organization and also because their diffuse multiplicity made contact with them very difficult to obtain. Moreover, to a very large extent the papacy had to rely on the co-operation of the bishops who lacked the necessary understanding and perception. Their response to the enlightened papal policy was on the whole very poor, for to them a non-conformist was a heretic to be damned; and when the target of criticism was the neglect of episcopal preaching and the like, the bishops' hostility was perhaps understandable from the human point of view. Where however the deviationists were concentrated in more or less closely circumscribed communities or localities, it was easier to get in touch with their leaders. This was, for instance, the case with the Humiliati in Northern Italy, the Poor Men of Lyons, the Trinitarians, and similar communities. In these circumstances certain compromise solutions were found and respectable sections of non-conformists were granted a living space within the framework of the Church.

Paradoxically enough, one might say that Innocent himself was converted to 'heresy' when he advised the Spanish sub-prior Dominic of Osma and Bishop Diego of Osma on their return journey from Rome to Spain (in 1206) to assume the same external manners which characterized the heretics, such as roaming about in tattered clothings, taking up the itinerant way of preaching and above all provoking the Waldensians and other heretics to public discussions, but yet at all times representing the orthodox doctrines. The first recorded encounter between Dominic-Diego and the heretics took place at Pamiers in Southern France in the early part of 1207. This can be reckoned as the beginning of the Friars movement, of the itinerant preachers who represented orthodoxy as well as poverty. The Dominican Friars (the Order of Preachers) developed from this rather insignificant incident; they were ecclesiastically recognized as an Order in the pontificate of Innocent's successor. In fighting the heretical movements the Dominicans were as great a force as the other group, that is, the followers of St Francis of Assisi (the later Order of the Friars Minor). They had an entirely different origin. In their beginning they were quite unorthodox. Their founder wholly absorbed the twin aims of apostolic poverty and preaching on a much more individualistic basis than the Dominicans had envisaged. Upon petition of Francis and the powerful support by Cardinal Ugolini Innocent raised no objection to the small group that had collected around Francis (1210), provided they remained responsible to their leader and he himself to the pope. The group rapidly increased, although to the less discerning bishops they could hardly be distinguished from heretics proper; regional resistance to the new group was at times fierce. Even in the Fourth Lateran Council the synodists took by no means a favourable view of the two new movements. It is nevertheless virtually certain that the two mendicant Orders prevented an otherwise exuberant growth of heresy in the thirteenth century. In the last resort it was the far-sighted policy of Innocent III which launched them on their successful career, however badly they fitted into the existing ecclesiastical organization. But because they had a flexible and easily adjustable framework they were able to establish contact with sections of the population which were hardly reached by the secular and especially the higher clergy or the monks, that is, the town population which was rapidly growing in the course of the thirteenth century.

In sharp contrast to this enlightened policy is Innocent's handling of the Albigensian heresy which comes not only as an anticlimax but also as a phenomenon which is difficult to explain by Innocent's own standards. For the crusade preached by him against the Albigensians was nothing but a solemn declaration of war against a European sect in France. Admittedly, the Albigensians were numerous in Southern France and counted an influential bourgeoisie among their followers; admittedly they (as Cathari) were avowed enemies of contemporary Christianity and stigmatized all its corporeal or material manifestations, such as the mass and sacraments, sacrilegious practices, however much the Albigensians themselves developed their own ritual; admittedly also their preachers – dedicated and zealous – had no difficulty in pointing an accusing finger at the luxury displayed by contemporary prelates; admittedly the practical application of some Albigensian views would have had serious repercussions in public and social life. It is also true that when the Albigensians spread and began to engulf larger and larger sections of the Southern French populace, Innocent dispatched special legates in the person of some Cistercians, but by their bearing and provocatively ostentatious way of living they only aggravated the situation. When, however, Peter of Castelnau, one of the papal legates was murdered, Innocent openly declared war on the whole region by proclaiming a crusade. Despite urgent entreaties Philip II remained adamant in refusing to become a crusader. The over-all leadership of the papal crusade lay in the hands of the legate, Abbot Arnald Amalrici, another Cistercian, while the armed forces came to be commanded by Simon de Montfort. The war was fought in a bestial manner on both sides and during the occupation of Béziers by the 'crusaders' unspeakable atrocities were committed (1209). The original purpose of extirpating the Albigensian heresy came to be pushed more and more into the background, and the foreground came to be taken up partly by the land-hungry aspirations of French barons, and partly by the prebend-hungry legates: Arnald, for instance, took the archbishopric of Narbonne once this had fallen into the hands of the 'crusaders'. From the point of view of the history of the papacy the campaign inflicted very great damage upon its prestige in these regions. Not until the fourteenth century was it possible to eradicate the most conspicuous manifestations of this heresy.

H

As for Innocent's proclaiming a crusade against Christians – though it should be stressed that he strongly condemned the excesses committed during the war – the explanation may partly lie in the example which was provided by Constantinople and the papal efforts to establish papal primacy over the Byzantine Christians, also labelled heretics, by, if necessary, military means (see above p. 150) and partly in the very conception of heresy as a crime of *lèse majesté*, as high treason, committed against the divine majesty, as he himself had expounded in a decretal some 10 years earlier. Here he declared that the offence against the divine majesty merited at least the same penalties which an offence against a secular majesty entailed. The ideological background of this was the Roman law crime of *lèse majesté* which furnished the jurist Innocent III with the necessary legal backing and armoury. To him, a confirmed and hardened heretic – and there was no doubt about the Albigensians in this respect though the lower local clergy and a great many lay people were their sympathizers – was no Christian in the sense in which he understood the term, because he deliberately defied the authority of the Roman Church. And in this Innocent moved entirely within the framework provided by Gregory VII who too had declared, possibly with a view to Constantinople, that 'he who disagrees with the Roman Church, shall not be held a catholic'.

However short a survey of this all-important pontificate is, it must include at least some reference to the benefits which the institution derived from it in purely legal matters. For Innocent III was the first pope to publish an official collection of canon law. Hitherto all collections, codifications, excerpts and summaries of canon law were purely private works, however official the individual papal decretal may have been. The need for collections containing the new papal law issued since Gratian's *Decretum* (see below p. 242) was clearly felt by the practitioners in the various chanceries and courts as well as in the law schools. The *Decretum* of Gratian was supplemented by a great number of exceedingly competent and exhaustive collections which came to arrange the enormous legislative output according to the subject-matter of the decretals themselves.

A governor of Innocent's calibre, experience and vision realized that for the proper functioning of the Christian body public throughout the length and breadth of Europe, the papal imprint concerning the law was imperative. That is to say, the Registers of Innocent III – the second almost complete set of Registers preserved, apart from Gregory VII's, all others having been destroyed or lost or preserved merely in later copies – were the only authentic as well as central source which contained the thousands of decretals dispatched to all parts of contemporary Christendom: but what the papacy had laid down as the law in a decretal sent to Durham in England could hardly be known at, say, Gnesen or Cracow in Eastern Europe. In other words, the exemplary state of Innocent's Registers enabled the pope to issue a special collection of those decretals which appeared relevant and important enough to serve as an official supplementation to Gratian. This papal collection was finished in 1210 and embodied decretals of the first 12 years of his pontificate. What is further-more significant about this collection is that it was sent to the university of Bologna. This indicates in what high esteem the law school there must have been held by the papacy. In fact, it seemed to be the only suitable medium by which a collection of this kind could be disseminated. The masters at Bologna had now an authentic text which could be used – to quote the pre-amble – in their lectures as well as in the courts. This step by the Innocentian chancery began the long distinguished line of official papal collections of canon law.

The crowning event of Innocent's pontificate as well as of his legislative work was the Fourth Lateran Council which held its first session on 11 November 1215. Attended by some 70 patriarchs and archbishops (from the West and East), nearly four hundred bishops and more than 800 abbots and priors and monastic representatives, this council assumes great significance because it was the first genuinely universal council in the medieval West and was intended to be equal in importance to the great councils of Christian antiquity. That indeed was the point stressed in Innocent's convocation edict. That this council was universal could be gathered by the invitation to, and participation of, the leaders of Christendom who came from various regions, estates and orders; they had assembled to discuss the common good of the Church. Hence in contrast to the twelfth-century Lateran councils the participants were not only bishops, but also abbots and provosts as well as the plenipotentiaries of the secular powers. They all 'represented' Christendom over which Innocent as vicar of Christ presided, because (as Alexander III had already pointed out quoting Bernard of Clairvaux) he had been given the power not only over the priesthood but also over the secular world. The assembly was an impressive testimony of the standing and function of the papacy as the monarchic instrument of governing Christendom. In other words, Innocent translated the pristine idea of the Church as the congregation of all the faithful into a concrete assembly by summoning the leaders of the two orders (laity and clergy) which constituted the Church.

The universality of this Council also found expression in its great and comprehensive legislative output of seventy decrees, some of which were lengthy legal expositions of difficult themes. They can be classed as a legislative summary of this pontificate. In the manner of the ancient councils, this too began with a fixation of the faith, so that the law itself now made possible a reliable differentiation between orthodox Christians and heretics. And consistently enough this was followed by the decree enacting the measures to be adopted in order to extirpate heresy and eliminate heretics. In some respects refining the decree of Lucius III (see above p. 202) this new canon also fixed the social isolation of those who were suspected of heresy and laid down that defendants sentenced as heretics must be handed over to the secular power for special treatment; if secular powers were remiss in purging their countries of heretics, Catholic princes were then to be ordered to move in and occupy the countries concerned. Detailed sanctions were to be applied to the 'fellow-travellers' of heretics. Other decrees made the convocation of annual provincial synods a legal duty while to the religious Orders, such as the Benedictines and Augustinians, instructions were issued to hold general chapters every three years. The creation of new Orders was prohibited – a momentary check on the nascent mendicant Orders – and the veneration of new relics was to be dependent upon papal approbation. Every Christian was enjoined to confess his sins and to receive communion once a year, preferably at Easter tide. A number of decrees dealt with the Jews who were ordered to wear distinctive marks on their clothing so as to prevent intercourse of Christians with Jewish women or Jews with Christian women. Special decrees referred to the forthcoming crusade as well as to the indulgences and the tax to be paid by the clergy (one-twentieth) while the pope and cardinals were to give one-tenth of their income. Wars between Christian princes were to cease for four years. No item of relevance or importance to the Church was omitted in these decrees which in their precision and diction revealed a remarkable skill of draftsmanship: preaching, the education of the clergy, conferment of prebends, elections, rites, matrimonial matters, tithes, discipline, jurisdictional and appellate issues, and so on, constituted the subject-matter of the bulk of decrees. The universal legislation of this council was in keeping with its ecumenical character.

At its zenith the papacy under Innocent III exhibited few original ideas or principles. What the observer finds is that a particular idea was clothed in a memorable phrase or term. For the programmatic ideas of the papacy had now grown to full maturity, culminating in the official function of the pope who from now on was and remained the vicar of Christ which, as already remarked, meant no substantial change in his position (see above p. 183). Innocent drew the manifest conclusions from this basic standpoint by declaring that in his official capacity he was placed between God and man and thus less than God but more than man. This was a statement which has not always been adequately understood. It expressed in a succinct and perspicacious manner the contemporary idea of the personal sovereignty of the pope who in his function as pope stood outside and above the Church that was entrusted to him, but from which he received no power. His powers were those which Christ had handed to St Peter for purposes of governing the Christian commonwealth. He was thus 'set above' the Church. This 'superiority' (= sovereignty) vis-à-vis the Church as the congregation of all the faithful was designated by the old term (of Leo I's coinage in the fifth century) of 'plenitude of power' which tallied exactly with the papal vicariate of Christ based as this was on the Petrine powers. Hence the frequent statements by Innocent that as monarch he alone had plenitude of power, parts of which on the principle of division of labour he distributed downwards so that the lower placed officers who had received some of his power could say of him as the gospel of St John said of Christ (1.16): 'And of his fulness have all we received.' This 'superior' status of the pope also explains why from now on the words of the prophet 'I have set thee over the nations and kingdoms' were found directly applicable to the pope in his official function: this too was no more than a way of expressing the monarchic power in biblical terms.

This plenitude of power manifested itself above all according to Innocent III in the papal claim to comprehensive jurisdiction. Precisely because the body of Christians was entrusted to the papacy, it was the pope's responsibility to govern it in such a way that it would eventually achieve its end, salvation. Therefrom resulted the papal demand to universal jurisdiction which Innocent based on the concept of sin as being destructive of Christian society. Hence whenever sin was involved, papal jurisdiction came into play. By reason of sin (*ratione peccati*) as he termed it, the papacy had the right to intervene judicially in any matter, however secular, temporal or mundane it might be. From this angle the papacy's claim to the control of secular Rulers will be understandable, as also its closely guarded, historically evolved prerogative to create its own universal protector in the shape of the emperor of the Romans. That the papacy therefore devoted great attention to the elaboration of the coronation ritual of the emperor is easily understandable. And Innocent himself ordered the composition of a new imperial rite that finally developed the symbolism employed in earlier rites. His rite presented the papal plenitude of power in symbolic fullness, and sharply accentuated the role of the pope as the sole organ that dispensed imperial power. It was the last papal rite for imperial coronations.

During the Innocentian pontificate this papal plenitude of power came to be particularly frequently expressed in allegories which could be hardly misunderstood by contemporaries. One of these allegories was the already mentioned two sword theme which was abstractly and finally formulated by Bernard and practically applied in Innocent's own imperial coronation ritual when on the occasion of the emperor's coronation the pope himself conferred the sword by girding the emperor with it to show symbolically from whom the emperor had received his physical strength. The sun and moon allegory also expressed the supreme monarchic power, according to which the moon – the emperor – received its light from the sun, the papacy. Sometimes the relationship between pope and emperor was depicted in the allegory of soul and body: to the soul as the vivifying element corresponded the law issued by the papacy for Christendom which here assumed the role of the body (corporate). The ideology underlying this allegory is one of the roots of the rule of law – a body public and corporate could (and can) live only by the law which here rested on the papally expounded faith.

There can be no reasonable doubt that at the time of Innocent III the medieval papacy had reached its apogee. Innocent appears indeed as the pope who with consummate skill would seem to have accomplished the programme of the papacy, the pope who realized after some seven centuries the innermost aspirations of the papacy to become the focal institution of Europe in religious, moral and governmental respects. The papacy was held to be the nerve centre of a singularly homogeneous society the ideological foundations of which rested on the papally fixed Christian faith. This very achievement was also apt to bring into the clearest possible relief the crucial problem of faith and law. The determined opposition to the papacy in some quarters – not so much to Innocent himself – would indicate that the Christian religion and the law as handled by the papacy were conceived to be incompatible with each other – the one purely internal and formless, the other external and formalized. The papal axiom of the compatibility of religion and law, nay, of the necessity that for the full realization of the Christian religion it must be complemented by the law, met with increasing scepticism and doubt. It was indeed the Innocentian pontificate which starkly revealed this most crucial of all crucial problems.

That reflexion together with the unshakeable axiom of Innocent that it was ideas alone which conquered reality may furnish some explanation for the indisputable fact that despite the sometimes brilliantly conceived strategy by the papacy, the actuality of success eluded it: the Fourth Crusade was, from any historical angle, an unmitigated disaster; the imperial, the German and Sicilian questions gaped wide open at the end of this pontificate; the crusading idea was debased by the Albigensian adventure which was soon to become a model for similar other undertakings; growing opposition to the centralism of the papal government in episcopal quarters was clearly noticeable; and so was despite the far-sighted policy of Innocent the growth of heretical sects; a number of kings, such as the French, felt apprehension about a papal policy which to them appeared vacillating, irresolute, if not devoid of principle, as instanced in the management of John's affair in 1213.

Yet the incontrovertible fact also remains that the prestige of the papacy as an institution of government and as the final arbiter in all matters affecting the essential fabric of contemporary Christian society was never higher than when Innocent III closed his eyes on 16 July 1216. His was a pontificate which revealed at once the strength and weakness of the papacy as an institution of government. Its strength lay in the formulation, fixation and application of medieval Christian doctrine, in its axiomatic belief in its ability to shape society by the Christian idea embodied in the law – a grandiose conception and an equally grandiose aim, but whose weakness was that it was hardly capable of being translated into reality. Reality and the natural frailty of mankind could not be mastered by ideas alone. In no other phase in the history of the medieval papacy was there so stark a contrast between actuality and the ideal Christian theme of a rebirth, of a veritable renaissance of mankind.

THE EARLY THIRTEENTH century provides a good vantage point from which to survey the institutional structure of the curia in the high Middle Ages. The term signified the totality of the offices, departments and special institutions which dealt with the legislative, financial, administrative and executive work of the papacy as the central point of Western Christendom. Further, the curia – as any other court – also contained departments which dealt with judicial business and the preparation of those cases which came before the supreme tribunal presided over by the pope, as well as those organizational and administrative sections which any Ruler – then as now – had to have in order to fulfil his functions. As the universal Ruler the pope was especially in need of a well-organized court, for to the papacy was subjected the whole of Christendom in one way or another. This itself necessitated a network of offices, quite apart from those which the administration of the city of Rome and of the papal state demanded.

As monarchic Ruler the pope claimed not only the ownership of all islands (on the basis of the Donation of Constantine), but he was also, as already indicated, the feudal lord of a great many countries. As the general 'overseer' (the *speculator*) he was entitled to depose princes, release subjects from their oaths of allegiance, confer crowns by making kings (as evidenced in Croatia-Dalmatia, Sicily, Armenia, Bulgaria, Lithuania, and so on) and to dispose of territories, as illustrated by Languedoc (after the Albigensian wars) and by Estonia, Russia, etc. In this same capacity as 'overseer' he could order the despatch of troops in support of a Ruler or prohibit further military engagements or refuse any additional armed help, as instanced in Georgia under Gregory IX. He could order the preservation of the legal systems of countries conquered or invaded, as was the case in Ireland. He could transfer one kingdom to another as shown in the case of Hungary in Gregory VII's pontificate and as also envisaged in later pontificates. By the same reasoning he considered himself entitled to annul certain laws, such as Magna Carta in England in August 1215 (on the ground of its interference with royal power) or later, the 'Mirror of the Saxons' in Germany (1274), because it attempted to restrict the papal right to excommunicate the emperor. As the focal institution of Christian Europe the papacy acted as a court which ratified treaties between kings and countries; hence also the right of the papacy to prohibit trade with certain localities and to impose an embargo on towns. Since public highways and rivers were under the special protection of the papacy, ecclesiastical censures were decreed against those who exacted extortionate tolls and customs. All these and similar measures were also brought under the general heading of the papacy's exercise of 'universal government' (what Gregory VII and Innocent III called the 'universale regimen') undertaken in the 'public interest' ('publica utilitas') of the whole Christian commonwealth. Considering the responsible and wide-flung as well as complicated nature of the government, it stands to reason that an official apparatus was necessary to cope with this activity.

In view of the powers of the man who was St Peter's successor and vicar of Christ, his creation was always a matter of intimate concern to the papacy as a governmental institution. The making of the papal monarch required detailed regulations. Even the shortest survey of papal electoral proceedings must point out that originally it was clergy and people of Rome who elected the bishop of Rome, but because of the aristocratic as well as imperial influence the synod of 769 fixed the Roman presbyters and deacons as the legitimate electors and restricted the right of the Roman lay aristocracy to a mere acclamation of the election. Throughout the earlier medieval period there existed a strictly observed prohibition against electing a bishop from another diocese (see above p. 112). The decree of 769 became more noteworthy in its breach than its observance. Especially during the Saxon and Salian reigns the making of the pope was a matter for the imperial government. The decisive breakthrough came – as already shown (above p. 136) – in 1059, which first put the election of the pope on a basis which took account of experience as well as of ideology and which also initiated the formation of the College of Cardinals.

Although the cardinal-bishops had according to this decree the decisive vote, they were soon to be joined in this activity by the much more numerous cardinal-priests and cardinal-deacons, a process that was clearly discernible by the end of the eleventh century. What is noteworthy is that aristocratic influence came in through the 'back-door', so to speak, that is, through the cardinals who themselves were members of the one or the other aristocratic faction (above pp. 173ff.). The grave defect of the decree of 1059 was that it provided no regulation for procedure to be used if the electors were divided.

This deficiency was remedied in the Third Lateran Council in 1179. It issued a decree which incidentally was one of the first medieval laws laying down a numerical majority rule. Now all cardinals of whatever rank were to be equal electors, and for the valid election a two-thirds majority was necessary. The Roman populace, the emperor and the Roman clergy were excluded from the procedure. The additional significance of this decree was that it made the election and its acceptance by the candidate the sole juristic criterion. Certain hitherto practised usages, such as the consecration (where necessary) and coronation were from the juristic viewpoint irrelevant. From the moment of election and acceptance the candidate had full governing powers. Very frequently elected popes were not even ordained priests, let alone consecrated bishops. Sometimes weeks and months passed before the pope was ordained or consecrated. The juristic nature of the papal office was thereby clearly demonstrated. The reason why the quantitative majority (and not the usual qualitative) principle was adopted was simply that in their function as electors there was no difference between the cardinals: hence only counting by heads remained. This decree of 1179 – *Licet de vitanda* – has been the basic norm for all subsequent papal elections down to the present day.

The papal name as distinct from the pope's Christian name indicated the change in the pope's personality from that of a simple Christian into the successor of St Peter. Just as the baptismal name was to indicate the ordinary Christian's rebirth, in the same way the papal name was to bring out the rebirth or renaissance of the pope. A number of refinements and modifications were made to the original decree of 1179. In the mid-thirteenth century Innocent IV ordered that the election should take place at the locality at which the papal see was vacated by death, and that nobody should be allowed to cast a vote for himself. Of great significance was the decree issued in the Second Lyons Council (1274) (*Ubi periculum*) which made the conclave for papal elections obligatory and prescribed detailed regulations down to the provisioning of the cardinals with food while in conclave. At the Council of Vienne (1311) Clement V issued further regulations permitting excommunicated or suspended cardinals to function as electors. In pursuit of their oligarchic aspirations the cardinals hit upon the device (in the mid-fourteenth century on the occasion of Innocent VI's election) of agreeing among each other while in conclave that if one of them were elected, he would adhere to a number of specifically enumerated points which imposed quite severe restrictions on the governmental scope of the future pope. Although these papal electoral pacts (*capitulations*, as they were called on the model of similar royal procedures) were solemnly sworn to in the presence of a notary and continued to be made right down to the sixteenth century with ever lengthening lists of detailed points, no pope implemented them, the reason advanced being that when he took the oath he was only a cardinal, but by becoming pope he had changed his status and the oath was no longer binding upon him.

As soon as the elected had signified his acceptance, the archdeacon of the Roman Church threw the scarlet robe over the pope, conferred the papal name and declared 'I invest you with the Roman Church' (the term 'invest' was here used in the original meaning of 'clothing in'). Thereupon two cardinals led the pope to the altar of the Lateran church (the pope's own) where he was enthroned, while the Lateran choir intoned the *Te Deum*. Seated on the throne the pope received homage from the cardinals who kissed his feet, whereupon as a sign of special favour he kissed their mouths. This over, the pope was then seated for a short while on the so-called *sedes stercoraria* (a night commode) to make real what was said in I Kings 2.8: 'He raiseth up the poor out of dust and lifteth up the beggar from the dunghill to set them among the princes', and then made to stand up erect to show the change symbolically. He was then led through all the halls and chambers of the Lateran to signify his taking possession of the palace as well.

After this tour he moved to the outside of the Lateran basilica where two curule chairs stood, the one symbolizing St Peter's, the other St Paul's, because the Roman Church was held to have been founded by the two apostles (above p. 10). According to the Donation of Constantine, these two chairs had been presented to the papacy by the emperor himself. The pope had to take up a recumbent position on the chairs to show that his position rested upon both apostles. After the archdeacon had given him a rod – the symbol of justice – the prior of the cardinal-deacons girded him with a red belt upon which hung 12 seals, symbolizing the 12 apostles: this was a clear demonstration of papalism *v.* episcopalism. If he was not yet bishop, his consecration took place the following Sunday in St Peter's basilica. Of the significant actions one is particularly noteworthy: the pallium – the sign of episcopal power – was taken from the altar of St Peter's and handed to the pope by the archdeacon, while the cardinal-bishops were ostentatiously kept in the background in order to prevent any suggestion that the pope had received power from a cardinal or a bishop. With the pallium on him, the pope said the first papal mass.

The papal coronation has few outstanding features. Again for understandable reasons the chief actor was the prior of the cardinal-deacons who removed the episcopal mitre from the pope's head and replaced it with the tiara or papal crown which was also called the *regnum*. Since the first recorded papal coronation in 1059 the papal crown – suggested in fact by the Donation of Constantine – was a kind of mitre modified by two rings which were the upper and lower trimmings of the gold lace of the mitre. They were to symbolize papal power in the two relevant spheres. The papal head-gear was to present the pope in a manner similar to an emperor, as Gregory VII had already claimed by appropriating a great many of the imperial garments for the use of the pope. Here indeed the parallelism between pope and emperor (both East and West) is noteworthy, for the emperor also had his mitre, but wore it underneath the imperial crown, whereas with the pope the mitre and the crown served two different purposes, as Innocent III made clear when he said that as supreme priest he wore the mitre, as temporal Ruler the tiara. Throughout the thirteenth century the papal crown came to be increasingly richly ornamented until in the early fourteenth it nearly attained the splendour of the Western imperial crown and had now three rings probably modelled on the three crowns of the Western emperor: that of Germany, of Lombardy, and of the empire, all of which were contained in one papal crown.

The main consultative body of the papacy was the College of Cardinals which by the end of the eleventh century had assumed its final structure: 7 cardinal-bishops, 28 cardinal-priests and 18 cardinal-deacons. They were no longer taken from the ranks of Roman families but came from virtually all European nations, since the regional needs, practices and customs were to be taken into account in the regular consistory, as the meeting of the pope with the cardinals was called. The supra-national composition of the College of Cardinals very well reflected the cosmopolitan character of the papacy. The creation of the cardinals was a personal prerogative of the pope, and in schismatic times the creation of two Colleges considerably added to the difficulties of bringing the schism to an end. The original liturgical duties of the cardinals virtually vanished from the early twelfth century onwards, though down to the end of the fourteenth it was still necessary for a cardinal to be resident in the curia. The main prerogatives of the cardinals were the election of the pope, their function as special papal legates, especially in connexion with difficult secular business, and their entitlement to the headship of important curial departments. The head of the cardinals was – and still is – the cardinal-bishop of Ostia (Hostiensis) who consecrated the pope and anointed the emperor. By the turn of the twelfth and thirteenth centuries the cardinals had their own chest and financial administration. They also participated in virtually all sources of curial incomes, sometimes receiving as much as half of the total income as well as certain percentages of such sources of income as Peter's pence and similar regular payments. In course of time individual cardinals came to accumulate a great many prebends the revenue from which must also be added to their income.

Yet although the College of Cardinals was the pope's consultative body – on the model of the Roman senate, as Peter Damian said – there were frequently enough severe tensions between pope and cardinals. These frictions were mainly concerned with the status of the cardinals: was the cardinalate an institution of divine or of human law? What rights did the cardinals have which were independent of any papal confirmation? Could the pope issue solemn 'Privileges' without the signature of the cardinals? Could he issue laws without their consent? How far could the College or individual cardinals press their opinions on the pope? What rights did they have during a papal vacancy? Since the creation of a cardinal was a papal prerogative, some popes preferred to avoid tensions by simply not filling vacancies and by letting the number of cardinals run down to literally speaking a handful, as happened in the mid-thirteenth century. The question of the divine or human origin of the cardinalate was finally settled in 1439 by Eugenius IV who laid down that the cardinalate was a jurisdictional office and instituted by St Peter; the cardinals formed 'part of the pope's body' – an expression modelled on the Roman law which laid down the same intimate connexion between Roman senators and the emperor – and therefore enjoyed special privileges and protection. Hence offences against them were crimes of *lèse majesté* because by offending against them the pope himself was offended. The other questions never received any official reply, but what they made clear was the oligarchic tendency which the College almost always exhibited and which came to full fruition during the Great Schism (below p. 296).

The papal legatine system was overwhelmingly operated by cardinals. They were, so to speak, the prolonged arms of the papacy representing papal interests to kings, emperors, patriarchs, provincial councils, and so on. Cardinal legates were called *legati a latere* (i.e. *pontificis*), that is, personal ambassadors of the pope. They usually had plenipotentiary jurisdictional powers, sometimes over-riding episcopal and archiepiscopal jurisdictions, except in the so-called major causes which were explicitly reserved to the pope alone. A papal legate not drawn from the ranks of the cardinals was called a *legatus missus* and had well-defined powers, whilst papal nuncios were dispatched for special missions. It cannot be said that papal legates always enjoyed great popularity in the countries in which they operated, because sometimes they were overbearing in their attitudes, sometimes they interfered in topical regional quarrels and sometimes held legatine synods which were frequently resented by local bishops. Apart from that, papal legates had to be maintained from local sources which was often a great drain on limited resources, especially as cardinal legates were wont to live in great style. Lower than these legates ranked the so-called *legati nati* who were of archiepiscopal status, but whose jurisdictional function was circumscribed: they received permanent legatine status through a special papal 'Privilege'; their main function was to act as a court of appeal; they enjoyed a certain honorary status and had some liturgical privileges. Among the more important *legati nati* were the archbishops of Canterbury, Rheims and Salzburg.

The papal legatine system was one of the vehicles by which the central government operated. Its counterpart was the close association of the bishops with the papacy. The episcopal oath which from Gregory VII onwards every newly consecrated bishop had to take, tied the episcopate firmly to the papacy (see also below p. 244). It was a very stringent oath of obedience which brought clearly into relief the descending theme of government in its hierarchical form. The oath also made regular visits to the papacy obligatory – this was the so-called *visitatio liminum* (scil. *apostolorum*). Its purpose was to report to the pope about the actual state of affairs in the dioceses, so that the central government was fully informed and in possession of all relevant facts. The law allowed the bishop to appoint a *nuncio* for making the report and out of this developed the more or less permanent proctors resident in the curia. They might be likened to episcopal legates and were thus the counterpart of the papal legates. From the late thirteenth century onwards a number of kings also maintained proctors in the curia who might be likened to modern ambassadors. Geographical distances and difficulties of communication accounted for the differences in the periods within which visits by the bishops had to be paid (varying from one to five years). Similarly, the pallium which the metropolitans (= archbishops) – and in a few cases bishops too as a special sign of papal favour – received directly from the pope, had the purpose of creating strong ties between them and the papacy: the conferment of the pallium had become a regular feature since the mid-ninth century. According to the papacy, the pallium juristically symbolized the legal dependence of the metropolitan on the papacy. This was to contribute greatly to the weakening of metropolitan power (see also below p. 245), since all episcopal matters as major causes belonged in any case to direct papal jurisdiction.

Seen from the closest quarters the papal primacy of jurisdiction expressed itself in different and yet related ways. In the first place there was the creation of law by the pope himself. In strictest legal theory, however, the papal law embodied as it was in the decretal letter, was not a law in the modern or late Roman sense, but a definitive binding ruling given in a particular case (or several individual cases) which by virtue of having been given by the papacy as a universal institution assumed of necessity universal character, that is, became universally binding and therefore the law for the whole of Christendom. In some respects the law of the papacy could be compared to the English case law. Laws in the late Roman or modern sense were issued by the general councils (see below pp. 239ff.). In laying down legal norms, the papacy was free and unfettered and its freedom was restrained only in one respect, that is to say by the divine law itself. For the doctrine of Gratian prevailed which maintained that it was the papacy which infused legal binding character to the canons and decrees and laws of other legislative organs, including councils.

What in this context needs emphasizing is that in issuing a decretal the papacy functioned in a threefold capacity: as a governing, legislating and judicial organ. In actual fact, the papal decision in an individual case was the exercise of jurisdictional power which, if it did not create new law, at any rate applied or modified or authoritatively interpreted alreadying existing law. Legislative and judicial functions were not only not separated, but were intrinsically and programmatically fused. But because the governing capacity of the pope as a Ruler also comprised judicial and legislative functions, 'law' and 'politics', to employ conventional language, were intertwined and interlaced.

At no time was the papacy bound by the law itself. Here the idea of a correctly understood sovereignty is paramount. No pope was bound by the rulings of a predecessor or a general council or any other organ, and by a stroke of the pen ancient and hallowed laws could be wiped out. Nevertheless, legislative wisdom and prudence prevented the papacy from exercising this sovereign right, and on the whole the decretal legislation was a testimony to the sense of realism and evolution animating the law-creating popes. They refined and modified and made explicit what might have been merely implicit. Instead of revolutionizing, the papal decretals embodied developing tradition. The basis of this wholly independent papal will was plenitude of jurisdictional power.

Papal primacy manifested itself also in the so-called 'Privileges'

and 'Dispensations'. It was common to both that the pope interfered with existing law. The 'Privilege' created law. It was an
exemption from the common law of the Church and conferred
rights, which would not otherwise have existed, upon persons,
groups or even things. This was instanced in immunities from
taxation, special kinds of protection, exemptions of monasteries
or Orders from episcopal control and the like. The 'Privileges'
were solemn and frequently lavishly executed documents; they
were sought by those who could afford a very expensive and
lengthy procedure. The 'Dispensations' on the other hand were
also exemptions from the law but only for one special person or a
specific case, and they therefore did not create law. Innocent III
often enough justified the dispensatory power of the papacy by
reference to the papal plenitude of power and his namesake, the
fourth Innocent in the mid-thirteenth century, added that the
papacy need not give any reasons for dispensation from the law.
Dispensations concerned the removal of impediments, such as
illegitimate birth, age restrictions, bodily infirmity, matrimonial
impediments, and the like. All three manifestations of papal
primacy – the decretal, the 'Privilege' and the 'Dispensation' –
adopted at least in theory the principle advocated by Bernard of
Clairvaux: the pope should keep in mind what was licit, expedient
and fitting.

Certain so-called major causes were reserved to the papacy
alone. They were matters concerning bishops, cardinals and
emperors, as well as physical offences committed against clerics,
and no delegation was possible in these cases which were dealt
with in full consistory. Further, there were other cases of 'Reservation', such as piracy on the high seas, embargo on food supply to
Rome and certain crimes within the papal state, which could only
be dealt with by the papacy and for which a special tribunal
functioned. In summary form the cases of 'Reservation' and their
censures were annually published on Maunday Thursday; hence
the respective papal bull began *In coena Domini*, the first instance
of which was in the pontificate of Honorius III.

Papal primacy manifested itself also in the final fixation of
general liturgical matters. The all-important episcopal liturgy in
regard to the bishop's divine services and functions originally
consisted of German and Roman component parts. The so-called
Roman-German Pontifical had by the late eleventh century

become simply the Roman pontifical which underwent a number of recensions until it received its final medieval form under Innocent III. Canonization was another liturgical measure which from the late tenth century onwards (John XV's canonization of Bishop Ulrich of Augsburg) gradually became the prerogative of the papacy. The creation of individuals as saints who were thus alone recognized to intercede with Christ, was a right exclusively reserved to the papacy. Innocent III plainly based this right on the papal plenitude of power. Until the early twelfth century popular 'elevations' to the status of saints as well as episcopal 'promotions', frequently with synodal participation, were common practices which as a result of papal centralization, were altogether abolished by the end of the century. Hand in hand with this went the papal fixation of feast days. Conspicuous examples were the Corpus Christi feast (introduced by Urban IV) and the special Trinity Sunday feast (introduced by John XXII in 1334).

Litigation of the common and garden kind began to reach the papacy in ever increasing numbers from all parts of Christendom; they concerned often trivial matters in which civil, religious and ecclesiastical issues were inextricably mixed up. In order to stem the flow of cases reaching the papacy, Alexander III ruled that the proper process of procedural law was to be maintained before the jurisdiction of the papal court was invoked. The papally appointed palatine judges and the chancery were no longer able to cope with the mass of cases, with the result that judges delegate were appointed to examine and decide cases on the spot. Usually the papacy employed ecclesiastics who had legal training, experience and also local knowledge, such as, in England, Baldwin of Worcester, John, abbot of Ford, etc. After their decision the case could then be brought on appeal to the papal court itself over which the pope himself frequently presided. He could also call on a large 'civil' service in the shape of the Auditors who were charged with the preparation of the cases. Most of the Auditors were young graduates of the law school of Bologna who thereby gained practical experience. In the fourteenth century the Auditors constituted their own court, the so-called *Rota Romana* which henceforth functioned as a court of appeal, the records of which are still to a large extent preserved.

Cases which were important either because of their subject-matter or because of the personages involved, were frequently treated in consistory. In modern parlance these cases might be said to have been international disputes. Thus the papacy could, as indeed it did, order belligerent parties to refrain from further belligerent action, or to enter into peace or truce negotiations. The papal court also ordered reprisals against townships or the confiscation of public property. By the verdict of the papal tribunal governments were changed and governing power transferred to other organs or Rulers. Kingdoms were established and new kings were set up by the sentence of the papal judicial tribunal. Municipal law was declared invalid, and the people of a particular region or country were forbidden to adhere to certain laws. This kind of comprehensive papal jurisdiction affected the whole of Europe, from the Iberian peninsula to West Russia, from Scotland and Scandinavia to Sicily, and in the thirteenth century also territories outside Europe, especially when the full effects of the crusades came to be felt. This was a veritable universal jurisdiction that had not been witnessed in antiquity. These judicial measures of the papacy were decisions made on a supra-regal, supra-national plane. To all intents and purposes the papal court was an international tribunal of justice.

Whereas papal decretals and 'Privileges' constituted one source of law, the synods or councils constituted another. Down to the mid-eleventh century the papacy had, as necessity demanded, summoned a so-called Roman provincial council in order to consult with the Italian prelates, but with the emergence of the College of Cardinals these provincial synods died out and their functions were taken over by the regular meetings of pope and cardinals in consistory which, as already indicated, had only consultative character. With the disappearance of these Roman synods another kind of synod began to make its appearance – the so-called plenary Roman council – which was initially held in the Lenten period, especially under Gregory VII and Urban II, and which had legislative powers; moreover the composition was widened so as to include also non-Italians: these new councils therefore exhibited the same cosmopolitan status as the College of Cardinals. It was these councils – usually held in the Lateran – which led to the four great Lateran Councils which are counted as general councils of the Church. They rested on the pseudo-isidorian demand that in order to be universal, a synod must be convoked and chaired by the pope and its decrees confirmed by him. With the appearance of the Lateran Councils the Roman plenary (or papal) synods fell into abeyance.

All the four great Lateran Councils were to mark a special phase in the development of the papacy. They were major legislative assemblies which dealt with all matters of universal concern to the whole of Christendom. Their decrees (or canons) constituted law in every sense of the term and are technically indistinguishable from a modern law issued by Parliament. Most of the decrees were incorporated in canonical collections and thus made easily available. The First Lateran Council (which was the Ninth General Council) in 1123 was to signify the formal end of the Investiture Contest by confirming the concordat of Worms (above p. 172). It also took the opportunity of issuing a number of disciplinary decrees, such as those against concubinage of clerics, and laid down the personal qualifications for the house-keepers of clerics from the sub-deacon upwards; the sale of ecclesiastical goods was declared a sacrilege; indulgence was offered to those who went out to defend Jerusalem against the Muslims; special papal protection was promised to pilgrims and crusaders; counterfeiters of money were threatened with excommunication; the canonical election of a bishop was to be presupposition for his consecration; there was strict regulation of ordinations and the re-iteration of monarchic episcopal power within the diocese. The Second Lateran Council (the Tenth General Council) was held in 1139 to mark the end of the schism between Innocent II and Anacletus. It also issued and re-issued disciplinary decrees, mainly concerned with married clerks and also threatened public sanctions (it should be remembered that celibacy among the lower rural clergy did not become a general rule until later in the century, and in Scandinavia, Spain and Poland still later); the retention of tithes was now declared a sacrilege; there was a prohibition against monks and regular canons studying secular laws and medicine for pecuniary advantages; there was also prohibition against contact with excommunicate persons (since they were held contagious); there was to be coercion of heretics by secular princes; all ordinations performed by the anti-pope were to be invalid; there was to be special clerical protection in the case of physical injury which became a 'major cause'.

In the Third Lateran Council held by Alexander III in 1179 at the end of his conflict with Frederick I and of the schism, the perhaps most important decree was the already mentioned canon regulating papal elections; other decrees concerned the fixation of the minimum age for priests to be consecrated bishops (30) and legitimate birth was a necessary condition; tournaments were forbidden, and visiting ecclesiastical superiors were entitled to proper provisions by the faithful in the diocese. One of the most influential and splendid ecclesiastical gatherings was Innocent III's Fourth Lateran Council in 1215 (about its character as a genuine ecumenical council see above p. 221). Not until recent times were there so many participants in a council. Attention has already been drawn to some of its decrees. Here it is only necessary to mention some others of importance, such as the redefinition of the inquisitorial power of the bishops or the prohibition of duels and ordeals; measures to prevent pluralism of ecclesiastical benefices; the redefinition of the jurisdictional limits of ecclesiastical and civil courts; restriction of the matrimonial impediment of consanguinity to the fourth degree (hitherto to the seventh degree); the amount of tithes to be fixed before other taxes had been deducted and control of interest payment to Jewish money lenders. The council finally appealed for a further crusade to recover the Holy Land.

The thirteenth century witnessed two further general councils, both held at Lyons. The First Lyons Council under Innocent IV in July 1245 was wholly overshadowed by the fierce and final conflict between the papacy and the Staufen emperor, Frederick II. The latter was solemnly excommunicated and deposed in this council which took the opportunity to issue a great number of purely disciplinary canons modifying, refining and supplementing earlier decrees in the light of experience. Other canons concerned procedural law, the fight against heretics and infidels, including the Tartars, and an appeal for a new crusade. The Second Lyons Council of 1274 under Gregory X counted a far greater number of participants than its predecessor and was a veritably ecumenical assembly. The union between the Western and Eastern churches formed its main topic and legislative enactment which thus ended the schism for a brief spell. Of the other 31 canons which deserve to be mentioned one dealt with the suppression of all religious Orders founded after 1215 and without papal approval which resulted in the death of some small mendicant congregations; another prohibited the 'commenda', i.e. prebends which were not held in order to carry out official clerical duties, but of which the cleric had the usufruct as an additional income without any corresponding office; a further canon emphasized that the bishop was the sole competent organ to administer the sacrament of confirmation; the suitability of ordinands formed the subject of another canon; there was also a canon condemning the view that Christ had forbidden the hierarchy to own property. In this council there were indications that the principle of voting according to nations was borrowed from the universities and adapted to ecclesiastical exigencies, a principle which was clearly in evidence in the next general council.

The Council of Vienne under Clement V (1311–12) was virtually forced on the papacy by the French king in order to deal with the matter of Boniface VIII and the Templars (see below p. 281), but it also managed to enact a number of decrees, of which the most important dealt with the Friars, their possessions, the question of poverty and their rights in relation to the parish clergy. In view of the now quite brisk missionary activity among Muslims and other peoples in Syria and North Africa, this council was alive to the need of strengthening missionary organizations and of mastering oriental languages. Hence it decreed the creation of chairs in oriental languages (including Arabic and Hebrew) in a number of universities, including Oxford and Salamanca. But what characterized this council quite pronouncedly was its awareness of the need for a more or less radical reform in all ranks of the ecclesiastical organism. This thread ran right through all the deliberations of this council, and from the historical angle this realization did not come too late.

The easy availability of a code containing an up-to-date edition of current law is nowadays taken for granted by students as well as by the practitioners and administrators of the law. But in the high Middle Ages this was far from being the case – and yet it was the papacy which had always proclaimed the crucial need for a law and always insisted upon its own status as a legal institution. The situation changed with the appearance of Gratian's *Decretum* at the one place that mattered, the university of Bologna. The rich flow of decretal material after the forties of the twelfth century was, it is true, the answer to the need to have a law for the whole of Christendom, but on the other hand this entailed the great difficulty of how to keep track of this new law (see above p. 220). It is therefore easily comprehensible why in the second half of the twelfth century there was quite a spate of collections of those decretals which, so to speak, 'walked outside the *Decretum*'. These were technically called 'extravagant decretals'. Because these collections (in which the English took a prominent part in the seventies and eighties) were all private works, they not only differed greatly in the subject-matter collected, but also in their scope and extent. The Bolognese Master Bernard of Pavia composed a systematic collection on the basis of all previous collections and his became known as *Compilatio Prima* (*ca.* 1190): it contained the decretal and conciliar material issued since Gratian. Bernard divided his work into five books, and this division became standard and remained so until 1918: (1) 'iudex' (constitutional and administrative law); (2) 'iudicium' (procedural law and tribunals); (3) 'clerus' (law specifically dealing with clerical discipline); (4) 'sponsalia' (matrimonial law); (5) 'crimen' (criminal law and penalties). This compilation was at once accepted in Bologna, and also in other law schools, though it all too soon was out of date.

It was succeeded by the compilations of Master Gilbert (finished early 1203) which contained the decretals issued between Alexander III and Innocent III (latest December 1202), and of Master Alan (both were Englishmen teaching at Bologna) finished in 1209 embodying decretals prior to Innocent III (and not in earlier collections) and of Innocent himself. As already seen, this pope issued the first official papal collection of canon law which is known as *Compilatio Tertia*, to be succeeded by the compilation of Master Johannes (a Welshman at Bologna) who had combined Gilbert's and Alan's into one compilation, so-called *Secunda*, because it contained decretal material earlier than the *Tertia*. But all these collections were again outdated by the decretal output of Innocent after 1210 and especially by the legislation of the Fourth Lateran Council. This uncertain state of affairs prompted a German, Johannes Teutonicus, also of Bologna, to compose the *Quarta* (1216) which in its turn was succeeded by the second official collection, the *Compilatio Quinta* by Honorius III in 1225. It needs little historical imagination to visualize the state of uncertainty in legal matters in the twenties of the thirteenth century. It was precisely this consideration which moved Gregory IX to appoint a commission under St Raimond of Pennafort charging it with the composition of one law-book to be made out of all the previous collections. This great task – modelled on Justinian's – was finished in 1234: on 5 September the *Liber Extra* (*extra* meaning outside Gratian's *Decretum*) was published and all antecedent collections were declared without legal force. It was an official and universal code of ecclesiastical law.

The very considerable legislative activity both by the papacy and the councils during the thirteenth century necessitated further collections of this new law resulting eventually in the *Liber Sextus* officially promulgated by Boniface VIII on 3 March 1298. Its name indicated that it was an appendix to the (five books of the) *Liber Extra*. The last medieval collection contained decretals and decrees of the Council of Vienne and, though published by John XXII on 25 October 1317, was called the *Clementines*, because it contained no material later than Clement V. In contrast to earlier collections, the *Clementines* did not invalidate decretals which were not embodied in it – in other words, the papal decrees concerning Philip IV of France retained their full force, although not incorporated in the *Clementines*. This whole corpus constituted the law of the Church and of the papacy until 1918.

Since education throughout the medieval period had been an ecclesiastical matter, the universities became a special concern of the papacy, notably when higher education in the twelfth century became fully organized. In fact, apart from Paris, Bologna, Oxford and Cambridge, in order to qualify for the name of university a higher educational establishment had to be founded either by an emperor or a pope. Notable papal foundations were Toulouse (1229), Rome (1244), Grenoble (1339). The close link of the papacy with Bologna has already been the subject of comment. For general educational purposes the University of Paris was always the object of specific papal solicitude, particularly by Innocent III and Gregory IX. Moreover, in most medieval universities the executive officers were high ecclesiastics; the statutes of universities were confirmed by the papacy which sometimes intervened in the working and practical interpretation of the statutes and was very concerned about the preservation of certain liberties and immunities which the universities enjoyed. This explains the establishment at a number of universities of the so-called 'Conservators' who were entrusted with protecting the university from infringement by other public organs. What active concern the papacy displayed in the universities and the teaching they provided can for instance be seen from its prohibiting the study of Aristotle at Paris University (until proper safeguards were found), or the promotion of oriental languages, and above all of jurisprudence.

This general interest evinced by the papacy in the universities may be nothing but an extension of the instruction which Eugenius II gave in 826 that schools must be under episcopal control. Hence also the direct interest of the papacy in granting the licentiate to teach which it considered to be an episcopal matter and for which stringent tests were prescribed. In the thirteenth century most universities deserving of the name (whether Master or Student universities made no difference) became in law ecclesiastical institutions eventually under papal supervision. Even the coveted right of the Doctor to teach everywhere (the *ius ubique docendi*) was made the subject of a decree by the papacy under Nicholas IV whereby the chief distinctive feature of any university came to be laid down: a university was a genuine ecumenical institution. The active support which the papacy always gave to the universities of Paris and Bologna reflected, so to speak, the papal primacy in its twofold forms. The primacy of teaching (*primatus magisterii*) evinced papal interest in Paris and its theological and philosophical teaching, whereas the papal primacy of jurisdiction (*primatus iurisdictionis*) provoked equally strong interest in Bologna which had no theological faculty before 1364.

The over-all supervision of education was however merely a segment of the universal power of control which the papacy exercised from the twelfth century onwards partly through the appropriate ecclesiastical officers, partly through cardinal legates in the various countries, and partly by the bishops who were tied to the papacy ever more strongly by the requirement of regular visits to Rome. This requirement (the *visitatio liminum apostolorum*) could be insisted upon all the more easily, as according to the doctrine current since Leo I, the bishop was called upon to partake in the pope's solicitude for the Church. The episcopacy – the most serious adversary of the papacy in the Middle Ages – became thus more and more dependent on, and under the control of, the papacy, a development which was greatly assisted by this doctrine and enacted in the oath of obedience to the papacy (and not merely to the pope) (see above p. 234). The intitulation of a bishop suggested by the late eleventh-century papacy – 'Bishop by the grace of God and by the grace of the apostolic see' – did not meet with general episcopal enthusiasm.

Hand in hand with this went the weakening of metropolitan power through the agency at the papacy. Its predilection for episcopal elections to be carried out by the cathedral chapters led to a great increase in papal influence concerning vacant bishoprics. If elections were controversial or if the chapter had elected an unsuitable candidate or someone with a canonical impediment, for instance, one below the required age or of illegitimate birth, the case was drawn into the papal court. The result was the development of the right of devolution (already enacted by Gregory VII in the Lenten synod of 1080) which enabled the papacy to make appointments to a vacant see in specific cases. Next to this was 'Postulation' whereby the electing body could 'postulate' (*i.e.* nominate) a candidate to the papacy, if he had a canonical impediment, but was otherwise suitable. In the thirteenth century there also developed the papal 'Reservations' according to which the popes 'reserved' to themselves the appointment to vacant clerical offices, if certain contingencies occurred, such as death of the incumbent at the curia, or his promotion or translation to another office. In close proximity to this were the papal 'Provisions' which were also based on the papal plenitude of power: begun under Celestine III but fully developed under his successor, this right entitled the pope to 'provide' someone for an already vacant prebend and also for those expected to become vacant (so-called 'Expectancies'). There can be no doubt that the direct papal appointments were in many instances beneficial, though on the whole they were greatly resented by the clergy, high or low, as well as by the secular powers; at the turn of the thirteenth and fourteenth centuries the papacy considered it prudent to restrict the 'Provisions' to some more or less well-defined contingencies. But this centralizing system had gone too far to be susceptible of effective limitations, and John XXII in the fourteenth century relied to a very large scale on either 'Provisions' or 'Reservations' in his actual government. The widespread and fierce resistance to this system in the fourteenth century was understandable, not only on general grounds, but also on grounds of finance because all these devices were sources of papal income.

It is not therefore surprising to find that the papacy devoted considerable attention to the development of financial departments in the curia. One of the oldest curial departments was in fact the Apostolic Chamber, the main task of which had always been the administration of the papal finances. At its head stood either a bishop or a cardinal. In view of the frequent financial litigations a special judicial-financial department existed within the Chamber. The Chamber acquired ever greater importance in the thirteenth century, when on the basis of the plenitude of power the papacy made increasing use of the right to levy a general tax upon the clergy. The system of tithes and crusading taxes was tightened up. The trend towards monopolization became clear when the papacy – unsuccessfully – prohibited secular powers from imposing their own taxes on the clergy. The ingenuity of the papal Chamberlains, the heads of the Chamber, in inventing new imposts and duties hardly knew any bounds. That this highly sophisticated fiscal policy of the curia caused grave apprehension leading to animosity and consternation is comprehensible, particularly when it is borne in mind with what regularity, if not also ruthlessness, the papal taxes were collected. Here only a few can be mentioned. Peter's pence paid by England, Ireland, Poland, Hungary, Norway, Denmark, Sweden, yielded quite respectable sums. The papal tithes produced the largest revenue from the late twelfth century onwards and actually formed the staple income of the papacy. Innocent IV instituted special papal collectors in the various countries. It is estimated that by the end of the thirteenth century this source yielded approximately 800,000 pounds which was about three times the income of the French king. The papal book called *Liber censuum* is a first-class record containing the sources of regular curial income (including rents, dues, taxes for the whole Church) at the end of the twelfth century.

Other sources of income were the so-called service tax (*Servitia*) and the Annates. The former was a tax paid to the Chamber by any prelate who had received a bishopric (or other prelacy) from the pope sitting in consistory provided that the annual income of the prelacy was more than 100 florins. This tax was also levied on those who received the pallium from the pope, as well as on bishops who were exempted from metropolitan jurisdiction. Furthermore, bishops whose election was confirmed by the papacy or who themselves were 'provided' by the pope, had to pay this tax. Its amount was a third of the first annual income, and this sum was equally divided between pope and cardinals. In addition to this service tax there were fees to be paid to the papal chancery for the relevant documentation. In the late thirteenth century a consecration fee was levied on bishops and prelates who were privileged to have been consecrated by the pope personally. This too amounted to a third of the annual income (for Cologne or Salzburg for instance this amounted to 10,000 florins). On the other hand, the Annates were fees to be paid for prebends which the papacy conferred outside the consistory, that is, the lower prebends. This tax was originally one half of the income of the first year – it was in this context that provisions and reservations became so important to the papacy, and John XXII went so far as to levy this tax on all prebends of the whole Church which became vacant between 1318 and 1321. By various means his successors were able to improve this device which became an oppressive tax.

For routine administrative acts in the curial departments, such as the chancery and later the Rota, from the second half of the twelfth century there were graduated fees for any official service performed in these departments. By the fourteenth century the papal financial system was not only the best organized European taxation system, however complicated its machinery and however numerous its officials but also a system that, precisely because it was so efficient, worked in a wholly inhuman manner and in complete disregard of individual circumstances: the penalties were always at hand. On the eve of the Reformation there was, indeed, hardly any matter including indulgences which was not in one way or another tied to money to feed the ever increasing papal apparatus of offices and departments.

The curial department which next to the Apostolic Chamber had an importance equal to none was the chancery. It was the nerve-centre of the papal government, because here the decretals, decrees, orders, verdicts, bulls, 'Privileges', in short every kind of documentary material was, literally speaking, manufactured, copied, issued and committed to archival memory in the papal Registers. The chancery was also the largest department of the curial offices, at least as far as its personnel was concerned. The head of the chancery was the vice-chancellor (the office of chancellor having been abolished by Honorius III) under whose supervision were the notaries, the scriptors, the correctors, the abbreviators, and the officials especially charged with the sealing of documents. The chancery personnel often topped the three-figure mark. All the numerous concrete manifestations of papal primacy in one way or another began or ended in the chancery, whether it was the issue of a solemn 'Privilege' or of a mere dispensation from some impediment, or so-called gratial (as distinct from judicial) matters or the appointment of bishops or metropolitans or an excommunication or a deposition or an encyclical or an appeal or the confirmation of an election or of immunities or the grant of a charter or the approbation of a new university and its statutes or the issuing of the thousands of decretals. During the thirteenth century over 50,000 documents issued from the papal chancery. It was also within the competency of the chancery to keep records and therefore to produce copies of earlier documents as well as to prepare, at the request of the parties and on payment of fixed fees, the material for litigation. In short, all the threads of the papal government were gathered up in this office which, from a purely technical angle, was a model of documentary reliability and an organizational achieve-ment that had no parallel in medieval Europe. That the chancery began to keep Registers of outgoing (and partly also incoming) mail from the fifth century onwards is proved, though before Innocent III only one original Register has survived – that of Gregory VII. Gregory I's whole Register is transmitted in a copy of the eleventh century and there are some fragments of official papal Registers of the ninth century. From Innocent III onwards almost all the thirteenth-century Registers have now been edited. The complex and varied nature of curial business necessitated in the fourteenth century the establishment of special Registers which contained specified matters only, *e.g.* political, secret, ordinary, financial, petitions, etc.

Whereas chancery and chamber were organs of administration, the proper judicial work was done in the papal tribunal which consisted of two departments, the Penitentiary (for cases of conscience, for the internal forum and for the reserved cases) and the court of the sacred palace (*audientia sacri palatii*). At the head of the former stood a penitentiary with a number of officers placed under him, and in the course of the fourteenth century the department had enlarged its competency for dealing with indults, dispensations, rectifications of irregularities, and the like. Judicial decisions in the strict meaning of the term were taken by the court which by the second half of the twelfth century had become one of appeal from lower courts, and especially from those of delegated jurisdiction. But even this restriction did not dam the flood of cases reaching the court, and only the adoption of drastic means of prohibiting an appeal altogether in certain cases (*appellatione remota*) ensured its proper functioning. Its personnel was greatly enlarged by the addition of Auditors, mainly taken from the ranks of the *capellani*, the recent graduates from the law schools. Of course, the court could always – and frequently did – submit important cases to the consistory. Electoral disputes and the 'major causes' were still reserved to the personal jurisdiction of the pope as the supreme judge. Under John XXII this court became in 1331 the *Rota Romana* which was competent to try civil and criminal cases.

Innocent III created a special department which was attached to the chancery, had judicial functions and usually operated in public. The function of this department – the *audientia litterarum contradictarum* – was to deal with the preliminaries of a case, to sift the documentary material of the litigants, to prevent further litigations by proposing compromise solutions and to appoint judges delegate. Apparently this department answered a need of the time and throughout the thirteenth century it grew considerably: it was given its own constitution and structure, and since oral pleadings greatly diminished (their place being taken by written pleas), the objections and exceptions put in by the parties, could be examined judicially in a calm atmosphere and apart from the bustle of the courts proper: compromise solutions could then be found more easily.

While virtually all curial offices were staffed by clerics, the household offices of the curia were regularly manned by laymen. The kitchen personnel of the pope as well as the numerous cooks (and kitchen assistants) employed by the cardinals were laymen. Lay people were also detailed for duty in the stables which were larger in extent than those of any Western king: here the grooms, the keepers and stable boys constituted their own association and organization within the curial personnel, for the up-keep of the pope's and the cardinals' horses and stables was essential for the maintenance of a proper system of communications no less than for housing the dozens of horses belonging to legations, messengers, proctors and parties arriving at the curia on business. The departments of the papal messengers, runners, the curial police as well as cleaners, domestic servants, blacksmiths, saddlers, tailors and ancillary services were of course entirely in the hands of laymen.

This very brief survey of the curia shows that it was one of the best maintained and impressive central administrations in medieval Europe. Its extent and the attention given to detail as well as the multifarious business transacted prove the universal character of the government itself. By constant adjustment and accommodation to newly arising contingencies this vast apparatus was able to function smoothly – and this, despite so many external crises and conflicts and vicissitudes and even frequent and prolonged absences of individual popes from Rome. The frictionless work of the papacy was in no small measure due to the inner strength, resilience and organization of the curia which it acquired in the course of a long historical process. What however the curia also makes abundantly clear is not only its continuity and slow evolution literally reaching back centuries, but above all else the spirit that always animated it and its numerous ramifications – the law, the idea of the rule of law and of justice. The historian of the modern period may heartily disagree with the use which the papacy made of the law, as indeed did a number of contemporaries in no uncertain terms, but nothing can erase from the subsequent historical development the legacy which the papacy handed on – the idea of order based upon the law.

THE POWER OF the papacy lay in the religious and intellectual field; this power exercised by the mind was at all times far more enduring and determinative than that exercised by physical force. In the thirteenth century the bond that held Europe together was a common faith, one that in its essentials was the one fixed by the papacy, despite certain regional or local differences, none of which however affected the substance of the faith. In the public field particularly the commonly held faith left an indelible imprint upon the unquestioned theocratic Rulership. Its basis was nothing but faith in the divinely instituted Ruler, the very theme which the papacy had upheld throughout its long history. This Rulership moreover was underpinned by an elaborate anointing and coronation ceremonial. And the papacy itself was built on exactly the same theocratic premisses to which was added a definite biblically verifiable statement made by Christ to St Peter whose heir the pope was.

These remarks are necessary in order to further the understanding of the measures which the papacy came to take in the thirteenth century against the already mentioned heretical movements. For although they were by no means anti-Christian or anti-religious, they nevertheless based themselves on assumptions which severely impugned the papally expounded and legally fixed faith. And some of the doctrines set forth by the sects struck at the very roots of the universally accepted faith, and in particular at the principle which was considered vital that the priesthood mediated divine favours or graces. The opposition to this principle gravely affected not only an essential dogma of the Catholic priesthood itself, but also began to cast grave doubts on the very institution of the papacy and for the same reason also on the pronouncedly theocratic Rulers. Priestly and royal authority had already begun to resist these attacks on their common bases: the joint decree of Pope Lucius III and the Emperor Frederick I was merely a first step (see above p. 202). Technically, the canon of the Fourth Lateran Council was merely a juristic refinement of that first joint measure.

The harmonious co-operation between papacy and secular Rulers in repelling heretical attacks had also other facets. Although it was the ecclesiastical court which pronounced the culprit a heretic, the penalty (the term in papal legislation was 'animadversione debita', meaning appropriate punishment) to be meted out was decreed, not by the ecclesiastical tribunal, but by secular justices. Leaving aside Justinian's decree on burning 'heretical books' and the isolated instances of burning heretics by the early Capetian kings, proper royal legislation did not begin until Peter II of Aragon, the pope's vassal, decreed the death penalty as the appropriate punishment for heretics, in 1198. The Emperor Frederick II not only issued severe laws against heretics in his imperial coronation edicts of November 1220, but also outlawed them and specifically decreed the death penalty for heretics by burning at the stake. The ecclesiastical procedure adopted was the inquisitorial kind, but the details of this procedure were not worked out until after the secular monarchs had decreed the death penalty.

The medieval Inquisition elaborated by the papacy during the pontificate of Gregory IX was not substantially an entirely new procedure, because since the early Middle Ages the bishops always had the right (and duty) to 'enquire' into matters of common concern, among which the purity of the faith naturally figured. This method of proceeding was also adopted by kings and came to be called Inquest. But in the prevailing circumstances of the thirteenth century the episcopal inquisition obviously appeared not only too slow and cumbersome, but also put additional strain on the bishops' already heavily taxed administration. The papal Inquisition therefore was meant to be – and to a very large extent remained – supplementary and complementary to the episcopal inquisition upon which papal legislation never in any way impinged. That in actual fact episcopal power implicitly and necessarily suffered as a result of the much more efficient papal Inquisition, was evident and was not a little resented by the episcopacy. What is however of immediate concern is that the pronouncedly theocratic Rulers, such as those of

France, Aragon, Castille, partly of Germany, Bohemia, Hungary, facilitated the work of the papal Inquisition in every way. The reason should by now be clear.

However much the papal device of the Inquisition was historic-ally explicable and situationally conditioned, the juristic prin-ciples which the procedure embodied, bore hardly any resemblance to those which were commonly accepted and consistently advo-cated by the papacy itself. Few items of the fully matured in-quisitorial procedure could be squared with the most primitive demands of justice. Yet on the other hand, there was very little, if any, popular opposition to inquisitorial methods; in fact, there was considerable demand for public executions of heretics. Part of the explanation why the papacy instituted proceedings which spelt horror and fear wherever the papal inquisitors made their appearance, was that the faith – the very rock and foundation of contemporary society – must be protected from attacks and main-tained in its purity. When heresy itself came to be considered 'high treason' against the monarchic position, that is, the majesty of the pope by denying his plenitude of power (as laid down by the papacy throughout the thirteenth century and especially clearly by Boniface VIII), the ordinary safeguards of judicial proceedings were abandoned. The situation was one calling for emergency treatment, and recourse was therefore allowed to means which would otherwise be rejected. That the individual Christian thereby suffered, was no doubt admitted, but what mattered was the health, the well-being of the whole society, of the whole Church, and not of the parts of society constituting it. The axiom that gave rise to this cosmology was that the member functioned only for the sake of the whole society. The individual who impinged on the one or the other article of faith, forfeited any rights which the law might have in other circumstances conceded to him. In any case, on the model of St Paul, a heretic was considered to be a subversive member of society which, it should be added, was not viewed from the angle of modern liberalism. The papal Inquisition must be understood from the contemporary medieval standpoint which knew no freedom of expression or thought in regard to matters touching the sub-stance of the faith. Hence aberration from faith as papally fixed was not only (as it was said) a sign of intellectual arrogance, but also, and more so, an act of rebellion against constituted authority which claimed a monopoly in all matters relating to the religious foundations of society. And according to papal reasonings, since heresy was held to be an infectious disease the danger always existed that it might spread and cause the collapse of the whole Christian society.

The essence of the papal Inquisition was that specially commissioned inquisitors taken mainly and understandably from the ranks of the mobile itinerant Orders, such as the Dominicans and Franciscans, were sent to regions to 'enquire' into any matters which might constitute a charge of heresy. Everyone in the locality was compelled to bring to the inquisitor's notice any manifestation or suspicion of heresy. The proceedings were secret, the suspected or accused individual did not know who the informants were, there was no means of cross-questioning witnesses who might have been convicted perjurors, excommunicate persons, criminals or even accomplices. The accused knew no details of the charge and no appeal to a higher court was allowed, because the inquisitors themselves functioned 'by apostolic authority' and their verdict was in reality a papal verdict. And none other than one of the greatest lawyer popes, Innocent IV, sanctioned the use of torture. This offered ample opportunity to display the ingenuity of the inquisitors. Torture was not employed to obtain the truth, but a confession, the only restriction in its use being that it could not be repeated against the same accused. This was easily circumvented by 'continuing' torture, if the accused happened to retract his confession made under torture. There never was an acquittal: all that occurred juristically was that no further proceedings took place.

There can be no doubt that the papal Inquisition was a measure which can be comprehended only if contemporary conditions are properly taken into account. Precisely because medieval Christianity reached right down into the furthest compartments of public and private life, it vitally affected everyone and everything. The papacy was held and considered itself the guardian as well as legislator of all matters belonging to faith, upon which indeed the whole of Christian Europe rested. No government worth its name would have tolerated the dissemination of opinions, views and ideas subversive and fundamentally inimical to society and its foundations. The papacy would have regarded it as a dereliction of a divinely imposed duty, if it had not taken steps to eradicate destructive movements and their instigators. However detestable by modern standards the means employed were, they were of late Roman parentage and can therefore be comprehended only against the historical background.

In the first half of the thirteenth century a very gradual, though clearly perceptible shift in papal politics became detectable. Prompted by the fierce conflict between the papacy and Frederick II the shift resulted in far closer relations than hitherto between the papacy and France governed as it was by what the papacy always referred to as the *rex christianissimus*. The conflict with the Staufen emperor was to all intents and purposes a continuation of the one which was fought out in the twelfth century, with this difference however that the issues had become more sharply defined and crystallized. It is true that initially it was the implementation of Frederick II's promise to undertake the crusade decreed in the Fourth Lateran Council, which was the point of friction between the papacy under Honorius III and Frederick. As envisaged in the council, the crusade made a start in 1217, but inept military leadership, unforeseen military obstacles, and the absence of supplies brought the undertaking to a virtual collapse. Frederick had stood aside, though he renewed his promise in 1220 and even sent some supply ships to Egypt which constituted too late and too little help.

This development cast a shadow on the mutual relations which deteriorated rapidly since – by a masterly diplomatic stroke in which he showed himself a true pupil of his guardian (Innocent III) – Frederick had his son Henry, already king of Sicily since 1212, also elected King of Germany (in return for which he made large concessions to the ecclesiastical princes), so that the very contingency which the papacy had always feared, that is, a union of Sicily with the empire, had quickly come about – and this despite Frederick's solemn acknowledgment of Sicily as a papal fief and (in accordance with an agreement he had made with Innocent in 1216) his own renunciation of a personal union between Sicily and Germany. That the two kingdoms were united not in the person of the father but in that of the son contradicted the agreement with Innocent III not in the letter but in spirit. Not even the long-awaited imperial coronation of Frederick by Honorius III in 1220 produced any change of plan on the part of the emperor nor any concrete preparations for the promised crusade. It was postponed again and again until at long last in 1227 it started in earnest, though a few days after sailing from Brindisi, dysentery of epidemic dimensions visited the fleet which had to return. To the papacy this was no more than a clever subterfuge and quite indefensibly it excommunicated Frederick for breach of the crusading promise. In the following summer the undertaking started under more favourable auspices, and the excommunicated emperor was able to take possession of a coastal strip in Palestine as well as Jerusalem, Bethlehem and Nazareth (1229). This very considerable success was achieved by diplomatic negotiations with the Sultan (Treaty of Jaffa). Frederick undertook not to molest or impede the Muslims in Jerusalem in any way. In a swift diplomatic move with a minimal naval and military force Frederick, the excommunicated crusader, succeeded where large military contingents formerly suffered shipwreck and defeat. As he was still excommunicated he crowned himself King of Jerusalem in the Church of the Holy Sepulchre (18 March 1229).

Instead of releasing Frederick from excommunication as a reward for his remarkable success, Gregory IX feared for the safety of the papal state, and papal troops began their attack in Apulia. The return of the emperor signalled a crushing defeat of the papal troops. The peace between the papacy and the (now absolved) emperor reached at Ceprano in 1230 was, however, no more than a truce. How could trust and confidence be restored after a period which had witnessed not only armed hostility but revealed also deep ideological differences? For Frederick's plan was to make real the idea of a Roman emperor, and one of the first steps in this direction was to abandon the emperor's role as an officer, as an auxiliary organ of the papacy. This could be achieved only by first gaining real, physical – as distinct from imaginary – control over Italy: hence Frederick's attacks on the Lombard cities in order to secure the imperial position in Northern Italy. Though supported by the papacy the Lombard forces were utterly routed at Cortenuovo in 1237. They did not however accept the imperial demand for unconditional surrender.

That in the meantime the relations between the papacy and Frederick had worsened again, was predictable – partly because of continued and successful imperial raids on the papal state, partly because of the marriage of Frederick's son Enzio with the Sardinian heiress (the emperor herein clearly following his grandfather's example), partly on account of the subsequent creation of Enzio as King of Sardinia which was, however, on the basis of the Donation of Constantine, claimed by the papacy as its own property and not at the disposal of the emperor, and partly because Rome itself was now to become the capital of the Roman empire presided over by a real (and not merely fictitious) Roman emperor. In other words, a historically and ecclesiastically conditioned ideology that was originally created by the papacy for its own interests, was now to be put into grim reality. The master of this idea – the papacy – was in danger of being swallowed up by the servant, who was no longer willing to play the role allocated to him by ideology, but was seeking in earnest to assume the role of the historic emperor of Roman-Christian antiquity. Frederick's design was of course powerfully assisted by the disappearance of the Eastern (Roman) empire from the political map: indeed, there was now really only one Roman emperor in the shape of Frederick II crowned by the apostolic favour of the papacy. Potently helped by very able 'ghost-writers' Frederick resuscitated in his official correspondence the ancient imperial metaphors, imperial virtues and bombastic phraseology of the ancient Roman-imperial chancery culminating in the semi-divinization of the emperor and the arrogation of ancient imperial attributes relative to his person, status and power. There could be no doubt that Frederick was resolved to turn the idea into reality.

The conspicuous danger to the existence of the papal state prompted the papacy to excommunicate Frederick II in a most solemn form on Palm Sunday 1239. This was the signal for the outbreak of an ideological war which in fierceness, ferocity and depth of passion and disregard of all the accepted norms of warfare, has few, if any, parallels in medieval history. It was a war *à outrance*. For whoever emerged as victor, would show no mercy to the vanquished. But from a different angle this conflict is particularly significant for three reasons. First, in contrast to the Investiture Contest, propaganda was now centrally directed, if not undisguisedly manipulated; on both sides the pamphlets, manifestoes, encyclicals were masterpieces of style, diction and language. They were no longer scholarly, pedantic tracts, as in the Investiture Contest, but articles aimed at whipping up emotions and creating an atmosphere which itself was only to be a presupposition for subsequent action. Secondly, the imperial propaganda advocated a governmental scheme which though impressive at the time, nonetheless unwittingly served a cause hostile to all theocratic-secular forms of government. For to Frederick his contemporary popes were the personification of Anti-Christ and ought therefore to be put on trial before a general council. It was not so much the papacy which formed the target of the attack as the personal turpitude of the office holder: thereby the whole ancient papal system was turned upside down by imperial propaganda, a system which had always put into the foreground the office to which the personality of the individual pope was secondary.

Moreover, the invocation of a general council was qnite especially significant, because it heralded the first rumblings which were later to emerge fully in the conciliar movement (below p. 299). Imperial propaganda left no doubt about the crucial theme of that movement: that is, that the pope received his powers from the whole Church, the whole congregation of the faithful, which acted through the general council and the College of Cardinals. Hence also the imperial government's plea to the cardinals that they should summon a general council. According to this standpoint papal power was located in the totality of Christians to whom the pope remained responsible and who could, through the instrumentality of the general council, depose him, should the necessity arise. On the other hand, the emperor himself could only be judged by God alone from whom he had received power directly. Within the framework of imperial propaganda therefore, the ascending theme of government applied to the pope; the descending theme on the other hand was applicable to the emperor, precisely because he was a Roman emperor. The time was not far away when the ascending theme was to be propagandistically exploited against all theocratic secular Rulership. In more than one way, therefore, this ideological standpoint foreshadowed a great deal of the later development.

Thirdly, his position as emperor of the Romans entitled him to safeguard the interests of all secular European kings: he was 'the lord of the world' – the *dominus mundi* – and the papal attacks on him were in reality directed against all secular Rulers. Hence Frederick's appeals to the kings and barons in the Western kingdoms to come to his succour in his fight against the popes. The appeals appear to have been singularly unsuccessful in England, and produced only a modicum of success in France.

This ideological war was accompanied by the clash of arms. Frederick occupied large parts of the papal state with spearheads directed against Rome, whilst the Venetians instigated by Gregory IX, tried to invade imperial Apulia. Eventually Gregory summoned a general council to Rome for Easter 1241 – the very measure which Frederick had suggested, but which he now rather effectively prevented by capturing more than a hundred prelates who were on their way to the council; among them were three legates, two cardinals and several archbishops and bishops. No less decisive was the sudden death of Gregory IX on 22 August 1241.

At exactly the time at which the two leaders of European Christendom were locked in a fratricidal battle, the Mongolians had advanced from Asia towards the European Continent, conquering Russia between 1231 and 1240 and Hungary in the spring of 1241 and intending to invade the southern part of Poland, Silesia and Moravia. This rapid advance was quite unforeseen and constituted a very acute danger to the rest of Europe which was only averted by internal Mongolian succession troubles. The emperor, Frederick II, appeared to have recognized the magnitude of the danger, though he himself was just then engaged in laying siege on Rome itself, where indeed he had found some support for his plans from the citizens.

In order to make sure that the election of the new pope was not unduly delayed or influenced by the populace, the Senator of Rome (the civil head of the administration) locked the cardinals up in an old building and kept them there until they had finished their election. This experience of the first papal conclave – the idea of locking electors up was first practised in some Lombard cities – left an indelible imprint on the cardinals, for, apart from the unbearable heat in Rome, the hygienic conditions and the behaviour of the Roman police guarding the dilapidated building, were indescribable. In fact, the stench caused by the unremoved excrements was insufferable. One of the cardinals died during the conclave and the cardinals were not permitted to leave the place to attend the funeral; neither doctors nor servants were allowed to care for the cardinals who had fallen ill. Yet despite these inhuman conditions to which they were subjected, they found it difficult to get a two-thirds majority. It was not until the Senator threatened to have the corpse of Gregory IX exhumed and shown to the Romans in full papal regalia that the Cardinal-bishop of Sabina – Celestine IV – was unanimously elected on 25 October 1241. The old man fell ill and died after 17 days. Immediately after this election the cardinals left Rome, lest worse befell them. The vacancy lasted virtually two years. The delay can be explained by the insecure conditions in Rome, by the efforts to get the release of the still imprisoned two cardinals and by the stringent conditions which Frederick attached to their liberation. In the event, on 25 June 1243 at Anagni Cardinal Sinibaldus Fliscus was unanimously elected as Innocent IV. He was thought to have been untainted by the earlier conflicts and, therefore, more in a position to find some accommodation with the emperor. Innocent IV – like Gregory IX – was a superb jurist and canonist.

Initial negotiations between the pope and the emperor broke down on the question of control of Lombardy and on the Sicilian problem, but these in reality were only subsidiary matters while the substantive issues – the imperial position and the role of the pope within the Church – remained wide open. Because of the conditions in Italy in the summer of 1244 the papal court fled to Lyons which was only nominally situated on imperial territory, and yet was not French. In order to put an end to the festering conflict, Innocent convoked a general council for July 1245 in which Frederick was to appear as a defendant on several charges. Formally a general council (the Thirteenth), the Lyons Council was far from being fully representative, because in the main there were only Spanish, French and some English prelates present. Frederick's counsel, Thaddaeus of Suessa, proposed an adjournment because the accused had had insufficient time to prepare his case, but the council overruled this submission and on 17 July 1245 proceeded to the solemn excommunication and deposition of Frederick, emperor of the Romans. He was found guilty of heresy, of breaking his oath as papal vassal and of criminally capturing and detaining prelates on their way to a general council (1241). All oaths taken to him were declared no longer binding and the electoral college in Germany was ordered to proceed to a new election.

Whether the verdict was prudent, will always remain a debatable question. That is was valid from the formal juristic viewpoint, is beyond doubt. In fact, as legal commentator Innocent

IV himself afterwards interpreted his own sentence, the underlying ideology of which was that Roman emperorship as conceived by the papacy was wholly irreconcilable with that role with
which the Staufen credited it. Innocent fully explained the application of the two-sword theory to the emperor who was created by
the papacy for specific purposes only and who therefore could be
dethroned and unmade by the papacy if he was found unsuitable.
According to Innocent IV the papacy was entitled to 'translate'
the empire to whomsoever it wished, and consequently could
offer the imperial office to, say, the French. The preaching of a
crusade against the 'apostate and heretical' emperor by the papacy
was from the papal standpoint understandable, though its wisdom
was also open to question. It was only some time after the death
of 'the arch-enemy of the Christian Church' (Frederick II) in 1250
that the papal court moved back to Rome from Lyons. And since
a Staufen as successor to Frederick was a contingency which the
papacy was by no means willing to face, the crusade against
Frederick was now expanded into a crusade against his son
Conrad IV, German king since 1237. The undignified angling by
the papacy for a 'suitable' future emperor by offering the position
to more or less unwilling or unsuitable candidates, resulted in the
so-called interregnum in Germany that lasted until the election of
Rudolf of Habsburg on 10 October 1273.

The deposition of Frederick by the council of Lyons made a
very deep impression upon contemporary Europe. And once
more in the last years of Frederick's life the imperial chancery
became extremely active. It let loose a whole spate of manifestoes
and encyclicals and appeals addressed to all sorts and conditions
of men. Their general tenor was that Europe should rise against
the Anti-Christ in the person of the pope – there was still no
suggestion that the target of the attack was the papacy as an
institution – and that the clergy, including the pope, should
return to apostolic poverty and the simplicity of life as exempli-
fied by Christ Himself. That this kind of appeal was bound to fall
on fertile soil, needs little imagination when due consideration is
given to the actual conditions in which popes, cardinals and prelates lived. But this internecine quarrel between the two leaders
prompted the French King Louis IX to offer his luckless mediation – this very attempt showed how little he was aware of the
unbridgeable gulf between the warring parties. The more fiercely

the emperor attacked, the more violent the reaction was. Apart from lavishing all the crusaders' privileges on those taking up arms against Frederick, the papacy went even so far as to employ every ecclesiastical censure against anyone critical of the papal position, and the means employed included also the withholding of papal dispensations in matrimonial matters. Seen from a purely historical perspective, the policy pursued by the papacy towards the Staufen emperor from the late twenties on could be called neither prudent nor statesmanlike.

On the part of the papacy the effect was a revision of its age-old policy towards Germany and the adoption of a decidedly French-orientated policy. For Europe the effect was a very noticeable loosening of the bonds which had tied its princes and peoples to the papacy. To all intents and purposes the end of the Staufen régime marked the end of the medieval empire as a universally conceived European factor, whether this was seen from the papal or Staufen standpoint. The empire became more and more a purely German matter. It went without saying that this process of shrinkage was bound to have repercussions on the papacy itself. But what was immediately far more important was that the end of the Staufen régime accelerated the trend towards a policy pursued by the papacy which began to show less consistency, less firmness, less coherence than its history would have suggested. Having abandoned well-trodden and well-tried paths the papacy became too much involved, if not entangled, in the squabbles of the individual kingdoms and principalities. The singlemindedness in its policy came to be replaced by several kinds of policies, not all of which were reconcilable with each other.

Nevertheless, despite the papal concentration in the thirties and forties of the thirteenth century on the Staufen problem and, in the immediately succeeding decades on French and English questions, the papacy continued to pursue the policy of expansion of its authority by the active encouragement of missionary efforts as well as by appeals to somewhat questionable undertakings labelled 'crusades'. The submission of North-East Europe to Christianity was completed in this period. The Teutonic Order, founded in the late twelfth century, was the main instrument in converting Prussia to Christianity. The papacy also directed the missionary enterprises in the Baltic lands. The erection of four Prussian bishoprics was sanctioned by the papacy through its legate William of Modena in the late forties and early fifties. It was also during Innocent IV's pontificate that Lithuania came to be finally christianized: upon order of Innocent its Ruler, Mindowe, was crowned King of Lithuania. But the papacy also directed its gaze far into Asia. The itinerant Orders were the special organs through which the papacy attempted the conversion of the Mongols in Asia who from the mid-thirteenth century on began to rule large parts of China and, having acquainted itself with the account of the Venetian Marco Polo, the papacy under Nicholas IV realized the great potentialities which existed there and dispatched Franciscans to the court of the Mongolian Ruler in China. By 1299 the city of Peking was visited by the first European, the Franciscan Arnold of Cologne. A few years later Clement V erected an archbishopric in China with a number of (mainly Franciscan) suffragan bishops.

The crusading idea escalated but also suffered a debasement. Crusades were preached by the papacy against Christians, such as the Stedinger peasantry in Germany, because they refused to pay taxes to their bishop, or against Frederick II himself and later against his son, Conrad IV, quite apart from the Albigensians in the early part of the century. In the Holy Land itself Jerusalem (conquered by the excommunicate Frederick II in 1229) was lost for good in 1244, and the European nations showed unmistakable weariness in the matter of a crusading zeal. Innocent IV correctly sensed this and abandoned the plan he originally had wished to announce at the council of Lyons in 1245. Instead of a crusade against the Mongols he dispatched Dominicans and Franciscans as papal emissaries to their Ruler – this indeed was the beginning of the missions which in practice replaced the crusades. Although Gregory X still harboured a crusading programme – after the crusading enterprise of Louis IX had come to an inglorious end in 1270 – and a new crusading tax was imposed by the Second Council of Lyons in 1274, the response of Europe to this appeal and impost was virtually nil. In the course of the next few years Palestine was finally lost to the Christians. Despite a formal crusading promise by the French and English kings in 1312–13 nothing was realized. For by that time other and more directly pressing problems had come to engage the papacy as well as the Western kingdoms.

The deadly enmity which the papacy entertained against the

Staufen dynasty made the papacy knit ever stronger ties with France which, indeed, was the homeland of some of the popes. The French orientation can be illustrated by the papal predilection for appointing Frenchmen as cardinals and the preference for Frenchmen in filling vacant curial posts. Above all, Charles of Anjou, Louis IX's brother, was offered by the papacy the crown of Sicily and Naples which he had first to conquer in bloody battles. The legitimate and last Staufen, Conradin, barely 16 years old, was captured and, together with his entourage, publicly hanged as a traitor in Naples on 28 October 1268. Although there is no evidence that the pope, Clement IV, had proposed this drastic end of the Staufen heir, the latter's plea to the pope asking him to intervene with his captors went unheeded. This entanglement of the papacy with the foremost European power, France, was hardly to the benefit of the institution. Moreover, though papal vassals, Charles of Anjou and his immediate successors cared less for papal and ecclesiastical rights than the Staufens did. But through his connexions Charles knew how to influence at least some of the cardinals, a fact which accounted for the inability of the College of Cardinals to reach a two-thirds majority after the death of Clement IV: the vacancy lasted nearly three years. Yet meanwhile there was still no king in Germany where public insecurity went from bad to worse; a number of important decisions which only a pope could make, had to be postponed, and they concerned ecclesiastical matters all over Europe; the situation in the Holy Land had become virtually untenable for the Christians. Since 1261 the 'Latin empire' of Constantinople had vanished from the landscape and the old 'Greek' empire under Michael Palaeologus (1261–82) came to be re-established.

A somewhat re-invigorated papacy under Gregory X tried to master this extremely difficult situation, and in two respects the papacy began to show some of its old fibre. The first was the peremptory order to the German electoral college to proceed to an election within a specified time, otherwise the papacy would translate the empire from the Germans to the French. The result was the election of the first Habsburg, Rudolf, as king of the Germans, though the papacy always maintained that it itself had 'nominated' (probably misunderstanding Innocent III) 'the king of the Romans'. For reasons irrelevant in this context Rudolf of Habsburg never received the imperial office and crown.

The second and, from the ecclesiastical as well as papal point of view, most decisive event of this pontificate was the Second Lyons Council in 1274 (the Fourteenth General Council) which apart from the already mentioned decrees (above p. 240) legislated on usury, immunity of churches, desecration of churches through commercial activities, reprisals and enacted two measures of greatest significance, the one merely temporary, the other lasting until this day. The first was the re-union of the Western and Eastern churches, a measure which evoked so much resistance and hostility in Constantinople that it proved abortive. The Greek legation fully acknowledged papal primacy, while the papacy tolerated Greek liturgy. Considering the most recent experience of Constantinople with the Latins as well as the historically and culturally conditioned gulf that divided East from West, one can only conclude that the Greek emperor's readiness to obtain the union was dictated by the extremely serious threat to the empire by the menace of the advancing Turks. The union was still-born, although the imperial government tried to implement it by brute force. The *coup de grâce* to the 'union' was in fact given by the papacy which, influenced by Charles of Anjou, asserted that the Greek emperor aided heretics and schismatics. This allegation served as a pretext for the insatiable Angevin to attack the empire with the aim of ousting it from the Mediterranean as a military force. The other conciliar measure concerned the obligatory conclave for the College of Cardinals. The measure has stood the test of time, although there was a unanimous protest of the cardinals at the council, probably because the canon decreed the cessation of all income for the cardinals while in conclave. But the other prelates present voted with equal unanimity for the adoption of the papally proposed decree. However, the main purpose of the decree, *i.e.* to speed up the election, was not always achieved, especially when once more the old Roman aristocratic families managed to have access to the College of Cardinals. During the latter part of the thirteenth century the powerful Colonna and Orsini families came more and more to the foreground.

In the history of the medieval papacy the second half of this century presents a picture of contrasts. On the one hand, as far as papal and curial administration went, the machinery worked with a smoothness, elegance and reliability which might well be the envy of many a government far beyond the medieval period. The efficiency of the organization was well-nigh perfect, resting on a well-lubricated machinery and a highly experienced and dedicated personnel. Yet on the other hand, the once observable fibre and élan, the dynamic impetus, the buoyancy and energy of the papacy were steadily declining in proportion to its organizational efficiency. There can be no doubt that in the closing decades of the thirteenth century the authority of the papacy gradually diminished all over Europe and in some parts suffered a veritable rebuff.

The explanation of this contingency lies only partly with the papacy itself. To begin with, there were the long vacancies, sometimes lasting two to three years, as well as a great number of popes. While in the forty years between the death of Innocent III and the accession of Alexander IV there were three popes, in the subsequent forty years (1254–94) there were no less than eleven popes, and no fewer than seven years in which there was no pope at all, whereas in one year (1276–7) there were three. It is self-evident that this situation was not conducive to a prosperous functioning of the institution. And from the historical point of view it is also important to bear in mind that during this period the cardinalate came to assume a position which was to flavour the subsequent history of the papacy to an ever increasing extent. Leaving aside the factions within the College of Cardinals, it was the long vacancies which whetted their appetite for an oligarchic form of government – a contingency which now only simmered under the surface but which came to erupt with elemental force exactly a century later. The issues which the Great Schism threw up, cast their shadows back to the second half of the thirteenth century.

To these factors must be added the manner in which the papacy as an institution and some popes as individuals dealt with the Staufen dynasty and the contingent political jobbery with the French (and English) kings, not to omit the papal offers to various kings in regard to Sicily and Naples. Nor should a proper assessment leave out of account the invocation of all ecclesiastical censures in the service of the French in Sicily after the native population had risen against the oppressive government of Charles of Anjou (Sicilian Vespers on Easter Monday 1282) and had elected Peter III of Aragon as Sicilian king. The papacy excommunicated him, laid Sicily under an interdict, did not refrain from preaching a crusade against him and as feudal lord deposed the new Ruler. None of these measures had any effect worth speaking of. But unperturbed by this fiasco and in order to assuage the French, the pope, Martin IV, now offered the kingdom of Aragon to Charles of Valois and once more appealed for a crusade to conquer Aragon as a papal fief. The military and naval operations soon ended in predictable disaster. These are merely examples (easily multipliable) of how the papacy conducted its affairs in the late thirteenth century, but it does not need much imagination to visualize how profoundly the authority of the papacy suffered. One might well say that the certainty of past success is not a good counsellor.

In proximity to these features stands the over-use (not misuse) of the papal plenitude of power. In substance this power was grounded in legal and theological considerations, and was therefore all the more potent in a thoroughly Christian society, but how and when and where to use it was not a matter of law and theology, but of simple wisdom and practical psychology. And the over-use of this power in connexion with financial and territorial questions created a climate of opinion which together with the full rigours of the papal Inquisition (itself a papal tribunal) could not but contribute to a weakening of the hold which the papacy had over contemporary Christians. The ecclesiastical censures became blunted, and gradually began to lose their effectiveness, quite apart from the paucity of penalties available which in any case excluded much refinement and subtlety. In short, the voices of doubt, which resulted in open criticism of the papacy as an institution, became more outspoken, louder and more insistent than had been the case at any time in the papacy's existence. In this context and in order adequately to assess the forces at work, due consideration should also be given to the great intellectual power houses of the universities, the *raison d'être* of which was precisely the cultivation of a critical spirit and this especially within the framework of jurisprudence so powerfully fostered by the papacy. Further, the laity began to take an ever greater share in public affairs and hence came into direct contact with the results of papal policy. The rapid growth of towns and the concomitant emergence of new lay classes within their walls provided additional sections of the population who viewed contemporary papal policy with detachment, if not open animosity. It was these new groups which formed the nucleus of the third estate – the bourgeoisie – unencumbered by tradition and free from the fetters which constrained the estates of the ecclesiastical and secular princes and lords.

In the second half of the thirteenth century there also occurred an intellectual revolution which at least indirectly contributed to the growing estrangement of contemporary Europe from the papacy. This intellectual revolution was the result of adjusting Aristotle's teachings to Christian doctrines, an adaptation that was primarily the achievement of St Thomas Aquinas. This led to the emergence of the conception of the individual as a citizen which strongly contrasted with that of the individual as a subject of higher authority. This entailed the removal of a great many of the presuppositions upon which the papacy had based itself in its relation to the members of the Church. It was a revolution which found a particularly fertile soil in the towns and the new lay classes. The conception of man as a product of nature ushered in humanism which no longer looked at the Christian as the primary object of concern, but at his natural humanity and natural being. The birth of humanism and the accompanying emergence of the citizen as bearer of inborn rights and duties gravely undermined the authority of the papacy as the institution from which Christians as mere subjects received the doctrine clothed in the law which as subjects they had to obey. Thrown against the background of discontent with the papacy, this intellectual revolution added grist to the mills of the papal critics. The theoretical exposition of Christianity by the papacy and the actuality of papal government showed discrepancies which no reflecting and alert contemporary could overlook. Hence the receptivity of the soil for the new political theories.

Another result of this intellectual revolution – and one that most directly affected the papacy as an institution of government – was the concomitant emergence of the concept of the State as a body of citizens. At least in theory next to the supra-human, supra-natural Church, there was now conceived to be a purely human, natural State. And it was this latter to which the papacy addressed itself with less and less response. By its own definition the papacy presided over an exclusively Christian body which pursued ends beyond this world, while the professed aim of the

State lay in this world. The faithful Christians as subjects received their law eventually from the papacy; the autonomous citizens made their own laws directly or indirectly through their chosen representatives. A great many of the basic presuppositions of the papacy could not be squared with the principles upon which the State rested. The one, the Church, realized the descending theme of government and law, the other, the State, realized its ascending counterpart.

Hand in hand with the revival of 'the natural man' and the appearance of the citizen and the State in the political field, went simultaneously the development of a properly understood natural science. Above all the encouragement and the spread of the vernacular and vernacular literature was a symptom of the growing awareness of the differences of the individual nations from each other. This astonishingly quick dissemination of vernacular literature including hymns and popular songs, not to speak of the translation of the Bible into the vernacular, was a feature which in itself had nothing to do with the papacy, but which nevertheless must be taken into account in an assessment of the reasons for the decline of papal authority. As a universal language Latin was one of the most potent factors contributing to the idea of universalism. The monopoly of Latin was broken by the ubiquitous spread of the vernacular, a process which could not but impinge upon both the idea and practice of universalism, and hence at least indirectly upon the papacy as a government of universal dimensions. The reduction and impoverishment of the empire as a force to be reckoned with at this very time and the simultaneous favouritism shown by the papacy to the monarchies of England and France and its entanglement with their policies, must also be adequately appreciated if the lowering of the prestige of the papacy by the end of the thirteenth century is to be understood. Moreover, the concentration of the papacy on imperial policy for well over a century made it overlook a number of issues in the kingdoms which had evoked its wrath against the emperors: in this way the monarchies were greatly strengthened.

Here also enters another reflexion which demands attention, that is, the gradual withering away of the hitherto purely objective standpoint, itself based on the view of an objective world order that was laid down once and for all. This objective standpoint came now to be replaced by the subjective point of view, a change which gravely affected the papacy from the end of the thirteenth century on and which made its tentative début in the polemical writings of the Frederician chancery (above pp. 257, 261). For what counted according to the unshaken papal theme propounded and acted upon by the papacy since the mid-fifth century, was not the person of the individual pope, but the pope's office, in other words, the institution as such. This crucial papal distinction between office and person was now beginning to be reversed. What began to matter was the personality of the pope, was whether he was a morally 'good' or 'bad' pope. It was the subjective evaluation of the man as pope that came to the foreground in the place of the objective platform in the shape of the papal law. The objective validity of the latter – its sole criterion – was replaced by the subjective assessment of the personality of the pope. In sum, then, what the observer of the papacy witnessed in the second half of the thirteenth century was a gradual, though clearly perceptible decomposition of Europe as a single ecclesiastical unit, and the fragmentation of Europe into independent, autonomous entities which were soon to be called national monarchies or states. But this fragmentation heralded the withering away of the papacy as a governing institution operating on a universal scale.

It is against this background that the papacy must be assessed and understood at the turn of the thirteenth and fourteenth centuries. Boniface VIII replaced the pope who appeared to fulfil the subjective requirements of the 'good' pope – the 'angelic pope', a figure of mystical vision – in the person of Celestine V who was clearly a compromise choice by the cardinals when after the death of Nicholas IV they were unable to agree on a candidate for 27 months. Celestine was no doubt a pious, holy, well-meaning hermit, but totally unsuited to be a governor since he was without experience or training and had a correspondingly cloistered outlook. Realizing his incapacity he resigned – possibly not without prompting by his successor – after a pontificate of five months' duration. In some respects Cardinal Benedict Gaetani – Boniface VIII – was an anachronistic figure, and yet in others a classic representative of the ancient papal axiom that facts could and should be mastered by ideas. There is no doubt that in him the papacy acquired a Ruler who on the grounds of experience as well as his mastery of the law knew what was demanded of a papal Ruler, that is to say, universal government both in scope and in subject-matter as far as the exigencies of Christendom warranted it. But his pontificate was heavily mort-gaged by the just mentioned antecedent developments and move-ments. With all the heavy armoury at his disposal Boniface tried to stem the tide perilously advancing against the papacy. Whether in Italy or farther afield, the papacy though employing all the old arguments and weapons, suffered defeat after defeat.

It was compelled to recognize formally the Aragonese domina-tion in Sicily. Florence was torn by the domestic fights between the 'Blacks' and the 'Whites', the former inclined towards the papal world-outlook, while the latter favoured a more secularized ideology: papal legates decided for the former and the latter were expelled. Dante's picture of the pope had a certain poetic justice. Yet it was the Florentines themselves who chased out Charles of Valois, the papal military defender of the 'Blacks'. Boniface met a similar rebuff in Denmark where he also imposed an interdict because of the opposition of the king to the archbishop of Lund who, despite the king's eventual accommodation with the papacy, was debarred by royal decree from returning to his see: the episode provided a marked contrast to the English scene at the beginning of this same century. Even in Hungary where the suc-cession was once more disputed, the pope was unable to assert his authority. In withering tones the English Parliament and Edward I rejected (1301) the papal claim that Scotland was a papal fief: this claim was 'unheard-of', 'strange', and 'prejudicial' to royal interests, and in support of this rejection the spurious and novelistic *History of the Britons* by Geoffrey of Monmouth greatly assisted, so that the papacy was defeated by the same weapon of 'historical precedent' which it always knew how to wield so effectively. In Germany Boniface had more luck though with little practical avail. Although at first stigmatizing Albrecht I of Austria as a rebel, the pope readily changed his tune when the king wholly subscribed to the traditional papal theme in regard to the making of an emperor and the rights of the papacy over the empire.

In fact, it was precisely because Albrecht I had been allied to Philip IV of France that Boniface saw him as a mere tool of France which rapidly was approaching hegemonial status in Europe. The contrast between the German and the French reaction to the papal advances was at once a symptom and an effect of the antecedent policy pursued by the papacy towards both kingdoms. While the German king wholly accepted the premisses and axioms cherished by the papacy, the French king when presented with the very same themes and demands, rejected them outright. Boniface was not only quite unoriginal – in fact not a single new idea emerged in his pontificate – but was a pope of a rather conservative complexion who, moreover, was quite oblivious of the profound changes that had taken place in the preceding decades.

The heir of the Staufens had become the Capetian king of France, precisely because the papacy had overlooked in France – and also in England – the very things which had aroused its wrath in regard to the empire before the mid-thirteenth century. What the papacy now attempted was to raise its status to that over-all commanding position in Europe which its programme had always postulated. But the opponent of the papacy was now not a papally created emperor, but a 'mere' king, one of those whom the papacy (and in its wake the emperors) had contemptuously dubbed 'kinglets' (*reguli*). None of the arguments so carefully manufactured through the centuries, so carefully preserved in the papal archives, so skilfully executed by the papacy from the eleventh century onwards, was applicable to a 'mere' king: he was not made by the papacy; of all European Rulers he had been addressed as 'the most Christian king' and had been singularly distinguished by the oil sent directly from heaven for the unction at his coronation (the so-called Clovis oil); the provisions of the Donation of Constantine were hardly fit to be applied to France; the sun-moon allegory was wholly irrelevant.

As already indicated (see above p. 213), an unwitting contribution to the strengthening of France had been made by Innocent III who distinguished Philip Augustus as a Ruler who did not recognize a 'superior in temporal matters'. This was nothing but a pontifical endorsement of French sovereignty and intended as a rebuff to the universal aspirations of the Staufens. This Innocentian standpoint was to bear fruit in the emergence of the concept of territorial sovereignty in the early fourteenth century. To these considerations must be added papal favouritism towards France throughout the thirteenth century. Finally, the malaise from which the papacy suffered – admittedly historically conditioned – became almost fatal now. The papacy could never deny its Roman parentage and its ineluctable ties with Roman ideology and the Roman past, which explains the attention given to 'Roman' matters such as the whole cluster surrounding imperial ideology. Kings were always regarded as a *quantité négligeable*. What mattered to the papacy was the Roman empire, because it was its own creation having been established as an instrument against the 'Roman' emperor in Constantinople. It was the incubus of this Roman inheritance which prevented the papacy from realizing the potentialities of 'mere' kings. The governmental programme of the papacy was thoroughly Roman – and in this respect almost wholly inapplicable to kings who were not, and were not aspiring to be, Roman emperors.

The conflict between the papacy and Philip IV of France concerned well-worn questions: the right of the king to tax the clergy and royal jurisdiction over clerics. In denying Philip these rights Boniface spoke old, if not stale language that had ceased to make much impact. The royal incidence of a tax on the clergy was prompted by the war against England. Philip was no doubt in need of this financial supply against the economically far better equipped Edward I. The papal prohibition issued (1296) in *Clericis laicos* (a statement of St Jerome transmitted in Gratian's *Decretum*, referring to the animosity which lay people always harboured against clerics) sternly laid down in general terms that no king had the right of taxing the clergy without first having obtained papal approval, whereupon Philip made short shrift of the matter. The export of gold and silver was forbidden – a serious blow to the papal finances – and the papal collectors were expelled. Edward I threatened the English clergy with outlawry, if they stopped paying the fifth which the great majority continued to pay. Although a compromise was found in 1297 – the papacy permitted voluntary gifts to the king's coffers – the truce settled nothing, and the conflict flared up again in 1301 when Bernard Saisset, the bishop of the newly erected diocese of Pamiers (established in 1295 by Boniface himself) was tried by a royal court under the chairmanship of the chancellor, Pierre Flotte, for treason, offensive statements against the king, simony and heresy, found guilty and handed over to his archbishop for detention under lock and key. The pope received a detailed report and was asked to depose and punish Saisset; without even inspecting the dossier sent to him Boniface flatly refused and demanded the immediate release of the bishop.

Meanwhile, however, severe friction had arisen within the curia itself. The cardinals belonging to the Colonna family were incensed by a papal decision which affected the estates of their family. In the Colonna cardinals the papacy had to fight bitter and determined enemies. That no schism occurred at the time was principally due to the tensions between the papacy and France. After deposing the Colonna cardinals, Boniface found himself charged by them for the part he had allegedly played in removing Celestine V – and it was now they, the Colonna cardinals, who appealed to a general council which they asked to try the pope: Frederick II obviously served as a model. The pope took the severest measures against the Colonna faction: their town of Palestrina was razed to the ground and the family was deprived of all its goods and estates – which were handed over lock, stock and barrel to their mortal enemies, the Orsini as well as to the Gaetani, the pope's own family. Only precipitate flight to the French court saved the Colonna's life.

In the history of the papacy and of the Church the jubilee of 1300 has no small significance. Impervious of the clearly discernible change of the religious climate, Boniface instituted a great theatrical show in Rome to celebrate the jubilee year 1300. This afforded him an opportunity of displaying papal 'pomp and circumstance' as of old and obviously served as a means of boosting his somewhat damaged reputation. It was the jubilee which moved this pope to grant the first general indulgence for a hundred years to the crowds that had flocked to Rome for 'the grand feast'. But it would not have been difficult for Boniface to sense the detachment from, if not animosity to, papal ideology in the higher echelons of royal governments. The intoxication of the jubilee year misled him into taking appearances for reality, and he now peremptorily demanded from Philip IV the release of the imprisoned bishop Saisset. Simultaneously all the privileges granted to the king were revoked. This was the signal for the French king to go over to the offensive at the beginning of 1302. The royal chancery – ably staffed by members of the newly arisen bourgeoisie and advised by the Colonna cardinals – in conjunction with members of the university of Paris began to flood the country with royal decrees and supposed replies to papal writs.

The chancery even went so far as to forge a papal letter which was burnt in public and it also concocted a reply starting with the following words addressed to the pope: 'Your utter fatuity may know that we (the king) are not subjected to anyone . . .' which was never dispatched. The chancery also fabricated a charge sheet containing some 29 serious accusations against Boniface himself, among others, blasphemy, simony, heresy, murder of Celestine V, fornication, and the like, culminating in an appeal for a general council. At the same time public opinion was fanned by a spate of pamphlets and other centrally directed propagandistic efforts which posed old problems in a new light and with new equipment. Members of the university also issued learned tracts in which Roman law and Aristotelian arguments combined to buttress the attack on the papacy in general and on the pope in particular. These years gave an advance warning of the propagandistic potentialities of which the well-served chancery of a determined government was capable.

Boniface managed to hold a council at Rome in November 1302. Despite discouragement 39 French prelates nevertheless took part. And in this council the famous *Unam sanctam* was published (18 November 1302). In contrast to the publicistic literature directed against the papacy by the French chancery, this papal decree contained not one single new argument. All that was new was the very skilful stitching together of statements made by Cyprian, Hugh of St Victor, Bernard of Clairvaux, canonists and Thomas Aquinas and the moulding of this synthesis into a coherent whole. The last sentence that for the purpose of salvation it was necessary for every human creature to be subjected to the rulings of the Roman Church, was actually a literal copying of one of Aquinas' statements. The document containing also a number of statements culled from spurious sources as well as the two-sword allegory in accentuated form, pithily summed up the papal programme of government in a Christian society – a programme which, at the time, had no more than historical interest. *Unam sanctam* was the sonorous, proud and self-confident swan song of the medieval papacy.

Yet at the very time this decree was issued, the French king and his advisers hit upon a very effective device, and one that made practical use of the then fashionable ideas concerning representation and participation by the third estate in important public

matters. In a very large assembly of all three estates in June 1303 –
its superb stage management should be noted – a number of
speeches were made by more or less eminent leaders, including
Friars and Masters of the university, the climax being reached in a
short speech by the king himself. All speeches repeated in various
keys the already mentioned charges against Boniface. The assembly resolved as a matter of public policy that the pope should
stand his trial before a general council. This resolution was
broadcast through the length and breadth of France, and towns
and villages were asked to sign the petition embodied in the
resolution. Of the religious Orders only 17 Cistercian and some
Dominican houses refused to bow to the demands of the royal
agents, and these incurred severe and drastic sanctions on account
of their refusal. What became known abroad was not the somewhat ruthless manner with which the royal officers had gone to
work, but the resolution of June 1303. Upon hearing it the curia
was in real dismay, because the opponent was no longer a king,
but apparently a whole nation – a propagandistic master stroke
on the part of the king and of William of Playsian. The distance
between *Unam sanctam* and the French resolution could not have
been highlighted more persuasively – the one summing up past
ideology in an examplary and lucid manner, the other confidently
pointing to the future. That the assembly was in reality a staged,
and a very well staged, affair, was not immediately apparent to its
participants. The king pretended to be the executive spokesman
of the French nation: it was his duty to take effective governmental action to put the will of the nation into reality. It was the
clever invocation of the amorphous multitude in conjunction
with the principle of representation which was the stroke of
genius on the part of the royal stage managers.

The only weapon that remained at the disposal of the papacy
was the solemn excommunication of the king and the release of
his subjects from their allegiance to him. Indeed, this step had
long been prepared, certainly for the last 18 months. The king
was determined to prevent the publication of the decree which
was planned for 8 September 1303 from Anagni. During the
night of 7–8 September a troop of soldiers led by William Nogaret
and ably advised by Sciarra Colonna stormed the papal palace at
Anagni, demanded the instant resignation of the pope and delivery
of his person to the soldiers, the restitution of the Colonna pos-

sessions, and the handing over of all the available moneys. Boniface refused every demand and instead offered his own life. While Colonna would not have abstained from accepting this last papal offer, Nogaret's greater wisdom prevailed, because a dead pope was of little use to him or his master. The outrage spread like fire through the town, and the inhabitants of Anagni liberated the captive pope and his entourage in the early hours of 8 September. A month later, on 12 October, Boniface died a broken reed and was buried in the mausoleum which he had himself erected.

The turn of the thirteenth and fourteenth centuries showed that the papacy – however ably led by a man who was a worthy equal of a Gregory VII, Innocent III or IV and who had the same universal vision that inspired them, though not their statesmanship – could no longer evoke the response which only half a century earlier would have been considered self-evident. The mere thought of an armed troop storming Innocent III's abode and demanding his imprisonment, would have seemed a plan born of criminal lunacy. But now less than 90 years afterwards a French force did precisely this – which reveals how radically reality had changed and how the authority of the papacy as an institution had suffered in the meantime. It was the already mentioned new intellectual movement and forces which, though in themselves by no means hostile to the papacy, cumulatively and in the particular circumstances inflicted damage upon it. No longer was the reconciliation of faith with reason a foremost problem, but it was nature and man's natural humanity which had cosmologically changed the outlook. In addition no alert contemporary could have escaped the conclusion that the highest curial dignitaries had reached a depth of moral turpitude which only two generations earlier would have been unthinkable. It was the Colonna cardinals no less than a papal cardinal-legate (Cardinal Jean le Moine) who had handed ideological ammunition to the French court. Moreover, the national monarchies had emerged as fully-fledged states to which the idea of universalism was alien and which lived by a brand of particularism that was nurtured by differences in language, culture and modes of living. The national states and the papacy began to show fundamental divergencies in aim and outlook. To the national argument the papacy had no answer. That was exactly what Philip IV sensed and what assured him his success. Paradoxically enough it was the papacy which since the eleventh century had mightily contributed to this development by underestimating the inherent strength of those whom already a Gregory VII had called mere 'kinglets' (*reguli*) and by its almost exclusive attention on the Roman empire and Roman emperor. The national kingdoms fostered a spirit which in the end was to prove the undoing of the papacy as a focal point in Europe. Boniface's pontificate ends one phase and begins another in the history of the papacy.

12 *Avignon, Rome and Constance*

THE VIOLENCE OF the conflict of the papacy with France and the eventual use of force against the pope personally, produced a traumatic effect in papal quarters. The shock was perhaps salutary. A week after Boniface's death a successor was chosen (Benedict XI). The papacy now entered a period which could suitably be headed: appeasement of France. Most of the measures decreed by Boniface against Philip were revoked and even the Colonna cardinals were released from excommunication, though not immediately restored to the College of Cardinals. Among the new cardinals created by Benedict XI in June 1304 was the English Dominican-General Walter Winterbourne who after the death of the pope in July 1304 was to play some role in the long and protracted conclave deliberating on a suitable successor: he had not, of course, had anything to do with the Bonifacian policy nor could he, as an Englishman, be accused of too great a leaning towards France. In short he was an outsider and 'an honest broker' to repair the damage that had been inflicted on the institution. Walter Winterbourne was indeed put up as a candidate after joining the conclave at Perugia in November 1304, but did not receive the required two-thirds majority. In the event, on 5 June 1305, the archbishop of Bordeaux was chosen by 10 out of 15 cardinals. In the circumstances this was a wise choice. Clement V was French by upbringing and outlook, but English as a subject of Edward I, and never having been a member of the curia, he was not in any way tainted as a partisan.

A deep shadow hung over the papacy. The threatened trial and exhumation of Boniface VIII was one of the most obstinately pursued aims of the French. It was a threat that Philip was resolved to make real, and he had a great deal of genuine and less genuine evidence collected against his dead enemy. But the papacy was equally adamant, even if only to avoid creating a precedent, in its determination to prevent this trial from taking place, because in addition to the ideological and political defeat there would have also been the spectacle of a public humiliation of that very pope who had acted and spoken and judged and decreed as God's vicar on earth as none had done before and few after him. The instrument which the French monarchy knew how to use to the best advantage was the Order of the Templars. It was an Order of Knights – their rule was given to them by Bernard of Clairvaux (1128) and they shortly afterwards became an exempted Order by decree of Innocent II (1139) – which after the loss of the Holy Land in the late thirteenth century, had few practical tasks. The Order was however prosperous and happened to be particularly wealthy in France. It had increased its membership and its houses, and with trade and commerce between the Levant and Western Europe expanding the Templars began to act like medieval merchant bankers. Moreover, many people had deposited their jewellery and other personal treasures with the Templars in France, so that the Order was likely to become a considerable economic force. And as an Order it in any case enjoyed many privileges and immunities.

Since Philip's financial position was not particularly secure, he hit upon the device of using the Templars – or rather their wealth – as part of a bargain: the Damocles sword of the posthumous trial of Boniface as a heretic, fornicator, and so on, hung over the head of the papacy. The suggestion that the trial might be averted, if the papacy showed itself accommodating in the question of the Templars, was received with some alacrity in curial quarters. The French court proceeded in a manner which showed once more what could be done even in an age which had no wireless, no daily press, no posters, nor other mass media. The screw was turned on the Templars in the very first year of Clement's pontificate by making charges of sodomy and blasphemy against some of their eminent members. And anticipating similar procedures in modern times, they were sentenced, and their houses as well as their possessions confiscated. It was soon to be the turn of the pope who after having been threatened with a charge of aiding and abetting heretics, ordered bishops and papal inquisitors in all countries to examine the Templars with a view to ascertaining their orthodoxy. Many a Templar ended his life at the stake. What Clement V had achieved was that the final pronouncement on the future of the Order was to be made by a general council which he convoked to Vienne, where indeed after some postponements it met in 1311.

Although there had never been an intention on the part of the papacy to forsake Rome – in fact, immediately after accepting the election Clement made preparations for moving from Bordeaux to Rome – Clement adjourned his departure from month to month, from year to year. He was a sickly man and did not wish to be exposed to the rigours of crossing the Alps. Hence he was enthroned and crowned at Lyons at All Saints in 1305: a wall which collapsed when the procession passed by, killed several dignitaries; the pope was thrown from his horse and lost a precious jewel from the tiara which having fallen from his head, rolled along the pavement. After his coronation he immediately appointed nine new cardinals, all bar one Frenchmen, and four were his nephews. Although never abandoning the idea of returning to Rome, Clement felt more at home in Gascony. He resided at Poitiers one and a half years and did not feel strong enough to give orders to move the whole curial apparatus back to Rome. The Colonna cardinals were now fully re-instated and *Unam sanctam* was declared inapplicable to France. Because of the geographical proximity of Vienne where the council was to take place, he took up residence at Avignon in 1309, though even then he had no intention to remain there. As a matter of fact, Clement himself lived at Avignon only for short periods, always preferring localities which were more suited to his frail health. The rapidity with which papal prestige, function and authority had declined, was perhaps best mirrored in Clement V, who remained a Gascon ecclesiastic despite his Roman-papal garb.

The Council of Vienne barely justifies its rank as a general council (the Fifteenth) of the Church. Although attended by nearly 300 prelates, in reality it had to deal with one point only, that is, the Templars and their wealth. The trial of Boniface hung like the sword of Damocles over the papacy owing to the resourcefulness of the French commission led by the astute Marigny; the papal commission was as anxious as before not to risk this public spectacle. It did not take the French commission long to achieve its aim through a purely administrative papal act: the dissolution of the Order. This papal decree of 22 March 1312 was then laid before the whole council which duly approved it (*Vox in excelso*,

3 April 1312). The reason for the dissolution as given in the decree was that the Order no longer fulfilled the tasks for which it was created, that it had lost its usefulness in the Holy Land and that its high reputation had been severely shattered in recent years. After much undignified wrangling its goods, estates, all its property, were by papal and conciliar decrees distributed amongst the Hospitallers and the French fisc. The price which the papacy paid for avoiding the trial against the dead Boniface was high indeed. No doubt the handling of this matter by the papacy must have gravely damaged its standing. It is surely legitimate to observe that only a modicum of statesmanship and a moderate implementation of some papal principles – which ironically enough had been proclaimed with such furore less than a decade before – could have saved a good deal of the papacy's prestige. Part – and it can only be part – of the explanation must be that the papacy was for the first time confronted by a determined and ruthless king who had recognized the Achilles heel of the contemporary papacy – its universality, its Romanism, and its attendant ideological unpreparedness vis-à-vis a national monarchy. It was a further symptom of the early fourteenth-century papacy that in the papal decree issued in 1313 (*Pastoralis cura*) it endorsed the idea of the national state and of its territorial sovereignty, in this case specifically applicable to Sicily, but easily extendable to other countries and regions.

Historically, the pontificates of Boniface VIII and of Clement V depict the two extremes to which the papal pendulum had swung. Ideologically they are a study in contrasts. For Clement's papacy was to all intents and purposes the very denial of the historically conditioned bases upon which Boniface's papacy had taken its stand. This is not to say that Boniface's policies had much chance of success, because the papacy in the anteceding decades had not come to terms with the new forces, but Boniface at least adhered to the traditional papal patterns, while in Clement's pontificate lack of statesmanship, experience, training and vision accounted for the veritable *volte face* of the papacy. What remained was little more than rearguard action which can hardly be called a programme. What was lost was the moral, spiritual and authoritative leadership which the papacy had built up in Europe over the centuries of minute, consistent, detailed, dynamic, forward-looking work. Yet, this is not the same as saying that through its

Avignonese sojourn the papacy became an appendix of France or of French policy. Nothing would be further from the truth, however much contemporaries may have believed it. But the papacy was now forced to pursue policies which in substance aimed at appeasement and were no longer directive, orientating and determinative.

It was also symptomatic of the early fourteenth century that the first book exclusively devoted to the concept of the Church appeared (written by James of Viterbo). The obvious conclusion to be drawn is that until then there was no need to devote a whole book to this subject, but that this need was now clearly felt. Moreover, it was in John XXII's pontificate when the papacy had firmly settled at Avignon that one of the ablest, most perceptive and persuasive books appeared which – and this really was its significance – using Aristotelian and Roman law arguments attacked the papacy as an institution and struck thereby at its very roots. The title of the book, *The Defender of the Peace* (1324) by Marsiglio of Padua, one time rector of the university of Paris (1311–12), as well as its contents made clear to contemporaries that in the writer's opinion it was the papacy which disturbed the peace of the world. This could be restored only by eliminating the institution as a governing authority. At the same time William Ockham attacked the institution from the theological angle and severely castigated the personalities of the contemporary popes. A little more refined but no less outspoken than Marsiglio's was the opposition to the papacy as such in the work of Dante entitled *Monarchy*, in which he denied the institution governmental character. Some preparatory work for this kind of polemical literature was found indeed in the already mentioned works of the French publicists at the very beginning of this century, but none of them, with the possible exception of John of Paris and Pierre Dubois, went as far as Dante, Marsiglio or Ockham in assailing the papacy and the popes.

Just as the Avignonese papacy had lacked effective means with which to accommodate the national states into its framework, in the same way it lacked an effective ideology with which to parry the attacks launched by these publicists. Condemnations and excommunications of the authors – Dante's book remained on the official papal Index of prohibited books until 1908 – and the regurgitation and emphatic reiteration of old, but rarely relevant

K

material, was assuredly not enough to stem the tide. Of course, there were contemporary writers such as Augustinus Triumphus or Alvarus Pelagius, who in a very scholarly and trenchant manner and with the help of all the accumulated papal-hierocratic armoury tried to set forth the programme of a universal papal monarchy, but these defenders took little account of the arguments of their opponents and, endowed with an admirable sense of logic, they oftentimes reached positions and conclusions which the papacy itself hardly claimed and was now, as the fourteenth century advanced, in no position whatever to implement. Evidently, there were numerous minor writers on either side, but reality was no longer mouldable by an ideology that was almost exclusively based on faith. When it was even said in philosophical quarters that what mattered was experience and observation of natural phenomena, and that credulity was not a safe enough or strong enough base from which to argue, the papal-hierocratic system had indeed lost some of its strongest supports. The rapidly rising naturalist school which in actual fact coined the very term of 'natural science' in the late thirteenth century in conjunction with the other ideological developments proved itself a very serious hurdle for the deployment of papal arguments.

When thrown against this ideological background, the conflict between the papacy and Louis IV, the Bavarian, was barely reminiscent of the days when empire and papacy had fought for principles. True, the same language, the same instruments of coercion, the same censures were used on both sides, but the whole was a blurred reflexion of previous conflicts. What gave the conflict its particular flavour was the escalation of papal demands, almost self-propelled, it might seem, by the inner logic of the papal arguments. A notable example was that the papacy alone was entitled to appoint a vicar in Italy and that in case of a vacancy in the empire the pope himself assumed the role of an imperial vicar over the whole empire. The contingency which provided an application of these theses was the double election in Germany of Frederick of Austria and Louis the Bavarian in 1314. Although both approached the papacy – and we should recall that the empire itself was by this time to all intents and purposes nothing more than a German principality – John XXII was sensitive on the Italian question. The security, if not the existence, of the papal state was once more at stake and it was the only worthwhile source of regular income for the papacy in Avignon. Hence the vicar for Italy appointed by Louis was deposed by the pope and in his place he appointed his own in the person of Robert of Naples, whose outlawry by the Emperor Henry VII only a few years earlier had prompted Clement V's notorious *Pastoralis cura* (see above p. 282). When Louis defeated his opponent in 1322 and thus, not unjustifiably, held himself the sole claimant for the imperial crown, John remained adamant in his rejection of Louis. Because of his protests against the inter-ference by the papacy and his exercising governmental authority without papal approval, Louis found himself excommunicated on 23 March 1324 and his subjects were forbidden to obey his government.

In the subsequent famous *Sachsenhausen* manifesto of May 1324 Louis appealed for a general council and bitterly criticized the papacy for using ecclesiastical censures in the pursuit of its own interests while the pope was called a heretic, because he had favoured the heretical faction of the Franciscan Order. The papacy replied sharply: deposition of the king, solemn excommunication and papal interdict on all his followers. Learned in law and doctrine as John was, he was able to invoke all the old hierocratic legal arguments, but in the changed circumstances they fell flat. At the same time the orthodox wing of the Franciscans was persecuted with ruthless energy by the papacy, so that Ockham, Marsiglio and Michael of Cesena (the head of the Franciscans) found them-selves exiles in Louis' court. Hardly ever had a royal court counted such a galaxy of talent amongst refugees from papal attack. No worthwhile advocate appeared for the papacy. In 1328 Louis deposed the pope on the grounds of his heresy and other crimes and deprived the papacy of Rome and the papal state. On the model of the Staufen Rulers Louis appointed his own pope in the person of Nicholas V, a Franciscan. Sciarra Colonna as city prefect and representative of the Romans crowned Louis at St Peter's; he was anointed by the excommunicated Bishop Alberti of Venice. Louis asked the anti-pope to repeat the corona-tion with a proper regard to the traditional ceremonial. The anti-pope Nicholas V withdrew from his somewhat exalted posi-tion after the pope at Avignon had appealed for a crusade against Louis, the emperor of the Romans. In the constitution *Licet iuris* (finally approved in 1338) the ancient rights of the papacy in regard to the empire and the emperor were severely curtailed. In it the papacy's right to examine the imperial candidate was denied and if the pope were to refuse to crown the king emperor of the Romans, any bishop or archbishop was entitled to do so. This was a preliminary step towards the *Golden Bull* (below p. 290).

The general lack of orientation, even in purely theological matters, revealed itself also in some views which John XXII held and for which he was censored by those qualified to pronounce upon them. It was a spectacle which the Christian world had not yet seen. The pope was called a heretic not only by political opponents, but also by properly qualified theologians. On his death-bed the nonagenarian renounced his erroneous opinions concerning the so-called beatific vision. There also seemed to be some substance in the charge of heresy committed by this pope, who was, nevertheless, one of the best canonists and a most acute expert in jurisprudence. This accusation concerned his views on the poverty of Christ, which were at least theologically debatable. Precisely because he was an excellent lawyer, John XXII was anxious to have the papal administrative apparatus thoroughly overhauled. This reorganization of the curial offices had become necessary as a result of the greatly increased business which reached the papacy.

Meanwhile the city of Rome and the papal state deteriorated economically and financially, while the court at Avignon swallowed up more and more money. Hence the papal curia made determined attempts to re-establish a proper organization in Italy, but for this too more money was needed. The way out was a considerable increase in curial taxation and an enlargement of offices and prebends specially reserved to the papacy in the case of a vacancy. The concomitant feature of this escalation of papal reservations was that more and higher fees had to be paid to the papacy. This in conjunction with the already latent anticlericalism and festering antipapalism, by-products of a heightened national feeling in England, led to anti-papal legislation under Edward III. The statutes of *Provisors* and *Praemunire* (1351-3) struck at the roots of these papal measures and were symptomatic of the strong detachment with which the papacy was viewed in England. It cannot cause much surprise that at the same time the

English Parliament revoked the grant which King John had made to the papacy: even nominally England ceased to be a fief of the papacy.

But it was the costly officialdom that was perhaps the most expensive item in the whole curia. The establishment personnel consisted of the hundreds of notaries, referendaries, registraries, scriptors, abbreviators, correctors, bullators, quite apart from the superior officers, such as vice-chancellor of the curia and his own staff. The registration and filing and dating and sealing of the thousands of documents demanded a highly geared up organisation. In particular the petitions for prebends or benefices ran into tens of thousands (for instance, under John XXII about 65,000; Clement VI over 90,000; Innocent VI some 30,000; etc.). Each petition had to be scrutinized by an intricate procedure before a final decision was reached. To this must be added the political correspondence of the popes with princes, kings and other potentates, which made the establishment of special Registers necessary, so that the different kinds of curial correspondence were easily and speedily available. Considering the crucial importance which finances had assumed, special attention was devoted to the Register of the Apostolic Chamber, the financial department of the curia. Here too the intricate mechanism of curial and papal income and expenditure made a re-organization necessary. The administrative and financial ingenuity of the Avignonese papacy had no limits. But it should also be borne in mind that the expenses of the curia at times reached astronomical figures. The city of Avignon became one of the important places in Europe and most banking houses had their branches there. The kitchens, the butteries, cellars, vestments and clothing of the personnel, jewellery, library, new buildings and repairs and upkeep of old ones, the equipment of the guards, payment of alms, charitable donations, and so on, absorbed considerable sums. The annual ordinary expenses at Avignon varied between 230,000 and 480,000 gold ducats to which must be added a great many extraordinary expenses, notably those which were incurred by the far-flung missions.

Among the non-recurrent expenditure was also the building of the papal palace at Avignon and the purchase of the county of Avignon from the kingdom of Naples in 1348 by Clement VI The French contingent in the College of Cardinals increased. Yet, the idea of the papacy returning to Rome was never far from the minds of the popes, though its realization in practice was a different matter. In fact, Rome itself tried to induce the papacy to return by a somewhat anachronistic attempt to raise the city to its previous splendour. Cola di Rienzo, a real people's tribune, if not demagogue, made himself the mouthpiece of the Romans and became the 'tribune of freedom, peace and justice, the liberator of the holy Roman Republic'. He managed to evoke nostalgic memories among the Romans and made them believe in their mission as creators of a world-wide empire. This revival of a Roman tradition was as pathetic as it was fruitless. The papacy was apparently too well lodged in Avignon to be induced by this clumsy device to return at once to Rome. The Cardinal-legate Bertrand de Deux represented papal interests in Italy. A very practical impediment to a return was the fury of the Black Death which made it improvident to embark on the journey. Between 1348 and 1352 death literally decimated the population; curial offices were orphaned; Orders, congregations, villages and towns shrank alarmingly in size. It was this terrible scourge which forced the papacy to turn its mind to the more practical task of how to survive the epidemic.

Meanwhile the last papal-imperial conflict had continued with unabated vigour. What John XXII was unable to achieve, was attempted by his successor Benedict XII whose efforts at a settlement miscarried because by now the papacy appeared to have lost all sense of reality. Ockham's particular venom was reserved for this pope whose stature was never in any case high. The conflict reached its concluding climax in Clement VI's solemn, and in its fierce tone hardly surpassable, repetition of Louis' excommunication, after he had rejected wholly unacceptable and enormously inflated papal conditions for a settlement (April 1346). It was a war of attrition from which both sides emerged very considerably weakened. In Germany which had lain under an interdict for nearly two decades, the conflict resulted in loss of respect for ecclesiastical authorities by the people who distrusted the clergy and felt betrayed by the papacy. The religious and moral state of affairs all over Europe suffered great damage, and anti-religious and anti-clerical sects sprang up everywhere. It was no doubt highly significant that after Nicholas V had relinquished his in any case somewhat pitiable role as anti-pope in 1330, Louis the

Bavarian did not bother to proceed to the creation of another anti-pope. And yet it was he who had deposed Pope John XXII, whom, however, he never 're-instated'. Louis was one of the few Rulers who died an excommunicate. What was left of a genuine religious zeal escaped into mysticism which began to flower abundantly from the thirties onwards. What had become clear was that the two contestants were mere shadows of their own past. The papacy was seen to fight only for its Italian interests; the empire was no more than a German kingdom which saw some of its Italian interests threatened by the papacy. But since the empire was reduced to a German principality, an embryonic and inchoate nationalism sprang up here too, with the inevitable consequence of an alienation from the papacy which was believed to be the tool of France. In addition to the loosening of the religious bonds, the historical ties which for centuries had yielded such close relations between German and papal interests, began to lose their force.

The increase in curial business at Avignon led necessarily to a form of oligarchic government in fact, though not of course in theory, because it became understandably increasingly difficult for the pope to keep control over the numerous departments. The consequence was that the cardinals gradually came to acquire powers which they certainly did not have while in Rome. In order to put this onto something approaching a constitutional basis, the cardinals devised the so-called electoral pacts (see above p. 230) or capitulations and put this device into practice on the occasion of Innocent VI's election in December 1352. They agreed among each other that if one of them were elected, he would adhere to the following points: the number of cardinals were to be restricted to not more than 20 at any one time; in creating a cardinal the pope was to be bound by a two-thirds majority of the cardinals; all curial incomes were to be divided equally between pope and cardinals; there were to be no influential posts for relatives of the pope. This was the first electoral pact to be followed by very many more. The practice continued beyond the Reformation and the pacts grew longer and longer with more and more restrictions placed on the pope – yet when once elected, no pope formally adhered to them, because they were held to be irreconcilable with the papal plenitude of power. Innocent VI himself refused to act in accordance with the oath he had taken in the conclave. In practice however a kind of oligarchic government continued.

What continued to cause justifiable concern to the Avignonese papacy was the state of affairs in the city of Rome and in the papal state which were by now outside papal control altogether. The real governors there were petty local tyrants. Innocent VI appreciated the qualities of one of his cardinals, Cardinal Egidio Albornoz who was a warrior, a constitutional lawyer and a diplomat. With only moderate military forces which he led very ably, he managed to reconquer the papal state and to give it a constitution (so-called Egidian Constitution) which stood the test of time and remained valid virtually down to the extinction of the papal state. The cardinal also allowed Cola di Rienzo who had meanwhile led a somewhat adventurous life, to return to Rome, after the pope had released him from the papal prison at Avignon; in a skirmish he was killed soon after his return (8 October 1354).

With Rome more or less securely in 'papal' hands, at long last a 'legitimate' imperial coronation could be performed: the Cardinal-bishop of Ostia acted on behalf of the pope as the coronator on 5 April 1355 of Louis IV's successor, Charles IV, who though 'emperor of the Romans' quickly left the city for Germany. The shadowy character of Roman emperorship was reflected in the coronation by a cardinal on behalf of an absent pope. It was probably in recognition of this stark and undeniable reality that Charles IV issued the so-called *Golden Bull* in 1356 which rested on *Licet iuris* (above p. 285). Its main point was that at the moment of his election the German king had a right to be crowned emperor of the Romans; the pope as a functionary, still less as one by whose favour the imperial crown was acquired, was not even mentioned in the whole long document. The hitherto so closely guarded right of the papacy to take a hand in the making of the emperor of the Romans, was tacitly brushed aside. That is the distance the papacy had travelled between Frederick II and Charles IV: its protest against the *Golden Bull* was unavailing. This law also shows that the emperor was no more than a glorified German Ruler. The idea of universalism had been dropped by both the papacy and the empire.

One of the most notable activities of the Avignonese papacy was the initiative it took in missionary enterprises and in continually supporting them. For instance, John XXII reorganized the Asian churches and himself erected a new province at Sultaniyah with six (Armenian) suffragans; one new diocese was established in India at Quilon. Ethiopia, too, came onto the horizon of missionaries; East Africa south of the Equator may have been a missionary target; papal legates reported on the success of the Asian missions, but the Black Death here also created gaps which could hardly be made good. In Europe the universities received a great deal of attention and also support from the Avignonese papacy. Vienna was founded in 1365 with the personal support of the pope, Urban V; a theological faculty (the first in Italy) was erected at Bologna; new privileges were conferred on Toulouse, Paris and Montpellier by the same Urban V.

It was also during his pontificate that the question of re-settling in Rome became particularly acute, because Charles IV and others including St Catherine of Siena, represented to the papacy in vivid colours the continuing harm which was done to the prestige of the institution by residing at Avignon; it was also represented to the curia that in the eyes of contemporaries the French monarchy exercised an overbearing influence on the papacy. Urban could hardly resist these cogent reasons, and in 1367 he and the court began the journey back, settling first at Viterbo and entering Rome in October 1367. The Lateran was exchanged for the Vatican as the official residence. Yet compared with the security and comfort and ease which the papacy had come to experience at Avignon, the sojourn at a Rome that had sunk to the status of a big village, proved unattractive, and the recent death of Albornoz robbed the papacy of an effective military defender who knew how to improvise. The resumption of hostilities between England and France (in the course of the Hundred Years War) persuaded Urban to return to Avignon where the curia considered that there were greater opportunities for mediation than in faraway Rome. On 23 September 1370 the curia was back, and less than three months later the pope was dead.

It was clear that the 'Roman' question had to be settled, especially as the Visconti troops tried to re-occupy papal territory. The settlement which Gregory XI reached with the rebels made an enemy of Florence, hitherto a supporter of the papacy. Florence was laid under interdict and Breton mercenaries ordered to attack it. This was a spectacle which testified to the lowering of standards all round. But the Gregorian papacy was not impervious to the entreaties of St Catherine of Siena and St Bridget of Sweden to leave Avignon for good. And indeed on 17 January 1377 the papacy re-entered the city of Rome, once more taking up residence at the Vatican which henceforward was to be the official seat of the papacy. The so-called Babylonish exile of the papacy had come to an end. The papacy's work at Rome was more occupied with the immediate questions of resettlement than with any general papal policy. The eleventh Gregory was to reign only 14 months: he died on 27 March 1378.

Throughout Europe the papacy had suffered an almost irreparable loss of prestige and authority. Paradoxically enough, the papacy itself greatly fostered the spirit of nationalism in Europe, partly through its economic and financial policy, partly through its alleged dependence on France, partly through 'providing' aliens, mainly Italians and also Frenchmen, with fat prebends in other countries, and partly also through the impersonal, if not heartless, manner in which the papal tax collectors went about their business. They too were for the most part foreigners in other countries. More and more did the papacy come to be looked upon as just another foreign power. What above all fanned the spirit of nationalism was the appointment of foreign prelates, including many cardinals to ecclesiastical positions in countries whose language they were even incapable of speaking. They cared little for those allegedly entrusted to their care or for the churches in their charge. This together with the reports received about the high standard of living in the curia from those who had cause to be at Avignon on business evoked not only contemporary protests but also a veritable aversion from the papacy in wholly unexpected quarters, and since educational standards had gradually increased – after all the fourteenth century was the age in which a great many universities as well as colleges and schools were founded – larger and larger sections of the populace came to question the very foundations, nay, the *raison d'être*, of the papacy as an institution. No writings of this period are extant which took up the cause of the contemporary papacy. Finally, as already indicated, the state of the city of Rome had degenerated into little more than an overgrown village. Grass grew on the steps of St Peter's basilica where goats also grazed. The city administration and organization was largely ineffective, and where it was effective, it was corrupt.

That was the background against which the election of a successor of Gregory XI took place. It was for nearly 80 years the first papal election to be carried out in Rome. The Roman municipal authorities urged the cardinals to elect a Roman or at least an Italian, in order to have some assurance that the new pope would not go back to Avignon, as was Gregory XI's clear intention. And when the cardinals were inside the conclave, the Roman mob, yelling and shrieking outside as only a Roman mob can do, vociferously demanded a Roman. The conclave lasted well into the night of 7 to 8 April 1378, when after long and mature deliberations all but four cardinals cast their vote for a non-member of the College. They elected the archbishop of Bari, Bartolomeo Prignano. The election – not at all unlike that of Clement V (above p. 279) – was one which steered a middle course. Prignano was neither a Roman nor an Italian nor a Frenchman, but a Neapolitan by birth and early upbringing (Naples through the house of Anjou had had strong connexion with France). Having left Naples in his early youth and having climbed very high in the ecclesiastical hierarchy, his outlook and bearing were not in any pronounced sense French or Italian or Roman. As chancellor of the curia at Avignon (where he had spent virtually all his working life) he had an enormous experience in administration. He had been, so to speak, the head of the papal civil service at Avignon and knew the working of the curia intimately having risen, as it were, from the ranks in the service of the curia. He was a reliable, highly efficient, hard-working official who had all the merits but also the demerits and limitations of a civil servant. Never at any time had he anything to do with policy making. As a matter of fact, he himself was outside the conclave among the clamouring crowd and did not know that his name stood in the forefront of the cardinals' choice. When he was summoned before the cardinals to say whether he would accept election, the crowd mistook the call, and instead of announcing him to the crowd, the cardinals were frightened and, making an octogenarian cardinal impersonate the newly elected pope, showed him to the crowd (he had to be propped up from behind to prevent him from collapsing) and 'enthroned' him in their full view. But in the afternoon of the following day the election of Prignano was repeated and confirmed in conclave.

Although conditions were most unruly outside the conclave,

there is no evidence at all that the cardinals were intimidated in their choice of the archbishop of Bari as pope. In fact, the very choice of Prignano – Urban VI – proved that they had resisted threats. Moreover, no riotous behaviour occurred when the election was formally announced on the following day; nor was there any opposition or allegation on the part of the cardinals or anyone else that the election was invalid because of popular pressure. On the following Sunday Urban VI was solemnly enthroned at St Peter's with all pomp and ceremony and acted as lawfully elected pope who presided over consistories and granted privileges to the cardinals, who did not cease to submit their humble petitions to him. In a word, Urban undisputedly acted and ruled as pope. But it was during these crucial weeks following his election that he showed his true weaknesses: an uncontrolled temper, megalomania and extreme rudeness in consistory. The burden of the papacy was obviously too great for a man who was not born a Ruler, but was an exemplary administrator. His aim as pope was to replace the oligarchy practised at Avignon by the monarchy of the pope. Whether he was justified in contemporary circumstances in pursuing this policy coupled as it was with some petty 'reform' measures (in fact dictated by the poverty of the Roman Church at the time) may be open to doubt. What can hardly be doubted is the tactlessness and unwisdom he displayed in pursuing his policy. Seen from the perspective of his later years, there were definite signs of mental derangement in Urban. His rise was too sudden and too steep from the top of the civil service to the supreme pontifical office.

The problem which confronted the cardinals – each of whom had become the target of rude, angry and slanderous papal remarks – was one for which the existing constitution provided no solution. What was to be done with a pope who proved incapable of governing? By the early summer months of 1378 the cardinals could not escape the conclusion that Urban was totally unsuitable to be pope – and since the law offered no other alternative than that of impugning the election itself, they seized upon this possibility and declared it null and void on the grounds that they had elected under duress and fear. That was the only possibility which the constitution allowed. One by one they left Rome, so that by 21 June all cardinals with the exception of four Italian cardinals had taken up residence at Anagni. From there they informed Europe in several manifestoes that Urban had been uncanonically elected, was therefore an intruder and that the holy see must be considered vacant. They also suggested to Urban that he should abdicate and return to private life. Despite a number of efforts to heal the breach between pope and his electors, the rift widened. Three Italian cardinals – the fourth was too old and infirm to travel and in fact died on 7 September – now also joined their colleagues who persuaded each Italian cardinal individually that he was to be the next pope. When eventually on 20 September at Fondi the College of Cardinals proceeded to an election, the emerging pope – Clement VII, who was Cardinal Robert of Geneva – was elected unanimously, because each of the three Italian cardinals abstained from voting believing that he was to be the future pope. Two months later, Pope Urban VI excommunicated Pope Clement VII who replied in kind. The excommunication by the pope of the anti-pope and vice-versa was to be repeated several times throughout nearly four decades.

The remarkable feature of this 'double election' was that one and the same College of Cardinals had elected two popes within a few months. In the numerous previous schisms this contingency had never occurred. The cardinals had acknowledged Urban VI as the rightful pope throughout the five months following the election; they had begged his favours even when they had repaired to Anagni and to Fondi. Clement's excommunication by Urban and the military attacks by Urbanist troops forced the Clementine curia to leave Italy and to take up residence at Avignon. The disarray, consternation and resultant conflict of loyalties through the length and breadth of Christendom is barely comprehensible to an observer in the twentieth century. There were now two popes fulminating against each other, and each claiming to be the sole vicar of Christ, and there were two Colleges of Cardinals. How was the ordinary Christian to decide who was the legitimate pope? The result was that some monasteries had two abbots and two priors, some parishes had two parish priests, and so on. Europe was split into two halves: France, Scotland, Aragon, Castille and Navarre adhered to Clement VII, while the larger part of Italy, Germany, Hungary, England, Poland and Scandinavia followed Urban VI; Portugal could not make up its mind for a long time; the Neapolitan kingdom was swayed from Clement to Urban and back again, after a number of Urbanist cardinals had migrated to Clement's curia. The Church universal witnessed the nadir of the papacy which was to have been its authoritative guide. The resultant anguish besetting the conscience of so many contemporary Christians is hardly imaginable today. What deserves at least a passing remark is that the papacy itself – once more unwittingly – contributed to the sharpening of the individual and private judgment, thereby not inconsiderably fertilizing the ground for a particular strand of Reformation Christianity.

The details of the Roman and Avignonese succession cannot be entered into here. It must suffice to state that the former proved as recalcitrant, obstinate and disingenuous as the latter in avoiding any genuine effort at an accommodation and bringing a scandalous situation to an end.

To say that the constitution of the Church and of the papacy was gravely at fault, is to state a truism. The cardinals were of course aware of this defect. Their plan was the establishment of a proper oligarchic government in which the pope was something approaching a *primus inter pares* or the equivalent of a modern prime minister. But this plan received no support at all outside the College of Cardinals and was tacitly dropped by them. The remedy that had the greatest appeal was to make the general council of the Church an effective and representative instrument of government. It was this idea which eventually prevailed and set in motion the train of events that was to end the Great Schism. Barely two years after its outbreak the first spate of pamphlets and literary products appeared which advocated the convocation of a general council – but the problem was, who was to summon it, since in order to be a general council, the assembly had to be convened by the pope. But which pope? The longer the schism lasted, the more opinion crystallized regarding the means by which it could be ended. Here was one more significant feature: the emergence of the universities and their masters as instruments through which public opinion was formed.

In the main three proposals were put forward: (a) the *via cessionis*: both popes should abdicate to create a vacancy and make an election possible – neither the Roman nor the Avignonese line of popes favoured this measure; (b) the *via concilii*: most universities favoured this which would have meant that a general council was to pronounce which was the rightful pope – the measure floundered on the canonical and actual difficulty just mentioned, and in any case throughout its existence the papacy was never favourably inclined towards a general council which it could not fully control; (c) the *via compromissi*, according to which each pope was to acknowledge the verdict of an arbitration tribunal – a proposal which never had many followers because of its impracticability. When none of these measures promised a way out, a fourth plan gained some ground: the followers of each pope should withdraw their obedience and allegiance from them. This, the *via subtractionis*, was urged by the university of Paris and the French king, and was even practically applied for a short time without any tangible result. Richard II of England was asked to support it. He relied on the advice given by the university of Cambridge (shortly to be followed by that of Oxford) which rejected this proposal for a number of reasons and counselled continuing adherence to the Roman papacy. These academic views sponsored as they were in the highest government circles, were accompanied by an unprecedented mass of literary productions throughout Western Europe. None of these took up the cause of papal monarchy – it was as stone dead as the conciliar theme was vigorously alive. Despite the overwhelming vociferous protestations for an escalated papal monarchy little more than a generation earlier, the papacy as such now found not a single defender. This was perhaps the clearest possible sign how much harm to its own governmental ideology the papacy had done by its actual practice of government as handled in the preceding decades. Or in different words: ideology and practice were cleft apart.

It seemed as if a solution was in sight when the Roman pope, Gregory XII, in accordance with the electoral pacts he had entered into, agreed to meet his Avignonese rival, Benedict XIII, but the legates of both sides failed to find a mutually convenient meeting place. When this attempt also came to naught, nearly all cardinals left Gregory in 1408 and appealed for a general council; they also dispatched letters to the European courts in which they appealed from the vicar of Christ Himself and hence to a general council. By now the conciliar idea had gripped everyone, even the Avignonese cardinals who met their Roman colleagues at Pisa in 1409 where indeed a council took place which counted among its participants some of the most distinguished scholars, such as Pierre d'Ailly, chancellor of the university of Paris, and Jean Gerson, his successor and one of the foremost theologians. The theory that supreme power was located in the council was now generally accepted: at Pisa there were assembled 24 cardinals, 4 patriarchs, 80 bishops and 102 episcopal delegates, 87 abbots and nearly 200 abbatial legates, over 40 priors, representatives of 13 universities, numerous delegates of cathedral chapters, of the mendicant Orders, and so on. The result was that the council declared both popes notorious schismatics and heretics, deposed both of them and elected a new one, Alexander V, archbishop of Milan and Cardinal of the Roman line. Christendom now had three popes, since neither of the two others recognized the validity of the Pisan council.

The scandal of three popes, three curial administrations, and three Colleges of Cardinals together with the other paraphernalia of a triple headship of Christendom was aggravated by the early death of Alexander V and the necessity for another election. It resulted in raising a superb military leader, fighter and general to the successorship of St Peter. John XXIII had won his laurels as a successful commander of papal troops, though later he acquired clerical status. From a pope of this calibre no reconciliation could be expected. As he was quite obviously incapable of holding his own without the help of a secular Ruler, he implored the assistance of King Sigismund of Germany, who indeed had earlier acknowledged the Pisan line. Persuaded by contemporary writings especially the eminent Dietrich of Niem, that in cases of emergency the Ruler should on the model of ancient Christian emperors convoke a general council, he followed this example: although merely a prospective emperor on 30 October 1413 (he was not crowned emperor until 1433) he summoned the council to Constance to begin its sessions in the autumn of the following year. In some respects this was a tangible application of history to a concrete problem. John's edict convening the council followed on 9 December. Gregory XII (the 'Roman' pope) and Benedict XIII refused to acknowledge this summons, and so did the Spanish kingdoms and Scotland.

After some inevitable initial delays the Council of Constance began its sessions on 5 November 1414 under the presidency of John XXIII. Although the number of participants was not great –

most displayed an attitude of 'wait and see' – the arrival of King Sigismund on Christmas eve and later the active part taken by him prompted many who had hesitated, to flock to Constance, so that early in 1415 there were 29 cardinals, 33 archbishops, 3 patriarchs, well over 300 bishops, numerous abbots and priors and doctors of theology and canon law, as well as the representatives of anointed and crowned heads. It was perhaps the most impressive council of the Middle Ages. Its importance is that its enactments represented the full-scale victory of conciliarism and the utter and most convincing defeat of the papal-hierocratic system.

The main point of conciliarism was that power was not located in the papal monarch but in the Church itself as represented by the general council. In this system the pope was merely a representative of the general council and eventually of the Church. It was the latter from which he received power and to which he consequently remained responsible. Hitherto the master of the Church, he was now turned into its servant. The pope became an officer, an organ of the Church which could restrict, modify and take away the power conferred on him by the general council. Conciliarism was the exact opposite of papal monarchy. Conciliarism was the application of the ascending theme of government and the rejection of the hitherto virtually unquestioned descending theme. Within the former the pope's powers rested upon the consent and will of the whole body of Christians (the Church) represented in the general council; within the latter the pope as vicar of Christ imparted rights to the Church and delegated part of his powers to certain officers, such as the bishops. Within the papal-monarchic system the rights of the Church and of its officers were ultimately the pope's who had conceded them – the application of the Petrine text; within the conciliar system the pope owed his position and rights to the Church through the medium of the general council, so that he became its chief officer. The one system was the denial of the other. Or seen from a different angle: sovereignty belonged to the pope alone (the papal-hierocratic standpoint); sovereignty belonged to the whole Church (the conciliar viewpoint). The one sovereignty was personal and individual; the other corporate and collectivist.

While the actuality of the situation – first a schism of two popes, then three popes, dividing Christendom and shaking it to its foundations – had certainly cultivated the contemporary soil for the reception of conciliarism, its basic ingredients were not formed during the schismatic period, but had a distinguished ancestry. There were the doctrines of the lawyers relating to the Church as a corporation, according to which the head of a corporation was bound by the decisions of the members; there were the political ideologies as set forth by Marsiglio of Padua, according to which all public and legislative power was located in the people; there was the theology of Ockham according to which questions of faith should be decided by the counsel of wise and mature men; there were the legal-constitutional theories propounded by Bartolus and his school based on the reality of the Italian city-states, according to which political power rested with the totality of the citizenhood acting through its parliament; and finally there was an ever growing awareness of the conditions in the primitive Church when people and clergy elected their officers. If one adds to this the general lowering of papal authority and wide-spread disenchantment with the practice of Christianity by prelates and popes, one will understand not only the upsurge of conciliarist pamphlets and books and tracts during the decades preceding Constance, but also the receptivity of the soil for these 'democratic' views.

Both the procedure and the enactments of the Council of Constance bear witness to the prevalent trends of thought. The three main topics on the agenda were: the ending of the schism, clerical reform, and the condemnation of certain heresies. The principle of voting by nations – already practised in earlier councils – was adopted and greatly refined: there were four nations – the French, the Italian, the English and the German – to which later a fifth, the Spanish, was added. All final votes were to be unanimous. John XXIII's hope that he would be elected as the one and only legitimate pope soon faded. When he sensed the general animosity he considered it wise to flee from Constance, but he was caught and held in honorary protective custody until December 1417. In July 1415 the Roman pope, Gregory XII, sent a legation which acknowledged the council and on his behalf offered his abdication. The Avignonese pope, the fiery Spaniard Benedict XIII, did not know when it was time to call a halt, took up residence on a small island off the Catalan coast, and not even the personal plea of King Sigismund could make him change his mind. The council finally deposed him by the decree of 26 July 1417, and the Spanish kingdoms which alone had hitherto recognized him, began to take part in the council proceedings. The field was at long last clear. By the required two-thirds majority the 23 cardinals present together with 6 representatives of each of the 5 nations in a conclave held in one of the large warehouses on the banks of Lake Constance elected Cardinal Oddo Colonna on 11 November 1417. Himself a participant of the Pisan Council and adherent to the Pisan line of popes, Martin V was the pope to emerge from the general council to end the schism. *The causa unionis* thus found a solution.

That the idea of a nation as a unit had received its particular imprint at the Council of Constance was one of the features which was to impress itself on all subsequent ecclesiastical and political life. The principle of voting by nations – in fact taken over from the universities – indubitably fostered national sentiments and feelings, especially when applied to such major issues as those with which Constance had to deal. It was the organisers and the administrative committees that patronized this principle and sanctioned it by giving it the final imprint of the universal Church. If one wishes to have a better understanding of the subsequent cataclysmic events in the sixteenth century – the Reformation and the rise of national churches – this feature should not be left out of account. Evidently, the utterly corrosive effect of the 'nation principle' was not then foreseeable, but the historical point of view warrants a remark on it, if its results are to be adequately assessed.

Of the decrees passed at Constance those which embody the full conciliar idea deserve special mention. One dealt with the character of the general council as such and its powers: the general council was a lawful assembly which represented the universal Church and had its power directly from Christ and consequently everyone holding an office, including the pope himself, was to be obedient to the council under pain of punishment, especially in questions concerning the faith, reform and the removal of the schism. It was hardly possible to put conciliarism into clearer language which also spelt the collapse of the papal-hierocratic system: the pope had to obey the assembled representatives of the Church – an incontrovertible victory for the ascending theme of government as propounded by Bartolus and Marsiglio a generation earlier and made palatable by Dietrich of Niem, Gerson, d'Ailly and a host of other luminaries. Whether this decree was to be part of the universal law of the Church or whether it was passed merely in respect of the contemporary contingency, is not quite certain.

The other decree of immediate importance stipulated that general councils should be regularly held, that is, the first five years after Constance, the next seven years afterwards and then every ten years. In the 40th and 43rd sessions (30 October 1417 and 21 March 1418) a number of consequential decrees were passed. They were the work of the relevant commissions and showed how thoroughly they had debated the individual issues. Among these decrees were measures to prevent a new schism; regulations concerned with the 'reform of the Church in its head and members'; the profession of faith to be made by a newly elected pope; abolition of all exemptions granted during the schismatic period; restriction of the right of papal taxation; re-enactment of earlier disciplinary laws relating to tonsure and clerical dress; the composition of the College of Cardinals and the number of cardinals to be taken from each nation; excommunication and indulgencies.

Some of these decrees formed part of special agreements made between Martin V and certain nations (the German including Poland and Hungary; the Latin including the French, the Italian and Spanish; and the English), and these agreements were for the first time called Concordats (*concordata*). Apart from their intrinsic importance in regard to the subject-matter, they are above all else a further indication of the significance which the individual nations had achieved. What *au fond* these Concordats signified was that the papacy hitherto always considering itself as standing above the kingdoms and nations and tribes, now by entering into these arrangements with the nations in matters of a specifically papal and ecclesiastical nature (such as the composition of the College of Cardinals, papal taxation, appointments, excommunication, indulgences) bound itself in a contractual manner. This was a step of greatest significance. The papacy did not consider itself as anything other than a power that stood on a level with certain specific nations which could in all propriety be called nation states. To this feature too little attention has been paid in the past: some of the antecedents of the fissure that was to occur exactly a century afterwards are to be sought in this development of the Concordats.

While both the Council of Constance and the papacy unequivocally endorsed the principle of the nation as an entity of its own and as a legal personality, this same council on the other hand issued decrees which aimed at the extermination of allegedly heretical views, though these latter were strongly tinged with national sentiments. The theological opinions of Jan Hus, the Czech professor of theology at Prague university, were stigmatized as thoroughly heretical. Under cover of theological speculation and disputation these views of Hus embodied a great deal of national feelings which contrasted sharply with the traditional universal doctrines of the papacy and generally held religious dogmas. It was the assembled wisdom of Europe at Constance which sentenced Hus as well as his companion Jerome of Prague to death by burning – the sentence was duly carried out – but which thereby inflamed national passions in Bohemia. It was perhaps the first time that theology and nationalism had formed a union. The sequel was a fierce revolt and a bitter anti-papal, highly nationalistic legacy throughout Bohemian lands. It was also this same Council which in furtherance of the *causa fidei* solemnly declared heretical certain teachings of John Wyclif (the Oxford scholar who had greatly influenced Hus) and ordered the exhumation of his body. Wyclif's teachings were suffused with national sentiments which enabled him vigorously to attack the papacy as an institution. His doctrines fell upon fertile soil in contemporary England. It is from this angle too that in conjunction with translations of the Bible into the vernacular the emergence of national churches appears historically conditioned. Perhaps nothing better illustrates how contemporaries viewed the papacy than the offer made by King Sigismund to Martin V asking him to take up his residence in Germany, and the similar offer of the French king asking the pope to return to Avignon. In the eyes of leading contemporaries the papacy had indeed sunk to just one more power in Europe.

Formally the papacy never confirmed the decrees of the Council of Constance. And few noticed this at the time, because everyone was gratified that after 40 disastrous years of schism there was at least one undisputed head of the Church. These four decades had not only wrought havoc on the authority and prestige of the papacy in Europe, but had also inflicted serious material damage on the institution. The city of Rome was occupied by the queen of Naples, Joanna II, and the rest of the papal state by military adventurers. It was not until 1420 and after numerous concessions that the papacy was able to return to Rome – a desolate place, forsaken by the wealthy, without hinterland for trade and commerce, viable only through the presence of the papacy; St Peter's basilica and the Lateran church were in a ruinous state. To these material difficulties facing the papacy on its return must be added the state of Italy itself. The prosperous towns, such as Venice, Genoa, Pisa, Florence, had become powerful and independent city-states, while in the South the kingdoms of Naples and Sicily gave France and Aragon an opportunity to play some role in the internal affairs of the peninsula. And as just mentioned, the papal state was in the hands of *condottieri*.

It was this perilous situation which impelled the returned papacy to employ all its resources for the re-establishment of law and order, and above all to restore the papal state as a territorial and material base of the institution itself. Despite severe handicaps in this latter respect the papacy was extraordinarily successful. The papal state was once more brought under effective papal control, at least for a short time, until a more final settlement under Eugenius IV. It was not therefore quite incomprehensible that Martin and the curia displayed little enthusiasm in enacting the decree of Constance that after five years a new council should take place. Indeed, to do formal justice to the decree Martin summoned a council for April 1423 at Pavia which because of an epidemic was transferred in June to Siena, but was soon dissolved because of the extremely poor attendance. The participants were so few that not a single reform decree was passed. Not discouraged, though hardly with zeal, Martin summoned as bidden by Constance, a council for 1431 to Basle: its president was to be Cardinal Cesarini. The lack of enthusiasm for the Pavia-Siena Council can partly be explained by the Hundred Years War between France and England having reached a decisive stage which kept the French and English prelates away; and among the German, Polish, Hungarian and Scandinavian prelates weariness had indubitably set in.

For the immediate aftermath of the Great Schism and of the impressive Council of Constance was lethargy, apathy and confusion. Clearly, this was a period of transition, in which the old was not yet old enough to be replaced by the new which was as yet too new to gain a firm footing. The twenties of the fifteenth century show the picture of a Christian world which smarted from the wounds of the calamity, the extent of which is difficult to assess in the modern world. Neither the papacy nor the College of Cardinals nor the prelates nor the great theoreticians of the preceding decades gave as yet any indication as to how the future of Christendom was to be shaped. The great question that was left unanswered was this: Was the pope to be the reforming organ or was it to be the general council? Was papal monarchy or the representative general council to be the future authority in whose hands lay the destiny and repair of torn Christendom? Was the government of the Church to be built on the descending theme of government – the traditional and until schismatic times hardly questioned axiom – or upon its ascending counterpart, the battle cry of the conciliarists and virtually everyone concerned with bringing the schism to an end? Was the *via antiqua* or the *via moderna* to be the path which European Christendom was to take? In the twenties and thirties of the fifteenth century it would have been impossible to give any sort of satisfactory answer to these questions which upon closer inspection concern, historically speaking, nothing less than some of the crucial factors which were to bring forth the cataclysm of the sixteenth century.

13 The Last Phase of the Medieval Papacy

THE PERIOD AFTER the Council of Constance suffered from its inheritance: confusion, religious inertia, ecclesiastical indifference, erosion of moral standards, uncertainty. The traditional landmarks had either disappeared or lost their meaning. The foundations of contemporary society had received a severe shaking. In particular the papacy was confronted by determined opponents, the radical conciliarists. With its immediate past record only too vividly in the memory of contemporaries, it was difficult for the papacy to appear as an effective promoter of 'reform in head and members of the Church'. For this had now in the post-Constance era become the watchword everywhere, and it does not need much historical imagination to visualize how much easier it was for the conciliarists to claim that the general council alone was better fitted to play the reforming agent than the monarchic papacy.

The antithesis of monarchic papacy and conciliarism was, however, overshadowed in the thirties of the fifteenth century by an entirely different problem. This was wholly independent of the squabble between the papacy and its opponents and concerned the perilous position of the Eastern empire gravely threatened as it was on all sides by the advancing Turks. The tremors which this menace set up throughout Europe were particularly keenly registered by the papacy. The Eastern empire played a decisive role in the initial stages of the papacy's development in the fifth century, and it was to play a similar, though less direct, role in the last phase of the medieval papacy exactly a millennium later.

In order to enlist Western help against the Turks, the Eastern emperor chose the means which he was certain promised success. He once more proposed a union of the Eastern and Western churches. To achieve this it was essential to acknowledge the papal claim to primacy. This it was which made understandable the conflicts between the papacy and the Byzantine empire in the fifth century; and this it was which caused the alienation between the two halves of Christendom and the eventual rupture between East and West, between New Rome and Old Rome, only temporarily patched up in 1274. Since the papacy had never abandoned its claim to universal primacy (in teaching as well as in jurisdiction) the offer of the Byzantine emperor in this hour of dire need appeared indeed the fulfilment of the aim which the papacy had pursued since the second half of the fifth century. Now that Byzantium was so hard pressed and its very existence as a Christian state at stake, it seemed almost certain that papal primacy would now at long last become reality in Constantinople.

It will be recalled that in accordance with the decree of the Council of Constance Martin V had convoked a council at Basle for 1431. After his death on 20 February of this year this legacy of Constance devolved upon his successor, Eugenius IV. So few had arrived by December 1431 (a mere three bishops, 14 abbots and about the same number of doctors of theology) that Eugenius dissolved the meeting, before in actual fact it was formally opened as a council. The wisdom of this action in the prevailing temper of the time, may well be open to doubt. At once the participants issued a sharply worded protest against this papal decision (with which a number of cardinals had disagreed), and it was due to the efforts of Sigismund that an open breach between council and pope was prevented. The Basleans supported by Germany, England, France, Scotland, Burgundy had already gone so far as to threaten Eugenius with deposition. In December 1433 he realized the wisdom of withdrawing his decision and he formally acknowledged the assembly as a general council. Indeed, at that juncture it did appear as if the Council of Basle whose numbers had greatly increased in the meantime, had all the appurtenances of a European parliament. A number of reform decrees were expedited, mainly concerned with clerical discipline, but also some which fixed the size of the College of Cardinals, dealt with the government of the papal state and reduced, if they did not virtually abolish, the taxes to be paid to the curia. The prudence of this particular decree may be doubted, because the income of the curia was severely curtailed. The pope took offence and thereafter the relations between pope and council rapidly deteriorated.

It was at this juncture that the proposal put forward by Constantinople of a union between East and West, began to affect decisively the crucial problem of papacy *v.* conciliarism. Although this link was purely coincidental, it was nevertheless causal for the subsequent development. The arrival of the Greek legation necessitated the fixing of a locality suitable for everyone. For historical and ideological reasons the papacy at once opted for an Italian place – Rome as the obvious and conspicuous choice was out of the question because of the considerable unrest and sporadic riots. Since after all, the primatial question was so overwhelmingly a 'Roman' problem it seemed to the papacy that to have a council anywhere else but in the Italian peninsula, was unacceptable. On the other hand, wholly untouched as they were by these considerations, the conciliarists at Basle wished for the council to continue to sit at Basle, or at Avignon or in a town in Savoy: indeed this was the majority opinion of those assembled at Basle, and the possibility that the French king, Charles VII, had influenced them in their choice, cannot be excluded. A minority at Basle falling in with the suggestion of the papacy proposed an Italian town, and this proposal was accepted by the papacy in May 1437. Demanding the trial of Eugenius for disobeying a conciliar decree, the conciliarists now began to fulminate in earnest against the papacy. Accepting the minority view of Basle as 'the weightier part' (*pars sanior*), the papal decree of 18 September 1437 officially transferred the council from Basle to Ferrara – the place where the Council of Union was to be held. The president of the Baslean Council, Cardinal Cesarini, and the minority, including Nicholas of Cusa, left the 'progressives' at Basle to join the traditional forces – the split was incontrovertible. Although this causal link between the proposed union and the fundamental question of pope and council is rarely seen, it is nonetheless important to draw attention to it, because this was the first event in a long and complicated chain which eventually led to some restoration of the papacy. At any rate, Constantinople once more proved of decisive importance.

Still in the full flush of the conciliar spirit the Basleans in the autumn of 1437 retorted angrily to the papal initiative. They threatened suspension of the pope from his office and demanded from him the official endorsement of certain articles, among which was the conciliarist credo that the council as a divinely inspired assembly was superior to the papacy. Obviously all this was merely a manœuvre and a challenge, and the result was predictable. Having refused the demands, Eugenius found himself deposed by the Council of Basle. Nevertheless, ignoring this measure he opened the Council of Ferrara in January 1438 where some fruitful discussions took place, but where the safety of the participants – slowly growing in numbers – was in jeopardy because of a local epidemic. Early in 1439 the council was transferred from Ferrara to Florence. Meanwhile, however, the Basleans registered a considerable success in the Hussite question. Since the crusading efforts against the Hussites achieved nothing, negotiations began between the council at Basle (represented by John of Ragusa, John of Palomar and Aegidius Charlier) and the Hussites (represented by John Rokycana, Procop the Great and Peter Payne) which eventually led to the accommodation reached in the so-called *Compactata* on 5 July 1436 at Iglau. They were ratified by the council at Basle, but never confirmed by the papacy.

The main, if not exclusive, task of the council at Florence was to negotiate a union with the East on terms which were not merely face saving formulae. The East had sent a powerful, very learned and versatile legation, led by Archbishop Bessarion of Nicaea and Archbishop Isidore of Kiev. On 6 July 1439 the long-awaited union was made public in the decree *Laetentur* signed by the Byzantine emperor himself and all the 43 members of the legation. But the fate of this union was in no wise different from its predecessor at Lyons in 1274. The cultural, religious, ecclesiastical and political gulf was too great and too long-standing to be bridged however acceptable the terms were to the chief negotiators. The opposition in Constantinople was too strong to be mastered by the Emperor John VIII. In the event, within another dozen years the once proud, glittering continuation of the ancient Roman empire in the East vanished from the landscape and became a prey to the Turkish hordes. An empire once rich in spiritual inheritance, seminal in cultural respects, and radiating a civilization unsurpassed anywhere in Europe, had come under the barbarous heel of the Turks. Among the contributory reasons for the collapse were the corrosive effects of the centuries-long tensions inside the empire and the ecclesiastical rift with the West: these had sapped the energies of the empire. The heir of Byzantium became Russia which arrogated to itself the imperial double eagle as the outward symbol of its continuing the 'Roman' empire. Ivan III (1462–1505) by virtue of his marriage to a niece of the last Paleaologue, laid claim to the successorship. The hitherto not unfriendly attitude of the Czars towards the papacy now gave way to open animosity which remained until the Revolution of 1917. From the point of view of the papacy, however, the union albeit ineffective, was a major achievement, although the council itself was far from representing Christendom. The prelates present were almost wholly Italians, apart from three Spanish, two Irish bishops and one bishop from Poland and Portugal. Only Burgundy and the Angevins had sent delegations.

Yet in far-away Basle matters did not progress at all well for the conciliarists. They elected in the place of the deposed Eugenius IV Duke Amadaeus of Savoy, a widower, who as Felix V became the last anti-pope in the history of the papacy – a symbol as well as a symptom of the state of affairs prevailing in the mid-fifteenth century. The Basleans received strong support from the French clergy and king whose inclination to favour the Gallican church found embodiment in the Pragmatic Sanction of Bourges (7 July 1438). It considerably increased royal influence in clerical appointments and categorically stated that superiority belonged to the council because the pope was simply its executive organ. The Sanction in fact turned not less than 23 decrees of Basle into French national law which served as the basis of Gallicanism. Indeed, one can understand why there was a community of interests between the Basleans and the French.

Nevertheless, despite this and other active support the Basleans' stock and reputation rapidly began to fall throughout Europe, not so much because their views appeared unacceptable, but primarily because their own most vociferous, staunch and leading spokesmen forsook their camp and went over to the papacy, the very institution they had attacked vigorously for years. The secretary of the Council, the later Pius II, was one such luminary to desert Basle and to seek his fortune with the papacy; Panormitanus, one of the great conciliarists and an eminent canonist, was another. When once this disintegration started, it could hardly be kept under control. At first it was the quality of the deserters which reduced the standing of the council, but it soon also declined quantitatively. In Germany the territorial princes declared themselves neutral in the conflict between pope and anti-pope (and therefore Basle) though it is difficult to say what in actual fact neutrality meant, especially when in March 1439 some Baslean decrees were adopted as law (the so-called *instrumentum acceptationis*). By the mid-forties some electoral and other territorial princes in Germany had openly joined the papacy which was well served by its legates, notably the later Pope Nicholas V. The empire and the curia concluded in February 1448 the so-called 'Vienna Concordat' which among other things signified a temporary success of the papacy. On the whole this agreement legalized a great many papal demands and made a number of sensible financial arrangements. In several respects the Vienna Concordat (which formally remained in force until 1803) was the exact opposite of the Pragmatic Sanction of Bourges.

There can be little doubt that by the mid-fifteenth century conciliarism had spent most of its force and that the real winner was the papacy which slowly and steadily recouped within a restricted sphere of action some of the position which it had recently lost. In order to see the matter in perspective, one ought to realize that, by the end of the Council of Constance, barely a shadow was detectable of the papacy's former authority and power. Yet within little more than 30 years the institution had once more assumed a position that gave it some respectable standing albeit far removed from that which it had enjoyed in the high Middle Ages. How is one to explain this partial recovery?

What seems certain is that the explanation cannot be sought in the papacy itself, but in conciliarism and its adherents. It was they who first vociferously propagated the scheme and then left the conciliarist camp to return to 'the old fold'. However much and however loudly the conciliarists proclaimed that original power was located in the Church, their concept of the Church was when put to the test, a rather narrow one. They meant by it the priesthood, that is, the ordained members. In other words, despite their highfalutin and 'progressive' claims the conciliarists were in reality little more than a refurbished edition of the old-fashioned episcopalists whose programme by no means greatly differed from that of the conciliarists. Their common link was aversion to the primatial-monarchic function of the pope, that is, their refusal to acknowledge the monarchic government of the papacy. But while the earlier episcopalists were on the whole inarticulate in their positive aim – their main, if not exclusive, concern was the government of their own dioceses without any interference by the papacy – the conciliarists proposed a positive programme by postulating control of the papacy by the general council. Yet this controlling council was in reality no more than an assembly of the higher clergy. The educated layman as such did not count. True enough, there were the delegates of the kings in Constance and in Basle, but they were there as delegates of theocratic Rulers who were, ideologically, more akin to the higher clergy than to the educated layman or lowly positioned ecclesiastic.

The danger which brought about the alliance between papacy and theocratic Rulers – the realization of this danger also partly explains the return of many conciliarists to the papacy – was the threat which conciliarism was seen to constitute to the traditional set-up of society. In actual fact, at numerous diets and princely assemblies in the forties of the fifteenth century the plea was made by many influential speakers that the adoption of conciliarism – a barely disguised form of the ascending theme of government – would lead to utter disorder and chaos in the public field: rebellion would be the result, and kings and princes would be constantly exposed to the factions and whims and demagogues of the people who instead of being governed would soon become the governors and masters of their lords, kings – and of the popes. In lurid language and with gloomy predictions the spectre of sedition and anarchy was raised in such diets as at Mainz, Frankfurt, Nürnberg, and elsewhere. 'Unspeakable and insufferable', so it was said, would be the effect if the principles enshrined in conciliarism became operational in the secular public field. In apocalyptic terms the calamitous consequences of making real the ascending theme of government were prophesied. And the speakers were supported by able writers. The result of this propaganda was the creation of real fear on the part of secular governments which saw themselves just as much exposed and menaced by the 'new-fangled' 'democratic' process as the papacy was.

The issue, in brief, was nothing else but the preservation of the *status quo* against the new and rapidly rising groups, classes and sections of the people – the effective rise of the third estate. The issue, in other words, was whether monarchic government in the traditional sense could hold its own against the swelling tide of 'popular' forces which included the educated layman, the educated lower clergy, the cosmopolitan and prosperous merchant, and the like. It was these new classes which drove the secular kings and princes and the papacy into one and the same camp. The absence of any quarrels on the old model between kings and popes throughout the rest of the fifteenth century was indeed no coincidence. Assuredly, there would have been plenty of explosive ammunition which in former times would have sparked off another of the fierce conflicts, but both the papacy and the secular monarchies were confronted by a common adversary, the rising educated and urban classes. Hence the readiness on the part of the papacy and the monarchies to conclude the concordats. This moreover was a feature which also showed that the papacy considered itself no more than one of the European powers that happened to be situate in Italy. Or seen from yet another angle, that Felix V was the last anti-pope ever – and the role he played during the tenure of his 'office' was pitiable by any standard – clearly indicated to what a low level the successor of St Peter had sunk. It was an office of dignity that was no longer considered attractive enough to aim at. Too little importance appears to be attributed to this single and yet highly significant feature.

The mid-fifteenth century and the following decades showed the determined attempts on the part of the 'Establishment' to keep at bay those sections of the populace which clamoured to have a share in the government of both the Church and the State. These were actually the incipient signs of the coming Reformation which though primarily affecting religious and ecclesiastical matters, nevertheless had also a great impact on the public and secular sector. What is therefore important to bear in mind is the still very powerful combination of the established forces which resulted in the attempted repression of the popular elements, precisely those to which the Reformers successfully appealed in the early sixteenth century. Wise management might have realized the potentialities of these popular forces and have harnessed them to a common and constructive new programme.

Furthermore, in their attempt to preserve the *status quo* the established forces paid little heed to the prevalent battle-cry 'reform in head and members of the Church'. The exclusive

attention which by virtue of its constitution the papacy was forced
to direct towards the restoration of a monarchic form of government, prevented it from dealing with precisely those deficiencies
which cried out for reform. And whatever intention there may
have been was thwarted by the role which the papacy was also
forced to play in Italy, partly through its attempts to maintain the
papal patrimony in a viable state, partly because it was drawn
into the internecine strife between powerful city-states, such as
Genoa, Venice, Milan; and partly because papal interests came
into direct conflict with the two great mediterranean powers,
France and Spain, through their prolonged arms in the Italian
peninsula. All this constituted for the papacy a *damnosa haereditas*
of the earlier historical development. Specifically both Spain and
France attempted a hegemonial position in the peninsula. These
facts make it understandable why the papacy was diverted from
vigorously tackling reform for which there was a general per-
sistent demand. In a word, the papacy shrank more and more to a
central-Italian power (this is evidenced in the grand Italian League
consisting of the papacy, Florence, Venice and Milan (1455)), and
had less and less opportunity to concern itself with universal and
fundamental questions, those very questions which in previous
times it had handled with masterly skill. Exactly a millennium
earlier Constantinople had begun, and since then continued, to
play a decisive role in the history of the medieval papacy as a
universal institution, and it was perhaps symbolic that the fall of
Constantinople coincided with the calamity which now began to
overtake the papacy as an institution of universal government.

In order to see the situation which faced the papacy in the
fifteenth century more adequately, it is advisable to refer to forces
which in themselves were wholly unconnected with the institution, and yet in a most direct manner impinged upon it in several
and adverse ways. For this was also the age in which humanism
and renaissance came to their full flowering. The feature which
was particularly responsible for the diminution of the papacy's
prestige and which was indissolubly linked with both humanism
and renaissance, was the attention given to the individual as such,
that is, to the individual just because he was a mere man (a mere
homo). What counted more and more was the natural *human*ity of
man, and not man as a baptized Christian (see also above p. 268).
What humanism effected was a re-birth of the natural man, that is,

a re-birth of that man who had been washed away by baptismal waters. The Christian and natural man were two quite distinct beings. The individual was seen in a dual role, in that of natural man and in that of a Christian. In his former capacity he followed his own judgment, followed the norms and laws which nature had implanted in him. He became, in a word, autonomous, and a citizen. In the latter capacity he was a mere subject and followed the laws as given to him by superior authority. The emergence of the individual as a citizen was coincidental with the emergence of the concept of the state, and both vitally affected the function, authority and standing of the papacy.

For the papacy was – as had been the papal theme since the mid-fifth century – primarily a governmental, that is, legal institution which laid down the law for the faithful subjects. But the re-emergence of natural man in the moral sphere and of the citizen in the public-political sphere, drastically altered the picture, and this especially after the troublous time of the Great Schism and the conciliarist efforts. For as a natural man (and citizen) the individual obeyed his own conscience, that is, he began in religious matters to arrive at his own judgments and reach his own conclusions which was the same as saying that the law of the papacy counted correspondingly less. It was therefore no coincidence that the fifteenth century also witnessed so much individualistic religious fervour, as evidenced in mysticism or in Thomas of Kempen's (or Kempis) *Imitation of Christ* or in the writings of John of Goch or of John Wesel or the highly individualistic preaching of John of Capestrano in Austria, Silesia and Bohemia. And there were numerous other manifestations of individual religiosity which showed aversion from the external-legalized and formal kind of religious observance and which propagated the personal, intimate and direct relationship with Christ – a relationship which could dispense with the priests as mediators between Christ and man.

The observer of the second half of the fifteenth century notices a conspicuous detachment from the orthodox and traditional 'collective' view in which Christianity expressed itself through the medium of the papacy, its laws and decretals. There was also a consequential turning towards the individual's own judgment and emphasis on his own responsibility before God for his activity on this earth. If one takes the other features already mentioned into account, one will realize that as the fifteenth century progressed, the papacy was beginning to be confronted by a tide which it was ill-equipped to control. The exuberant growth of humanism and renaissance and of its manifestations were potent factors which weakened the influence of the papacy and powerfully prepared the way for the programme of the Reformers in the sixteenth century. For the hold which the papacy had come to have over the faithful through the law, diminished in proportion to the growth of individualistic humanism. More and more was the *raison d'être* of the papacy as an institution of *public* government questioned, because religion and the individual's link with divinity and his conscience were with increasing emphasis no longer held to be susceptible of regulation by the blunt instrument of the law. In conjunction with the all-too-vivid memories man had of the not so distant past, this detachment from the papacy clearly signified the (reborn) individual's goal which was the liberation in religious matters from fetters imposed upon him. Thereby he was able to establish direct communion with God.

Even in its most immediate external environs the papacy had to contend with some of the aspirations at liberation. More immediately important was that the city of Rome became once again the platform from which republican ideas of government were advocated, this time by the humanist Stefano Porcaro. The rebellion was suppressed by sharp measures which included the public execution of all the ring-leaders in Rome. All this contrasted sharply with the splendour and pomp that could be witnessed only a year earlier when the first Habsburg underwent the last imperial coronation performed in Rome (19 March 1452). This event was perhaps symbolic. For the last time Old Rome was the scene of an imperial coronation – the very year before New Rome finally vanished (1453). It is as if these two events marked the end of medieval Romanism in both its ecclesiastical and secular forms. Bologna had made itself virtually independent which was, rightly, taken as a danger signal by the papacy. The existence of the papal state was threatened, and at once measures were implemented to prevent its disintegration.

One cannot refrain from remarking how powerful was the pull of humanism and renaissance in their purely cultural manifestations, for the papacy itself came to be drawn into their orbit and proved itself one of the foremost promoters of the cultural expressions of contemporary humanism and renaissance. The papacy itself acted as host for a number of writers and thinkers, and the encouragement of critical scholarship by the papacy was particularly noteworthy. Humanists, such as Poggio and Lorenzo Valla, were invited to work in Rome, even though Valla (and also independently of him Nicholas of Cusa) was to establish incontrovertibly that the notorious Donation of Constantine was a huge fraud. Numerous classical, patristic, Greek and Latin manuscripts came to be assembled in Rome. In Nicholas V's pontificate well over a thousand and still more during Sixtus IV's reign were added to the Vatican Library which became the greatest and best organized centre of all available manuscript material. It was due to Nicholas V that a great many manuscripts of St Augustine, Bonaventure, and Thomas Aquinas, are still extant. As soon as orderly conditions were restored, and quite in the spirit of a cultural renaissance, the papacy entered upon a massive rebuilding of the city of Rome – it was largely in ruins – and the erection, and, when necessary, a reconstruction of its fortifications which were needed in view of hostile neighbours. The renovation of a number of basilicas proved to be the artists' paradise, and some of the greatest painters among whom were Perugino, Rosselli, Botticelli, Pinturicchio, and many more received a call to Rome. One of the most impressive renaissance palaces, i.e. the Palazzo Venezia, was started and remains to this day one of the most imposing Roman buildings. The restoration of the Roman water supply (Acqua vergine) was a further achievement of the renaissance papacy. It was this same papacy which built the Sistine Chapel as well as a number of churches, such as S. Maria del popolo, or S. Maria della pace. And by the turn of the fifteenth century calls went out to Michelangelo and to Raffael and to Bramante (and others) to come to Rome to put at the disposal of the papacy their talents which in many ways have made Rome what still it is in the eyes of the marvelling visitor.

But it would be eroneous to think that the pull of humanism was confined to its cultural manifestations only. Mainly Italians, the popes were quite understandably and to a particular extent attracted to humanism in all its variegated forms. And it was precisely this release of 'humanity' and its liberating effect, even on the popes, which is capable of at least partly explaining the state of affairs on the eve of the Reformation. For what one witnesses then is a veritable reversal of things. Formerly it was the institution which absorbed the individual pope who was no more and no less than an officer (see above pp. 20ff.). Now, however, by virtue of the role and function which the individual had come to assume, the former officer stepped into the place of the institution, with the result that the papacy as an institution faded so much into the background that of its authority and standing as an organ of government only mere traces remained.

It is advisable to point to this state of things prevailing in the late fifteenth century. It was the personalities of the popes which counted and set the tone, and it was a tone which had all the merits and demerits of fifteenth-century Italian humanism. It was no longer the impersonal office with its powers that was determinative, but the personal character of the individual pope, his 'humanity' – precisely the axiom which papal ideology from the mid-fifth century onwards had strenuously and successfully denied. It is this reversal which explains why the gulf between this period and the high Middle Ages was so conspicuous. Previously the law or verdict of the papacy as an institution was decisive, no matter what sort of person the pope was; but when the institution of the papacy and its authority had to all intents and purposes reached a vanishing point, there remained only the law of the pope as an individual – and that was indeed an entirely different proposition. Once his actions and conduct were scrutinized, they were seen at that period to be frequently enough of a lower order than those of his far less exalted contemporaries.

Even the briefest of surveys will show the effects of the reversal of pope and papacy. In implementing the concordats the papacy had to appoint a certain number of cardinals from specified kingdoms. This at once resulted in the formation of factions inside the College of Cardinals where national animosities sometimes came quite markedly to the fore – the effects were not at all dissimilar to those of the local Roman aristocratic infiltration in an earlier age (see above pp. 113, 120). Now in order to create an effective counterweight against royal influences the popes resorted to the stratagem of nepotism, which had an inevitably demoralizing effect on the popes as well as on the curia itself. Calixtus III, for instance, elevated two youngsters, both his nephews, to the cardinalate, one of whom was a Borgia, the later

Alexander VI; Sixtus IV created no less than five of his nephews cardinals, while shortly afterwards Innocent VIII appointed as a cardinal a thirteen-year-old offspring of the Medici family, who was to become Leo X.

Nepotism practised on a large, almost professional, scale, and by no means restricted to the College of Cardinals, also led to the adoption of corruptive practices throughout the many departments of the curia, involving in fact the highest officers and dignitaries. Bribery and simony were common enough features of the late medieval curia. Personal secretaries of popes and other highly placed officers forged papal decrees, privileges and bulls in return for respectable sums of money. The bearing and public and private conduct of virtually all popes at that time not only failed to inspire respect, but produced contempt everywhere. While Pius II had only one illegitimate son, Innocent VIII had a son and a daughter to whom and to whose interests he devoted more care than to the papal office: the pleasure he derived from arranging the wedding festivities of his legitimized son with a daughter of the Medici family in the Vatican palace reflected well on his paternal-carnal instincts but hardly on the paternal-spiritual office he occupied. It is hardly surprising that he mortgaged the papal tiara and almost all the papal treasures. And less than two years later (in November 1488) the same pope gave another huge wedding party in the Vatican for his granddaughter Peretta (daughter of Theodorina, the pope's daughter) who married the wealthy Genoese merchant Usodimare. The notorious Borgia, Alexander VI, openly boasted of his simoniacal acquisition of the pontifical office, and his liaison with Vanozza de Cataneis, a married aristocrat whose palace was only a stone's throw from the Vatican palace, was public knowledge; the result of this liaison, four children, was no less well known; their own scandals were covered up by their father, Pope Alexander, even when one of them poisoned a cardinal and robbed papal vassals of their property. One can hardly wonder that fervent preachers and advocates of drastic reforms and changes met their fate at the stake – that Alexander was at least partly responsible for the death of Girolamo Savonarola is beyond doubt. It was as if Innocent III had sentenced Francis of Assisi to death, although in the case of Savonarola internal Florentine politics played some part. That pluralism was practised to an hitherto unknown extent by and in the curia, appears as a mild affliction in comparison with the other diseases endemic at the turn of the fifteenth century. The involvement of the renaissance popes in domestic Italian squabbles, intrigues and conspiracies including financial scandals with bankers, completes the picture of a – by any standards – thoroughly demoralized succession of popes.

These are but a few examples illustrating the calibre of the popes during the heyday of Italian humanism. And since by the principles of humanism it was the individual who was the primary, if not sole object of judgment and evaluation, it is wholly understandable why contemporaries concentrated on the evaluation of the popes themselves, and far less on the papacy. The debasement of the institution itself was a consequence of the reversal of the relative position of the office and the pope, and in this reversal the popes themselves were instrumental. This was clearly demonstrated in the utter failure of the papacy to exercise any influence in areas where it had always been active. In the fifties and sixties the papacy was quite well aware of the danger which the Turkish advance constituted for Europe. But the papal appeal to the national kingdoms for a crusade against the Turks fell flat, although the pope, the Catalan Calixtus III, had equipped a small fleet. A fierce opposition arose especially in Germany (which for historical reasons had still some interest in the papacy and Italian matters), and the papal imposition of another crusading tax found an angry response with the result that a spate of enraged protests against both papacy and popes was let loose. How little the popes counted could be gauged from the – in itself perfectly justified and well-intentioned – attempt to convoke a European congress of heads of states at Rome for 1458: the summons issued by Calixtus was a fiasco. The idea was nevertheless revived by his immediate successor, Pius II, who at Mantua from late 1459 to early 1460 presided over a European Congress which was only significant for the paucity of participants. Leaving aside a few pretty speeches nothing was done. Quite clearly, a united Christian Europe barely existed in theory, while the pope's authority was non-existent.

Meanwhile conditions inside the curia (as well as generally among the higher clergy) went from bad to worse. Great store was therefore set on the just mentioned new pope, who was the former fiery conciliarist and splendid public orator, Aeneas

Silvius. Successively bishop of Trieste and Siena and immediately before his pontificate a cardinal, Pius II could well be expected to know where a start with the indispensable reform work should be made. He was familiar with the temper of the clergy and laity, both high and low, as he had moved in circles to which only a few mortals then had access; as a cardinal he was familiar with the malpractices in the curia; as a man of genuine scholarship and historical learning he had sufficient knowledge of the means which might have halted the downward trend of the papacy. But none of the expectations was fulfilled, though he did commission Cardinal Nicholas of Cusa to draft a plan of reform: nothing came of it. Although in 1461 the French formally retracted the Pragmatic Sanction of Bourges upon persuasion by Pius, the king, Louis XI, to all intents and purposes restored 'the Gallican liberties' to their old status only a few years later. When reminded of his conciliarist past, Pius' reply was tart: 'Reject Aeneas, accept Pius' ('Aeneam rejicite, Pium recipite'). It was assuredly an anti-climax when the former conciliarist threatened with excommunication anyone who demanded the convocation of a general council. The wheel had come full circle. The Bohemian king, George Podjebrad, was threatened with excommunication in 1462, because of his continued adherence to the utraquist section of the Hussites: this action on the part of a former Baslean was especially liable to cast doubt on his character, since the Council of Basle itself had explicitly approved communion in both forms (see above p. 309). Nevertheless, Bohemia was vital, geographically and militarily, for the crusade against the Turks who had advanced as far as Hungary, and no one was more emphatic about this crusade than the same Pius II who, a poor imitator of Gregory VII, announced his intention of personally leading the crusade against Islam – a fantastic detachment from reality. His death on 15 August 1464 thwarted this intention. It was at this same time that Podjebrad actively pursued his plan of a Con-federation of European States as the only effective means to ward off the Turkish menace. The motto was not war, but *pax et iustitia*, but the plan also came to grief.

The low state of affairs inside the curia during the latter part of the fifteenth century was also faithfully reflected in the depart-ments and offices constituting it. Above all, the papal chancery presented a deplorable picture. Since the times of the schism its paradigmatic organization had greatly suffered, and half-hearted attempts to restore a strict code within it merely resulted in useless half-measures. The chancery personnel mirrored this state of affairs: absenteeism, pluralism, and above all venality and corruption at an unprecedented scale were notorious. Sales and purchases of official positions in the curia were practised without a serious effort to disguise the nature of the transaction. The registration of official papal documents suffered correspondingly – and this despite changes in the system of registration – and to the present day the enquiring historian does not derive great pleasure from consulting and searching through the fifteenth-century Registers of the papacy. The relegation of the papacy as an institution to a secondary place could hardly find a more persuasive manifestation than in the depth to which the curial offices had sunk.

In several respects the picture which the papacy presents in the last decades before the great revolution, was one of a leading Italian Renaissance court. The pope was an Italian prince whose interests were local and purely egoistic, a shadow of the past, mechanically using weapons which belonged to a different era altogether and which had completely lost their meaning. Thus when the Bohemian King George Podjebrad was excommunicated and deposed by the pope in 1465, one of the most vital links in the crusading plan against the Turks was lost: Paul II now appealed for a crusade against him. Fierce nationalistic outbursts were the reaction to these papal moves, civil war broke out, and new social and economic programmes came to be propagated (for instance, Peter Cheltschizki's agrarian reform programme; the Bohemian Brothers; etc.). Once more unwittingly, the papacy was instrumental in raising forces which only a modicum of statesmanship could have harnessed to the needs of the papacy and the advantage of European Christendom. Instead, the popes created revolutionaries and martyrs. But this Bohemian case was no isolated instance. Similar national reactions could be observed in England, and as already mentioned in France and Germany proper. The pope, in a word, had shown himself an Italian prince who was treated as such by the nations. The higher and the lower clergy in the kingdoms demonstrated a considerable degree of independence from the popes who earned in some quarters not unmerited vituperation and contempt.

However paradoxical it may seem, the College of Cardinals was somehow alive to the urgent need for not only talking about reform, but doing something concrete to eliminate at least the worst excesses of corruption and bribery. They tried to make the pope – Paul II – keep his sworn electoral capitulations, but in vain: as pope he disavowed his own oath. Yet despite their 'humanity' so ostensibly demonstrated, the popes of the late fifteenth century more insistently and emphatically than ever appealed to their functions as vicars of Christ and to the plenitude of power in their hands in conjunction with all the outworn epithets. This sense of unrealism and above all the chasm dividing the central message and core of Christianity from the practice of the official heads of organized Christianity, was too wide not to be noticed by even the most dull-witted contemporaries. It is understandable, furthermore, that the decades before the Reformation showed a remarkable and steady growth of opposition to the papacy and the popes, and this opposition was far more articulate, hard-hitting and acute than had earlier been observable. It is nevertheless also true that some writers made a valiant attempt to defend the papacy, but what they reveal is a quite incredible intellectual poverty and naivity. Their writings demonstrated an almost unparalleled dullness, paucity of arguments and insensitivity to the urgent and real needs of the time. All they did was to regurgitate the stale and by now wholly irrelevant and ineffectual hierocratic matter as it was produced in the twelfth and thirteenth centuries. And most of them had not even taken cognizance of Aristotle. If ever the term 'reactionary' was applicable, it was they who merited this opprobrious stigma. Even the papacy under Alexander VI – in contrast to its defenders – was alive to the needs of a properly thought-out reform programme. A high-powered commission of able cardinals and theologians appointed by Alexander produced a workable scheme and reduced its recommendations to a papal reform decree which was however never issued.

It is perhaps symbolic that on the threshold of the modern age the Donation of Constantine was made to serve for the last time in a decisive and useful way, and in the hands of none other than Alexander VI. It was he who in two official letters (though not decrees or bulls) of 1493 used the Donation as a basis when he suggested a division of interests of the Spanish and Portuguese overseas discoveries and missions. As their territorial interests conflicted, Alexander proposed (and both Spain and Portugal accepted) a line of demarcation which prevented one of the earliest colonial wars. Present-day Spanish and Portuguese interests in South America still bear witness to this settlement resulting from a practical (and the last) application of the Donation. A similarly long-lasting, though by no means as beneficial, bequest, of this pontificate was French intervention in Northern Italy. In order to fortify his own position in central Italy Alexander instigated the French king, Charles VIII, to invade Italy in the North, a step which left a legacy down to the nineteenth century.

Despite internal curial tensions the papacy under Julius II tried (on the model of Innocent III) with inadequate means to restore authority in the papal state by regaining lost territories and attempted to set on foot a programme which to all intents and purposes embodied the idea of Italian unification. But these aims embroiled the papacy with other European states and entangled it still more in internal Italian feuds as well as in actual warfare, notably against Venice. It was indicative of the curial state of affairs on the eve of the Reformation that the College of Cardinals recalling the relevant decree of Constance cited Julius II before the council which they had convoked in 1511 at Pisa. They charged him with breaking his promise he had given before his election to summon a general council. Crafty as only a renaissance pope could be, Julius after realizing that the Emperor (elect) Maximilian I and Henry VIII were not at all averse to this Pisan Council and that France was as firmly opposed as before to any papal interference in royal matters or in the kingdom, now hastily convoked a council of his own at the Lateran for the following year.

No less symptomatic of the state of affairs in the early sixteenth century was the plan of the Emperor (elect) Maximilian I to take possession of the papacy himself. One month after convoking the Lateran Council Julius II suddenly fell seriously ill on 17 August 1511; his early demise was generally assumed. That was the moment when Maximilian revived earlier plans (pursued in 1493 and 1503) which were now concretely formulated to serve his Italian interests. He was either to become pope himself or, at the risk of a schism, anti-pope. The essential point was that the

German church would then be headed by either himself as pope or by a German patriarch. It was precisely in this context that the Pisan Council was useful to Maximilian who saw in the French ecclesiastical arrangements a model to be imitated. The probable originator of this plan was the bishop of Gurk in Carinthia (Matthew Lang) who negotiated with France and Spain about its realization. The total cost involved in the planned transaction reached the astronomical figure of over 500,000 ducats. The recovery of Julius II, the Spanish and French withdrawal of support from Maximilian and above all the debacle of Pisa, brought to naught a plan which could well have served as an epilogue to the late medieval papacy.

On 10 May 1512 Julius II solemnly opened the Fifth Lateran Council, the last medieval council. Its main achievement was the confirmation of the Concordat (1516) between the curia and France. The French revocation of the Pragmatic Sanction was however bought at a very high price by the papacy. It now formally conceded to Francis I the right to nominate all French archbishops (10), bishops (82), and virtually all abbots and priors (nearly 500); the king bound himself to nominate only suitable men, a duty the limits of which he himself fixed. A great many economic advantages also accrued to France from this settlement. Appeals to the papacy were permitted in only the so-called 'major causes' – a stipulation which in view of the royal nomination amounted to very little. It is no exaggeration to say that with active assistance by the pope the Gallican Church was given a firm constitutional base. Even so, the arrangements evoked some strong opposition on the part of Paris university which considered the settlement a virtual sell-out to the papacy. In any event on 19 December 1516 the Lateran Council fully confirmed this condordat which displayed its effects right down to the French Revolution, if not beyond to 1906.

This Fifth Lateran Council also enacted a number of long over-due reform decrees. In themselves they were quite modest in scope, for instance, reorganization of certain curial departments, canonical impediments to appointments, holding of regular diocesan synods, restriction of cumulation of prebends, and the like. It seemed as if this kind of legislation was no more than routine window dressing. The papacy here showed itself in perhaps its worst light: instead of insisting upon the enforcement of the law it dispensed from the observation of these decrees. And in so doing the whole panoply of papal weapons including the plenitude of power, was invoked. In a way, the fifth Lateran Council was a conciliar swan song of the medieval papacy and a precursor of Trent later in this same century.

For while the Fifth Lateran Council was still in session, Martin Luther began his attack on the Roman Church on grounds and in language which at the time found an immediate and favourable response. But the papacy, the council and the exalted members of the hierarchy considered themselves secure, immune and shielded. Totally unaware of the changed temper of the time and its trend, they paid no attention to the German opponent whom they all believed fitted into their own preconceived pattern of just one more rebellious heretic who could be dealt with in the accustomed manner. But it was Luther who sensed the winds of change correctly – and acted accordingly. His invectives were little more than the articulation of the sentiments of a great many of his contemporaries: nationalistic, anti-papal, anti-Roman, economic, financial; and he tuned his attacks to suit the very groups and sections and classes of contemporary society which were directly affected by the policy of 'Rome'. A century earlier the assessment by the Establishment might well have been right, but conditions had rapidly altered to the detriment of the pillars of the established order. Instead of keeping under control the interests of universal Christendom by consistently pursuing the plan of a crusade against the Turks Leo X displayed active and keen concern in these very same and crucial years in one matter only – the acquisition of the duchy of Spoleto for his nephew Lorenzo. This was the background to the attempted assassination of the pope by a conspiracy of cardinals. It was a Leo who by the principles he evolved set the medieval papacy on its triumphant career, and it was a Leo in whose pontificate the papacy ingloriously ended the phase initiated by the Great Leo. These two reigns were separated by just over a millennium of hard struggles, splendid successes, and dismal failures.

At this juncture the question must be faced: how can one explain the progressive slipping of the institution into the abyss as the fifteenth century advanced and the sixteenth opened? The same question may be asked differently: why did the Reformers of the sixteenth century succeed with comparatively speaking little effort where numerous others before had failed? In what way can the papacy itself be said to be a factor contributory to the success of Luther and the other Reformers?

Part of the answer lies not in the papacy as an institution, but in those to whom the institution and herewith the whole Church was entrusted, the popes and specifically the personalities of the popes. The calibre of the popes just reviewed was decidedly not one which was conducive to inspiring or even maintaining confidence in their ability as leaders of Christendom. Certainly, in preceding centuries there had been popes who were worthy equals of their fifteenth-century successors, but there was hardly ever such a long continuous line of unworthy individuals. And in any case, the conditions were entirely different, say, in the tenth century as compared with the fifteenth. What, however, is rarely noticed is that humanism itself spelt the death of the institution, for as already noted what now mattered was not the objective law, the impersonal order, the formalized constitution, the external institution and apparatus of the papacy but the worth of the individual irrespective of the office or the institution, in brief, the man himself. It was this idea that had been simmering under the surface for a long time, sometimes coming into the open and bringing forth mystical, sometimes visionary models, such as the 'Angelic Pope' (see above p. 270). But the fifteenth century showed on the one hand the individual's liberation from fetters imposed by an objective world order, and that process affected the popes themselves as individuals (who also became liberated), and on the other hand the progressive elimination of objective, institutionalized organizations and establishments. One incontrovertible effect of liberating humanism was, if not the abolition, at any rate the drastic diminution in efficacy of the existing objective and institutionalized forms of government, and this effect first and foremost hit the papacy, because it was the papacy which was avowedly and existentially built on the cosmology of an objective divinely established order. (In parenthesis it may be remarked that all theocratic forms of government were exposed to this danger, though by no means to this immediate degree as the papacy.) Humanism focused attention on the man-made order. The collective, corporate and impersonal order of things was replaced by the individual, personal and internalized order.

These reflexions should make understandable why contemporaries came to launch such well-articulated, well-aimed and virulent attacks on the personalities of the popes. They in turn demonstrated the severe weakness of the papacy. No provision had been made for the contingency of a pope who turned out to be incapable or utterly unsuited. But while this weakness erupted dramatically in Urban VI, the other deficiency – one might well call it creeping paralysis – was the relationship between pope and cardinals. This was an unresolved problem, and in the background stood the much larger problem of the relations between the papacy and the episcopacy – another unsolved question. Did the bishop, or did he not, receive his powers of government from the papacy? The repercussion of this problem could be felt until recent times. But what these main constitutional deficiencies showed was that the monarchic papacy was no longer capable of coping with the increasingly complicated problems which late medieval society posed. The papal monarchy had become an object of attack from the mid-thirteenth century onwards. From Frederick II through the intermediate stage of Boniface VIII's conflict with his cardinals down to Urban VI, and specially throughout the fifteenth century, there was one theme detectable: oligarchic aspirations of the cardinals *versus* the preservation of the monarchic status of the papacy. On more than one occasion the College of Cardinals appeared to take up a more responsible and sensible line than the popes, certainly in the fifteenth and early sixteenth centuries. In the early and high Middle Ages it was indubitably the monarchic form of government that in prevailing social and political and cultural conditions produced the best results which only goes to prove that the monarchic form of the papal government was time-conditioned. It was obviously incapable of effectively coping with an intricate and involved social mechanism that faced the papacy from the late thirteenth century onwards.

But to the fashionable concentration on the individual and the simultaneous aversion from institutionalized Christianity must be added the ever widening gulf between what was thought to be Christian and what was practised. The alert individual Christian was forced to query the hitherto unqueried role of clerics and especially of popes as mediators of sacraments. There was an unbridgeable and wide gap between the word and the deed, between dogma and conduct, between what the papacy stood for as an institution and the actions of the pope. More and more critical attention was turned to the Scriptures upon which dogma, theory and doctrine were alleged to be based, and with this attention given to the Bible an inevitable result emerged – criticism of the mode of living of the professional expositors of the Bible. In other words, the Bible as the individual's sole source of inspiration and faith came to play from the fourteenth century onwards a role that it had not and could not have played before, partly because the papacy was credited with the role of the authoritative interpreter of the Bible, partly because the Bible was not available in the vernacular, and partly because it was virtually inaccessible to the ordinary mortal. All this had now changed. The role of the papacy was if not denied, at least questioned; the Bible was available in the vernacular and thus provided a firm enough basis upon which the papacy and the popes were capable of being judged; the invention of printing at that very time altered the situation quite drastically. Not only was the Bible produced in increasing numbers, and therefore could find its way into hands which had hitherto little opportunity of possessing it, but above all scholars, thinkers, writers and propagandists were able to disseminate their ideas – as well as their attacks on the papacy – to an extent which only a few decades before was literally speaking, undreamt of. The papacy had lost its dynamic initiative which now belonged to forces which had little in common with the institution, whether in religious, ideological or political respects.

Yet the papacy had nothing with which to stem the tidal advance of new ideologies and above all of the new orientation in religious and ecclesiastical matters. All that remained was to resort to the old, worn and musty arguments, antiquated blunt ecclesiastical censures and rusty sanctions which, if they were not considered irrelevant, at any rate failed to make much impression. The very medium of communication used by the papacy was not attuned to the multitudes: Latin was the language of the scholar and of the scholastic exercise, but new currents had gripped the multitudes, had attracted, and penetrated into, circles of the populace which had hitherto stood aside, because they had no standing or say in ecclesiastical, public or religious affairs. The preacher and speaker and propagandist was able to reach those

new and 'liberated' masses, precisely because he addressed them
in the vernacular. It was also this same preacher who was able
to appeal in an articulate manner to the sentiments and emotions
which his audience had only dimly and amorphously felt and
grasped. The most potent ally of humanism was indubitably the
vernacular language. What Luther taught and wrote and
preached, was no more than what a great many of his contemporary compatriots had already unreflectingly felt, and he did it
in their own language. For the papacy in the fifteenth century
time had stood still, and the enormous intellectual development
and re-orientation that could be observed throughout the century,
had bypassed the popes who lived in a world that was by then
merely historical.

The blindness, deafness and detachment from reality made
the papacy under Leo X view Luther with sublime contempt.
The papacy failed to realize the potentialities of the new brands
of Christianity which were advocated and which engulfed with
alarming rapidity ever more influential circles and classes of
society. It was a fatal sense of security that enveloped the
papacy which was wont to look backward and had now become the victim of its own history. The papacy suffered from
the incubus of its own tradition and history from which it was
unable to escape. It was the harnessing of history which had
always so potently assisted the papacy – it was its own history
which prevented the papacy's finding an accommodation with,
and adjustment to, new forces. In a word, the papacy's own past
prevented its own 'liberation', however much the popes themselves had been liberated by the tide of humanism.

The success of the Reformers was not primarily due to the
inner strength of their programme but to the clear articulation
and enunciation of grievances felt by many contemporary
Christians, and secondly to the appeal to the very sections and
classes of Christendom which despite their proper qualifications
had still not gained any access to the governmental machinery of
the Church: participation and decision-making had been denied
to them on no longer valid grounds. It was the lower clergy and
the educated and politically alert bourgeoisie which was particularly aggrieved by the continued rigidity, 'authoritarianism'
and monarchic structure of Church government. That, indeed, is
one of the reasons why even two generations earlier the Reformers

would have failed to elicit a similar response. For one should bear in mind that in the fifteenth century great strides had been made in all kinds of self-government, particularly in municipal administration, in the town corporations, and especially in the organization and structure of the estates of the various kingdoms, in the *Reichstag*, and so forth. There the very elements, notably the lower knightly class and the educated bourgeoisie, which were excluded from playing any role in ecclesiastical matters, had risen to prominence. The self-governing universities and colleges, too, must be taken into account to show how widespread the practice of self-government had been in the fifteenth century.

Once more it can be said that a vital development had bypassed the papacy which had at its disposal only blunted and ineffectual disciplinary measures when the ideological and ecclesiastical onslaught did eventually come in all its fury. The papal ideological defence was a mechanical regurgitation of doctrines which were constructed for entirely different conditions. These doctrines were hardly relevant to the new kind of Christianity which could not but fail to be attractive by its very opposition to the legalized, formalized brand of Christianity as enunciated by the papacy. The bonfire which Luther made of the law-books of the papacy was more than a mere symbolic protest. It was the affirmation that what mattered for salvation was not the fulfilment of a legal duty imposed by the papacy, but the direct communion of the Christian with God and obedience to His commands in accordance with the individual conscience. And within this religious framework there was indeed little room for the papacy, as it understood itself and was understood in the Middle Ages. Only after passing through a depression and crisis of unsurpassed severity and after slowly accommodating itself to the changed conditions, could the institution re-emerge in a cleansed state, though with a different kind of influence.

It was not the Reformation that set the seal on the medieval papacy, but the papacy itself in the fifteenth century when the institution receded into the background and its place was taken by a succession of individuals who were no more than wealthy Italian princelings and whose qualification for the office was, by any standard, open to doubt. Or seen from yet another angle, the papacy was unable to recover in time from the severe illness that afflicted it in the Great Schism; and the medicine that was proposed to prevent a recurrence of this disease – conciliarism – was a means that merely sapped the papacy's energies without curing its endemic disease. The papacy had entered the historic scene as a monarchic institution, but failed to adjust itself to new situations and contingencies, ironically enough brought about largely by itself. There, then, is a paradox of veritably historic dimensions: it was through the operation with the unadulterated monarchic role of the pope that the papacy became Europe's focal point in the Middle Ages; and it was the operation with this self-same monarchic function which on the threshold of the modern period reduced the papacy to a power situated in central Italy.

Abbreviations

ABA	*Abhandlungen der bayrischen Akademie der Wissenschaften*
Abh	*Abhandlungen*
AD	*Archiv für Diplomatik*
AHP	*Archivium historiae pontificiae*
APA	*Abhandlungen der preussischen Akademie der Wissenschaften*
ASP	*Archivio della società romana di storia patria*
AUF	*Archiv für Urkundenforschung*
Bettenson	H. Bettenson, *Documents of the Christian Church* (1948 and reprints)
BECH	*Bibliothèque de l'école des chartes*
bibl.	Bibliography; bibliographical
Caspar	E. Caspar, *Gesch. des Papsttums* (1930–3)
ch(s)	Chapter(s)
CMH	*Cambridge Medieval History*
CR	W. Ullmann, *The Carolingian Renaissance* (1969)
CSEL	*Corpus scriptorum ecclesiasticorum latinorum*
DA	*Deutsches Archiv für die Erforschung des Mittelalters*
DAC	*Dictionnaire d'archéologie chrétienne et de liturgie*
Decreta	*Conciliorum oecumenicorum decreta*, ed J. Alberigo et al. 2nd ed (1962)
D(D)	*Diploma (ta)*
Docs	Documents
EHR	*English Hist. Review*
Epp.	*Epistolae*
ET	English translation
FM	A. Fliche-V. Martin, *Histoire de l'église*

Gesch.	Geschichte
Hdb	*Handbuch der Kirchengeschichte* (*Handbook of Church History*)
hist.	historical; historisch; histoire
HJb	*Historisches Jahrbuch*
HL	J. Hefele-H. Leclercq, *Histoire des conciles*
HZ	*Historische Zeitschrift*
Jbb.	*Jahrbücher*
JE, JK, JL	*Regesta pontificum Romanorum*, ed P. Jaffé (Ewald; Kaltenbrunner; Loewenfeld)
JEH	*Journal of Ecclesiastical History*
JTS	*Journal of Theological Studies*
KGD	A. Hauck, *Kirchengeschichte Deutschlands* (8th ed 1963)
KRG	H. E. Feine, *Kirchliche Rechtsgeschichte* 4th ed (1964)
LdL	*MGH Libelli de lite*
lit.	Literature
LP	*Liber Pontificalis*, ed L. Duchesne (& C. Vogel)
M.	J. D. Mansi, *Sanctorum conciliorum amplissima collectio*
MA	Middle Ages; Moyen Age; Mittelalter
MGHAA	*Monumenta Germaniae Historica: Auctores antiquissimi*
— Conc	*MGH Concilia*
— Const	— *Constitutiones*
— DD	— *Diplomata*
— Epp	— *Epistolae*
— SSRRGG	— *Scriptores rerum Germanicarum*
MIOG	*Mitteilungen des Instituts für österreichische Geschichtsforschung*
Mitt.	*Mitteilungen*
NA	*Neues Archiv*
OCP	*Orientalia Christiana Periodica*
OR	*Ordo Romanus*
PG	W. Ullmann, *The Growth of Papal Government in the MA*, 3rd–4th ed (1970)
PGP	W. Ullmann, *Principles of Government & Politics in the MA* 2nd ed (1966)

PGr	*Patrologia Graeca*
PL	*Patrologia Latina*
Pullan	B. Pullan, *Sources for the history of medieval Europe from the mid-eighth to the mid-thirteenth century* (1966)
QFIAB	*Quellen & Forschungen aus italienischen Archiven und Bibliotheken*
QRG	E. Eichmann, *Quellen zur kirchlichen Rechtsgeschichte*, 2nd ed (repr. 1968)
Rahner	H. Rahner, *Kirche & Staat im frühen Christentum* (1961)
RHE	*Revue d'histoire ecclésiastique*
RHEF	*Revue d'histoire de l'église de France*
Reg	Register
RNI	*Regestum Innocentii papae super negotio Romani imperii*
RQ	*Römische Quartalschrift*
RSC	*Rivista di storia della chiesa in Italia*
SavKA	*Zeitschrift der Savigny Stiftung für Rechtsgeschichte: Kanonistische Abteilung*
SavRA	*— Romanistische Abteilung*
SB	*Sitzungsberichte*
SCH	*Studies in Church History*, ed G. J. Cuming and D. Baker
Schubert	H. v. Schubert, *Geschichte der christlichen Kirche im Frühmittelalter* (repr. 1962)
Seppelt	F. X. Seppelt, *Geschichte der Päpste*
SG	*Studi Gregoriani*, ed G. B. Borino
St. Grat.	*Studia Gratiana*, ed A. M. Stickler
ST	*Studi e Testi*
ThQ	*Theologische Quartalschrift*
TRHS	*Transactions of the Royal Hist. Society*
trsl.	Translation; translated
TU	*Texte & Untersuchungen zur Gesch. der altchristlichen Literatur*
VI	*Liber Sextus*
WL	Wattenbach-Levison, *Geschichtsquellen des Mittelalters*

X	*Liber Extra*
Z	*Zeitschrift*
ZKG	*Zeitschrift für Kirchengeschichte*

All other abbreviations are self-explanatory.

Bibliographical Notes

GENERAL

Sources

Ph. Jaffé, ed F. Kaltenbrunner, P. Ewald, S. Loewenfeld, *Regesta pontificum Romanorum* (to 1198), 2nd ed (repr. 1956)

A. Potthast, *Regesta pontificum Romanorum* (1198–1304) (repr. 1957)

J. v. Pflugk-Hartung, *Acta pontificum Romanorum inedita* (to 1198) (repr. 1958)

Ae. Friedberg (ed), *Corpus Iuris Canonici* (1879–82)

J. D. Mansi, *Sacrorum conciliorum nova et amplissima collectio* (1759–98; repr. 1962)

J. Alberigo *et al.* (ed), *Conciliorum oecumenicorum decreta*, 2nd ed (1962)

Liber Pontificalis, ed L. Duchesne (repr. 1955); suppl. vol. by C. Vogel (1957)

C. Eubel, *Hierarchia catholica medii aevi ab anno 1198 usque ad annum 1431* (1913–14)

E. Eichmann, *Quellen zur kirchlichen Rechtsgeschichte und zum Kirchenrecht*, 2nd ed (repr. 1968)

K. Mirbt, *Quellen zur Geschichte des Papsttums und des Katholizismus* 6th ed by K. Aland (1967): this does not supersede the 5th ed (1932), cf. H. Fuhrmann, 'Der alte und der neue Mirbt' in *ZKG* 79 (1968) 198–205

C. Silva-Tarouca, *Fontes historiae ecclesiasticae medii aevi: Fontes saeculorum v–ix* (1930)

H. Denzinger–A. Schönmetzer, *Enchiridion symbolorum*, 34th ed (1967)

C. Kirch–L. Ueding, *Enchiridion fontium historiae ecclesiasticae antiquae*, 8th ed (1960)

Literature

(a) K. Bihlmeyer–H. Tüchle, *Kirchengeschichte*, I (13th ed) (1962); II (17th ed) (1963)

337

E. Caspar, *Geschichte des Papsttums* (to *ca* 750), 2 vols (1930–3)

A. Fliche and V. Martin, *Histoire de l'église*, 15 vols to the end of the medieval period (1934–63)

J. Haller, *Das Papsttum: Idee und Wirklichkeit*, 5 vols (1950–3)

C. J. Hefele–H. Leclercq, *Histoire des conciles*, 8 vols in 15 to the end of the medieval period (1909–1917)

H. Jedin (ed), *Handbuch der Kirchengeschichte*, 3 vols (1964–8) (ET in progress under the title: *Handbook of Church History*)

Ch. Poulet, *Histoire du christianisme*, 3 vols (1932–7)

H. v. Schubert, *Geschichte der Kirche im Frühmittelalter* (repr. 1962)

F. X. Seppelt, *Geschichte der Päpste*, 6 vols (1939–58); for the medieval period: vols I–IV

W. Ullmann, *The Growth of Papal Government in the Middle Ages*, 3rd–4th ed (1970)

H. E. Feine, *Kirchliche Rechtsgeschichte*, 4th ed (1964)

G. Le Bras, *Histoire du droit et des institutions de l'église: Prolégomènes* (1955)

A. M. Stickler, *Historia iuris canonici* (1950)

A. van Hove, *Prolegomena ad codicem iuris canonici*, 2nd ed (1945)

(b) Reference works: *Dictionnaire du droit canonique* (1935–65)

Dictionnaire d'histoire et de géographie ecclésiastiques (in progress)

Dizionario ecclesiastico (1953–8)

Lexikon für Theologie und Kirche (with suppl. vols) (1957–68)

New Catholic Encyclopedia (1967)

Reallexikon für Antike und Christentum (in progress)

Sacramentum mundi (in progress)

CHAPTER I

(A) Sources

JK 182–618; *Codex Theodosianus* (repr. 1954); Eusebius, *Historia ecclesiastica* (1903–8) (ET 1965); C. H. Turner, *Ecclesiae orientalis monumenta iuris antiquissimi*, 2 vols (1899–1930); Ed. Schwartz, 'Die Kanonessammlungen der alten Reichskirche' in *Gesammelte Schriften*, IV (1960) 159–75; O. Seeck, *Regesten der Kaiser und Päpste 311–476* 1919); *Collectio Avellana*, ed in *CSEL* XXXV.

(B) Literature

P. Batiffol, *La paix constantienne* (1929 and reprs.); Caspar, I.103–617; Ed. Schwartz, *Konstantin und die Kirche*, 2nd ed (1936); H. Doerries,

Konstantin d. Gr. (1958); J. Gaudemet, *L'église dans l'empire romain* (1959); S. Calderone, *Costantino e il cattolecismo* (1962)

4 Edict of Milan: Lactantius, *De morte persecutorum* c. 48, in *CSEL* XXVII.228–33; part ET in Bettenson 22f.

5 Incorporation: A. Ehrhardt, 'Das Corpus Christi und die Korporation im spät-röm. Recht' in *SavZRA* 70 (1953) 299–347; 71 (1954) 25–65.

5 Monotheism and monarchy: E. Peterson, *Theologische Traktate* (1951) esp. 60–95; W. Ullmann, 'The cosmic theme of the Prima Clementis and its significance for the concept of Roman Rulership' in *TU* (1971) = *Studia patristica* XI (1971) 93–102.

6 Arles: M.2.470–1.

6 Nicaea: canons in *Decreta* 4–15; participants: C. H. Turner 1.36–91, 97–101; I. Ortiz de Urbina, *Nicée et Constantinople* (1963), with trsl. of decrees 260–5 and bibl. 295–300; Ed. Schwartz, 'Die Bischofslisten der Synoden von Chalkedon, Nicaea und Konstantinopel' in *Abh. Bayr. Ak.* 1937.

8 Exemptions: some docs in Bettenson 23–6.

8 Sardica: canons in C. H. Turner 1.452–86 (Greek); 489–531 (Latin); Hamilton Hess, *The Canons of the Council of Sardica* (1958).

8 Liberius: Caspar, 1.176–80, 588–9.

9 Theodosian decree: *Cunctos populos* in *Cod. Theod.* 16.12 (= *Cod. Just.* 1.i.1); ET in Bettenson 31.

9 New Rome: M. Fuhrmann, 'Die Romidee der Spätantike' in *HZ* 207 (1968) 529–61 (from 4th to the 6th cents).

9 Council of Constantinople: canons in *Decreta* 20–34.

10 Damasus and the *sedes apostolica*: P. Batiffol, *Cathedra Petri* (1938) 151–68; H. Rahner in *Z. kath. Theol.* 69 (1947) 3–36; L. M. Dewailly in *Mélanges de science religieuse*, 5 (1948) 141–59; *PG* 4–7; for the *apostolicus* see esp. M. J. Wilks in *JTS* n.s. 13 (1962) 290–317; 14 (1963) 311–54.

11 Petrinological theme: *PGP* 94–6.

13 Vulgate: G. Violardo, *Il pensiero giuridico de s. Girolamo* (1937); W. Ullmann in *Settimana Spoleto*, 10 (1963) 181–228.

13 Petrine succession and Bible: A. Rimoldi, *L'apostolo san Pietro* (1958); F. Refoulé, 'La primauté de Pierre dans les évangiles' in *Revue des sciences religieuses* 38 (1964) 1–41.

13 Epistle of Clement: W. Ullmann, 'The significance of the Epistola Clementis' in *JTS* n.s. 11 (1960) 295–317 (here also bibl. details); id., in *TU* 79 (1961) 330–8. For the development of the idea of law in the early Church see esp. L. Buisson in *SavZKA* 52 (1966) 1–175.

16 Decretals: A. van Hove, 137–44; *KRG* 93–6; J. Gaudemet, *La formation du droit séculier et du droit de l'église aux IVᵉ et Vᵉ siècles* (1957).

18 Zosimus and Boniface I: *PL* 20.676 (also in *Avellana* 115–16) and cols. 777–8; Celestine I: *PL* 50.437.

18 Ephesus: canons in *Decreta* 52–6; Y. Congar, *Le concile et les conciles* (1960); legate's statement: M.4.1295 (*topoteretes = locum tenens*).

19 Leo I: W. Ullmann, 'Leo I and the theme of papal primacy' in *JTS* n.s. 11 (1960) 25–51; for the stimulus which Leo's theses gave to liturgical venerations of St Peter see F. Susmann, 'Il culto di s. Pietro a Roma dalla morte di Leone a Vitaliano, 461–672' in *ASP* 84 (1964) 1–192; of purely hagiographical interest is O. Bertolini, 'Leone I Papa' in *ASP* 89 (1967) 1–23 (who is quite unaware of modern literature).

20 Office and person: *PGP* 38–42.

22 *Principatus (princeps)*: P. Batiffol, *Cathedra Petri* 169–98; J. Gaudemet, 'Le régime impérial' in *Studia et documenta historiae et iuris* 26 (1960) 282–322.

24 Byzantine coronation: O. Treitinger, *Die oströmische Reichs- und Kaiseridee*, 2nd ed (1956) 16–43; A. Michel, *Die Kaisermacht in der Ostkirche* (1959) 132ff.

25 Chalcedon: canons in *Decreta* 59–79; A. Grillmeier–H. Bacht (eds), *Chalkedon*, 2 vols (1953); P.-Th. Camelot, *Ephèse et Chalcédon* (1962) with trsl. of texts 228–33; bibl. 241–8; W. de Vries, 'Die Struktur der Kirche gemäss dem Konzil von Chalkedon' in *OCP* 35 (1969) 63–122, esp. 98–118.

25 Peter and Leo: details in M.6.937–82.

26 Chalcedon ch. 28: P. Stephanou, 'Sedes apostolica, regia civitas' in *OCP* 33 (1967) 563–82.

27 Valentinian's decree: text in *Novellae Valentiniani III*, tit. 16 in G. Haenel, *Corpus iuris Romani anteiustiniani* (1844), fasc. 6, 172–6. The diction of the preamble (at 173) may well have served as the model for the synodists' acclamation in 535, below 43.

CHAPTER II

(A) Sources

JK 619–1063; *LP* 1.255–311; A. Thiel, *Epistolae Romanorum pontificum genuinae* (1862); *Avellana* in *CSEL* xxxv; *Pelagii I Papae Epistolae*, ed P. M. Gasso and C. M. Batlle (1956).

(B) Literature

P. Batiffol, *Cathedra Petri* (1938); L. Duchesne, *L'église au VIe siècle* (1925); G. Every, *The Byzantine patriarchate* 451–1204 2nd ed (1961);

Schubert 17–221; F. Dvornik, *Byzance et la primauté romaine* (1964) (ET 1966); L. M. Hartmann, *Geschichte Italiens im MA*, 11.1.1–159; H. St B. Moss in *CMH* IV (1966) 3–42; FM. IV; HL. 11.881–1185; III.1–237.

29 Alienation of East and West: H. Steinacker, 'Die römische Kirche und die griechischen Sprachkenntnisse des Frühmittelalters' in *MIOG* 62 (1954) 28–66.

29 Imperial attributes: L. Bréhier et P. Batiffol, *Les survivances du culte impérial romain* (1920) (fundamental); W. Ensslin, 'Gottkaiser und Kaiser von Gottes Gnaden' in *SB Bayr. Ak.* (1946); *PG* 16 n. 3, 24 n. 1; O. Treitinger (above 24); A. Michel, *Kaisermacht* (above 24) with copious lit.

29 Monophysites: W. H. C. Frend, *The growth of monophysitism* (1971).

30 Henotikon: text in Evagrius, *PGr* 86.2 cols 2620–5; Caspar 11.22–39, esp. 35 (marking the transition to cesaropapism).

30 Felix III: Duchesne in *LP* 1.253 n. 2.

30 Gelasius I: *PG* 17–28, 462–3, 473; some relevant docs ed and trsl. by H. Rahner, *Kirche und Staat im Frühmittelalter* (1962) nos 19–20c, pp. 250–63; A. S. McGrade, 'Two fifth-century conceptions of papal primacy' in *Studies in Medieval and Renaissance History* 7 (1969) 3–45. ET of the more important Gelasian texts in Pullan 45–7.

31 Acacian schism: Ed. Schwartz, 'Publizistische Aktenstücke zum akazianischen Schisma' in *Abh. Bayr. Ak.* 10 (1934).

35 Pseudo-Denys: B. Altaner, *Patrologie*, 5th ed (1958) 466–7; U. Riedinger, 'Der Verfasser der ps. dionysischen Schriften' in *ZKG* 75 (1964) 146–52; cf. also W. Ullmann in *TU* (above 5).

36 Legend of Silvester: text in B. Mombritius, *Sanctuarium seu vitae sanctorum* (ed 1910) 508–24, partly also in C. B. Coleman, *Constantine and early Christianity* (1914) 217–27; *PG* 70–81 (further lit.).

37 Clovis: Caspar 11.126–8, 762; J. M. Wallace-Hadrill, *The Long-Haired Kings* (1961) 163–85, *Early Germanic Kingship* (1971), 18ff.

38 Laurentian schism: R. Cessi in *ASP* 42 (1919) 5–229; 43 (1920) 209–31 (fundamental); Caspar 11.87–106, 758–61; W. Ensslin, *Theoderich d. Gr.* (1947); L. Duchesne, *L'église* (as in (B)).

38 Symmachan forgeries: L. Duchesne in *LP* 1.cxxii, cxxvi, cxxxiii–cxli.

39 Zosimus, Boniface I, Celestine I: above 16, 18.

39 *Liber Pontificalis:* admirable characterization by L. Duchesne in his introduction to the *LP*; additional observations now in vol. III, ed C. Vogel (1957), incl. the MS at Tortosa with an improved text for the twelfth century (143–71). See also H. Leclercq, s.v. in *DAC* IX.354–459.

40 Hormisdas and the settlement: relevant docs in *Avellana*, nos 89, 90, 116b, 159 (at 338–43, 520–2, 607–10); cf. for textual problems Caspar 11.764–5; W. Haacke, *Die Glaubensformel des Papstes*

Hormisdas (in *Analecta Gregoriana*, 20 (1939)); also R. Cessi, *ASP* 43 (1920) 209ff.

41 Justinian: Ed. Schwartz, 'Zur Kirchenpolitik Justinians' in *Gesammelte Schriften* 4 (1960) 276–328; *PG* 31–8, 463f.; H. Rahner (above 30) 281–96; *CMH* IV.2 (1967) 55–63, 105–30.

43 Acclamation by council of 535: M.8.969. Cf. above 27.

44 Justinian's legislation: references in *PG* 34 n. 2; further F. A. Biener, *Geschichte der Novellen Justinians* (repr. 1970).

44 Justinian's division of labour: *Novella* 6, preamble.

45 Ceremonial: O. Treitinger (above 24); F. Dölger, *Byzanz und die europäische Staatenwelt* (ed 1964) 9–33; 70–115.

45 Justinian's divine mouth: *Cod.* I.xvii.1 (6); his law as a 'divine precept' in *Novella* 13, Epilogue.

46 Papal reaction: some docs ed and trsl in H. Rahner 298–332.

46 'Three chapters': Facundus in *PL* 67.527–854; W. Pewesin, *Imperium, ecclesia universalis* (1937) 3–18, 150–8; E. Stein, *Histoire du bas empire* II (1949) 632–88; R. Haacke, 'Die kaiserliche Politik in den Auseinandersetzungen um Chalkedon' in *Chalkedon* II (1953) 95–177 at 164ff. and A. Grillmeier, ibid. 806–34.

46 Vigilius: Ed. Schwartz, 'Vigilius-Briefe' in *SB Bayr. Ak.* (1940); Caspar II.234–86 (fundamental); H. Rahner doc no. 28 at 334–443; Facundus ibid. nos 24–6 at 302–22.

47 Fifth General Council: *Decreta* 83–98; R. Devréesse, 'Le Vᵉ concile et l'ecumenicité' in *Misc. G. Mercati* III (1946) 1–15.

50 *Liber Diurnus:* Th. Sickel, *Der Liber Diurnus* (1889); lit. in *PG* 329 n. 2 and R. Buchner in WL, *Die Rechtsquellen* (1953) 55–7. The letter by the Emperor Honorius to Boniface I in 419 is the earliest secular intervention in papal election mechanics: *Avellana* 83–4.

CHAPTER III

(*A*) *Sources*

JE 1066–2257; *LP* 1.312–425; Register of Gregory I: ed in *MGH Epp* I, II.

(*B*) *Literature*

Caspar II.306–740; L. Bréhier, *Grégoire le Grand, les états barbares et la conquête arabe* (1938); id., *Le monde byzantin* (repr. 1970); J. Haller, *Papsttum* I.247–361; I. Herwegen, *Antike, Germanentum und Christentum* (1932); K. F. Stroheker, *Germanentum und Spätantike* (1965); A. Michel, *Die Kaisermacht in der Ostkirche* (1959); FM. v; HL. III.238–600.

51 Gregory I: S. Brechter, *Die Quellen zur Angelsachsenmission* (1942); P. Batiffol, *Grégoire le Grand* (1929) (ET 1929); Caspar II.373–514;

Schubert 189–201; *PG* 36–52, add. lit. 465; C. Dagens in *Recherches de science religieuse* 58 (1970) 273–88, Wallace-Hadrill, *Germanic Kingship*, 28ff.

55 Isidore of Seville: *PL* vols 81–84; *Etymologies*, ed W. M. Lindsay (1911); further lit. in WL fasc. 1, 81–91 at 86–7.

56 Quarrel with John IV: *PG* 37 n. 3. Note that popes had in early sixth century been addressed as 'universal patriarchs' or 'patriarchs of the whole world' ('universi orbis terrae patriarcha'), e.g., *Avellana* in *CSEL* xxxv.565, 614, 616 etc. (Hormisdas).

59 Heraklius: G. Ostrogorsky, *Gesch. des byzantinischen Staates* 3rd ed (1964) (ET 2nd ed 1968); further H. Rahner 347ff.

60 *Ekthesis:* M.10.992–5.

60 *Typos:* M.10.1029–30.

60 Martin I: *LP* 1.336–42; JE 2057–81; Lateran Council of 649: M.10.863–8; Caspar in *ZKG* 51 (1932) 75–156; arrest: JE 2078–81; H. Rahner 354–6; report of his trial: ibid. (with German trsl) 366–91.

61 Situation in exarchate: A. Guillou, *Régionalisme et indépendence dans l'empire byzantin au VIIe siècle: l'exemple de l'exarchat et de la pentapole d'Italie* (1969).

62 Maximus: trial report, sentence and exile: H. Rahner docs 30, 31 at 392–435.

63 Sixth General Council: canons in *Decreta* 100–6.

63 Sergius I: *LP* 1.371–82.

63 Council of 692 (*Trullanum* and *Quinisexta*): M.11.921–38.

64 Attempted arrest of Sergius: *LP* 1.372–3; also in Rahner doc 32.

64 Pope Constantine at Constantinople: *LP* 1.389–95 at 390–1.

65 Phillipikos Bardanes and Roman unrest: *LP* 1.391–2.

66 Anglo-Saxons and the papacy: W. Levison, *England and the Continent in the eighth century* (1948 and repr.) (fundamental); Th. Schieffer, *Winfried-Bonifatius und die christliche Grundlegung Europas* (1954); H. Loewe, *Die karolingische Reichsgründung und der Südosten* (1937).

66 Boniface: his letters in *MGH Epp* iii.215–433; G. W. Greenaway, *Saint Boniface* (1955).

68 Dilemma of the papacy: penetrating observations by H. Steinacker in *MIOG* 62 (1954) 28–66 at 61–3.

CHAPTER IV

(A) Sources

JE 2153–2544; *LP* 1.396–523; 11.1–51; F. Böhmer–E. Mühlbacher, *Die Regesten des Kaiserreichs unter den Karolingern* 2nd ed (1908); *MGH Epp*

III.469–657; IV.19–29, 127–38, 144–6, 187–9, V.1–104; *MGH Concilia* II.1; J. Haller, *Quellen zur Gesch. der Entstehung des Kirchenstaates* (1907); H. Loewe in *WL* fasc. 2 (1953); R. Buchner, ibid. *Die Rechtsquellen* (1953).

(B) Literature

P. Brezzi, *Roma e l'impero medioevale* 774–1252 (1947); E. Caspar, *Das Papsttum unter fränkischer Herrschaft* (1964); H. Beumann, *Karl d. Gr.: Persönlichkeit und Geschichte* (1965); L. Halphen, *Charlemagne et l'empire Carolingien* 2nd ed (1949); L. Duchesne, *Les premiers temps de l'état pontifical* (1908; also ET); Schubert 288–390; Seppelt 11. 2nd ed (1955); *PG* chs 2, 3; FM VI.17–70, 153–228; *Hdb* III.1 chs 1–4, 10–15; HL III.1001–1145.

71 Iconoclastic controversy: E. Caspar, 'Papst Gregor II. und der Bilderstreit' in *ZKG* 52 (1933) 29–86. Relevant texts of papal letters (and German trsl) in H. Rahner 438–59; M. Anastos, 'Iconoclasm and the imperial rule' in *CMH* IV (1966) 61–104; G. Ostrogorsky (above 59) ch 3.

75 Papacy and Pippin: *LP* 1.440–62; *Annales regni Francorum* (ed *MGHSSRRGG*); *Clausula* in *MGHSSRRMerov.* 1.465 (ET in Pullan 7–8); *Codex Carolinus* in *MGH Epp* III.469–657 at 479–507; L. Levillain, 'L'avènement de la dynastie carolingienne et les origines de l'état pontifical' in *BECH* 94 (1933) 225–95; J. Haller, 'Die Karolinger und das Papsttum' in his *Abh. zur Gesch. des MA* (1944) 1–40; M. Wallace-Hadrill, *Kingship* (above 37), 99ff.

76 Byzantine embassy: *LP* 1.444–6.

76 Ponthion and unction: *PG* 52–74.

77 Donation of Constantine: new ed by H. Fuhrmann in *Fontes Iuris Germanici antiqui* 10 (1968); use in papal chancery: *PG* 59 n. 1, 60, 65 n. 3, 73 n. 2, 466, 480.

79 Identification of Christians with Romans: e.g., Boniface in *MGH Epp* III.341, no. 73, lines 19f.; other sources *PG* 62 nn. 1, 2.

79 Charlemagne and the papacy: *Cod. Carol.* in *MGH Epp* III.469ff. at 559–636; Einhard, *Vita Karoli* (ed *MGHSSRRGG* 1905); *MGH Concilia* I.110–71 (Council of Frankfurt); *LP* 1.486–523, II.1–48; P. Classen, 'Karl d. Gr., das Papsttum und Byzanz' in *Karl d. Gr.* (as under (B)) 1.537–608 (new ed 1968) (fundamental); *PG* ch 3.

80 *Dionysio-Hadriana:* details in P. Fournier–G. Le Bras, *Histoire des collections canoniques* I (1933) 94–8; H. Mordek, 'Dionysio-Hadriana und Vetus Gallica' in *SavZKA* 55 (1969) 39–63.

81 Leo III and Paderborn: H. Beumann in *HZ* 185 (1958) 515–49; description of programme in *MGH Poetae Latini* 1.366ff. and Einhard, *Vita Karoli*, c. 32; coronation: sources assembled by H. Dannenbauer, *Die Quellen zur Geschichte der Kaiserkrönung Karls d. Gr.* (1931); R. Folz, *Le couronnement impérial de Charlemagne* (1964);

L. Falkenstein, *Der Lateran der karolingischen Pfalz zu Aachen* (1966); relevant texts in ET in Pullan 11–17.

81 Pope not justiciable: statement made by assembly in Rome: *LP* 11.7; cf. W. Ullmann in *SG* IV (1952) 111–28 at 116f.; oath of Leo: *LP* loc cit.; and *MGH Conc.* 11.226; cf. P. Classen 578 n. 200; H. Zimmermann, *Papstabsetzungen des MA* (1968) 30–7.

84 Source reporting 'adoration' by pope: *Annales regni Francorum* at 112.

84f. Byzantine coronation: O. Treitinger (above 24).

85 Roman emperor West and East: W. Ohnsorge, *Das Zweikaiserproblem* (1947); significance of coronation: *CR* ch 6.

87 Papal action at Rheims: *PG* ch 5 and esp. E. Eichmann, *Die Kaiserkrönung im Abendland* (1943) 1.39–50; unction and its meaning: *CR* ch 4; Eva Müller in *HJb* (1938) 317–60; Dr J. L. Nelson's unpublished Cambridge dissertation (1967) and ead. in *Studies in Church History*, VII (1971) 41–60.

87 Visigoths and Franks (unction): *CR* 69 n. 1 (sources and lit.).

89 Imperial and royal unction: *PG* 148–56, 225–7, 253–61; royal unction: *CR* 71ff., 91–2; M. J. Wilks (below 268) 242.

CHAPTER V

(*A*) *Sources*

JE 2545–3673; *LP* 11.49–245; *MGH Epp* V.581–614, VI.257–765, VII.1–329, 334–70; *MGH Concilia* 11.2; R. Elze (ed.), *Ordines coronationis imperialis* in *Fontes iuris Germanici antiqui* (1960); *Annales Fuldenses* (ed *MGHSSRRGG*); Regino of Prum, *Chronicon* (ed *MGHSSRRGG*); H. Loewe in WL fasc. 3 (1957) and 4 (1963); D. Lohrmann, *Das Register Papst Johannes' VIII.* (1968); H. Zimmermann, *Papstregesten 911–1024* (1969).

(*B*) *Literature*

Gina Fasoli, *I re d'Italia 888–962* (1949); *CR* chs 2, 3, 6; W. Ohnsorge *Abendland und Byzanz* (1958); F. Dölger, *Byzanz und die europäische Staatenwelt* (repr. 1964), esp. 34–115, 282–369; D. Hay, *Europa: the emergence of an idea* (1957); A. Lapôtre, *L'Europe et le s. siège à l'époque carolingienne* (1895); FM VI.273–302, 367–412, VII.15–50; *Hdb* III.1, chs 16–18, 21, 22, 27; HL IV.1–786.

92 Constitution of 824 and papal elections: W. Ullmann in *Cambridge Hist. J.* 11 (1953) 114–28; questionable premisses in O. Bertolini, 'Osservazioni sulla constitutio Romana...dell' 824' in *Studi medievali in onore di A. Stefano* (1956) 43–76.

93 Episcopalism *v* papalism: *PG* ch 4; now esp. R. L. Benson, *The Bishop-Elect* (1968).

94ff. Imperial coronations: E. Eichmann (above 87) 1.45–108; *PG* ch 5.

97 Leo IV: about his Register fragments see W. Ullmann, 'Nos si aliquid incompetenter' in *Ephemerides iuris canonici* 9 (1953) 312–36.

98 Clergy in Frankish realms: C. Nissl, *Der Gerichtsstand des Clerus im Frankenreich* (1886) (still fundamental).

99 Pseudo-Isidore: ed P. Hinschius, *Decretales Pseudo-Isidorianae* (repr. 1963); R. Buchner, *Die Rechtsquellen* (1953); Fournier–Le Bras, *Hist. des collections canoniques* 1.127–230; A. M. Stickler, *Historia iuris canonici latini* (1950) 117–43; *KRG* ch 17; E. H. Davenport, *The false decretals* (1916); J. Haller, *Nikolaus I. und Pseudoisidor* (1936); *PG* 167–89; H. Fuhrmann, 'Ps. Isidor in Rom vom Ende der Karolingerzeit bis zum Reformpapsttum' in *ZKG* 78 (1967) 15–66; id. in *QFIAB* 49 (1969) 313–39 (mainly historiographical).

102 Nicholas I: *LP* II.151–71; *MGH Epp* VI.257–690; E. Perels, *Nikolaus I. und Anastasius* (1920); K. Brandi, 'Ravenna und Rom' in *AUF* 9 (1926) 1–38; H. Fuhrmann in *SavZKA* 44 (1958) 353–8; *PG* ch 7; Y. Congar in *RSC* 20 (1967) 393–410; id., *L'ecclésiologie du haut MA* (1968) 206–25.

104 Marriage affair of Lothar: *MGH Epp* VI.209–40, 300–51; E. Ewig in *Hdb* III.1, 148ff. (best recent account).

104 Hincmar of Rheims: H. Schrörs, *Hinkmar von Reims* (1884) (still fundamental); further *CR* ch 4; M. Andrieu, 'Le sacre épiscopal d'après Hincmar' in *RHE* 48 (1953) 22–73.

105 Byzantium: *MGH Epp* VI.433–610; synodal canons of Constantinople: H. G. Beck in *Hdb* III.1, 197; J. Hergenröther, *Photius, Patriarch von Constantinopel* (repr. 1968) (fundamental); F. Dvornik, *The Photian schism* (1948); G. T. Dennis, 'The "anti-Greek" character of the Responsa ad Bulgaros of Nicholas I?' in *OCP* 24 (1958) 165–74 (not anti-Greek); D. M. Nicol, 'The Byzantine view of Western Europe' in *Greek, Roman and Byzantine Studies*, 8 (1967) 315–36.

108 Intellectual level: M. L. W. Laistner, *Thought and Letters in Western Europe*, 2nd ed (1957) 251–385.

109 Circular letter: *CR* ch 6.

110 Arabs: F. E. Engreen in *Speculum* 21 (1946) 318–30; E. Ewig in *Hdb* III.1, 152–60.

110 Eighth General Council: canons in *Decreta* 142–62.

111 Papal election decree (898): M.18.225, cap. 10; *HL* IV.7–8, 716–17.

112 Formosus: J. Duhr, 'Le concile de Ravenne en 898: la réhabilitation du pape Formose' in *Recherches de science relig.* 22 (1932) 541–79; esp. H. Zimmermann, *Papstabsetzungen* (above 81) 53–73.

311 Papal state: W. Kölmel, *Rom und der Kirchenstaat im 10. Jahrhundert*

(1935); B. Hamilton in *Studies in Medieval and Renaissance History* 11 (1965) 263–310; H. Zimmermann, op. cit. 74–7.

114 Cluny and Alberic: A. Rota, 'La riforma monastica del "princeps" Alberico' in *ASP* 79 (1965) 11–23.

114 Papal name: F. Krämer, 'Ueber die Anfänge und Beweggründe der Papstnamensänderungen im MA' in *RQ* 51 (1956) 148–88, here 154–6.

114 Hungarian incursions: G. Fasoli, *Le incursioni ungare in Europa del secolo X* (1946); C. A. Macartney, *The Magyars in the ninth century* (repr. 1970); G. Ostrogorsky (above 59) 194–224.

CHAPTER VI

(A) Sources

JL 3674–4468; *LP* 11.246–80; J. M. Watterich, *Pontificum Romanorum ... Vitae* (1862) 1.38–235, 623–739; M. Boye, 'Quellenkatalog der Synoden Deutschlands und Reichsitaliens' in *NA* 48 (1930) 47–96; Liutprand of Cremona, *Opera*, 3rd ed in *MGHSSRRGG*; R. Elze, *Ordines* (as in v (A)). J. Deér, *Das Papsttum und die süditalienischen Normannenstaaten 1053–1212* (1969) (ed of all relevant docs).

(B) Literature

Jules Gay, *Les papes du XIᵉ siècle et la chrétienté* (1926); R. Folz, *La naissance du saint-empire* (1967) (numerous texts trsl 185–354); R. Holtzmann, *Gesch. der sächsischen Kaiserzeit* (1943 and repr.) (fundamental); P. E. Schramm, *Kaiser, Rom und Renovatio* (repr. 1957); R. Morghen, *Rinnovamento della vita europea e riforma della chiesa nel sec. XI* (1958); A. Cartellieri, *Der Aufstieg des Papsttums 1047–1095* (1936); FM VIII.51–176; *Hdb* III.1, chs 27, 28, 32, 42; HL IV.777–1249; *PG* ch 8.

117 Otto I's coronation: E. Eichmann, *Kaiserkrönung* (above 87) I.129–149; P. E. Schramm, *Kaiser, Könige und Päpste* (1969) III, 153ff., at 169–75.

118 Byzantium and S. Italy: R. Holtzmann 136–52, 184–201.

118 Otto I as Roman emperor: *MGH Dipl.* 1.318, 322, 324, 329, 346.

119 Otto's compact: W. Ullmann, 'The origins of the Ottonianum' in *Cambridge Hist. J.* 11 (1953) 114–28.

119 Deposition of John XII: H. Zimmermann (above 81) 77–98, 235–72.

120 John XII's death: Liutprand, *Historia Ottonis*, c. 20 (ed *MGH-SSRRGG* at 173–4); *LP* 11.264: this 'infelicissimus' pope 'spent most of his life in adultery and debauchery'.

M

120 Otto III: M. Uhlirz, *Jbb. des deutschen Reichs unter Otto III.* (1954).

122 Council of Pavia in 1022: M.19.343–56 (esp. concerned with concubinage, priests' sons, and similar matters); for identical efforts in the German church see synod of Seligenstadt, M.19. 396–404.

125 Missions to Slavs: A. P. Vlasto, *The entry of the Slavs into Christendom* (1970); K. Bosl, 'Der Eintritt Böhmens und Mährens in den westl. Kulturkreis' in *Collegium Carolinum* (1958); missions to Denmark and Sweden: W. Seegrün, *Das Papsttum und Skandinavien* (1967) 18–64.

125 Magdeburg: R. Holtzmann 182–5, 231–3, 415; Gnesen, 359–64.

125 Hungarian ecclesiastical organization: G. Györffy, 'Zu den Anfängen der ungarischen Kirchenorganisation' in *AHP* 7 (1969) 79–113.

127 Sutri: H. Zimmermann (above 87) 114–39 (with exhaustive bibl.).

128 Popes between 955 and 1057: L. Santifaller, 'Zur Geschichte des ottonisch-salischen Reichskirchensystems' in *SB Vienna* 1954 (new ed 1964) (most detailed bibl.); also O. Köhler, 'Die ottonische Reichskirche' in *Adel und Kirche: Festgabe für Gerd Tellenbach* (1968) 141–204.

129 Leo IX and Lorraine circles: H. Hoffmann, 'Von Cluny zum Investiturstreit' in *Archiv für Kulturgeschichte* 45 (1963) 165–209.

129 Cluniacs: J. Leclercq, *Aux sources de la spiritualité occidentale* (1964) 91–173; H. E. J. Cowdrey, *The Cluniacs and Gregorian Reform* (1970); also Seppelt III.9–49.

130 Humbert: *Contra simoniacos* ed in *LdL* 1.95–253; A. Michel, *Die Sentenzen des Kardinals Humbert* (1943); id. in *SG* 1.65–92; W. Ullmann in *SG* IV.111–28; J. J. Ryan in *Medieval Studies* 20 (1958) 206–38. Relevant texts in ET in Pullan 58–63.

131 Council of Rheims in 1049: M.19.738C (main decrees against simony, divorce (c. 12) and demand for election by clergy and people, cols 741–2).

132 Schism of 1054: Cornel. Will, *Acta et Scripta* (1861); A. Michel, *Humbert und Kerullarios* (1926–30); id. in *L'église et les églises* 1 (1954) 341–441; M. Jugie, *Le schisme byzantin* (1940); Cf. H. Steinacker in *MIOG* 62 (1954) at 40: the schism 'ist nur der sinnfällige Abschluss einer Entfremdung, die schon im 5. Jahrhundert einsetzt und im 9. Jahrhundert wesentlich beendet ist.'

133 Validity of excommunication: E. Hermann in *OCP* 8 (1942) 209–18 (book review).

135 Nicholas II: details of election and lit. in J. Wollasch, 'Die Wahl des Papstes Nikolaus II.' in *Adel und Kirche* (above 128) 203–20. Now also D. Hägermann, 'Zur Vorgeschichte des Pontifikats Nikolaus II.' in *ZKG* 81 (1970) 352–61.

135f. Synod of 1059: *MGH Const* 1.382 at 539–40; 384, at 547–8; H. G.

Krause, *Das Papstwahldekret 1059 und seine Rolle im Investiturstreit* (1960 = *SG* VII); W. Stürner, 'Salvo debito honore et reverentia' in *SavZKA* 54 (1968) 1–56.

136 Cardinals: J. B. Sägmüller, *Die Tätigkeit und Stellung der Kardinäle bis auf Bonifaz VIII.* (1896) (fundamental); H. W. Klewitz, 'Die Entstehung des Kardinalskollegiums' in *SavZKA* 25 (1936) 115–221; S. Kuttner, 'Cardinalis' in *Traditio* 3 (1945) 129–214; M. Andrieu, 'L'origine du titre cardinal' in *Misc. G. Mercati* (= *Studi e Testi*, 126) V (1946) 113–32; C. G. Fürst, *Cardinalis* (1967).

137 Curia: K. Jordan, 'Die Entstehung der römischen Kurie' in *SavZKA* 27 (1939) 96–152; id. in *SG* I.111–35; J. Sydow in *DA* 11 (1954) 18–73.

137 Hildebrand: G. B. Borino, 'L'arcidiaconato di Ildebrando' in *SG* III (1948) 463–516.

138 S. Italian enfeoffments: oaths of Robert Guiscard and Richard of Capua in the collection of canon law by Deusdedit, III.285–6 (ed W. von Glanvell 393f.). For Norman background esp. H. Hoffmann, 'Die Anfänge der Normannen in Süditalien' in *QFIAB* 49 (1969) 95–144. For sources J. Deér (as in (A)).

139 Coronation of pope: F. Wasner, 'De consecratione, inthronizatione, coronatione summi pontificis' in *Apollinaris* 8 (1935) 86–125, 249–81, 428–39; E. Eichmann, *Weihe und Krönung des Papstes* (1952).

CHAPTER VII

(*A*) *Sources*

JL 4469–7177; *LP* II.281–326, 331–79, III.143–69; J. M. Watterich, *Vitae* (as in VI (A)) I.239–620, 470–7, II.1–153; *Registrum Gregorii VII*, ed E. Caspar (repr. 1955); *MGH LdL* I–III; C. Erdmann, *Die Briefe Heinrichs IV.* (1937); *Codex Udalricus*, ed Ph. Jaffé in *Bibliotheca rerum Germanicarum* V (1869) 38–388; E. E. Emerton, *The correspondence of Gregory VII* (1932).

(*B*) *Literature*

H. X. Arquillière, *Saint Grégoire* (1934 and repr.); R. Morghen, *Gregorio VII* (1952); A. Brackmann, 'Gregor VII. und die kirchliche Reformbewegung in Deutschland' in *SG* II.7–30; W. v. den Steinen, *Canossa, Heinrich IV. und die Kirche* (1957); *PG* ch 9; A. Becker, *Urban II.* (1964–); S. Runciman, *History of the crusades* (1951 and repr.); E. Voosen, *Papauté et pouvoir civil à l'époque de Grégoire VII* (1927); FM VIII.13–390; *Hdb* III.1, chs 42–45, 49; HL V.13–644.

142 Papal banner: C. Erdmann, *Die Entstehung des Kreuzzugsgedankens* (1936 and repr.) 166–84.

144 Pattarini: H. E. J. Cowdrey, 'The papacy, the Patarenes and the

church of Milan' in *TRHS* 5th series, 18 (1968) 25–48; G. Miccoli, 'Per la storia della Pataria milanese' in his *Chiesa Gregoriana* (1967) 101–60.

147 Gregory's election: *Reg.* I.1–3; see also W. Goez below 154.

150 Military campaign against the East: *Reg.* 1.46; 11.31, 37, 49.

151 Salomo and Geisa (Hungary): J. Deér, *Die heilige Krone Ungarns* (1966) 72–9, 193–9; also G. Stadtmüller in *HJb* 70 (1951) 65–110.

151 Translation of a kingdom: Gregory's *Reg.* 11.70.

151 Principle of totality: *PGP* 33–7, 97–8; this was the *universale regimen* as claimed in *Reg.* 11.44, 51, IV.2 and 24, VIII.21 etc.

151 Collections of law: Fournier–Le Bras, *Hist. des coll. can.* 11.4–54; *PG* 359–73; A. M. Stickler, *Hist. iuris can. lat.*

152 Dictates of the pope: *Reg.* 11.55a; K. Hofmann, *Der Dictatus papae Gregors VII.* (1933); G. B. Borino, 'Un ipotesi sul D.P. di Gregorio' in *ASP* 67 (1944) 237–52; K. Hofmann in *SG* I.531–7; S. Kuttner, ibid. 11.387–401.

153 Pope as sanctus: W. Ullmann, 'D.P. 23 in retrospect and prospect' in *SG* VI (1961) 229–64.

154 Promulgation of prohibition of investiture in 1075: G. B. Borino in *SG* VI.329–49.

154 Ultimatum and German reaction: *Reg.* III.8; *MGH Const* 1.58–63 at 106–111; *Briefe* nos 10–13. The Worms sentence is closely analysed by W. Goez concerning the kernel of truth of the allegations: 'Zur Erhebung und ersten Absetzung Papst Gregors VII.' in *RQ* 63 (1968) 117–43.

155 Excommunication and provisional deposition of Henry IV: *Reg.* III.10a.

156 Tribur and Oppenheim: J. Fleckenstein, 'Heinrich IV. und der deutsche Episkopat' in *Adel und Kirche* (above 128) 221–36.

157 Crossing of the Alps: vivid description by Lampert of Hersfeld in his *Annales* (ed 1957 with German trsl) 394–401.

157 Canossa: sources conveniently assembled by K. Langosch, *Die Briefe Heinrichs IV.* (1955) 113–27; H. X. Arquillière, 'Grégoire VII, à Canossa a-t-il réintégré Henri IV dans sa fonction royale?' in *SG* IV (1952) 1–26. Descriptive narrative by Lampert, ed cit., 402–13 (to be used with caution). 'Matter in suspense': *Reg.* VI.12 ('ita adhuc totius negotii causa suspensa est'); Henry styled as 'king' by Gregory after Canossa in *Reg.* IV.22, 24, V.7, 16, VI.1, 17a (2), 22, etc. Cf. *Reg.* VII.3.

158 Publicistic literature: C. Mirbt, *Die Publizistik im Zeitalter Gregors VII.* (repr. 1965) (fundamental).

159 Final deposition and excommunication of Henry: *Reg.* VII.14a.

162 Gregory on history and faith: G. Ladner, 'Two Gregorian letters' in *SG* V (1958) 225–42.

163 Roman law: *PG* 382–7; W. Ullmann, 'Juristic obstacles to the emergence of the concept of the state in the MA' in *Annali di storia del diritto* 13 (1969) 41–64 (= *Memorial volume for F. Calasso*).

164 Urban II's advice: S. Loewenfeld, *Epp. pontificum Romanorum ineditae* (1885) no. 126 at 61f.

165 Settlement of the Investiture Conflict: Th. Schieffer, *Die päpstlichen Legaten in Frankreich 870–1130* (1935); H. Hoffmann, 'Ivo von Chartres und die Lösung des Investiturstreits' in *DA* 15 (1959) 383–440; A. Becker, *Urban II,* 1.187–226; English settlement: A. L. Poole, *From Domesday Book to Magna Carta* (1951) 177–84; N. Cantor, *Church, kingship and lay investiture in England 1089–1135* (1958); Z. N. Brooke, *The English Church and the Papacy* (repr. 1969).

165 Spain: P. Kehr in *APA* (1926) nos 1 and 2; (1928) no 4.

165f. Crusade: A. Waas, *Gesch. der Kreuzzüge* 2 vols (1966); H. E. Mayer, *Gesch. der Kreuzzüge* (1966); S. Runciman (as under (B)). About the spurious encyclical of Sergius IV appealing for a crusade (fabricated probably *ca.* 1096) see A. Giesztor in *Medievalia et Humanistica* 5 (1948) 3–23, 6 (1950) 3–34. Crusaders' obligations: J. A. Brundage in *Traditio* 24 (1968) 77–115; id., *Medieval canon law and the crusader* (1969). Sources of the crusades: *Documents relatifs à l'histoire des croisades,* publ. by *L'Académie des inscriptions et belles-lettres* (in progress: so far 9 vols published).

166 Roman primacy in Constantinople: Gregory VII's *Reg.* 11.31.

169 Paschal II and Henry V in 1111: *MGH Const* 1.83–101 at p. 134–52; E. Eichmann, *Kaiserkrönung,* 1.222–5; *KGD* 111.897–905.

169 *Pravilegium:* text in *MGH Const* 1.399, p. 571–3; M.21.74–6: excommunication of Henry V for perjury, sacrilege as 'alter Judas' and threat of schism in the Council of Vienne in 1112; Lateran synod of March 1116: M.21.145–51.

170 Settlement with Germany: sources of Worms conveniently assembled by W. Fritz, *Quellen zum Wormser Konkordat* (1955). For the background esp. important M. J. Wilks, 'Ecclesiastica and Regalia' in *SCH* VII (1971) 69–85 (significance of *potestas ordinis* and *potestas iurisdictionis* of bishop); further R. L. Benson, above 93.

CHAPTER VIII

(A) Sources

JL 7181–14056; Boso in *LP* 11.379–446; Watterich, *Vitae* (as in VI (A)) 11.157–649; *Codex Udalrici* ed Ph. Jaffé (as in VII (A)) v (1869) 388–469; relevant docs also in *QRG* 11 and in S. M. Onory, *La crisi del sacro romano impero* (1951).

(B) Literature

A. Cartellieri, *Der Vorrang des Papsttums zur Zeit der Kreuzzüge* (1941); *KGD* iv.114–324; H. Beumann (ed), *Heidenmission und Kreuzzugsgedanke in der deutschen Ostpolitik des MA* (1963); R. Folz, *L'idée d'empire en Occident du V*^e *au XIV*^e *siècle* (1953) (ET 1969); Seppelt iii.165–318; FM. ix.1, 42–102, 132–49; ix.2, 5–188; *Hdb* iii.2, chs 1, 3, 8, 11; HL v.645–1114.

174 Honorius II's election: *vita* in *LP* iii.170–1.

174 Southern block: about the Greek church and its 'union' with the Roman church, see P. Herde, 'Das Papsttum und die griechische Kirche in Süditalien vom 11. bis zum 13. Jahrh.' in *DA* 26 (1970) 1–46.

175 Schism of 1130–8: F. J. Schmale, *Studien zum Schisma des Jahres 1130* (1961) (fundamental).

176 Innocent II in Germany: F. J. Schmale, 'Bemühungen Innozenz' II. um seine Anerkennung in Deutschland' in *ZKG* 65 (1954) 24–68.

178 Abelard: lit. in M. Grabmann, *Gesch. der katholischen Theologie* (repr. 1961) 288–9; J. G. Sikes, *Peter Abailard* (1932); A. Giuliani, *Abelardo e il diritto* (1964); D. Luscombe, *The school of Peter Abelard* (1969).

178 Arnold of Brescia: G. W. Greenaway, *Arnold of Brescia* (1937); A. Frugoni, *Arnaldo da Brescia nelle fonti del secolo XII* (1954); also J. Benzinger, *Invectiva in Romam: Romkritik vom 9. zum 12. Jahrh.* (1968).

179 Gratian: A. van Hove, *Prolegomena* (as under 'General' Lit.) 337–48; A. M. Stickler, *Hist. iuris can. lat.* 200–17; S. Kuttner, *St. Grat.* 1.15–29; relevant papers ibid. i–xiv; *KRG* 276–83.

180 Great lawyer popes: R. James Long, 'Utrum iurista vel theologus plus perficiat ad regimen ecclesiae' in *Medieval Studies* 30 (1968) 134–62.

181 Supply of jurists: *PG* ch 11.

181 St Bernard: *De consideratione* in *PL* 182.727–808; newly ed in *S. Bernardi Opera* (1963); Bernard on government: *PG* 426–37; full bibl. in H. Wolter, *Hdb* iii.2, 16–18. Some texts in ET in Pullan 63–6.

182 Vicar of Christ: history of the title: M. Maccarrone, *Vicarius Christi: storia del titolo papale* (1952) esp. 85–154.

183 Eugenius III: H. Gleber, *Papst Eugen III.* (1936).

183 Northern mission: W. Seegrün (above 125) 146–99.

184 Arnold: see above 178.

185 Western empire and Roman law: P. Koschaker, *Europa und das römische Recht*, 2nd ed (1958); W. Ullmann in *L'Europa e il diritto romano* (1954) 1.99–136; H. Appelt, 'Friedrich Barbarossa und das römische Recht' in *Römische Hist. Mitt.* 5 (1962) 18–34; id. in *SB*.

Vienna 252 (1967); relevant fascicles in *Ius romanum medii aevi* (in progress).

186 Imperial theme: R. Folz (as under (B)); W. Ullmann, 'Reflexions on the medieval empire' in *TRHS* 5th series 14 (1964) 89–108.

187 Pauline-Isidorian theme: *PGP* ch 3.

187 Enthronement: imperial coronation orders, ed R. Elze (above v (A)).

188 Adrian IV: Boso in *LP* 11.388–97; W. Ullmann, 'The pontificate of Adrian IV' in *Cambridge Hist. J.* 11 (1955) 233–52.

189 Irish conquest (*Laudabiliter*): W. Ullmann, 'On the influence of Geoffrey of Monmouth in English history' in *Speculum historiale* (1966) (= *Festschrift für J. Spörl*) 257–76, at 268–75; J. A. Watt, *The Church and the two nations in medieval Ireland* (1970) chs 1 and 2.

190 Frederick I: M. Maccarrone, *Papato e impero dalla elezione di Federico I alla morte di Adriano IV* (1959) (fundamental); M. Pacaut, *Frederic Barbarousse* (1968) (ET 1970); P. Munz, *Frederick Barbarossa* (1969). Manuel Comnenos: P. Lamma, *Comneni e Staufer*, 2 vols (1955–7); P. Classen, 'La politica di Manuele tra Federico I e le città italiane' in *Popolo e stato in Italia* (1970) 265–79. Imperial coronation: Boso, p. 392 lines 6ff.; Maccarrone 105–40. Curial approval of Federick's election: *MGH Const* 1.139, p. 194; H. Simonsfeld, *Jbb. unter Friedrich I.* (1908) 102; *KGD* IV.198; Seppelt III.206; H. Wolter in *Hdb* III.2, 71; Maccarrone 24–8; significance not noticed by P. Munz and Pacaut. Treaty of Constance: Maccarrone 41–81.

190 Incident at Besançon: W. Ullmann, in *Misc. Historiae Pontificiae* 18 (1954) 107–26; Maccarrone 179–85; for the vital link between *beneficium* and *favor apostolicus* see *PGP* 58–68; of this necessary link is unaware W. Heinemeyer, 'Beneficium – non feudum, sed bonum factum' in *AD* 15 (1969) 155–236.

191 Roncaglia and Roman law: above 186.

192 Alexander III: *LP* 11.397–445; *PL* 200.70f. (vivid description of his election); Rahewin, *Gesta Friderici* (in *MGHSSRRGG*) c. 60, pp. 293, 297–307; M. Pacaut, *Alexandre III* (1956); D. Hägermann, 'Cluny und das Papstschisma 1159' in *AD* 15 (1969) 237–50, at 240–3.

193 Pavia Council: *MGH Const* 1.181–90, pp. 251–69. Numbers present (50): Rahewin at 319.

193 English and French recognition of Alexander III: Mary G. Cheney in *EHR* 84 (1969) 474–98 esp. 480–7; J. Haller, II.2, 149–50, 560–1 (not at Toulouse in the autumn of 1160, cf. *KGD* IV.258).

195 Rouen–Würzburg: *MGH Const* 1.223–6, pp. 314–21.

195 Charlemagne's canonization: R. Folz, *Le souvenir et la légende de Charlemagne* (1950) 203–38; id., 'La chancellerie de Fréderick I et la canonisation de Charlemagne' in *Moyen Age* 70 (1964) 13–31.

195 'Unus Deus, unus papa, unus imperator': *MGH Const* 1.182, p. 253.

197 Peace of Venice: *MGH Const* 1.259–73, pp. 360–73.

197 Becket dispute: C. R. Cheney, 'The punishment of criminous clerks' in *EHR* 51 (1936) 215–37; Ch. Duggan in *Bulletin Institute of Hist. Research* 35 (1962) 1–22; id., 'Richard of Ilchester' in *TRHS* 5th series, 16 (1966) 1–21 at 9–19; id. in *Ampleforth J.* 75 (1970) 365–74; D. Knowles, *Thomas Becket* (1970).

199 Alexander as a canonist: *KRG* 279–83; also J. de Ghellinck, *Le mouvement théologique du xiie siècle*, 2nd ed (1948) 203–13.

200 Proprietary church and patronage (advowson): Gratian, xvi.vii. 30; Roland in his *Summa* (ed F. Thaner) 56ff.; Alexander's decretals: *X*: 111.xxxviii.3ff.

200 Alexander and Frederick: balanced assessment in *KGD* iv.314–16.

CHAPTER IX

(*A*) Sources

JL 14507–17678; P. 1–5316; J. M. Watterich, *Vitae* (as in vi (A)) 11.650–741; *Gesta Innocentii* in *PL* 214.xvii–ccxxxviii; Innocent III's Registers in *PL* 214–16; O. Hageneder and A. Haidacher (eds), *Die Register Innozenz' III.* (first pontifical year) (1964); *Regestum super negotio romani imperii* (ed F. Kempf (1947) and W. Holtzmann (1948)); C. R. Cheney and M. G. Cheney (eds), *The Letters of Innocent III concerning England and Wales* (1967).

(*B*) Literature

P. Zerbi, *Papato, impero e respublica christiana dal* 1187 *al* 1198 (1955); Ch. Duggan in C. H. Lawrence (ed), *The English Church and the Papacy* (1965) 63–117; F. Kempf, *Die Register Innozenz' III.* (1945); A. Luchaire, *Innocent III*, 6 vols (1904–8); D. Waley, *The papal state in the thirteenth century* (1961); Seppelt 111.291–389; FM ix.2, 198–230; x; *Hdb* 111.2, chs 11, 13, 15, 18–22; HL v.1114–1408; *KGD* iv.686–775.

202 Verona: the decree *Ad abolendam* is in *X*: v.vii.9.

203 Henry VI as 'Caesar': understandably the papacy always refused the creation of a co-emperor on the Byzantine model: W. Ohnsorge in *SavZGA* 67 (1950) 309–39 esp. 328–32.

203 Gregory VIII: W. Holtzmann, 'Die Dekretalen Gregors VIII.' in *Festschrift L. Santifaller* (1950) 113–24.

204 Frederick I and Constantinople: Ansbert, *Historia de expeditione Friderici* (ed in *MGHSSRRGG*) 49–50; *TRHS* (above 186) 101–3 (further sources); G. Ostrogorsky (above 59) 335–8.

205 Henry VI and the curia: W. Ullmann, 'Dies ortus imperii' in *Atti Accursiani* (1968) II.661–96 at 680–3.

206 Double election and Innocent: E. Winkelmann, *Jbb. unter Philip von Schwaben und Otto IV*. (1873) (still fundamental) esp. 131–271; F. Kempf, 'Die zwei Versprechen Ottos IV.' in *Festschrift E. Stengel* (1952) 359–84; full bibl. in H. Wolter, *Hdb* III.2, 171–2, 178–80.

208 Election and early pontificate: *Gesta* (as under (A)) xviiff. His *De contemptu mundi* newly ed by M. Maccarrone (1955). About his style and diction see esp. L. Buisson in *Adel und Kirche* (above 128) 458–76.

208 Recuperations: J. Ficker, *Forschungen zur Reichs- und Rechtsgeschichte Italiens* (1869) II.284–492 (fundamental).

209 'King of the Romans': this feature has escaped attention, cf. W. Ullmann, 'Dies ortus imperii' (above 205).

210 Innocent, Staufen and Guelfs: *RNI* nos 14, 18, 21, 29, 61. ET in Pullan 191–206.

211 Translation of empire: W. Goez, *Translatio imperii* (1958) 137–98 at 157–68.

212 Adolf of Cologne: now called by Innocent a perjuror, traitor, corrupted by money, etc., in *RNI* 116, after having relied on him, *RNI* 16, 55; the idea of creating an anti-king was Adolf's (not Innocent's) who had even pawned his cathedral's treasures in order to further his plans, see *RNI* 26.

212 Innocent's ordo and Otto's coronation as emperor: R. Elze, *Ordines* (above v (A)) no XVIII, pp. 69–87; E. Eichmann, *Kaiserkrönung* 1.253–96.

212 Otto's defection: Innocent in E. Winkelmann, *Acta imperii inedita* (1880) no. 1009, p. 677 (18 Jan. 1210); *Reg.* XIII.193; XV.20, 115, 189; excommunication and exact dates: A. Haidacher in *Römische Hist. Mitt.* 3 (1960) 132–85; 4 (1961) 26–36; 11 (1969) 206–9.

213 Golden bull of Eger: *MGH Const* II.46–51, pp. 57–63.

213 England: C. R. Cheney (ed) and W. H. Semple (trsl), *Selected Letters of Pope Innocent III concerning England* (1953); Canterbury election: M. D. Knowles in *EHR* 53 (1938) 211–20 (best account); interdict: C. R. Cheney in *TRHS* 4th series, 31 (1949) 129–50; id. in *Bulletin John Rylands Library* 31 (1948) 295–317; id., 'The alleged deposition of King John' in *Studies presented to F. M. Powicke* (1948) 100–16.

214 Bulgaria: *Reg.* VII.1, see also H. Hirsch (below 227) at 26–8.

214 Spain: L. G. Valdeavellano, *Historia de España* (1952) 1015–69; P. Linehan, *The Spanish Church and the Papacy in the thirteenth century* (1971) (exhaustive bibl.).

214 Portugal: H. Livermore, *A new history of Portugal* (repr. 1969) 61–80.

215 Papal fiefs: H. Hirsch (below 227) 9–11.

215 Ottocar of Bohemia: *Reg.* VII.49, 52, 54, 55.

215 Hungary: J. Deér, *Die heilige Krone Ungarns* (above 151) 200–10; L. Tautu, 'Le conflit entre Johannitsa et Eméric roi de Hongrie 1201–1204' in *Mélanges Eugène Tisserant* (= *ST* 233, 1964) III. 367–93; *CMH* IV (1966) 567–91.

215 Fourth Crusade: A. Frolow, *Recherches sur la déviation de la quatrième croisade* (1955); S. Runciman (above VII (B)) III.III–46; D. M. Nicol in *CMH* IV.1, 275–330; H. Roscher, *Innozenz III. und die Kreuzzüge* (1969). Innocent's reaction to the capture of Constantinople: *Reg.* VII.203; VIII.19, 24, 26; *RNI* 113, etc.

216 Latin empire: W. de Vries, 'Innozenz III. und der christliche Osten' in *AHP* 3 (1965) 87–126; J. Hussey in K. M. Setton, *History of the Crusades* 2nd ed (1970) II.123–52, and R. L. Wolff, ibid. 153–276; also P. Herde in *DA* 26 (1970) at 15–19 (in regard to S. Italy).

216 Heresies and Innocent III: H. Grundmann, *Religiöse Bewegungen im MA* (new ed with new appendices 487–567) (1961) 70–169 (fundamental); M. Maccarrone, 'Riforma e svilluppo della vita religiosa con Innocenzo' in *RSC* 16 (1962) 27–72.

216 Latin patriarchate: R. L. Wolff, loc. cit.

218 Innocent, Diego and Dominic: *Reg.* VII.76.

219 Albigenses: A. P. Evans, 'The Albigensian crusade' in K. M. Setton (above 216), II.277–324.

220 Heresy as crime of *lèse majesté*: W. Ullmann, 'The significance of Innocent III's decretal "Vergentis" ' in *Études d'histoire du droit dediées à Gabriel Le Bras* (1965) 729–43.

220 *Compilatio Tertia:* S. Kuttner, *Repertorium der Kanonistik* (1938) 355–69; *KRG* 285f.

221 Fourth Lateran Council: canons in *Decreta* 203–48. Full bibl. in H. Wolter, *Hdb* III.2, 206–8; further, R. Foreville (below 239). 'General council': A. Hauck, 'Rezeption und Umbildung der allgemeinen Synode im MA' in *Hist. Vierteljahrschrift* 10 (1907) 465–82 at 468–75 (fundamental).

222 Application of St John 1.16 to pope: *Reg.* 1.230.

223 Governmental axioms: *Reg.* II.123, 202, 220; VII.42; *RNI* 2, 18, 46; *Sermo* 2 in *PL* 217.657 (pope less than God but more than man: *medius constitutus*); A. Hof, 'Plenitudo potestatis und "imitatio imperii" zur Zeit Innozenz III.' in *ZKG* 66 (1955) 39–71; *PGP* part 1, chs 3, 4; B. Tierney in *Speculum* 37 (1962) 48–60. Some texts in ET in Pullan 67–76.

224 Two sword theory: H. Hoffmann, 'Die beiden Schwerter im hohen MA' in *DA* 20 (1964) 78–140 (here also details of A. M. Stickler's relevant papers); *PG* 430–7; soul and body: W. Ullmann, *Individual and Society in the MA* (1967) 46–9, 146; id., *Papst und König* (1967) 37–41 (addit. sources).

CHAPTER X

227 Curia: *KRG* 321-7 (lit.); further B. Rusch, *Die Behörden und Hofbeamten der päpstlichen Kurie des* 13. *Jahrhunderts* (1936); K. Jordan, 'Die Entstehung der römischen Kurie' in *SavZKA* 28 (1939) 97-152.

227 Deposition of Rulers: O. Hageneder in *AHP* 1 (1963) 53-95; a special case (Sancho II of Portugal) analysed by E. Peters, *The Shadow King* (1970) 135-69. For the creation of kings by popes see H. Hirsch, *Das Recht der Königserhebung durch Kaiser und Papst im hohen MA* (repr. 1962). General powers: *Acta pontificia iuris gentium,* ed G. B. Pallieri and G. Vismara (1946); further evidence in *PGP* 82-6. In general see G. Le Bras, *Institutions ecclésiastiques de la chrétienté médiévale,* 2 vols (1959-64); also B. Tierney in *Medieval Studies,* 27 (1965) 227-45; further W. Ullmann, 'The medieval papal court as an international tribunal' in *Virginia Journal of International Law* (1971) (Essays presented to Judge H. C. Dillard).

228 Papal election: *KRG* 319-21. ET in Pullan 47-56.

229 *Licet de vitanda: X:* 1.vi.6.

229 Papal name: above 114. Rebirth: see Innocent III below 231.

230 Conclave: *VI:* 1.vi.4; *Clem.* 1.iii.2.

230 Capitulations: W. Ullmann, 'The legality of the papal electoral pacts' in *Ephemerides Iuris Canonici* 12 (1956) 312-46.

230 Election procedure: E. Eichmann, *Weihe* (above 139); F. Wasner (above 139).

231 Investiture and taking possession of the Lateran: J. Hortal Sanchez, *De initio potestatis primatialis Romani pontificis* (= *Analecta Gregoriana* 167 (1968)) 37-70; for texts and the *sedes stercoraria* see M. Andrieu, *Le pontifical romain au MA* (1940) 11.526; here also the deacon who asks the elected pope by what name he wishes to be known, 111.667-8, although in the twelfth century the name was still imposed by the prior of the Roman deacons, see also the Ordo of Cencius in J. M. Watterich (above VI (A)) 1.13-14 (here further details). Innocent III confirmed the latter practice: *Reg.* IX.136.

231 Coronation: in addition to F. Wasner, see J. Hortal Sanchez (loc. cit.) at 71-89, 145-58; for the archdeacon and the pallium see M. Andrieu (op. cit.) Ordo XIII A 6, p. 370.

231 Papal crown: J. Braun, *Die liturgische Gewandung im Okzident und Orient* (repr. 1964) 502-9; E. Eichmann, *Weihe* (above 139) 56-8.

232 College of Cardinals: above 136. For the twelfth century see V. Pfaff, 'Die Kardinäle unter Coelestin III.' in *SavZKA* 52 (1966) 332-69 (with copious lit. for the whole century at 332-3); for the fourteenth century see G. Mollat in *RHE* 46 (1951) 22-212, 566-94. Divine or human origin of cardinalate: W. Ullmann, 'Eugenius IV, Cardinal Kemp and Archbishop Chichele' in *Medieval Studies* *presented to Aubrey Gwynn* (1961) 359–86; about non-curial cardinals see K. Ganzer, *Die Entwicklung des auswärtigen Kardinalats im hohen MA* (1963).

233 Legates: *KRG* 327f. (lit.); K. Walf, *Die Entwicklung des päpstlichen Gesandtschaftswesens* 1159–1815 (1966). Conferment of legatine powers on kings: J. Deér, 'Der Anspruch der Herrscher des 12. Jahrhunderts auf die apostolische Legation' in *AHP* 2 (1964) 117–86 (esp. important for Sicily) (*Monarchia Sicula*).

234 *Visitatio liminum:* J. B. Sägmüller in *ThQ* 82 (1900) 69–117 (fundamental); Th. Gottlob, *Der kirchliche Amtseid der Bischöfe* (repr. 1963).

234 Proctors: R. Heckel, 'Das Aufkommen der ständigen Prokuratoren an der päpstlichen Kurie' in *Misc. Francesco Ehrle* (= *ST* 38 (1924)) II.290–321; also P. Herde (below 236) 80–100.

234 Pallium: J. Braun, *Liturgische Gewandung* (above 231) 620–63.

235 Gratian on force of decretals; D.p.c. 16, C. xxv, i. Cf. Justinian in *Cod.* i.xvii.1 (6).

235 Sovereignty of the pope: W. Ullmann, 'The papacy as an institution of government' in *SCH* 11 (1965) 78–101.

236 Papal diplomatic: R. L. Poole, *Lectures on the history of the papal chancery* (1915); C. R. Cheney, *The study of the medieval papal chancery* (1966); W. Ullmann, 'On the heuristic value of medieval chancery products with special reference to papal documents' in *Annali della fondazione italiana per la storia amministrativa*, 1 (1964) 117–36; P. Herde, *Beiträge zum päpstlichen Kanzlei- und Urkundenwesen im 13. Jahrhundert*, 2nd ed (1967). Further lit. in *KRG* 325, 335–6 (Privilege and Dispensation).

237 Canonization: E. W. Kemp, *Canonization and authority in the Western Church* (1948).

237 Judges delegate: Ch. Duggan, *Twelfth-century decretal collections* (1963) chs 1 and 2 (here also further lit.). Auditors and capellani: R. Elze, 'Die päpstliche Kapelle' in *SavZKA* 38 (1950) 145–204; P. Herde, *Audientia litterarum contradictarum: Untersuchungen über die Justizbriefe und die päpstliche Delegationsgerichtsbarkeit vom 13. bis zum 16. Jahrhundert* (1970); J. E. Sayers, *Papal Judges Delegate in the Province of Canterbury* (1971).

238f. General Councils: First Lateran: canons in *Decreta* 166–70; Second: canons ibid. 173–9; Third: canons ibid. 187–201; Fourth: canons ibid. 206–47; First Lyons: canons ibid. 254–77; Second Lyons: canons ibid. 285–307; Vienne: ibid. 312–77. The introductions to the texts of the decrees contain very useful bibliographies. There are translations of the decrees of the four Lateran Councils in R. Foreville, *Latran I, II, III et Lateran IV* (1965) at 167–78, 187–94, 210–23, 342–86; here also useful lists of participants 387–95 and bibl. 407–19; trsl of Vienne decrees in J. Lecler, *Vienne* (1964) 187ff. For the internal arrangements of councils see the

Roman ordo in M. Andrieu, *Le pontifical romain* I (1938), Ordo XXXVI, p. 255–60. See further, R. Foreville, 'Procédure et débats dans les conciles mediévaux du Latran' in *RSC* 19 (1965) 21–37.

240 Fourth Lateran Council: see also above 221. S. Kuttner and A. García y García, 'A new eye witness account of the Fourth Lateran Council' in *Traditio* 20 (1964) 115–78; M. Maccarrone, 'Il IV concilio Lateranense' in *Divinitas* 2 (1961) 270–91. ET of some canons of IV Lateran in Pullan 88–98.

241f. Canon law: A. van Hove, *Prolegomena* 338–69; *KRG* 276–93; J. Gaudemet, 'Droit canonique' in *Introduction bibliographique à l'histoire du droit et à l'ethnologie juridique*, ed J. Gillissen, vol. B (1963); B. Paradisi in *Studi Medievali* 6 (1965) 1–133.

243 Universities: H. Rashdall (ed F. M. Powicke and A. B. Emden), *The Universities of Europe in the MA* (1936) 1 (for Paris and Bologna); 11 (for the other continental universities); A. B. Cobban, 'Episcopal control in the medieval universities of Northern Europe' in *SCH* v (1969) 1–22; G. de Vergottini, *Lo studio di Bologna: l'impero e il papato* (1954). See now esp. P. Classen in *Heidelberger Jbb* 12 (1968) 72–92 (with copious lit.).

244 Papal and episcopal power: Leo I in his *Ep.* 14, c. 1; *PG* 8, 291; M. J. Wilks in *JTS* n.s. 8 (1957) 71–91, 256–71; R. L. Benson, above 93.

245 Expectations, reservations, provisions: *KRG* 340f. K. Ganzer, *Papsttum und Bistumsbesetzungen von Gregor IX. bis Bonifaz VIII.* (1968).

246 Apostolic chamber: E. Fabre-L. Duchesne, *Le Liber censuum* (1889–1910); V. Pfaff, 'Der Liber censuum' in *Vierteljahrschrift für Sozial- und Wirtschaftsgeschichte* 44 (1957) 78ff., 105ff., 220ff.; 46 (1960) 71ff; 48 (1961) 360ff. (annual income according to the *Liber censuum* was about 100 pound of gold); W. E. Lunt, *Papal revenues in the MA*, 2 vols (1934); P. Partner, 'Camera papae: problems of papal finance' in *JEH* 4 (1953) 55–68. Detailed lit. in *Hdb* III.2, 413 and *KRG* 350–1.

247 Chancery: F. Bock, 'Die erste urkundlich greifbare Ordnung des päpstlichen Archivs' in *MIOG* 62 (1954) 317–35; *KRG* 334–5. For procedure in chancery see P. Herde (above 236) 101–76. For papal Registers see above 210; for Gregory VII's Register *PG* 276 n. 2 and additional lit. 472; also A. Murray in *Traditio* 22 (1966) 149–201. Most meritorious is E. Pasztor, 'Per la storia dei registri pontifici nel due cento' in *AHP* 6 (1968) 71–112. For the organization of the chancery in the 14th century see *Dietrich von Niem: Der Liber cancellariae apostolicae vom Jahre 1380 und der stilus palatii abbreviatus*, ed G. Erler (repr. 1970).

248f. Judicial tribunals: T. Majic, 'Die apostolische Pönitentiarie' in *RQ* 50 (1955) 129–64; G. Mollat, 'Contribution à l'histoire de l'admini-

N

stration judiciaire de l'église romaine au xive siècle' in *RHE* 33 (1936) 877–928; G. Barraclough, *Public notaries and the papal curia* (1934); J. Reetz, 'Kuriales Prozesswesen um 1340' in *AD* 10 (1964) 395–414 (a concrete case). Further lit. in *KRG* 326–7. Rota: W. Ullmann in *St. Grat.* XIII (1967) 457–89 (further lit.).

CHAPTER XI

(*A*) *Sources*

P 5317–25448; P. Pressutti (ed), *Regesta Honorii Papae III* (1888); Registers (not complete) from Gregory IX to Boniface VIII ed by *L'école française de Rome; MGH Epistolae saeculi XIII e regestis pontificum Romanorum selectae*, 3 vols (1883); J. F. Böhmer–J. Ficker, *Acta imperii selecta*, 2 vols (1870); E. Winkelmann, *Acta imperii inedita*, 2 vols (1885); *MGH Constitutiones* II–IV.1 (to no 119, p. 96): J. L. A. Huillard-Bréholles, *Historia diplomatica Friderici II*, 11 vols in 6 (1852–61).

(*B*) *Literature*

Seppelt III.390–578; FM X.271–340; 427–60, 487–504; *Hdb* III.2, chs 25–8, 31, 34–5; HL V.1409–1710, VI.1–467; L. Buisson, *Potestas und Caritas: die päpstliche Gewalt im Spätmittelalter* (1958).

251 Heretical movements: A. S. Turberville, *Medieval heresy and inquisition* (1920); A. C. Shannon, *The popes and heresy in the thirteenth century* (1949); H. Maisonneuve, *Études sur les origines de l'inquisition*, 2nd ed (1961); W. Ullmann, Historical introduction to H. C. Lea, *A history of the Inquisition in the MA* (1962). Early Capetians and the stake: M.19.373–4 (anno 1017). ET of some relevant decrees in Pullan 90–4.

252 Frederick II's anti-heretical laws: *MGH Const* II.85, pp. 107–9.

256 Coronation at Jerusalem: *MGH Const* II.120–3, pp. 160–7.

256f. Frederick II and the papacy: *MGH Const* II nos 116, 119, 126–49, 176–82, 224–34, 236–59, 262; *KGD* IV.777–886.

259 Papal conclave: K. Hampe, 'Ein ungedruckter Bericht über das Konklave von 1241 im römischen Septizonium' in *SBHeidelberg* 1913; K. Wenck, 'Das erste Konklave der Papstgeschichte, August bis Oktober 1241' in *QFIAB* 18 (1926) 101–70.

260 First Lyons Council: *MGH Const* II.399–401; Ph. Pouzet, 'Le pape Innocent IV à Lyon: le concile de 1245' in *RHEF* 15 (1929) 281–318; S. Kuttner, 'Die Konstitutionen des ersten allgemeinen Konzils von Lyon' in *Studia et documenta historiae et iuris* 6 (1940) 70–130; id., *L'édition romaine des conciles généraux et les actes du I concile de Lyon* (1940); cf. *Decreta* 259–77.

260 Deposition of Frederick II: text in *Decreta* 254–9.

261 Innocent IV as legal commentator: J. A. Watt, *The theory of papal monarchy in the thirteenth century* (1965).

261 Manifestoes and encyclicals: *MGH Const* 11.215, pp. 290–8; 224, pp. 308–12; *MGH Epp sel*. 1.672, p. 567; 11.184, p. 247; E. Winkelmann, *Acta* (as under (A)), 1.25, pp. 23–5; 28, pp. 25f.; nos 30–31, pp. 28–36; nos 43, 46, 48–9, pp. 44–7, 49–51, 52–4. The decree *Eger cui levia* (ibid., 11.1035, pp. 696–703) and its authenticity is disputed with good reasons by P. Herde, 'Ein Pamphlet der päpstlichen Kurie gegen Friedrich II. von 1245–6' in *DA* 23 (1967) 468–538 (here also new ed of text); W. Ullmann, 'Reflexions on the opposition of Frederick II to the papacy' in *Archivio storico Pugliese* 13 (1960) 1–17.

262 France and the papacy: G. Zeller, 'Les rois de France candidats à l'empire' in *Revue historique* 173 (1934) 273–311, 498–534.

262 Missions: B. Schumacher, *Geschichte Ost- und Westpreussens* 3rd ed (1958) 21–66; R. Hennig, *Terrae incognitae* (1938) III nos 125–28, 131–3, 135, 149; G. Soranzo, *Il papato, l'Europa cristiana e il Tartari: un secolo di penetrazione occidentale in Asia* (1930); C. Dawson, *Mongolia: the Mongol mission* (1955).

264 Michael Palaeologus: D. J. Geanokoplos, *Emperor Michael Palaeologus and the West* (1959).

264 Gregory X: L. Gatto, *Il pontificato di Gregorio X* (1959).

265 Second Lyons Council: S. Kuttner, 'Conciliar law in the making' in *Misc. Pio Paschini* (1949) 11.39–81; B. Roberg, *Die Union zwischen der griechischen und lateinischen Kirche auf dem zweiten Konzil von Lyon* (1964); Byzantine reaction: D. Nicol in *SCH* VII (1971) 113–46 (with copious lit.). Canons of the council in *Decreta* 285–307.

266 Sicily: E. Pontieri, *Ricerche sulla crisis della monarchia siciliana nel secolo XIII*, 3rd ed (1959); Registers of the Angevins: *I Registri della cancellaria Angioina*, 17 vols (1951–67).

267 Spain: P. Linehan (above 214).

268 Intellectual revolution: *PGP* 231–79; *Individual and Society* 99–152; M. J. Wilks, *The problem of sovereignty* (1963) (also important for the assessment of Aristotle's impact).

269 Subjectivism: *PGP* 102–8.

270 Celestine V: F. X. Seppelt (ed), *Monumenta Coelestiniana* (1921); A. Frugoni, *Celestiniana* (1954).

270 Boniface VIII: G. Digard, *Philippe le Bel et le s. siège*, 2 vols (1936) (fundamental); H. Wieruszowski, *Vom Imperium zum nationalen Königtum* (1933); full bibl. in *Hdb* III.2, 340–2.

271 Scotland as papal fief: W. Ullmann in *Speculum historiale* (1965), 257–76 at 264–8.

274 Publicistic literature: main sources in P. Dupuy, *Histoire du differend d'entre le pape et Philippe le Bel roy de France* (repr. 1963);

J. Rivière, *Le problème de l'église et de l'état au temps de Philippe le Bel* (1926); R. Scholz, *Die Publizistik zur Zeit Philipps des Schönen* (repr. 1970); Marion Melville in *RHEF* 36 (1950) 56–66.

275 *Unam sanctam:* text in *Extravagantes communes*, I.viii.1; also in Mirbt 5th ed no. 372 and in Denzinger *Enchiridion* no. 468.

276 Anagni: H. G. Beck, 'William Hundleby's account of the Anagni outrage' in *Catholic Hist. Rev.* 32 (1947) 190–225 (text with ET).

CHAPTER XII

(*A*) *Sources*

S. Baluzius, *Vitae paparum Avenionensium*, ed G. Mollat, 4 vols (1916–22); H. Finke, *Acta Aragonensia*, 3 vols (1908–23); Register of Clement V, 8 vols (1885), indices (1948–57); Ed of *Lettres secrètes et curiales* of Innocent VI, Urban V and Gregory XI (relative to France) (in progress); *Repertorium Germanicum*, ed G. Tellenbach, E. Göller, U. Kühne (1916–62); *Analecta Vaticano-Belgica* (1924–32); *Vatikanische Quellen zur Geschichte der päpstlichen Hof- und Finanzverwaltung* (in progress).

(*B*) *Literature*

G. Mollat, *L'administration des états de l'église au xive siècle* (1964); id., *Les papes d'Avignon* 10th ed (1965) (ET 1963); FM XIV.3–199; Hdb III.2, chs 37–40, 46–9; HL VI.484–1406, VII.1–582; Seppelt IV.3–365.

279 Walter Winterbourne: W. Ullmann, 'Curial exequies for Edward I and Edward III' in *JEH* (1955) 26–36, at 28 n. 2.

279 Clement V: G. Lizerand, *Clement V et Philippe le Bel* (1910); J. H. Denton, 'Pope Clement V's career as a royal clerk' in *EHR* 83 (1968) 303–14.

280 Templars: H. Finke, *Papsttum und Untergang des Templerordens*, 2 vols (1907) (fundamental); H. Neu, *Bibliographie des Templerordens* (1965); C. R. Cheney, 'The downfall of the Templars and a letter in their defence' in *Medieval Miscellany* (ed. F. Whitehead *et al.*, 1965) 65–79.

281 Council of Vienne: canons in *Decreta* 336–77; condemnation of the Templars: 312–36. E. Müller, *Das Konzil von Vienne* (1934) (fundamental); J. Lecler, *Vienne* (1964).

282 *Pastoralis Cura:* text in *Clem.* II.xi.2; F. Calasso, *I glossatori e la teoria della sovranità*, 2nd ed (1951); K. Hitzfeld, 'Die letzte Gesandtschaft Heinrichs VII. nach Avignon und ihre Folgen' in *HJb* 83 (1964) 43–53; W. Ullmann, *A history of political thought in the MA* 2nd ed (1970) 195–200.

282 Territorial sovereignty: the Golden Bull (below 290) strongly endorsed this concept in chs 8 and 11: no appeal was allowed outside the confines of Bohemia and the territories of the electoral princes.

282 Avignon: G. Mollat (as under (B)); Y. Renouard, *La papauté à Avignon* 2nd ed (1962); B. Guillemain, *La cour pontificale d'Avignon* (1963).

283 James of Viterbo: H. X. Arquillière, *Le plus ancien traité de l'église: Jacques de Viterbe* (1926); M. J. Wilks, 'The idea of the Church as "unus homo perfectus" and its bearing on the medieval theory of sovereignty' in *Misc. historiae ecclesiasticae* (1961) 30–49.

284 Augustinus Triumphus: M. J. Wilks, *The problem of sovereignty in the later MA* (1963) gives an exhaustive analysis as well as synthesis of the development of political ideas in the first half of the fourteenth century.

284 Papacy and Louis IV: H. S. Offler, 'Ueber die Prokuratorien Ludwigs des Bayern für die römische Kirche' in *DA* 8 (1951) 461–87; id., 'Empire and Papacy: the last struggle' in *TRSH* 5th series 6 (1956) 21–47; O. Berthold (ed), *Kaiser, Volk und Avignon* (1960); F. Bock, *Reichsidee und Nationalstaaten* (1943).

285 Sachsenhausen manifesto: text in *QRG* 11.179f.

286 Provisions and finance: G. Barraclough, *Papal provisions* (1935); W. E. Lunt, *Financial relations of the papacy with England to 1327* (1939); M. McKisack, *The Fourteenth Century* (1959) 272–305.

288 Cola di Rienzo: E. Dupré-Theseider, *I papi di Avinione e la questione romana* (1939).

290 Egidio Albornoz: J. Beneyto Perez, *El Cardenal Albornoz* (1950); his constitutions of 1357 ed by P. Sella (1912). A. Erler, *Aegidius Albornoz als Gesetzgeber* (1970).

290 Golden Bull: text in K. Zeumer, *Quellensammlung* 2nd ed (1913) 1.192–214.

291 Missions: see also above 262.

293 Urban VI: Great Schism: W. Ullmann, *The origins of the Great Schism* (repr. 1967); K. A. Fink, 'Zur Beurteilung des grossen abendländischen Schismas' in *ZKG* 73 (1962) 335–43; R. G. Trexler, 'Rome on the eve of the Great Schism' in *Speculum* 42 (1967) 489–509; A. Esch, 'Bankiers der Kirche im grossen Schisma' in *QFIAB* 46 (1966) 277–398; M. Souchon, *Die Papstwahlen in der Zeit des Grossen Schismas* (repr. 1970).

297 Richard II and the Schism: W. Ullmann, 'The University of Cambridge and the Great Schism' in *JTS* n.s. 9 (1958) 53–77 (here also ed of the university's official reply).

298 Council of Pisa: HL VII.1–70, M. Harvey in *SCH* VII (1971) 197–209.

299 Conciliarism: E. F Jacob, *Essays in the conciliar epoch*, 3rd ed

(1963); B. Tierney, *Foundations of conciliar theory* (repr. 1968); id., 'Pope and Council: some new decretist texts' in *Medieval Studies* 19 (1957) 197–218; K. A. Fink, 'Die konziliare Idee im späten MA' in *Vorträge und Forschungen* 9 (1965) 119–35; W. Ullmann, 'De Bartoli sententia: Concilium representat mentem populi' in *Bartolus de Sassoferrato: Studi e documenti per il VI Centenario* (1962) 11.705–33 at 730–2; for Zabarella see *Origins of the Great Schism* (above 293) 191–231; B. Tierney, *Foundations* 220–31; T. Sartori, 'Un discorso inedito de Franciscus Zabarella a Bonifacio IX sull' autoritá del papa' in *RSC* 20 (1966) 375–88 (revealing position of a conciliarist); J. Gill, 'Representation in the conciliar period' in *SCH* VII (1971) 177–95.

300 Constance: H. Finke, *Acta concilii Constanciensis*, 4 vols (1896–1926); exhaustive bibl. by K. A. Fink in *Hdb* III.2,545–7; also by J. Gill, *Constance et Bâle-Florence*, here also trsl of important texts and canons; B. Tierney, 'The problem of "Haec sancta"' in *Essays presented to Bertie Wilkinson* (1969) 354–70; further W. Brandmüller, 'Besitzt das Dekret "Haec sancta" dogmatische Verbindlichkeit?' in *RQ* 62 (1967) 1–17.

302 Concordats: W. Bertrams, *Der neuzeitliche Staatsgedanke und die Konkordate des ausgehenden MA* (1942); texts in A. Mercati, *Raccolta di concordati* (1954).

302 Martin V: announcement of his election to the University of Cambridge in *JTS* (above 297) 75–7; W. Brandmüller, 'Der Uebergang vom Pontifikat Martins V. zu Eugen IV.' in *QFIAB* 47 (1967) 596–629. Papal state: P. Partner, *The papal state under Martin V* (1958); cf. also A. Esch, *Bonifaz IX. und der Kirchenstaat* (1969).

303 Hus: M. Spinka, *John Hus at the Council of Constance* (1965) (with trsl of Latin and Czech texts).

CHAPTER XIII

(A) Sources

Concilium Basiliense: Studien und Quellen zur Geschichte des Conzils von Basel, 8 vols (1896–1936); Aeneas Sylvius Piccolominus, *De gestis Concilii Basiliensis commentariorum* (ed D. Hay and ET by W. K. Smith) (1967); J. Haller in *HZ* 74 (1895) 385–406; *Concilium Florentinum, documenta et scriptores* (in progress); Vespasiano da Bisticci, *Vite di uomini del secolo XV* (ed 1893) (ET 1963); L. Pastor, *Ungedruckte Akten zur Geschichte der Päpste 1376–1464* (1904).

(B) *Literature*

J. Haller, *Papsttum und Kirchenreform* (1908); Seppelt IV.240–453 (with copious bibl. 455–504); *Hdb* III.2, chs 50, 51, 53, 55–7; HL VII.663–1052; L. Pastor, *Geschichte der Päpste* 2nd ed and reprints, vols I–III (also ET); F. du Boulay in C. H. Lawrence, *England and the Papacy* (1965).

306 Byzantium: Ostrogorsky in *CMH* IV (1966) 379–87.

307 Eugenius and the councils: K. A. Fink in *Hdb* III.2, 573–84; H. Angermeier, 'Das Reich und der Konziliarismus' in *HZ* 192 (1961) 529–83; E. F. Jacob, 'Reflexions on the study of the general councils in the fifteenth century' in *Bulletin John Rylands Library* 41 (1958) 26–53; id., Giuliano Cesarini, ibid., 51 (1968) 104–26; A. Black, *Monarchy and Community: political ideas in the later conciliar controversy* 1430–50(1970). For financial relations between Eugenius and Florence see J. Kirshner, 'Papa Eugenio IV e il monte comune' in *Archivio storico italiano* 127 (1969) 339–82.

308 Councils of Ferrara (Florence) and Basle: canons in *Decreta* 431–567. Florence: J. Gill, *The Council of Florence* (1959); id., *Constance et Bâle-Florence* (1965); Basle: P. Ourliac, 'Sociologie du concile de Bâle' in *RHE* 56 (1961) 5–32; A. P. J. Meijknecht, 'Le concile de Bâle, aperçu général sur les sources', ibid. 65 (1970) 465–73; A. N. E. Schofield 'Some aspects of English representation at the Council of Basle' in *SCH* VII (1971) 219–29 (with further relevant lit. and lists of members of the delegations); A. J. Black, ibid., 229ff. For the new conciliar arrangements at Florence see R. Kay, 'The conciliar ordo of Eugenius IV' in *OCP* 31 (1965) 295–304 (newly discovered texts).

309 *Laetentur:* Latin and Greek texts in *Decreta* 500–4.

309 Hussites: M. Spinka, *John Hus' concept of the Church* (1966); F. G. Heymann, *John Žižka and the Hussite Revolution* (1955); Johannes de Ragusa: A. Krchnak, *De vita et operibus Ioannis de Ragusio* (= *Lateranum* n.s. 26) (1960); J. Kubelik, 'Jean de Raguse' in *Revue des sciences religieuses* 41 (1967) 150–68.

310 Pragmatic Sanction: N. Valois, *Histoire de la pragmatique sanction de Bourges sous Charles VII* (1907) (fundamental). Neutrality: H. Angermeier (above 307) at 569–73.

311 Conciliarism and the papacy: A. Black, *Monarchy* (above 307) 85–129. Laymen and participation: W. Ullmann, 'The papacy and the faithful' in *Recueil de la société Jean Bodin* 25 (1965) 7–45 at 34–45.

311 Concordats: A. Mercati above 302.

313 Attempts at reform: J. Haller (as under (B)); H. Jedin, *History of the Council of Trent* (1958) 3–115; A. A. Strnad, 'Francesco Todeschini – Piccolominis Politik und Mäzenatentum im Quattrocento' in *Römische Hist. Mitt.* 9 (1969) 102–425 (fundamental; with copious lit.).

314 Humanism and the citizen: K. A. Fink in *Hdb* III.2, 625–33; W. Ullmann, *Individual and Society in the MA* ch 3.

316 Last imperial coronation: E. Eichmann, *Kaiserkrönung* 1.303–8; F. Wasner, 'Päpstliches Zeremonienwesen im 15. Jahrh.' in *AHP* 6 (1968) 113–62 at 143–52 (important new texts).

319 Savonarola: K. A. Fink in *Hdb* III.2, 664 at n. 23; L. Bolzono in *RSC* 23 (1969) 428–40.

320 Pius II and his conciliarist past: H. Diener, 'Enea Silvio Piccolominis Weg von Basel nach Rom' in *Adel und Kirche* (above 128) 516–33.

321 Pius II and Congress at Mantua: vue d'ensemble by A. A. Strnad, 'Johannes Hinderbachs Obödienz–Ansprache an Pius II.' in *Römische Hist. Mitt.* 10 (1968) 43–183 (with copious lit.).

321 Curial reform: R. Haubst, 'Der Reformentwurf Pius des Zweiten' in *RQ* 49(1954) 188–242 (ed of reform decree at 205ff.).

322 George Podjebrad: F. G. Heymann, *George of Bohemia, king of heretics* (1965); J. Macek, 'Der Konziliarismus in der böhmischen Reformation, besonders in der Politik Georgs von Podiebrad' in *ZKG* 80 (1969) 312–30.

322 Bohemian social programme: P. Brock, *The social and political doctrines of the Unity of Czech Brethren* (1957); H. Kaminsky, 'Peter Chelcický: Treatises on Christianity and the social order' in *Studies in Medieval and Renaissance History*, ed W. M. Bowsky (1964) 1.104–79.

323 Alexander VI and the Donation of Constantine: L. Weckmann, *Las Bulas Alexandrinas* (1949); A. Garcia-Gallo, *Las bulas de Alejandro VI y el ordenamiente* (1958).

324 Maximilian I as pope: H. Wiesflecker, 'Kaiser-Papst Plan Maximilians i. J. 1511' in *MIOG* 71 (1963) 311–32.

324 Julius II and the Council of Pisa: relevant docs in O. Raynaldus, *Annales ecclesiastici* (ed Bar-le-Duc 1873) 30.537–53; detailed legal opinions by Philippus Decius and the council's secretary, Zacharias Ferrerius, in Melchior Goldast, *Monarchia* (ed 1668) II.1753–82; D. S. Chambers, *Cardinal Bainbridge in the Court of Rome 1509–1514* (1965); C. Fusero, *Giulio II* (1965). Further W. Ullmann, 'Julius II and the schismatic cardinals' in *SCH* ix (1972).

325 Fifth Lateran Council: canons in *Decreta* 511–631; concordat of 1516: A. Mercati (above 302) at 235–52; O. de La Brosse, *Le pape et le concile: la comparison de leurs pouvoirs à la veille de la Réforme* (1965).

326 Leo X: K. M. Setton, 'Pope Leo X and the Turkish peril' in *Proceedings of the American Philosophical Society* 112 (1969) 367–424.

List of Medieval Popes

This list is based on *Annuario pontificio* (ed 1971) which is derived from A. Mercati in *Medieval Studies*, 9 (1947) 71–80. Of the two dates given at the beginning of a pontificate, the first refers to the date of election, the second to ordination or consecration (coronation). The names of anti-popes are in brackets.

Melchiades, 2.VII.311–11.I.314

Silvester I, 31.I.314–31.XII.335

Mark, 18.I.336–7.X.336

Julius I, 6.II.337–12.IV.352

Liberius, 17.V.352–24.IX.366
(Felix II, 355–22.XI.365)

Damasus I, 1.X.366–11.XII.384
(Ursinus, 366–367)

Siricius, 15 or 22 or 29.XII.
384–26.XI.399

Anastasius I, 27.XI.399–19.
XII.401

Innocent I, 22.XII.401–12.III.
417

Zosimus, 18.III.417–26.XII.
418

Boniface I, 28 or 29.XII.418–4.
IX.422 (Eulalius, 27 or 29.
XII.418–419)

Celestine I, 10.IX.422–27.VII.
432

Sixtus III, 31.VII.432–19.VIII.
440

Leo I, 29.IX.440–10.XI.461

Hilarus, 19.XI.461–29.II.468

Simplicius, 3.III.468–10.III.
483

Felix III, 13.III.483–1.III.492

Gelasius I, 1.III.492–21.XI.496

Anastasius II, 24.XI.496–19.
XI.498

Symmachus, 22.XI.498–19.VII.
514 (Laurentius, 498, 501–
505)

Hormisdas, 20.VII.514–6.VIII.
523

John I, 13.VIII.523–18.V.526

Felix IV, 12.VII.526–22.IX.530

Boniface II, 22.IX.530–17.X.
532 (Dioscorus, 22.IX.530–
14.X.530)

John II, 2.I.533–8.V.535

Agapitus I, 13.V.535–22.IV.536

Silverius, VI.536–11.XI.537

Vigilius, 29.III.537–7.VI.555

Pelagius I, 16.IV.556–4.III.561

John III, 17.VII.561–13.VII.
574

Benedict I, 2.VI.575–30.VII.
579

Pelagius II, 26.XI.579–7.II.590

Gregory I, 3.IX.590–12.III.604

Sabinianus, 13.IX.604–22.II.606

Boniface III, 19.II.607–12.XI. 607

Boniface IV, 25.VIII.608–8.V. 615

Deusdedit or Adeodatus I, 19. X.615–8.XI.618

Boniface V, 23.XII.619–25.X. 625

Honorius I, 27.X.625–12.X.638

Severinus, 28.V.640–2.VIII.640

John IV, 24.XII.640–12.X.642

Theodore I, 24.XI.642–14.V.649

Martin I, VII.649–16.IX.655

Eugenius I, 10.VIII.654–2.VI. 657

Vitalian, 30.VII.657–27.I.672

Adeodatus II, 11.IV.672–17. VI.676

Donus, 2.XI.676–11.IV.678

Agatho, 27.VI.678–10.I.681

Leo II, 17.VIII.682–3.VII.683

Benedict II, 26.VI.684–8.V.685

John V, 23.VII.685–2.VIII.686

Cono, 21.X.686–21.IX.687 (Theodore, 687) (Paschal, 687)

Sergius I, 15.XII.687–8.IX.701

John VI, 30.X.701–11.I.705

John VII, 1.III.705–18.X.707

Sisinnius, 15.I.708–4.II.708

Constantine, 25.III.708–9.IV. 715

Gregory II, 19.V.715–11.II.731

Gregory III, 18.III.731–XI.741

Zachary, 10.XII.741–22.III.752

Stephen II, 23.III.752–25.III. 752

Stephen III, 26.III.752–26.IV. 757

Paul I, iv, 29.V.757–28.VI.767 (Constantine, 28.VI, 5.VII. 767–769) (Philip, 31.VII.768)

Stephen IV, I, 7.VIII.768–24.I. 772

Adrian I, 1, 9.II.772–25.XII.795

Leo III, 26, 27.XII.795–12.VI. 816

Stephen V, 22.VI.816–24.I.817

Paschal I, 25.I.817–11.II.824

Eugenius II, 11–V.824–VIII.827

Valentine, VIII.827–IX.827

Gregory IV, 827–1.844 (John, –1.844)

Sergius II, 1.844–27.I.847

Leo IV, 10.IV.847–17.VII.855

Benedict III, vii, 29.IX.855– 17.IV.858 (Anastasius, The Librarian, VIII.855–IX.855, d. (*ca*) 880)

Nicholas I, 24.IV.858–13.XI.867

Adrian II, 14.XII.867–14.XII. 872

John VIII, 14.XII.872–16.XII. 882

Marinus I, 16.XII.882–15.V.884

Adrian III, 17.V.884–IX.885

Stephen VI, IX.885–14.IX.891

Formosus, Bishop of Porto, 6.X.891–4.IV.896

Boniface VI, IV.896–IV.896

Stephen VII, V.896–VIII.897

Romanus, VIII.897–XI.897

Theodore II, XII.897–XII.897

John IX, 1.898–1.900

Benedict IV, I–II.900–VII.903

Leo V, VII.903–IX.903

(Christopher, VII or IX.903–I.904)

Sergius III, 29.I.904–14.IV.911

Anastasius III, IV.911–VI.913

Lando, VII.913–II.914

John X, III.914–V.928

Leo VI, V.928–XII.928

Stephen VIII, XII.928–II.931

John XI, II–III.931–XII.935

Leo VII, 3.I.936–13.VII.939

Stephen IX, 14.VII.939–X.942

Marinus II, 30.X.942–V.946

Agapitus II, 10.V.946–XII.955

John XII, 16.XII.955–14.V.964

Leo VIII, 4, 6.XII.963–1.III.965

Benedict V, 22.V.964–4.VII.966

John XIII, 1.X.965–6.IX.972

Benedict VI, 19.I.973–VI.974

(Boniface VII, VI–VII.974; again VIII.984–VII.985)

Benedict VII, X.974–10.VII.983

John XIV, XII.983–20.VIII.984

John XV, VIII.985–III.996

Gregory V, 3.V.996–18.II.999

(John XVI, IV.997–II.998)

Silvester II, 2.IV.999–12.V.1003

John XVII, VI.1003–XII.1003

John XVIII, 1.1004–VII.1009

Sergius IV, 31.VII.1009–12.V.1012

Benedict VIII, 18.V.1012–9.IV.1024 (Gregory, 1012)

John XIX, IV–V.1024–1032

Benedict IX, 1032–1044

Silvester III, 20.I.1045–10.III.1045

Benedict IX (for the second time), 10.IV.1045–1.V.1045

Gregory VI, 5.V.1045–20.XII.1046

Clement II, 24, 25.XII.1046–9.X.1047

Benedict IX (for the third time) 8.XI.1047–17.VII.1048

Damasus II, 17.VII.1048–9.VIII.1048

Leo IX, 12.II.1049–19.IV.1054

Victor II, 13.IV.1055–28.VII.1057

Stephen X, 3.VIII.1057–29.III.1058 (Benedict X, 5.IV.1058–24.I.1059)

Nicholas II, 24.I.1059–27.VII.1061

Alexander II, 1.X.1061–21.IV.1073 (Honorius II, 28.X.1061–1072)

Gregory VII, 22.IV, 30.VI.1073–25.V.1085 (Clement III, 25.VI.1080. 24.III.1084–8.IX.1100)

Victor III, of Benevento, Dauferius (Desiderius), 24.V.1086–16.IX.1087

Urban II, 12.III.1088–29.VII.1099

Paschal II, 13, 14.VIII.1099–21.I.1118 (Theodoric, 1100, d. 1102) (Albert, 1102) (Silvester IV, 18.XI.1105–1111)

Gelasius II, 24.I, 10.III.1118–28.I.1119 (Gregory VIII, 8.III.1118–1121, d. ?)

Callixtus II, 2, 9.II.1119–13.XII.
1124

Honorius II, 15, 21.XII.1124–
13.II.1130 (Celestine II,
XII.1124)

Innocent II, 14, 23.II.1130–24.
IX.1143 (Anacletus II, 14,
23.II.1130–25.I.1138)
(Victor IV, III.1138–29.V.
1138, d. ?)

Celestine II, 26.IX, 3.X.1143–8.
III.1144

Lucius II, 12.III.1144–15.II.
1145

Eugenius III, 15, 18.II.1145–8.
VII.1153

Anastasius IV, 12.VII.1153–3.
XII.1154

Adrian IV, 4, 5.XII.1154–1.IX.
1159

Alexander III, 7, 20.IX.1159–
30.VIII.1181 (Victor IV, 7.
IX, 4.X.1159–20.IV.1164)
(Paschal III, 22, 26.IV.1164–
20.IX.1168) (Callixtus III,
IX.1168–29.VIII.1178)
(Innocent III, 29.IX.1179–
1180)

Lucius III, 1, 6.IX.1181–25.IX.
1185

Urban III, 25.XI, 1.XII.1185–
20.X.1187

Gregory VIII, 21, 25.X.1187–
17.XII.1187

Clement III, 19, 20.XII.1187–
III.1191

Celestine III, 30.III, 14.IV.
1191–8.I.1198

Innocent III, 8.I, 22.II.1198–16.
VII, 1216

Honorius III, 18, 24.VII.1216–
18.III.1227

Gregory IX, 19, 21.III.1227–
22.VIII.1241

Celestine IV, 25, 28.X.1241–10.
XI.1241

Innocent IV, 25, 28.VI.1243–7.
XII.1254

Alexander IV, 12, 20.XII.1254–
25.V.1261

Urban IV, 29.VIII, 4.IX.1261–
2.X.1264

Clement IV, 5, 15.II.1265–29.
XI.1268

Gregory X, 1.XI.1271, 27.III.
1272–10.I.1276

Innocent V, 21.I, 22.II.1276–22.
VI.1276

Adrian V, 11.VII.1276–18.
VIII.1276

John XXI, 8, 20.IX.1276–20.V.
1277

Nicholas III, 25.XI, 26.XII.
1277–22.VIII.1280

Martin IV, 22.II, 23.III.1281–
28.III.1285

Honorius IV, 2.IV, 20.V.1285–
3.IV.1287

Nicholas IV, 22.II.1288–4.IV.
1292

Celestine V, 5.VII, 29.VIII.
1294–13.XII.1294 (d. 19.V.
1296)

Boniface VIII, 24.XII.1294,
23.I.1295–11.X.1303

Benedict XI, 22, 27.X.1303–7.
VII.1304

Clement V, 5.VI, 14.XI.1305–
20.IV.1314

John XXII, 7.VIII, 5.IX. 1316–
4.XII.1334 (Nicholas V, 12,
22.V.1328–25.VIII. 1330,
d. 16.X.1333)

Benedict XII, 20.XII.1334, 8.I.
1335–25.IV.1342

Clement VI, 7, 19.V.1342–6.
XII.1352

Innocent VI, 18, 30.XII.1352–
12.IX.1362

Urban V, 28.IX, 6.XI.1362–19.
XII.1370

Gregory XI, 30.XII.1370, 5.I.
1371–26.III.1378

Urban VI, 8, 18.IV.1378–15.X.
1389

Boniface IX, 2, 9.XI.1389–1.X.
1404

Innocent VII, 17.X, 11.XI.
1404–6.XI.1406

Gregory XII, 30.XI, 19.XII.
1406–4.VII.1415 (Clement
VII, 20.IX, 31.X.1378–16.IX.
1394) (Benedict XIII, 28.IX,
11.X.1394–23.V.1423)
(Alexander V, 26.VI, 7.VII.
1409–3.V.1410) (John

XXIII, 17, 25.V.1410–29.V.
1415)

Martin V, 11, 21.XI.1417–20.
II.1431

Eugenius IV, 3, 11.III.1431–
23.II.1447 (Felix V, 5.XI.
1439, 24.VII.1440–7.IV.1449)

Nicholas V, 6, 19.III.1447–24.
III.1455

Callixtus III, 8, 20.IV.1455–6.
VIII.1458

Pius II, 19.VIII, 3.IX.1458–15.
VIII.1464

Paul II, 30.VIII, 16.IX.1464–26.
VII.1471

Sixtus IV, 9, 25.VIII.1471–12.
VIII.1484

Innocent VIII, 29.VIII, 12.IX.
1484–25.VII.1492

Alexander VI, 11, 26.VIII.
1492–18.VIII.1503

Pius III, 22.IX, 1, 8.X.1503–18.
X.1503

Julius II, 31.X, 26.XI.1503–21.
II.1513

Leo X, 9, 19.III.1513–1.XII.
1521

Index